School, State, and Society

School, State, and Society

The Growth of Elementary Schooling
in Nineteenth-Century France—
A Quantitative Analysis

Raymond Grew and Patrick J. Harrigan

Ann Arbor
THE UNIVERSITY OF MICHIGAN PRESS

Copyright © by the University of Michigan 1991
All rights reserved
Published in the United States of America by
The University of Michigan Press
Manufactured in the United States of America

1994 1993 1992 1991   4 3 2 1

Library of Congress Cataloging-in-Publication Data

Grew, Raymond.
   School, state, and society : the growth of elementary schooling in nineteenth-century France : a quantitative analysis / Raymond Grew and Patrick J. Harrigan.
     p.   cm.
   Includes bibliographical references and index.
   ISBN 0-472-10095-5
   1. Education, Elementary—France—History—19th century.
2. Education, Elementary—France—History—19th century—Statistics.
3. Education and state—France—History—19th century.
4. Education, Elementary—Social aspects—France—History—19th century.   I. Harrigan, Patrick.   II. Title.
LA693.G74   1992
372.944—dc20   91-23529
                                                                        CIP

British Library Cataloguing in Publication Data

Grew, Raymond
   School, state and society : the growth of elementary schooling in nineteenth-century France : a quantitative analysis.
   1. France. Primary education, history
   I. Title   II. Harrigan, Patrick J. *1941–*
   372.944

ISBN 0-472-10095-5

Acknowledgments

Erik Austin and Jerome Clubb of the University of Michigan gave invaluable encouragement and guidance for the establishment of this project, and James B. Whitney of the Department of Statistics, University of Waterloo, worked closely with us in the selection and analysis of statistical procedures. Victor Neglia helped program the data and provided technical advice. Rod Day, Robert Gidney, Wyn Millar, R. R. Palmer, and Maris Vinovskis offered sage advice at different points; and we were generously helped by André Burguière, William B. Cohen, François Furet, Emmanuel Leroy Ladurie, and Jacques Ozouf. Gail Heideman and Julia Routson meticulously typed some of the manuscript and the daunting tables; Carol Cooper assisted in some of the bibliographic searches and proofreading. All but a small part of the project's funds came from the Social Science and Humanities Research Council of Canada. We are grateful to all these individuals and institutions and to the editors of the scholarly journals in which parts of this study first appeared for their initial interest and their willingness to let us use some of the same material here (much of chapter 2 first appeared in the *Journal of Interdisciplinary History*, of chapter 3 in *Annales: Économies, Sociétés, Civilisations*, and of chapter 4 in the *Journal of Modern History*).

Contents

1. Historical Problems and Statistics — 1
2. The Availability of Schooling — 31
3. French Students in School, 1829–1906 — 55
4. The Catholic Contribution to Universal Schooling — 91
5. The Schooling of Girls — 121
6. *Instituteurs* and *Institutrices* — 147
7. The System Circumscribed — 181
8. The Balance Sheet — 207
   Tables — 245
   Index — 315

Figures

1.	The availability of schools in the departments of France	36
2.	The western wedge of fewer schools	41
3.	The departments of France that achieved fulfillment by 1829, 1837, 1850, and 1863	43
4.	Mean enrollment in departments grouped by octiles based on enrollment in 1832	58
5.	Octiles and quartiles of departments based on enrollments in 1832	74
6.	Best cluster fit of departments based on enrollment, 1832–81 and on *certificats d'études*, 1882–1907	75
7.	Seven clusters based on schools in 1821, enrollment in 1837, summer attendance in 1876, and *certificats d'études* in 1886	76
8.	Seven clusters based on the percentage of primary school pupils enrolled in Catholic schools, 1850–82	93
9.	Percentage of school-age girls and of school-age boys enrolled in primary school	125
10.	Three clusters based on girls enrollment compared to that of boys, 1837–76	126
11.	Seven clusters based on the percentage of school-age girls enrolled in school, 1837–76	135

CHAPTER 1

Historical Problems and Statistics

Popular instruction was one of the compelling visions of the nineteenth century, and the persistent efforts of its advocates made schools, like steam engines and newspapers, symbols of the century. From one end of the European continent to the other, enlightened opinion believed education essential to progress, political and economic; to creating and sustaining a healthy nation; and to social peace. The campaigns for accessible elementary schools were strikingly similar though waged in countries where conditions were very different, and they established a current of writing that has continued to the present day. To the academies, institutes, societies, and newspapers that sponsored articles, essays, pamphlets, and books on education, its benefits were so obvious that neither the justifications for schooling nor the pedagogy to be employed was the principal topic. Rather, practical issues of how schools should be organized, their costs controlled and paid for, teachers selected and supervised, buildings given proper air and light, and sanitary conditions maintained, were the issues treated in detail. The quite different examples of Prussia and Boston were admiringly cited, with the lessons deduced then used to support local programs. This literature was international, comparative (in the assumption of a common path to progress that would put some societies ahead of others), and filled with numbers that counted pupils and calculated budgets. Its volume and high seriousness makes a historical point, for it testifies to the enormity of the task being advocated. To a considerable extent, these concerns early in the century set the course both for the actual development of schooling—understood as essentially an organizational problem— and for historical accounts of that development, written in terms of its steady progress. By the latter part of the century, histories of education, like the ever more elaborate inquiries into its current operation, were largely the work of professional educators. Such efforts tended to be detailed, to emphasize formal structures, legal requirements, and statistics, and to be rather unquestioning about the social significance of what had happened.

From the turn of the century on, and especially after World War I, political historians were increasingly drawn to the history of education, and this established a second current in the historiography. Education had often been the battleground on which left and right, church and state, chose to fight;

closer study of the defeats, victories, and compromises that followed could elucidate the course of national politics while describing the history of education. Interest in nationalism and its relationship to public schools widened the historical canvas. Education was moving nearer to the center of general national histories. The history of education gained further importance after World War II with the attention given in all the social sciences to modernization, the view that a whole array of interconnected social changes (in which the state played a major part) constituted a process that brought about "modern" society, which welcomed change, was flexible and mobile, individualist but highly organized, rational, and productive while supporting a high degree of political participation. Literacy but also formal education were seen as critical to this process, psychologically and intellectually as well as economically and technologically. A third stream in the historical writing on education opened up.

The establishment of universal, compulsory primary instruction was clearly one of the fundamental changes in modern life. For Europe and North America, that transformation had occurred in the nineteenth century. In every society that achieved it, universal education required impressive expenditures, not a little compulsion, and the creation of an elaborate system to get children into schools, train teachers, and provide the facilities needed for mass education. Understandably, the subject has come to attract more and more attention from historians. Using theories and findings from research on modern education and armed now with a more theoretical framework, historians began to raise new questions about education, especially about its role in the process of social change. There was special interest in professionalization (which schools certified for society and school systems embrace for teachers), technological innovation (which educational systems were discovered to constrain as well as spur), and social mobility (for which school systems served both as a means and a barrier).

Historians, however, are inclined to study even large-scale processes in terms of concrete behavior. Often aided since the 1960s by penetrating techniques of quantitative analysis, their investigations of particular groups in specific places frequently challenged common assumptions about social processes. The tendency was reinforced by the rising tide of social history and wide-ranging efforts to rethink social relations. Applied to the history of education, these interests constitute a fourth current in the historiography, one composed of many parts. There has been renewed interest in what really went on in the classroom and school yard in the nineteenth century and in how teachers were selected and socialized. Heavy and fruitful borrowing from sociology and anthropology and from the writings of Foucault, contemporary Marxists, and feminist thinkers has resulted in impressive studies showing educational systems to have been an important part of the process of class formation, powerful instruments of cultural reproduction, and a major means of defining and maintaining gender roles.

Each of these currents reflects the educational preoccupations of the era in which it was formed; but all are still alive, their contributions more lasting than the hope or disillusionment from which they grew. The findings of these diverse approaches do not necessarily contradict. If education is central in so many theories, that obviously reflects its place in contemporary thought but also perhaps its historical signficance. In all these historiographical currents, much of the attention is on education as a measure of something else—civic consciousness, political disagreement, the growth of the state, the inculcation of nationalism, the process of modernization, the nature of social control, the institutionalization of class differences, and the maintenance of gender discrimination. Like a national anthem or constitution, a universal system of primary education appears to be the direct expression of a national state, which prodded local governments, passed laws, and spent money to make education available to all and then insistently used it. Even general histories of education now move beyond issues of educational policy to reveal a history of selfish interests and social fears, good intentions ill informed, and bitter social conflicts only partially resolved—all essentially guaranteeing that the proclaimed goals of education would never be fully met.

In all these interpretations, France has been of major importance, and for a number of reasons. From Victor Cousin to Pierre Bourdieu, French intellectuals have helped to frame international discussion of how educational institutions do (and should) function. French historical writing, influential and admired in so many fields, includes an extensive literature on the history of education, based on sources as voluminous, well organized, and accessible as any in the world. Absorbed and contributed to by many others, especially British and American historians, that historiography is international. Most of all, historical experience itself gives the history of education in France its particular vigor and relevance. By the nineteenth century, France had a well-established national culture with one dominant national language, had long been a national state, and enjoyed or was burdened by a relatively efficient and highly centralized political administration. At the same time, there remained important differences among regional cultures and dialects, there were frequent and important changes in political regimes, and there were deep religious cleavages. The delicate balance between national uniformity and local variation, between administrative continuity and political change may in the case of France be unusually visible in the spotlight of political conflict and therefore accessible to analysis. A society preoccupied with its own divisions and intensely concerned with education[1] quickly felt the contradictions that may be inherent in educational systems everywhere. No wonder, then, that a subject on which so much has already been written continues to attract exciting new research and interpretations.[2]

The tendency to view education through the state has been especially strong in the literature on France. Despite changes of regime, the efficient, uniform Napoleonic apparatus had an entire century of continuity in which to establish and enlarge a notoriously centralized educational system. If national politics and administration provided the framework for much of the literature,[3] that emphasis has often transfixed foreign analysts.[4] The statistics on elementary instruction may tell us something about what to make of this emphasis, by letting us test some connections between national policy and local schools and by giving some measures of how uniform schooling became.

The century-long struggle between church and state also looms very large in the history of French education. Even before the open warfare of the Third Republic, much about educational policy had been determined by the Bourbon Restoration's closeness to the church, the July Monarchy's more distant relations, and Louis Napoleon's initial accommodation (codified in the Falloux Law) and more independent tack during the Liberal Empire (when Victor Duruy was in charge of public instruction). The conflicts that led to the Law of Associations and the separation of church and state in 1905 rang with arguments about education. Republican historians have echoed these debates in their emphasis on the necessity in France for the state to take the initiative in making instruction universal, free, and laic.[5] Biographies of leading politicians of the Third Republic—Jules Simon, Jules Ferry, Léon Gambetta, René Waldeck-Rousseau—have emphasized their preoccupation with education and their sensitivity to its political implications. Historians of the Church, on the other hand, have stressed its contributions to education from before the Revolution through the nineteenth century and its role in the struggle for liberty of education.[6] In a reedition of what remains the standard work on the topic, Mona Ozouf points out the risk in this literature of relegating education itself to a secondary concern.[7] Perhaps we would see these issues in a different light if the educational statistics can tell us when and where elementary schools became free, where Catholic schools were, and how many children went to them.

French education's part in social change has been explored with vigor. Some of the results have been striking. French schools, it turns out, did foster scientific and technological development; and the view, dominant for more than a generation, that by the 1840s France lost an early lead in these fields due to cultural prejudice and inadequate instruction, has essentially been overturned.[8] In light of these findings, consonant with reassessments of France's industrial growth in the nineteenth century, we might well look to see if statistical evidence indicates whether or not elementary schooling in general was similarly well grounded in French society. The innovative role of the Third Republic has faired less well in recent research. Important work on schooling in the old regime and on the development of literacy has given education, too, its *longue durée*, emphasizing the continuity and social roots of its development.[9] Against republican lore, which saw universal instruction as the Third Republic's achievement at the end of the century of goals established by the Revolution, historians currently tend to stress the Revolution's failure to replace the institutions it abolished and France's subsequent slowness in repairing the damage.[10] Continuity, change, and pace are relative matters, but they have a quantitative dimension; perhaps statistical data can tell us whether elementary schooling developed where it had been before or started anew and when it grew rapidly or slowly.

Historians currently tend to look with critical skepticism at the purposes and practices of France's educational system. Whatever its Weberian advantages, professionalization brought more than specialization and efficiency, and schools cooperated eagerly enough with semiclosed elites preoccupied with their own interests. Following the lead of sociologists,[11] historians, too, have wondered whether schooling was less a source of change than a means to sustain and reproduce the differences of class and gender that marked French society in the nineteenth century. Here the results of research have often been subtler and more complicated than the initial questions, an important point in itself. Schooling's connections to society are intricate and often contradictory, and its effects on society rarely push in a single direction. Schools did guard the gates of access to the professions and many other middle-class occupations, and anyone not in the upper third of society was severely disadvantaged at almost every step. Even so, individual instances of access and mobility were numerous enough to have social significance, given the small number of secondary school students.[12] There is reason to ask whether elementary instruction increased opportunities or effectively closed them off.

The recent work on women's education has not only brought into focus one half of the population historians often slighted but has brought a broader, more anthropological vision to the study of schooling. Although not intended to prepare women for careers, girls schools did broaden horizons and raise ambitions. Curricula, textbooks, role models, and rituals conveyed and acted out an elaborately articulated vision of women's domestic place in society. They also exposed its restrictiveness.[13] The elementary instruction of girls thus also takes on new interest, for that can tell us whether many even had the chance to go to school (the picture in the secondary literature is mixed), who provided those schools, and whether society seemed to welcome or reject them.

Even when offered, schooling for the people was not simply a matter of progress. Efforts to promote enlightenment and hygiene were also efforts to denigrate dialect and erode local custom, and recent writing has tended to underscore the resistance schooling met.[14] Social historians, interested in the daily life of village and classroom, have constructed a compelling and frequently pessimistic picture of indifferent pupils, dilapidated schools, and lonely, ill-paid teachers, often deeply committed but subject to distrust and abuse in the isolated worlds they were supposed to transform.[15]

Resistance, hardship, and inadequate funds were constant themes of the educators of the Third Republic too: Contemporary analysis, however, differs from theirs in its doubts about the efficacy of education. These doubts may reflect the late twentieth century more than the nineteenth; but historians have found a great deal of testimony that standards were often low and that many pupils acquired little useful knowledge. They have shown that schools sought to inculcate values useful for social order—patriotism, work, thrift, respect for authority, the domestic duties of women—as attentively as they taught writing or arithmetic. By probing memoirs, newspapers, and archives, with new questions and sometimes new methods, historians have vastly enriched and complicated our understanding of France's educational system, and they have done this both in studies of particular topics and in an impressive array of local histories.

What, then, can one more study, primarily a quantitative analysis of a single large collection of data although enriched by archival research, bring to this understanding? Clearly, there is much of importance to which it can hardly speak. Yet the elaborately assembled numbers, themselves a product of the forces and interests that built the national system, touch on most of the institutional aspects of primary instruction. By bringing to them questions that arise from this extensive literature and probing them with computer-assisted techniques, it may be possible to make these data, like any other kind of historical document, reveal more than their compilers (perceptive though they were) intended, more than would emerge from the daunting task of simply reading the hundreds and hundreds of printed tables. Final judgments on issues of education, perhaps more than on most subjects, often rest on whether the glass is seen as half-full or half-empty, on what is expected of schooling or thought possible. But the proportions can easily be lost sight of in the blaze of colorful descriptions, however insightful and valid, or the heat of engagement, whether the passionate debates of the nineteenth century or the exciting theses of modern scholarship. The analysis of statistical data is not a substitute for any of this, but its measures can usefully set a range and define a context within which limitations and achievements can be better understood. We think there are some controversies and misconceptions that this study comes close to resolving. There are many others on which it casts useful light. Assembling evidence in a different way, we will try to pose some fresh questions, seek consistent answers to them, and offer some alternative arguments and interpretations.

There are even some advantages to the limitations this data base imposes. We will use statistics gathered by that sometimes overweening state to study the development not of state policy but of primary schooling, and we will treat elementary schooling alone, almost in isolation. That is, after all, how the vast majority of French citizens experienced it. The existing literature, however, has given much closer attention to other levels of instruction, and general studies usually follow the whole Napoleonic university up and down its table of organization from universities and *grands écoles* to kindergarten. We will be studying the statistics of change and thereby gain, should the data support it, a certain independence from the political chronology that necessarily informs legislative and administrative accounts. Unable to measure the great successes or dismal failures of individual schools, teachers, inspectors, or pupils, we will have to focus on the nation as a whole as described by educational data that record the shifting balances among its departments. Our study begins in the decades before the Guizot Law of 1833 (which made the establishment of public schools in every commune France's national policy) and continues to 1906 (just after church and state were formally separated and Catholic schools officially abolished), when primary school enrollment in France neared a peak not to be surpassed until after World War II.[16]

We begin in chapter 2 by exploring the number of elementary schools. When does France acquire the number its nearly forty thousand communes required? Are they established rapidly or slowly? Schools are an institutional measure of a community's commitment to intruction, and so it is important to know if their numbers suggest enthusiasm in some departments and reluctance in others, if their creation seems dependent upon legislation and pressure from Paris or other forces. We will want to look at departments for the effects of their differences in wealth, urbanization, administrative structure, and regional culture. If the data permit, it may be possible to suggest the rate and patterns by which schools spread across France, providing a basis for subsequent investigations.

We then analyze enrollment, asking many of the same questions. Did tuition-charging schools effectively exclude large parts of the population? If peasants, the majority of Frenchmen, resisted the cost in time and money that educators sought to impose upon them, that should show in enrollments. Religion, occupation, or region may make a great enough difference in people's willingness to learn to speak, read, and write French to be apparent even in departmental figures. The chronology of enrollments may help to measure the push and pull between national policy and individual behavior, mediated by local institutions and customs. If the patterns identified seem to hold, our picture of how elementary schooling developed across the nation can be further refined, and we will want to think again about wealth, literacy, administrative areas, and regional cultures.

To this point, our investigation lumps together all the different types of primary schools, only glancing at differences among those that were Catholic or lay, public or private. But the historiography is decisive: the question of whether school should be taught by men and women in religious orders was socially and politically explosive. That is the topic of chapter 4. Is it possible to even roughly assess the relative importance of national policy and local preference in determining the kind of schools children attended? Did the most Catholic departments consistently provide the highest proportion of Catholic attendance, or were other factors at work and are they in turn identifiable? And what of the uneven history of independent primary schools? They sometimes appear to have been a mere stopgap, sometimes a strong local tradition, sometimes laic, and sometimes the vehicle of Catholic resistance to public schools. Rates of change will be especially important here. Enrollment in independent schools tells something about the popularity of public schools; a sudden rise or fall in Catholic enrollments may indicate the power of public policy, slower changes the persistence of personal preference. After growth itself, the greatest transformation in French schooling during these years came with increased reliance on religious orders and then their rejection as teachers of French children. Placing those developments within the larger picture of schooling could put the competition between Catholics and anticlericals in another context.

We know that nineteenth-century society viewed the education of girls and boys very differently, but statistics can reveal little about how their classrooms differed in values and tone. They can, however, tell us how girls enrollment compared to that of boys and a good deal more. Chapter 5 looks to see if parents were less willing to pay for their daughters' instruction and whether departments differed significantly in their acceptance of girls schooling. Did differences increase or diminish as schooling for boys became universal, accepted as an economic necessity while girls education remained a kind of luxury or even a cultural threat? Maybe France really had two patterns of schooling, discriminating as sharply between peasant girls and boys as the *grands écoles* did between young men and women from the middle class. Elementary enrollment, in short, may provide important evidence of social behavior affecting women and attitudes underlying it.

The historical studies of elementary teachers, both religious and the famed *instituteurs* and *institutrices*, are especially strong, and we can add little to what they reveal of teachers' lives at normal school and in the classroom. Nevertheless, some important issues, ones that lend themselves to quantitative analysis, remain. A national educational system required a large number of qualified teachers, and we need to see at what pace it supplied them. Were normal school graduates, the official model, scarce in practice? Were they concentrated in favored departments or spread more evenly across the nation? There were other programs for training teachers, and their popularity may be a measure of the attractiveness of teaching. Because the relative qualifications of teachers, measured by the *brevet*, varied in different periods and regions, the percentage of teachers so certified can also indicate the spread of national standards. Teaching as an occupation for women developed differently, and it is a topic as important for the history of women as for the history of education. We will want to see if French girls were relatively reluctant or eager for that secular career, whether and when elementary school teaching came to be accepted as an occupation for women.

From the beginning, elementary schools taught a wider range of students than children six to thirteen years of age. Pupils were often younger and older, and in the course of the century, kindergartens and adult classes were often added. What was the pace of such developments, and did they continue, in an expansive process of ever widening ambitions and opportunities? Chapter 7 examines these questions and also the links between elementary education and further instruction. The path from preschool to university became an avenue in the twentieth century on which an individual's progress, including the side roads taken and barricades met, supposedly resulted from choice and talent. Did the achievement of free, universal primary schooling start France on this later course. Were there signs that students wanted more instruction or that society could provide it?

In the final chapter, we take up expenditures. Budgets are often, perhaps too readily, taken as the ultimate measure of political and social commitment. So, there is good reason to look at what France spent on public schools, especially to see if expenditures fluctuated or steadily rose and when the greatest increases came. We will look at expenditures in per capita and departmental terms for evidence of the effects of public policy and the local economy. The investigation of expenditures thus serves as an additional test of our general arguments, and we will look to see whether wealthier departments spent more on schooling or provided more of it. We also ask whether increased expenditures tended to produce higher enrollment or follow from it so that the discussions of patterns of growth and regional variation also serve as summary and conclusion.

These, then, are the kinds of questions we will be asking. Some of them have long haunted the literature on French schooling, some emerge from recent scholarship, and some grow out of the research undertaken here. We will not be able to answer all of them, and most of our answers will be in terms of trends and proportions, less definitive in tone than many of the (often contradictory) assertions found in descriptive accounts but consistently grounded in a comprehensive survey of national schooling as it changed over the years. Before beginning our explorations, however, two questions deserve an immediate answer: Are these data reliable, and how will they be analyzed and manipulated?

I

The statistics on French elementary schooling were systematically collected from the 1830s on, with sketchier efforts providing information from the late years of the First Empire. Collecting such data was an important expression of larger trends, in all of which France was a leader. Throughout Europe, governments of the post-Napoleonic era found in statistics a way to know their population and to increase their own effectiveness; intellectuals found in them an anthropological portrait and the materials for building a science of society. As assembled and analyzed by reformers, economists, and officials, social statistics fed the great discussions of social questions; and the techniques for dealing with such data had become quite sophisticated by the time the July Monarchy expanded official involvement in collecting, assessing, and publishing social data to make it a sizable, continuing operation with its own office and staff. For all who dealt with such matters, no topic was more important than popular education, and special efforts were made to gather data on it.[17] From the 1830s on the educational data were thus quite systematically gathered and are quite coherent from year to year. When the 1876 survey was published, a retrospective volume was added containing ninety-two tables, each of which treated a particular topic and listed by department the results from all the earlier major national inquiries. Thereafter, surveys were conducted every five years. More frequent and regular, they also became more elaborate, adding new items to their remarkable questionnaire. So many national surveys provide, in discriminating statistical detail, intricately interconnected descriptions of change in the educational system. For almost every important category, we have departmental data for thirteen different dates from 1829 to 1906—1829, 1833, 1837, 1850, 1863, 1867, 1876, 1881, 1886, 1891, 1896, 1901, and 1906. For many items, there is information for other years. Rows and columns were meticulously totaled (and compared), and, to make this massive amount of information more comprehensible, the statisticians of the Third Republic often calculated percentages and sometimes provided striking and useful graphs and maps. One of the reasons that these data, public and well known to historians, have not been more extensively used is in fact their very massiveness. It takes months just to absorb their range and general drift, and even then scholars were left to pick and choose the totals that seemed significant. It is simply impossible without the modern computer to attend consistently to every department of France at every data point on every variable. Our project began with the daunting and expensive task of putting this vast amount of printed statistical information in machine-readable form for computer analysis.[18]

Statistics, like sentences, are a form of generalization; but as evidence, verbal statements are more familiar and expressive, carry more of their own context, and can be more conveniently combined and weighed. Numbers proclaim their own abstractness and require an analysis that is limited by its very formality and remains vulnerably explicit. Understandably, students of French education have felt more confidence in historical documents presented in words by identifiable authors than in those consisting of numbers assembled by thousands of faceless compilers. To argue, as we do, that these statistics provide a useful measure of French education also seems to contradict some widely accepted impressions, the origins of which need to be understood. There is legitimate concern as to whether the numbers are accurate and whether the categories into which they fall really mean what they seem to. There is a suspicion that the picture the statistics form is more positive than the statements of inspectors, which have become a part of historical lore, and there is reluctance to abandon not so much an interpretation as a tone repeated through much of the writing on French schools.

The classroom teachers, heads of schools, rectors, and inspectors who filed the reports from which these data were compiled undoubtedly varied in their meticulousness and even in their understanding of what the questions meant, especially in the earlier surveys. Indeed, the editors of the published statistics warned of internal errors, but their helpful caution can be misleading. Positivists where numbers were concerned, they did not think in terms of any acceptable margin of error and apologized even for a discrepancy of less than ten among four million. Their concerns should be a source of confidence rather than doubt, for historical analysis looks at general patterns and is not undermined by random shifts of a few percentage points (let alone a few tenths or hundredths of a point) in the recorded figures. Although early data remain estimates, we are confident that they are representative, and the figures become more certain with subsequent surveys, as the system became more organized and its minions more accustomed to filling out forms. What François Guizot called the "first inspection générale et approfondie" of primary education took place in 1833. Twenty years earlier, a mere fifty-one of eighty-five departments had reported.

Computer analysis provides one useful check upon the sober civil servants who assembled these data. Any columns that added up incorrectly, horizontally or vertically, were flagged in the process of coding. Few did.[19] Our research in effect compares the data for each department against all others at a single date and each department against itself in all the other surveys, providing a check on the probable accuracy of each entry. We have found remarkably few statistical anomalies. The overall picture that emerges, department by department at one moment and over time, is extraordinarily internally consistent. By historical standards, even the early data are excellent, their weaknesses made evident by still better data for later dates.

Thus, the strongest reason for crediting these data comes from the data themselves. Literally millions of numbers are assigned to hundreds of variables (schools, public and private, religious and secular; classes, by size and type of school; students, by age and sex in various schools, summer and winter; teachers, by sex and school and level of certification; and expenditures, regular and extraordinary, by commune, department, and state). These numbers are listed for each department over a period of more than seventy years. The local inspectors and teachers who provided most of these figures normally had little access to earlier reports or to data in other categories from their own department let alone from the rest of France. Yet, in each category, the numbers for any one date generally make a neat progression from earlier to later dates, the data for one category correlate at a high level with the data from other categories (by tests contemporaries could not have made), and totals for each department sustain consistent rankings among all the other departments. Such impressive coherence on so large a scale implies that the numbers printed in all those columns reflect a reality sufficiently clear and well defined that different people in different places and on different dates were in fact counting the same things.

Undoubtedly, close local study will find many instances in which the figures reported to communal council, prefect, and inspector and then tabulated in Paris were exaggerated or incomplete. That may prove important for local or regional educational history, especially for its precise chronology, but it is difficult to imagine errors so great and so consistent that they would negate national trends. Where we have checked local sources, we have found no significant discrepancies. Take, for example, the Department of the Lozère, reputed to be both more backward and poorly reported than most. In the national statistics, it was often out of phase with most other departments. The local school inspector's report of 1835 was printed in the *Mémoires* of the department's learned Academy.[20] He lists the usual, basic statistics (numbers of schools and students by the various types) for each arrondissement. The notables who were members of the Academy would be sure to have had a good idea of the number and nature of schools in their district, and we can be confident they took statistics very seriously (the same issue of their bulletin published a report on the number of wolves killed in the past fourteen years—by arrondissement, male, pregnant female, nonpregnant female, and cubs—soberly establishing the average at "48.315" per year). National statistics were tabulated in 1834 and 1837; in every category, the figures in this local study for 1835 fall between those recorded for the Lozère in the national reports.[21]

In similar spot checks of local reports from a score of departments, reports to be found in the national archives or in secondary works based on local archives, we have consistently found the printed statistics confirmed.

Many small errors must in effect have cancelled each other out. In general, there were more reasons for teachers and inspectors to inflate the numbers of schools, students, and teachers than to shave them, although the opportunities were limited. Public schools had to account for public funds, and most charged tuition until the end of the Second Empire, which forced a certain rigor in record keeping, a tendency supported by a general belief in the importance of statistics and a widespread commitment to education. Figures for private schools, it was alleged, were less reliable and more likely to be exaggerated. On the other hand, isolated schools and "clandestine" ones, those taught by unofficial or itinerant teachers, were incompletely reported. And some students (but only a small proportion of the total) received primary instruction in *écoles maternelles*, lower classes of a secondary school, and other institutions not included among the elementary schools. These uncertainties, which occurred more in some categories than others, will be considered further where they matter, but on the whole there is little reason to believe them sizable enough to have very serious effect on the overall analysis of patterns.

A second limitation is historically more interesting. Terms like school, enrollment, or *brevet* (certification that a teacher was qualified) could refer to quite different phenonmena even at the same date and tended to change their meaning over the century. What counted as a school could be a distinctive high-ceilinged room dedicated to the purpose and adorned with a crucifix or tricolor or the dingy quarters of a poorly paid *instituteur*. The official statistics of French primary education are evidence primarily of the evolution of a national institution. The compilers of these statistics worried about the variety subsumed in a given category, and officials tried by gathering more and more information to probe behind the global figures. Their efforts provide us with categories more and more refined and reliable as the century progressed. For reasons related to this improvement in the statistics, critical terms tended to be applied with a firmer and more universal standard. Part of the development we study, those trends need to be kept in mind. Even the broader meanings should be important to the social historian, however. An identifiable place called a school, someone recognized as a professional teacher, students registered at school or town hall, and all of this operating under the eye of the mayor were important social facts in themselves. The numbers of schools and students, of teachers who had some training, and of francs and centimes spent on schooling have their own significance, especially when departments are compared with each other and one period with another, even though they tell us very little about the teaching and learning that went on.

The fact remains that the picture emerging from these structured statistics contrasts with a common impression that primary schooling in France was for a long time inadequate, progressed slowly and late, and had to overcome great local resistance. Ironically, that dark picture comes primarily from the inspectors themselves, the very men who gathered these statistics, and from the way historians have used their reports. They were written by men with a mission who believed like Camille Montalivet in 1829 that "primary schooling is a means to accelerate in France the progress of civilization, the perfecting of social order. . . ." With him they saw "popular education . . . as a story of intelligence, customs, general well being."[22] Like the director of a provincial normal school in 1833, they evoked the praise of local notables and indeed of all men of progress as they averred again and again that here was a "battle engaged between light and shadow," that "primary instruction is a counterweight necessary to social order; it is the true basis of liberty." And they promised that the pupil "returned to the masses" would "become an adept worker, intelligent farmer, intrepid and enlightened soldier, good father, good husband, excellent citizen."[23] Men who could promise so much met failure with moral indignation. Their self-consciously held bourgeois vision distanced them from the people they served but strengthened their tie to the likeminded men to whom they sent their reports. As local officials and beginning bureaucrats (often with some prospect of a career ahead), they had every incentive to stress the difficulty of their task, to show that their personal standards remained at Parisian levels, and to establish that local weaknesses were not their fault. Often, teachers, mayors, and inspectors joined in making their reports an occasion for vigorous lobbying for higher local taxes and more outside support.

Paul Lorain's influential *Tableau de l'instruction primaire*, written in 1837 and perhaps the most negative account of all, set the tone for a century of reports with its emphasis upon areas of almost universal illiteracy, uneven attendance totaling only three or four months a year, *hameaux* that were "sauvages," and recalcitrant parents who removed their children from school at the age of ten.[24] In 1839, the Conseil General of the Hautes-Alpes declared that only 18 of 222 public schools were in an "état passable," and the department was granted a one thousand franc subsidy that became twenty thousand francs a year by 1843 and forty thousand a year thereafter. In 1843, however, the inspector rated the "tenus et discipline" of 128 public schools as "bonnes" and of 65 as "mediocre," with only 25 "mal dirigé." Such shifting categories are hard to assess, but one suspects that the Conseil's low estimates were more directly tied to the subsequent subsidies than to any such dramatic improvement.[25]

Even as conditions improved, inspectors' aspirations leaped ahead, and at the end of the century, they remained as proudly distant from the peasants and workers whose children flocked to school as they had been at the beginning. The inspector of the Ain in 1864 complained of the absentees there in familiar rhetoric; Duruy himself estimated that 40 percent of the students left school without knowledge of the three R's; and the inspector of the Cher was indignant in 1878–79 that one of every ten boys between six and thirteen failed to attend school that year. Yet, the inspectors' reports that Lorain compiled estimate students to be making "satisfactory" progress in about two-thirds of the cases; the Ain was generally above the national average; Duruy's estimate is suspiciously (and self-servingly) close to the national level of adult illiteracy and three times what his own inspectors reported in 1866; and the Cher apparently had nine-tenths of its boys in school, an impressive achievement before legal compulsion.[26]

This does not mean that the inspectors are to be disbelieved (although some historians who have looked closely at their reports warn of their exaggerations and biases).[27] Rather, their rhetorical outrage and memorable tales about classrooms warmed by the adjacent stable or the *instituteur* who cooked his meal while teaching must be seen in the larger context that these same reports also provide. Usually, in even the most pessimistic accounts, the negative tone does not really contradict the statistical evidence or the impression it gives of general expansion and improvement. And there is a significant shift in the subjects of concern—from the absence of schools to the conditions of classrooms, from the competence of the teachers to the content of the curriculum, from sporadic and partial attendance to regular attendance but only for a few years—even though there was little change in the tone of pained condescension with which these matters were treated (the reports of 1878 are much more negative than those of 1869 despite undisputed progress). An impressive anthology could be compiled from reports as early as those of 1829 or 1843 about the "quite reassuring" spread of schools and generally "rapid and continual" progress. The reports of 1864 and 1869 are sometimes lyrical about the universality of instruction in departments like the Meuse, Moselle, Manche, Cher, Eure-et-Loir, and Doubs.[28] One M. L. Deries summed up the problem clearly in reporting on the Manche. In matters of education as elsewhere, he said, there were optimists and pessimists: "The former see a part of the reality, the others another . . . forgetting that progress is slow."[29] In fact, the majority of inspectors' reports during the half-century between Lorain and Ferry were positive.

Somehow that is not what stands out. Year after year the reports that reached Paris, even while noting the gains that were achieved, remained heavy with disappointment that the better society they sought had not been realized despite the continued efforts of enlightened legislators, overworked administrators, and schools that were understaffed and ill equipped. The apathy and indifference of ignorant parents became a standard lament (and perhaps an excuse). Indeed, that attitude in itself may be one of the by-products of the institutionalization and professionalization of education. It is certainly what inspectors reported in 1863 when specifically asked to explain why (some) students did not attend school,[30] and it is a view of peasants that many historians have accepted.[31] Rather like the nineteenth-century reformers, whose values they are likely to share, they have found the most pessimistic reports to be the most striking and have eschewed the statistics with their rather different overall message.

Combined with the political historian's concern about legislation—all the more justified in centralized France—the despairing view of France's educational progress became something of a historiographical tradition. Politicians like Guizot, Duruy, and Ferry saw themselves imposing progress at considerable cost. When social transformations were slow to follow from their efforts, there was a tendency to rediscover Lorain's regret at the "inexplicable torpor" of rural France. Republican historians set a lasting tradition in building their histories on "les grandes lois scolaires." The tendency has been to watch from the top, along with the administrators, as the promises of legislation were unevenly fulfilled.[32] In a historical tradition attuned to the recalcitrance of the masses, it was easy to overlook the fact that the inspectors were explaining the absence of just 10 percent of the prospective students or that they cited poverty, weather, the lack of warm clothing, distance, and the demands of work far more often than parental resistance.[33] Inspectors' comments on the positive demand for schooling have gone largely unreported.[34] In this historiography, unchallenged by attention to the statistics and focused on the great political battles surrounding the efforts of the state, the question of whether the growth of primary schooling often preceded major legislation or marched forward independent of it did not arise.

One might have expected the vitality of social history and of radical perspectives in the current generation to have rejected this older picture as class slander. Historians of labor, for example, have established that there was a strong and informed desire for education among workers in France and elsewhere during the nineteenth century. In the late twentieth century, however, after more than one hundred years of almost limitless expectations about the benefits of education, there is a tendency now to disparage the whole effort. For those disillusioned with what universal schooling accomplished, school systems are better understood as instruments of social control, and resistance to them becomes understandable, maybe even admirable. Much recent and skeptical historical writing, like the republican histories it would replace, has been prepared to find an intrusive state confronting reluctant masses. As this perspective is partially absorbed into studies on other topics that devote some space to education, it sustains a picture of France as having so inadequately and slowly taken to universal education that statistics to the contrary can scarcely be credited.[35] One scintillating work has proven so influential, especially among American and English historians, that it must be given special attention. In Eugen Weber's rich study, *Peasants into Frenchmen*, his chapter "Civilizing in Earnest: Schools and Society" provides a dizzying trip through descriptions of schools in the eighteenth century, teachers in mid-nineteenth century, and individual schools in the 1870s. His archival references come, as is to be expected, from departments our study labels as "laggards" and cite inspectors' descriptions of districts or particular schools within them. Although proof that there remained many makeshift schools, poor teachers, students left ignorant, and parents who did not care, this evidence needs to be placed in the context of the real achievement, of earlier and steady change, and in the larger picture for whole departments and the entire nation. Only then can we advance beyond the perspective of those ministry officials who, on receiving local reports, marked (usually with blue or red pen) the troubling passages, the passages still likely to catch the researcher's eye. If the historiographical tradition helps to remind us that mere numbers do not equal education, these carefully collected statistics can also provide a sense of proportion. They can encourage historians digging in the cartons of backward departments to go beyond the negative report about a particular school in Puy-de-Dôme to discover reports about the average school year in the department (ten and one-half months) and about "good schools," "important schools," and "intelligent masters." In Tarn-et-Garonne, often cited as retrograde, only 4 of 194 communes lacked schools in 1876 and the largest of those communes had 294 inhabitants. One can well believe the report that in the Haute-Loire the population spoke patois but should not forget the rest of the sentence: they also speak French.[36]

Among recent studies of education in France, there is much to suggest that the social roots of schooling were deep. Seeing schools in light of their history in the ancien régime can even make "the reforms of the nineteenth century seem singularly thin."[37] An impressive diversity of schools enjoyed social support early in the nineteenth century, too.[38] Robert Anderson has found that bad schools were the exception by the time of Duruy's administration in the 1860s and that examples of them were almost always drawn from backward departments.[39] And there are touching stories from throughout nineteenth-century France of parents' trust in the teacher to whom they sent milk and wood along with their "amazingly dutiful" children, and of children who like mountain climbers made a safety line to guide their daily hike through several kilometers of snow. Such scenes could occur in a place where it was said that "the peasants conserve with tenacity their old habits," in an area where one inspector suggested that one-third of the schools were "so deplorable and unhealthy" that they should be closed in the "name of humanity," although another, less dispeptic, observed that the inhabitants "are not so ignorant as is generally thought."[40] None of this prejudges what the statistics will show. In fact, the results will undoubtedly be mixed, but there is reason to consider with an open mind what they can be made to tell.

II

From this vast amount of statistical information, we have collected in a separate file more than two thousand statistical variables. Although some were selected from the *Statistique générale de la France*, primarily data on population and the economy, most of these variables come from the published *Statistique de l'enseignement*. We chose those that seemed most likely to prove revealing and that have information for many if not all of our data points across the century. With entries for each variable for each department at all these data points, we worked with something in the order of two million statistical items. It was important to observe certain principles.

The data were put into machine-readable form exactly as they appear in the printed sources. Some convenience could have been gained and economies won by combining categories before entering data, but where the variables are so numerous, there is a risk of later confusion and a likelihood that categories combined with one purpose in mind will come to be analyzed for another. Except in an occasional instance when the compilers' calculations contained an error (all totals and percentages were recalculated; their figures were rarely wrong), the computer data and the published data are the same. Sometimes for a single variable at certain dates we had alternative figures from archival records, other printed primary sources, or works by other scholars. Rarely were the discrepancies large enough to make any difference. When it seemed that they might, we used the two sets of data separately, and if the new results could affect interpretation, that is reported.

We generally resisted the temptation to improve the data. A good case can often be made for creating data, filling a gap at a certain point by interpolating from data before and after (and in a few instances, we felt it necessary to do something of the sort, a fact indicated on each table where it occurs). Similarly, a researcher may believe he knows that in a certain period data on a particular variable tended to be underreported or exaggerated. It can seem only sensible to adjust that variable by a few percentage points, but to do so can be very dangerous for several reasons. We do not really know what the percentage adjustment should be, and we certainly do not know that it applies equally to every department. A well-intended adjustment adds new and unknown distortions likely to be compounded when several variables are used at once; yet the results look as solid as any other. Indeed, the effects disappear from view so quickly that there is a tendency to make the correction again anyway when analyzing results, with some comment to the effect that of course in this period the figures are incomplete or exaggerated. Whenever we know of reasons to think these data may be high or low, we report that. In a few cases where some researchers have argued for some consistent bias in the statistics, we ran experiments with adjusted figures (usually to discover that the differences were statistically less significant than their description made them seem), and we mention the results of these experiments. They do not become part of further calculations, however; the data being used remain unchanged. The attentive reader should make allowances for margins of error as other evidence indicates.

Changes in France's frontiers between the Restoration and 1906 led to the addition, loss, or alteration of a few departments. In addition, data are occasionally not available on some variables for one or more departments. Whenever more than just a few departments are missing (and it is not a common problem), that is indicated. When our analysis refers to specific dates, it is based on all the departments of France at that time; when comparing all departments across time, we omit those not part of France through the entire period. A number of statistical techniques, none of them especially complicated, could have been used to compensate for this variation in boundaries, but all of them would have strengthened the correlations on which much of our findings are based, and we thought it wiser once again not to risk confusion between manipulating data and analyzing results.

When data are used for comparison between departments (at the same time or over different dates), as in almost all of our analysis, they are normalized, that is, calculated in relation to some other common factor: schools per population, students per school-age population, teachers per students, and so forth. Thus, analysis of a single variable in practice involves at least two variables, and these are always named. In each topic, particular questions about the effects of normalization tend to arise, and these will be treated chapter by chapter. Some general points should be made here. Obviously, normalization makes it possible to compare heavily and sparsely populated departments, but it does much more. Changes in boundaries (for example, the gain of Nice and Savoy in 1860 or the loss of Alsace-Lorraine in 1870), changes in departmental population (a few departments increased or declined significantly in this period), and demographic changes that affected school-age population are automatically taken into account.[41] Such factors may well need to be borne in mind when analyzing results, but they do not need to be separately estimated. Essential for meaningful comparison, normalization can nevertheless be misunderstood. The statisticians who worked on the *Statistique de l'enseignement* recognized the need for it, and with what must have taken enormous effort, they sometimes calculated enrollment as a percentage of a department's school-age population. On occasion, that produced results greater than 100 percent, which embarrassed the editors of the published volumes and has been cited off and on ever since as evidence of the *Statistique*'s unreliability. It is nothing of the sort. To say that enrollment equals 100 percent of the school-age population is to say only that the two numbers are the same, not that all children of school age are enrolled. By the same logic, if all of them are enrolled and then in addition there are some children under six in the lower grades and some over thirteen stay on for an extra year or two, there is no reason at all that enrollment might not be greater than school-age population. In fact, it often was.

Determining school-age population, used in a number of variables, presented subtler problems, although the French census gives those figures for boys from 1821 on and for all children from 1850 on. Until 1876, school age was defined as five to fifteen year olds but was changed in 1881 to those from six to thirteen. Both make sense, and we have dealt with it in two ways. First, we have adjusted the two definitions of school age by the straightforward 7:10 ratio (70 percent rather than by 71.5 percent that would have allowed for an aging population from 1876 to 1881). Similarly, we used a simple linear adjustment to arrive at school-age population between 1821 and 1850. Second, we have analyzed nearly all data by both total population and school-age population. From 1850 to 1906, Pearson correlations between these measures range from .89 to .97, indicating both national continuity and significant variation among some 10 to 20 percent of the departments (when the number of schools or enrollments are normalized by these two measures, correlations never fall below .82). Having noted changes in official categories wherever relevant, we generally use the population of six to thirteen year olds unless otherwise stated; it represents the conception of primary schooling toward which the system moved. We indicate in text and footnotes the few analytic discrepancies we encountered and look more closely at those departments with greatest changes in population and unusually high or low proportions of young people.

Before discussing the statistical devices we most frequently use, two limitations of the *Statistique*'s presentation of the data need to be addressed. Not all the data points are evenly distributed, and the absence of data between 1840 and 1850 and again between 1850 and 1863 is especially regrettable, for these were important periods of rapid change. Statistically, of course, one can adapt somewhat by calculating the annual percentage of change, and we do that, but the figure is more descriptive over a five-year than a thirteen-year period. Sometimes other information, contemporary comments or annual expenditures, indicate that the change was greater in certain years within these longer periods. We report that and consider it in our conclusions when it seems important. Beyond that, there is little to do except warn that when our periodizations emphasize changes in such a period (as they often must), the period and not a specific year marks the change. Nevertheless, the distribution of data points is extraordinarily good as historical data go, and comfort can be found in the statistical fact that many points unevenly distributed make patterns of regularity somewhat less likely to emerge, adding credibility to those that do.

The data on these two thousand variables are reported as a total for each department. There are many departments (between eighty and ninety throughout our period), which means that even low correlations tend to be statistically significant. Geographically, they are relatively small—it was supposed to be possible to cross any department on horseback in a single day, which makes them good units (when grouped in different ways) for testing some traditional assumptions about regional differences. For social analysis, they are less satisfactory. Even departments with sizable cities included some very rural parts and quite isolated communities, and most included areas extremely diverse in the very characteristics we would like to observe, such as the level of literacy, ease of communication, religious practice, economic structure, and per capita wealth. Thus, data aggregated by departments mask much that we want to study. In this respect, too, that may mean that when correlations do emerge, they are all the more significant, a relationship between schooling and some other social factor strong enough to show through the social averaging that department's effect. The fact remains that departments lump a lot of elements together. Correlations seeking to isolate particular factors are more telling, therefore, when they identify departments similar on that one measure but quite varied on most others (not, for example, from the same region of France).

We study the quantitative data on schooling in many internally diverse departments by comparing them on single measures of schooling. The comparisons must be sensitive to each department's relation at a given moment to all the others and also to each department's place in the changes that occur over time. Many approaches are available. We use correlations a good deal, and they are easily explained. The Pearson or product-moment correlation indicates how close the actual data points are to the straight line, the line of least squares, that best fits two sets of data (most simply in this study each department's enrollment, normalized by population, at two different dates). The result is reported as the coefficient of correlation, r. A perfect positive correlation is 1.0, a perfect negative correlation is -1.0, no relationship would produce an r of 0.0. The first variable is said to explain the second in proportion to the square of their correlation; with a correlation of .8 the first explains two-thirds (0.64) of the second, but with a correlation of .5 the first predicts a quarter (0.25) of the second. One of the important advantages of such correlations for this study is that each variable includes all departments. Correlations compare the distribution of all departments on one variable at one time to their distribution on another variable at another time, and the effect of any changes between two dates in the way the data were gathered or recorded is therefore minimized. The comparison is between the relationship of France's departments to each other on two variables rather than just between two sets of raw numbers. Because our variables compare many units (eighty-some departments), even a small correlation is said to be statistically significant. We generally ignore the lower correlations. As a check, we also often calculated another kind of correlation, the statistically less informative Spearman or rank-order correlation. Rank-order lists of all departments create a huge number of opportunities for changes in rank between the two lists (nearly 1,700,000 possibilities among eighty-five departments), and this measure might be expected to produce quite different and much lower correlations because the normalized scores of many departments will usually be close together and tend to move closer over time. Generally, we did not find important differences between the two types of correlation. Some of those differences are reported and discussed in chapter 2; otherwise, we use Pearson correlations, more sensitive because of their weighting factor, throughout this study.

We also often analyze in terms of octiles. They, too, are based on the rank of departments on a specified, normalized variable in a given year. They are convenient because it is easier to follow or graph the movement of eight groups than more than eighty. We often do something else, however, keeping departments in the octiles into which they fell at a first date. Then for later dates the mean is calculated for each of these eight groups. If the initial rankings of these departments was fortuitous or if in their later development they leapfrogged over each other, the means of these octiles should crisscross or cease to be distinguishable. When the initial octiles preserve their relative position as schooling develops, that indicates regularity in the process of growth.

Several standard statistical measures are used to indicate the degree to which departments differed. Standard deviation in effect defines a range; two-thirds of the departments fall within the standard deviation above and below the national mean. The coefficient of variation is useful for taking into account even the most extreme cases but does not distinguish so clearly between cases in which a few departments stand very far from the mean and many are scattered but nearer to it. Calculated by summing the squares of the difference between each department and the national mean, it is expressed in percentages. The cluster analyses we use are described more fully where they occur. In essence, they place departments into groups (the number of groups can be chosen by the investigator, and they are not necessarily of equal size) in such a way as to arrive at the smallest possible coefficient of variation within each group.[42] Because tradition and the mind's eye tend to group departments in regional formations, cluster analysis is especially helpful in making us look in a different way at which departments really have most in common on selected variables.

The most familiar summary statistics—percentages, means, and normalized variables—provide an abstract but useful sense of the national condition measured on a specific variable. If that variable is well chosen, the results can give a valuable sense of proportions and probabilities; they do not directly describe local reality. Beyond that, most of our analysis and most of these statistical tools are devices for discovering and measuring relations among departments and for identifying patterns of change. It becomes possible to ask not only whether there were national patterns of growth but whether those patterns also applied to individual departments. Because the numbers are very large and relationships among them are what matters, differences of a few percentage points in the raw data would usually have little effect on the larger findings. We have tried to base our analysis primarily on statistical relationships strong enough to remain valid even if inaccuracies were many times larger than we believe them to be. Where the indicators are strong, these measures can effectively establish that a certain pattern obtained. They do not in themselves prove that our explanations for it are correct except in the sense that multiple tests of a hypothesis can create an increasingly strong presumption in its favor. Allowing for some margin of error and remembering that official categories encompassed varied circumstances, these data can stand as the single most valuable source from which to establish the major trends in the national development of primary schooling in France. This, then, is primarily a book about patterns and directions of change and the process that seems to explain them.

While reading it, the tables at the back should get frequent attention. They are arranged in sets, by chapter (and there are numerous cross references to them in the text); but within each set, the tables are ordered by an independent logic, beginning with the most straightforward statistics and proceeding in increasing analytic complexity. Similarly constructed tables therefore occupy comparable positions within each set of tables, facilitating their comparison across chapters. Readers will want to assess the quality of support for different arguments, which necessarily varies, and look for explanations we may have missed. In doing that, we hope they will also share our sense of excitement in probing this quite extraordinary set of data for the historical insights it can provide.

Notes

1. The long history and intensity of that concern is reflected in the vast and useful catalogue of periodical publications assembled by the Institut national de recherche pédagogique under the direction of Pierre Caspard: Pénélope Caspard-Karydis, André

Chambon, Geneviève Fraisse, and Denise Poindron, *La presse d'éducation et d'enseignement, XVIIIᵉ–1940*, 3 vols. to date (Paris, 1981–).

2. Recent review articles of this burgeoning literature testify to its vitality and variety, in which all the major currents continue. They include a traditional view set forth in light of the anniversary of the Ferry Laws by Maurice Crubillier in *Histoire de l'éducation*, "Ou en l'histoire de l'école primaire" (April, 1982): 1–22, and "L'histoire en crise d'une école en crise" 18 (April, 1983): 29–48; a special section by three reviewers in *History of Education Quarterly*, no. 26 (Summer, 1986): 257–86, reviewing ten books and commenting on recent historiographical trends—on France, see especially the reviews by John M. Burney and Barry H. Bergen; Françoise Mayeur's wide-ranging survey, "Recent Views on the History of Education in France," in *European Historical Quarterly* 14 (January, 1984): 93–102; Pierre Caspard, "L'Institut National de Récherche Pédagogigue, centre de ressources sur l'histoire de l'éducation française," *French Historical Studies* 16 (Spring, 1989): 222–25; Linda Clark, "Approaching the History of Modern French Education: Recent Surveys and Research Guides," ibid., 15 (Spring, 1987): 157–65; Richard Wolff, "European Perspectives on the History of Education: A Review of Four Journals," *History of Education Quarterly* 26 (Spring, 1986): 87–94. See also Patrick J. Harrigan, "Historians and Compilers Joined: The Historiography of the 1970s and the French Enquêtes of the Nineteenth Century," in Donald N. Baker and Patrick J. Harrigan, eds., *The Making of Frenchmen: Current Directions in the History of Education in France, 1679–1979* (Waterloo, Can., 1983) 3–21. French education also became the subject of a multivolume history of its own, L.-H. Parias, ed., *Histoire générale de l'enseignement et de l'éducation in France*, 4 vols. (Paris, 1981). In its most recent biannual bibliography, *Histoire de l'éducation*, nos. 43–44 (September, 1989), lists 1,383 books and articles on French schooling.

3. Among important general histories Maurice Gontard, *L'enseignement primaire en France de la Révolution à la loi Guizot, 1789–1833: Des petits écoles de la monarchie d'Ancien Régime aux écoles primaires de la monarchie bourgeoise* (Paris, 1959); Paul Gerbod, *La condition universitaire en France au XIXᵉ siècle* (Paris, 1965); Félix Ponteil, *Histoire de l'enseignement en France: Les grandes étapes, 1789–1965* (Paris, 1966); Antoine Prost, *Histoire de l'enseignement en France, 1800–1967* (Paris, 1968); John Talbott, *The Politics of Educational Reform in France, 1918–1940* (Princeton, 1969); Robert Anderson, *Education in France, 1848–1970* (Oxford, 1975); Joseph N. Moody, *French Education since Napoleon* (Syracuse, 1978); Pascale Gruson, *L'état enseignant* (Paris, 1978); E. Plenel, *La république inachevée: l'état et l'école en France* (Paris, 1985).

4. Jacob L. Talmon, *The Rise of Totalitarian Democracy* (Boston, 1952), and Alfred Cobban, *Dictatorship* (London, 1938), stated the theme most baldly; and it has had a prominent life in the treatment of French education: Carlton J. H. Hayes, *Essays on Nationalism* (New York, 1926); idem, *France: A Nation of Patriots* (New York, 1930); James E. Coleman, ed., *Education and Political Development* (Princeton, 1965), especially his introductory essay; Michalina Vaughan and Margaret S. Archer, *Social Conflict and Educational Change in England and France, 1789–1848* (Cambridge, 1971).

5. See Louis Legrand, *L'influence du positivism dans l'oeuvre scolaire de Jules*

Ferry (Paris, 1961), and Pierre Chevalier, *La séparation de l'église et de l'école: Jules Ferry et Léon XIII* (Paris, 1961), but also Katherine Auspitz, *The Radical Bourgeoisie: The Ligue de l'enseignement and the Origins of the Third Republic, 1866-1885* (Cambridge, Eng., 1982).

6. Jean Maurain, *La politique ecclésiastique du Second Empire de 1852 à 1869* (Paris, 1930); Adrien Dansette, *Religious History of Modern France*, vol. 1 (New York, 1961); André Latreille and René Rémond, *Histoire du catholicisme en France*, vol. 3 (Paris, 1962); Gérard Cholvy and Yves-Marie Hilaire, *Histoire religieuse de la France contemporaine*, vol. I, 1800-80, and vol. II, 1880-1930 (Toulouse, 1985-86).

7. Mona Ozouf, *L'école, l'église, et la République, 1871-1914* (Paris, 1963 and 1982).

8. Maurice Lévy-Leboyer, "Innovation and Business Strategies in Nineteenth and Twentieth-Century France," in *Enterprise and Entrepreneurs in Nineteenth and Twentieth-Century France*, ed. Edward Carter, Robert Forster, and Joseph Moody (Baltimore, 1976): 87-135; Charles R. Day, *Education in the Industrial World: The Ecole d'Arts et Métiers* (Cambridge, 1987); Robert Fox and George Weisz, eds., *The Organization of Science and Technology in France, 1808-1914* (Cambridge, Eng., 1980); Terry Shinn on the Polytechnique, *L'Ecole Polytechnique, 1794-1914* (Paris, 1980).

9. Roger Chartier, Dominique Julia, and Marie Madeleine Compère, *L'éducation en France du XVIe au XVIIIe siècle* (Paris, 1976); François Furet and Jacques Ozouf, *Lire et écrire: L'alphabétisation des français de Calvin à Jules Ferry*, 2 vols. (Paris, 1977); Harvey Chisick, *The Limits of Reform in the Englightenment: Attitudes toward the Education of the Lower Classes in Eighteenth-Century France* (Princeton, 1981); Jean de Viguerie, *Une oeuvre d'éducation sous l'ancien régime* (Paris, 1976).

10. Robert R. Palmer, *The Improvement of Humanity: Education and the French Revolution* (Princeton, 1985).

11. Pierre Bourdieu and Jean-Claude Passeron, *Les héritiers: Les étudiants et la culture* (Paris, 1964), and *Le reproduction: Éléments pour une théorie du système d'enseignement* (Paris, 1970); Louis Althusser, "Idéologie et appareils idéologiques d'état (notes pour une recherche)," *La pensée* 151 (1970): 3-38; Michel Crozier, *The Bureaucratic Phenomenon* (Chicago, 1964); Victor Karady, "Educational Qualifications and University Careers in Science in Nineteenth-Century France," in Fox and Weisz, *Organization of Science*, 95-124; ibid., "Normaliens et autres enseignants à la Belle Epoque: Note sur l'origine sociale et la réussite dans une profession intellectuelle," *Révue française de sociologie* 12 (1972): 35-58; ibid., "L'expansion universitaire et l'évolution des inégalités devant la carrière d'enseignmant au début de la IIIe République," in ibid. 14 (1973): 443-70; Viviane Isambert-Jamati, *Crises de la société, crises de l'enseignement: Sociologie de l'enseignement secondaire français* (Paris, 1970).

12. Christian Baudelot and Roger Establet, *L'école capitaliste en France* (Paris, 1971); Patrick J. Harrigan, *Mobility, Elites, and Education in French Society of the Second Empire* (Waterloo, Ont., 1980), and *Lycéens et collégiens sous le Second Empire* (Paris, 1979).

13. Françoise Mayeur, *L'enseignement des jeunes filles* (Paris, 1976); and her "L'éducation des filles en France au XIXe siècle: Historiographie récente et prob-

lématiques," *Problèmes d'histoire de l'éducation*, Collection de l'Ecole française de Rome, no. 104 (Rome, 1988): 79–90; Linda Clark, *Schooling the Daughters of Marianne: Textbooks and the Socialization of Girls in Modern French Primary Schools* (Albany, 1984); Dominique Maingueneau, *Les livres d'écoles de la République, 1870–1917 (discours et idéologie)* (Paris, 1979).

14. Eugen Weber, *Peasants into Frenchmen* (Stanford, 1976); André Chevel, . . . *et il fallut apprendre à écrire à tous les petits français: Histoire de la grammaire scolaire* (Paris, 1981).

15. Jacques Ozouf, ed., *Nous, les maîtres d'école: Autobiographies d'instituteurs de la Belle Epoque* (Paris, 1967); Danielle Delhome, Nicole Gault, and Josian Gonthier, eds., *Les premières institutrices laïques* (Paris, 1980); Fabienne Reboul-Scherrer, *La vie quotidienne des premiers instituteurs, 1833–1882* (Paris, 1990).

16. Enrollment was 5,451,094 in 1905–6; it rose by 24,690 in 1911–12, then fell sharply not only during World War I but in the 1920s (when it was under 4,000,000) before rising to 5,436,554 in 1937–38.

17. An ordinance of 1816 called for annual statistics on education and one of 1821 proposed collecting data on primary education every three years and an annual accounting of expenditures. The system for annual reports was set up in 1820, but they were not regularly collected until 1830; the report of the following year was published. Bernard-Pierre Lécuyer, "The Statistician's Role in Society: The Institutional Establishment of Statistics in France," *Minerva* 25, no. 1–2 (Spring–Summer, 1987): 35–55; Jacques Ozouf, "Les Statistiques de l'enseignement primaire au XIXe siècle," *Pour une histoire de la statistique*, vol. I, *Contributions* (Paris, 1977): 139–54.

18. The retrospective volume is Ministère de l'Instruction Publique et des Beaux-Arts, *Statistique de l'enseignement primaire*, vol. II, *Statistique comparée de l'enseignement primaire (1829–1877)* (Paris, 1880). In addition, there are departmental data on many items for 1813, 1821, 1832, and 1872, and there are national data for a number of other years, including 1826, 1840, 1843, and 1847—all of which we included. The educational data were part of a much larger project that put the *Statistique générale de la France* into machine-readable form, a project conducted in cooperation with the Ecole des Hautes Etudes en Sciences Sociales by the Interuniversity Consortium for Political and Social Research, the Center for Political and Social Studies, and the Center for Western European Studies at the University of Michigan. The project was funded in the United States by the National Endowment for the Humanities and the National Science Foundation, Jerome M. Clubb and Raymond Grew, principal investigators.

19. Minor discrepancies crop up during the Second Empire (1 percent from the summary data in the *Statistique*) and during the 1870s (.5 percent).

20. "Instruction primaire, resumé statistique de 1835 d'après le rapport de M. l'inspecteur des écoles primaires du département," *Mémoires et analyse des travaux de la Société d'Agriculture, Science et Arts de la Ville de Mende, chef-lieu du département de La Lozère* 8 (1834–35): 121–22.

21. Later local reports now in the departmental archives are cited by Guillaume Géraud, *Notes sur cent ans d'histoire en Lozère* (Mende, 1969), 19–23; all conform to the published figures.

22. "Introduction" to the *Statistique des écoles*, 1829, 1–2.

23. M. Jegaud, directeur de l'école normale primaire du département et membre de la Société, *Société d'Agriculture, Commerce, Science et Arts de la Ville de Mende*... 8 (1834–35): 43, 45, 47. One of the important effects of the Guizot Law of 1833 was to occasion such panegyrics and unleash such local enthusiasm.

24. Paul Lorain, *Tableau de l'instruction primaire* (Paris, 1837), 13, 70.

25. Henri Thivet, *La vie publique dans les Hautes-Alpes ver le milieu de XIXe siècle* (La Tronche-Montfleur, n.d.), 259–60, 267.

26. The proportion leaving school without having acquired basic skills was thought to be about 13 percent (ranging from 1 percent in the Moselle to 25 percent in Morbihan), *Exposé* (1867), 23; the original reports are in the Archives Nationales, F17/10357. The proportion is consistent with the literacy statistics for *conscrits* in the *Statistique de l'enseignement*, II:clvi–clx. Comments on the Eure (*Etat* [1864], I: 296, 862) and on the Gard a decade later (*Rapports* [1878], II:156) similarly show indignation about a small proportion of absentees. Contrast Duruy's pessimism about the lasting effects of instruction (in *L'administration de l'instruction primaire de 1863 à 1869* [Paris, 1870], I:152–56, and in *Notes et souvenirs* (Paris, 1907), 1:207) with his own admission that many students temporarily absent from school would return (*Exposé* [1867], 22) and with the inspectors' belief that many whose school leaving was said to be "non-facultatif" would return to acquire further skills—a point at least eleven of them made explicitly (ibid. I: 59, 118, 448, 745; II: 46, 68, 241, 455, 490, 717, 987).

27. Dominique Julia, "L'enseignement primaire dans le diocèse de Reims à la fin de l'ancien régime," *Annales historiques de la Révolution française* 42 (1970): 284; Anderson, *Education in France*, 161 (although by page 167 he accepts the picture of rural apathy); Colin Heywood, *Childhood in Nineteenth-Century France: Work, Health and Education among the "classes populaires"* (Cambridge, Eng., 1988), 191, notes that many middle-class observers also exaggerated the demoralization and immorality among the working classes as well. Carl F. Kaestle and Maris A. Vinovskis, in *Education and Social Change in Nineteenth-Century Massachusetts* (Cambridge, Eng., 1980), 10, point out that much of the pessimism about the success of education in New England results from the exaggerated expectations of reformers like Horace Mann. The same holds true for Ontario where the reports of Egerton Ryerson were uncritically accepted by historians for a century, R. D. Gidney, "Making Nineteenth-Century School Systems: The Upper Canadian Experience and Its Relevance to English Historiography," *History of Education* 9 (1980): 101–16. Similarly, see David Tyack and Elizabeth Hansot, *Managers of Virtue: Public School Leadership in America, 1820–1980* (New York, 1982).

28. *Statistique des écoles* 1829, 4; *Rapport* (1843), 2, 31–33. Only the mentally handicapped failed to attend in the Meuse, the physically and mentally handicapped in the Manche, 1 percent in the Eure-et-Loir, according to the inspectors. In the Moselle, enough students finished a nine-year course, and in the Doubs only eight thirteen-year-olds remained "ignorant," *Etat* (1864), I: 118, 319; II: 283, 563. The report of 1869 is in the Archives Nationales, F17/9376.

29. *Etude statistique de l'enseignement primaire de la Manche* (1896), 3–4. In

1864, the inspector of the Isère explained that enrollment would grow with wealth, that with each generation better-educated parents would encourage their children more, *Etat* (1864), I:761.

30. *Statistique de l'instruction primaire 1863*, 3, 10, 15, 30.

31. Anderson, *Education in France*, 167, concurs that "the final obstacle to the progress of education was the 'indifference' or apathy of parents and local opinion. It was the most frequently appealed to by Duruy's officials, who saw it as the root of all their others." Moody, *French Education*, 73–75, accepts this judgment which Gontard, *L'enseignement primaire*, 538, shared a generation earlier. Prost reports a peasant father's comment that he had gotten along just fine without being able to read and sees it as an example of the "grand argument de la force d'inertie on retrouve tout au long du XIXe siècle," Prost, *Histoire de l'enseignement*, 99.

32. From Gabriel Compayré, *Histoire critique des doctrines de l'éducation en France depuis le seizième siècle* (Paris, 1879), that tradition has continued through Alexis Léaud and Emile Glay, *L'école primaire en France*, 2 vols. (Paris, 1934), to Maurice Gontard's valuable and revealing study titled *L'enseignement primaire en France de la Révolution de 1789 à la loi Guizot* (Paris, 1959); Felix Ponteil, *Histoire de l'enseignement en France: les grandes étapes, 1789–1965* (Paris, 1966); Paul Gerbod, *La vie quotidienne dans les lycées et collèges au XIXe siècle* (Paris, 1968); Pascale Gruson, *L'état enseignant* (Paris, 1978); and Mayeur, *L'éducation en France*, with its chapter on "Les grandes lois scolaires." Compayré, *Histoire critique*, II:381, declares that after the Guizot law "all communes would have a school," Gruson, "Du monopole napoléonien à la république des professeurs," these du 3e cycle (University of Paris, 1970), 70, that it "opened education to those who could not attend a lycée" and mistakenly thinks that it made primary schools free. This emphasis on the state leads Ponteil, *Histoire de l'enseignement*, 290, to show that the Ferry Laws increased enrollment by comparing the figures for 1876 and 1886, when both the *Statistique de l'enseignement* and the *Annuaires* give yearly figures establishing that the greatest growth preceded the law of obligation. Léaud and Glay, *L'école primaire*, II:98, believe that the *certificat d'études* was created in 1882 whereas that is merely the date at which departments were required to institute it. Most had done so a few years before; once again, national legislation confirmed local initiatives. These are admirable studies by able historians, which makes it all the more important and sobering to see how far a general perspective has shaped interpretation.

33. See *Etat* (1864), I:449 (Savoie). In the archival reports and the summary reports of 1864, 1869, and 1878–79, inspectors most often cited these outside pressures, ibid.; Archives Nationales, F17/9376 (for 1869); *Rapports* (1878–79).

34. *Etat* (1864), I: 6, 18, 578, 587, 635; *Rapports* (1878), 39, 49, 123, 143, 193, 246, 262, 272, 285, 409, 516, 540, 562, 592, 610. Eugen Weber, *Peasants into Frenchmen*, 311, notes that demand for schooling existed even in backward areas. Major series of reports are in the Archives Nationales, F17/9306–20, 9367–72, 10368–407 (July Monarchy); 9251–85 (1850–90); 9279–85, 9321-59, 9376 (Second Empire); 10408–719 (Third Republic).

35. David Pinkney, *Decisive Years, 1840–1847* (Princeton, 1986), comments that peasants "saw little value in education and resisted sending their children to schools. . . ."; he is arguing for these as years of transition, but the familiar picture is

as likely to be remembered as the chronology. Similar assumptions about the attitudes of English workers toward education are now being challenged, J. S. Hurt, *Elementary Schooling and the Working Classes, 1860–1918* (London, 1979), 34; Trygve Tholfsen, *Working Class Radicalism in mid-Victorian England* (New York, 1977), 61–65.

36. Archives Nationales, F17/9271 (1880), 9265 (1877).

37. Willem Frijhoff and Dominique Julia, *Ecole et société dans la France d'ancien régime: quartre exemples, Auch, Avallon, Condom et Gisors* (Paris, 1975), 93. Note also Jean Perrel, "L'enseignement féminin sous l'ancien régime; les écoles populaires en Auvergne, Bourbonnais, Velay," *Cahiers d'histoire* 23 (1978): 193–210, and of course Furet and Ozouf, *Lire et écrire*.

38. For a convenient sample, see three articles in Baker and Harrigan, *Making of Frenchmen*: Gérard Cholvy, "Une école des pauvres au début du 19e siècle: 'pieuse filles,' béates ou soeurs des campagnes"; Gabriel Désert, "Alphabétisation et scolarisation dans le Grand-Ouest au 19e siécle"; Robert R. Palmer, "The Central Schools of the First French Republic: A Statistical Survey."

39. Anderson, *Education in France*, 153.

40. Mona Ozouf, ed., *La classe interrompue: Cahier de la famille Sandre, enseignants 1780–1960* (Paris, 1979), 165–67; Romy Chastel, *La Haute Lozère, jadis et naguère* (Paris, n.d. [1976]), 129–30; Géraud, *Cent ans d'histoire*, 20.

41. Population figures themselves, we all know, are never absolutely correct. When normalizing other data by population, we took both from the same year, except for the 1813 data, which are greatly inferior. Data for 1813 are normalized by population in 1821 but excluded from all sophisticated statistical analysis.

42. Cluster analysis begins with variance tests to determine the total variation among all departments in the usual way. The variation accounted for by grouping is the total variation minus the sum of within-group variation (the sum of the squares of the deviations among departments within a group from that group's mean). The proportion of the variation removed by grouping (R^2) is the ratio of the variation accounted for by grouping to the total variation. Obviously, the greater the number of groups, the greater the R^2 would be; if every department constituted a group, R^2 would be 1. The Fastclus procedure used to create the groups is discussed in the *SAS User's Guide—Statistics*, Version 5 (Cary, N.C., 1985); the SAS statistical package was used to implement the Fastclus procedure.

CHAPTER 2

The Availability of Schooling

The history of primary education as a national institution begins with the establishment of schools. However meager the immediate result, the creation of a school was a significant social event. It meant a prescribed space (that could then be moved, improved, or enlarged and that the commune and state or church, parents, and donors were responsible for) and an assigned teacher (whose pay, preparation, and pedagogy could be prescribed). The creation of that school was the beginning of a competitive pressure among communes and families and the beginning of a kind of instruction in itself, teaching parents that at a certain age their children should be given over to the care of others. The fact that learning took place away from home in a new environment had great psychological implications and was part of the revolution in patterns of learning which many have studied.[1] Schools gave that process an increasing regularity, attaching it to certain hours of the day, seasons of the year, and years of childhood. To establish and expand these patterns the school itself was the central instrument, whether it was a school for boys or girls or both, private or public, taught by religious or lay teachers or by men or women.

There were about thirty-six thousand schools in France by 1829, and twice that many in 1906. Even these crude figures reveal that the growth of schools during the nineteenth century was enormous and that it primarily took place early in the century—during the Restoration and the first dozen years of the July Monarchy. Even allowing for some underestimate of the number of schools in the first two decades, table S.1 shows a clear pattern of rapid growth in the early years of the Restoration, which slowed during its second decade, was followed by growth (5 percent per year on average) from 1829 to 1837, and then gradually declined to 1843, remaining slower but fairly steady thereafter. Never again would the schools of France so rapidly increase in number.[2]

Although growth followed upon the Guizot Law of 1833, that law in fact came midway in a period of rapid growth and must have reflected as well as encouraged increasing social demands for schooling. Distinct periods of somewhat more rapid growth rates occurred in the Second Empire and again between 1876 and 1886.[3] Once again, major legislation on education—the Ferry Laws—was promulgated in the middle of a period of growth. By 1886,

France had all the schools it would have in 1906, although some growth occurred before the anticlerical laws in 1901 led to the closing of many private schools. These figures alone are important, for each school created reflected considerable effort and local expenditure. To know what schools meant for the availability of schooling, however, requires that the number of schools be understood in terms of the population to be instructed.

Table S.2 contains some surprises. Adjusted for population, the number of schools increased less from 1833 to 1837, following the Guizot Law, than one would have expected. Three-quarters of the apparent growth rate was the result of counting girls schools in 1837 and not in 1833. (If some mixed schools had now split into separate schools for boys and girls, some boys schools were counted for the first time in 1837 although they had existed earlier.) By 1837—before the revolution of 1848 and the prosperity of the Second Empire—France had 62 percent of the ratio of schools to population that it would have at the high point of 1901, and 82 percent of that ratio in 1867 before the beginning of the Third Republic. Important as it was, the Guizot Law had a rather less dramatic effect on the number of schools than the general literature has asserted.[4]

The famed Ferry Laws that so divided the nation had a miniscule effect on the number of schools per one thousand Frenchmen—a 5 percent increase in the next five years and 9 percent over the next quarter century. This law, which required every school-age child to go to school and made schooling free, demanded little increase in the number of schools despite what some historians have asserted and others implied.[5] The Ferry Laws and other contemporary measures did favor public over private schools and secular over religious teachers, which certainly led to the opening of some new schools and the closing of some old ones, but the significant point here is that the new laws required so little increase in the total number of schools. This argues that French society may have managed to provide the schools that universal education required earlier and more by way of local initiative and internal momentum than as the direct result of the most famous measures of governmental compulsion.

In the case of France, those of school age were proportionally a larger part of the total population earlier in the century than later, as a low birth rate led to an older population. Although more significant in a few, specific departments (as we show later), for the nation as a whole the ratio of schools to school-age population yields only slightly different results than the ratio of schools to total population, giving somewhat higher growth rates until 1882 (the Ferry Laws) and a more stable, declining growth rate thereafter. Normalized by school-age population, a more refined measure, the trend toward providing universal access to schools shows up even earlier. If one takes as a target the ratio of schools to school-age population in 1901 and 1906 (note that the ratio in these years is the same by this measure), France had reached over half that goal before the Guizot Law took effect, over two-thirds by the end of the July Monarchy, and over three-quarters by 1863.[6]

But can the number of schools in France really be taken as a measure of the availability (and response to) universal education? The simplest test is whether children attended schools once they were established. If one correlates the number of schools in each department of France with the number of children enrolled in schools, the results are striking (table S.9). The number of schools and enrollment correlate closely, predicting most of the total enrollment by department throughout the century, but the correlation declines slowly and drops abruptly at the turn of the century. Three suppositions present themselves. First, in the July Monarchy (and to a large extent up to the Third Republic), when schools were established, students went to them. There is little hint in these figures of recalcitrant parents withholding their children but rather the suggestion of so ready a response to new schools as to imply that parental demand, if not necessarily that of the children themselves, preceded the creation of schools. Undoubtedly, schools were built primarily where they were already wanted or at least where the population was sufficient to assure a good enrollment. Second, the increasing number of schools meant their establishment in more isolated hamlets and in areas of scattered population, so that additional schools brought much less by way of additional enrollment. Third, under the Third Republic, much of the increase in the number of schools must have represented further refinements (such as the division of a mixed school into separate schools for girls and boys) that brought little or no increase in enrollment. By then, access to school was no longer the critical issue, and the number of schools became a poorer measure of the availability of schooling. For some extended period, then, the number of schools can be taken as an indicator of the availability of schooling.[7]

When schools were established, they attracted many students, and the example of those students drew others. A department in which schools were established early was likely years later to have larger enrollments and greater interest in developing other levels of instruction (table S.10). Well into the Third Republic, nearly half the variation in school enrollments by department was predicted by the number of schools in that department thirty years earlier. There is also the double hint that this relationship became less important around 1876 and declined sharply by the turn of the century. Thus, the number of schools at a given time both correlates with enrollment at the same period and predicts later growth. This can also be shown by looking at these figures from the other direction. Taking the number of schools per population in each department in 1906 as our standard, these figures correlate at very high levels (but with a smooth decline) to the ranking of departments by their ratio of schools to population in earlier years before midcentury.[8] The *model* of a school system (as measured by the number of schools it required) that was operating in 1906 had been attained by 1876. Although less close, the pattern was very similar in the period from 1850 to 1867. Prior to that, the pattern was different, though not unrelated.

To test and refine the emerging periodization, we used cluster analysis based on the number of schools normalized both by population and by school-age population within departments. It confirms these trends.[9] In both analyses, an early period, 1821 to 1834, was grouped, the special case of 1837 (when the census changed) was isolated, and a second group, 1850 to 1867, and a third, 1876 to 1906, were selected. The national history of the growth of primary schools in France falls into three periods: rapid growth from 1821 to 1837; moderate growth from 1837 to 1867; and slight growth (with the needed number of schools largely achieved) from 1876 to 1906.

If in the early period schools were built primarily in towns and cities, they should have tended to be large. If, in a middle period, schools spread to scattered populations, their number should have had little relationship to total enrollments. And if the additional schools late in the century represented a more differentiated system, schools would have become smaller. The correlation of school size to total enrollment produces the results in table S.11. The analysis of schools by size rather than number also suggested three stages of development.

The division among periods should not be treated as absolute, but other data also roughly fit our periodization. It was suggested earlier that much of the effort in the middle period may have been devoted to adding schools in sparsely settled areas where new schools would consequently have tended to be small. There is no direct measure for that hypothesis in the national statistics, but there is an approximate one. The number of communes without any schools at all is given a great deal of pained attention in the printed volume for the period before 1876. Seen from Paris, those numbers told of intransigent violators of the law, backward communes to be added up by department in a roll of dishonor. For France, as a whole the figures are given in table S.3.

The number of communes that acquired their first school between 1837 and 1850 accounted for more than one-third the total number of schools added in that period; between 1850 and 1863, they were more than one-fifth the number of all new schools; less than one-fifth between 1863 and 1876, they were a negligible part of increases after that. Presumably, in a nation where a majority of the population lived in agglomerations of fewer than two thousand people, many of the other new schools added in the middle period represented the addition of a second or third school in communes with scattered populations. Even by the time of the Guizot Law, the number of schools in a department had a negative correlation with the percentage of the population that was urban, and that negative relationship increased with time. Thus, the more schools a department had, the fewer communes it was likely to have with no school at all, but that relationship declined sharply after 1850.[10]

The analysis of the number of schools by department thus does establish some clear patterns and a chronology for them, and it suggests something of the social significance of the increasing number of schools in each of the three periods. It suggests, too, that although national legislation was important, local initiatives stimulated the steady growth in schools, presumably in response to social pressures and eventually to demands from within the educational system itself. Most clearly of all, these data show that whatever the quality of those schools may have been, the government of the July Monarchy, the ministers of which were so committed to universal primary education, came to power in a society that already had more than half the ratio of schools to school-age population that it would need by the end of the century. Furthermore, at least according to the ministry's own estimates, those schools were not so bad as the historical literature had implied. In 1833, 46 percent of the schools were rated as good and only 11 percent bad. By 1863, 67 percent were considered good, with the proportion of bad schools still 11 percent.[11]

The discussion so far has treated France as a single unit, using national means. But the fact that the data on French education were aggregated by department, as in nearly all official statistics, makes possible a more discriminating and geographically sensitive analysis. When one compares the number of schools (normalized by school-age population) in the different departments of France, two points stand out, one hardly surprising, the other more unexpected. In the first stage, when schools meant the availability of schooling, there was a trend toward a common national norm. Thus, the difference between the department with the most schools per school-age population and the department with the fewest shrank, and the differences in departmental means, best measured by a coefficient of variation, declined until 1850. In the second and third stages, departmental differences—in the dispersal of population and in the range of schooling offered—maintained diversity in the ratio of schools to school-age population. A similar pattern is apparent in the variance among departments in the size of their schools, except that in this case there was less change in the early periods (schools just filled up) and increasing diversity in the third period (when diverse population densities required, and increased choices about the school system permitted, greater variation) [table S.4].

The same point is represented graphically in figure 1. Half the departments of France fall into the two boxes which become somewhat more compact before 1863; the lines above and below represent the range among the top

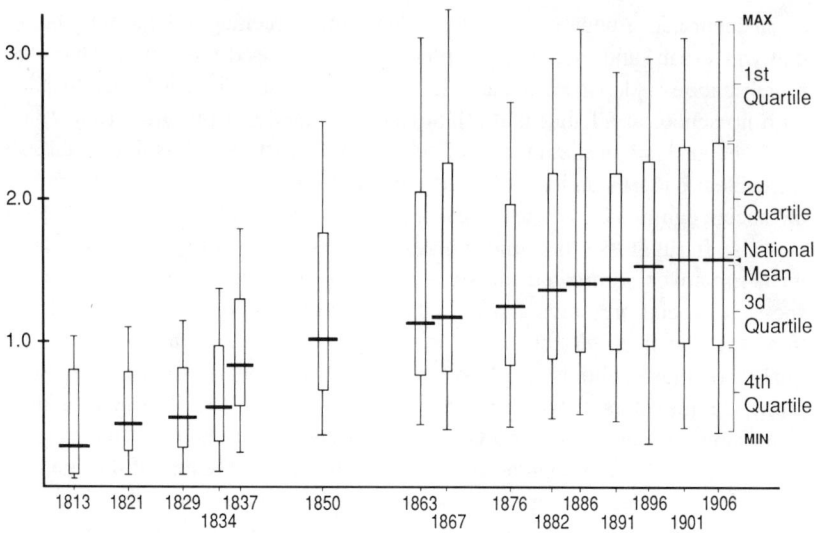

Fig. 1. The availability of schools in the departments of France (schools per hundred school-age population)

and bottom quartiles. Until 1867, the bottom quartile becomes more compact—that is, less diverse in the number of schools for every hundred students of school age. The top quartile by contrast becomes more diverse.

The second and less expected point that emerges from a comparison of the availability of schooling among the departments of France is that their ranking in relation to each other maintained remarkable continuity. Given all the regional diversity of France (in social and local attitudes as well as terrain, demography, and wealth), and given the great changes that occurred in the nineteenth century (in education itself as well as through urbanization and industrialization), one could imagine that departments fluctuated wildly in relation to each other. In reality, few did, an important further sign of an educational system well rooted in local conditions and established earlier than usually assumed by historians or contemporary reformers. (The latter were as horrified that schools were not better, more welcome, and more uniform as they were that few people in the provinces spoke French according to middle-class Parisian standards.) This indigenous quality can be shown by comparing the rank order of departments, by availability, over time. When departmental means are close together, however, very slight changes in one department may move it misleadingly far in the overall ranking. Therefore, the range of standard deviation is a more telling measure. From 1821 to 1906, nearly half the departments of France moved less than one standard deviation, and most of the movement was in the earlier period.[12]

From 1821 to 1834, most of the large changes in departmental ranking came as some departments suddenly extended their school systems and caught up to the national standard (or resulted from earlier underreporting where populations were dispersed). In the period 1850 to 1876, much of the change reflected departments with dispersed populations that had unusually large numbers of schools in proportion to their school-age population. Much of the change in the period from 1876 to 1901 simply reflected shifts in population. Not surprisingly, then, departments in mountainous regions with dispersed populations that had few schools in the earliest period changed the most by the measures of availability.[13]

But regions are composed of much more than topography. Could variations among the departments in nineteenth-century France be explained by a cultural and political heritage from the old regime? As a very crude test, the departments were assigned to their old provinces as if the prerevolutionary map were superimposed over the modern one. By rank order the "province" of Brittany was the lowest in the availability of schools of any in France for every year from 1813 to 1906 except for one, 1829, when it was next to last. Among others that markedly maintained their position across the century, Alsace–Lorraine–Franche Comté and Champagne-Brie remained high, Orléanais, Auvergne-Limousin, and Bourbonnais remained in the lower third, and Normandy stayed at about the middle. As to rates of growth, the Auvergne-Limousin "province" was consistently high, the "provinces" of Picardy and the Ile de France consistently low.[14]

There are few surprises in this, and the patterns that emerge could probably be accounted for by the similarity of neighboring departments in demography and wealth. In any case, there is little trace in these figures of a provincial and inherited educational culture that was then sharply disrupted to make "provinces" more alike.

Another form of regional groupings might be expected to have significantly shaped French elementary education: the academies—regional groupings of from three to six departments, the boundaries of which were established in 1808, altered in 1815, and again in 1854 when seventeen academies were established. As part of this last reform, the rectors of the academies were given greater powers over the inspection of schools and greater involvement in the decisions of departmental and communal councils. Presumably, then, departments within a single academy might have felt some pressure to maintain a common standard. In the middle years, at least, the rank order of the academies is relatively stable (as if they pursued independent policies), and when availability at each date for each academy is calculated, variance within academies becomes lower than within "provinces"—but this phenomenon occurs before 1854, before these academies were created! Whatever cohesion in availability academies achieved preceded their formal organization. This may support the view that availability had been largely achieved by 1850, but the effect of administrative decisions applied to an entire academy appears to have been far less significant than older, local and departmental, initiatives.

Perhaps the most famous way of dividing the geography of France is along an imaginary line drawn from St. Malo to Geneva. The concept of such a line has a long history. In 1823, Conrad Malte-Brun, a Danish geographer and the founder of the *Société de géographie*, wrote of this line above which lay "une France éclairée." And ever since, those attracted to the idea of such a division have not doubted on which side progress was to be found. Many of the early nineteenth-century students of society, moralizers enthralled by science and statistics (the very sort of men to whom we owe the existence of the *Statistique Générale de la France* and the educational *enquêtes*), made use of the St. Malo–Geneva line. Privat, Dupin, Guérry, and d'Angeville all described a France divided between north and south, with inhabitants in the north taller and more long-lived, law abiding, and orderly (d'Angeville's famous distinction between crimes against people, in the south, and crimes against property, in the north, rested on this geographical division). Many connected these differences to greater industry in the north (usually treated as a result of superior moral qualities), and some insisted that a crucial factor was the greater strength of religion in the north.[15]

By the time that Louis Maggiolo put new emphasis upon the St. Malo–Geneva line in his report on the history of literacy in France, the division was well known, heavily associated with social statistics and moral reform, and already enriched with mythical conflicts between Latin and Frankish culture. Maggiolo, incidentally, hoped to prove that the French Revolution had not been the boon to education that its partisans claimed it to have been. The line thus has been forever attached to the history of public education and of literacy and, interestingly enough, often continued to connote a faintly Catholic, positivist, conservative, and racist attitude. From Siegfried to Le Roy Ladurie, to Furet and Ozouf, it has maintained its place among the serious tools of regional analysis.[16] There is reason for this survival (tables S.5 and S.6). Mean availability of schooling was higher in the north than the south for every year except the last. Comparable differences hold up on other measures.[17]

Yet these statistically satisfying contrasts may tell us less than they appear to. They make clear that the differences between north and south were greatest in the early period. And by pointing to earlier (probably prerevolutionary) patterns in the north, the use of the St. Malo–Geneva line emphasizes the much greater growth rate in the south. Moreover, the data for the earlier period are the least reliable and particularly subject to underreporting (even more so in the dispersed south than the north).[18]

In any case, the two groups do not provide the best of comparisons. The northern group contains half as many departments as the southern. A still smaller group, roughly north of a line from Rouen to Chartres to Dijon and Besançon, would include the early leaders among the northern departments, plus a few others. The southern group was far more diverse in climate, terrain, and population density. Mean availability north of the St. Malo–Geneva line was twice the mean south of it in 1829; yet the nine leading departments of France, two of which were in the south, had a mean availability nine times that of the eleven lagging departments in Brittany and the center of France. The St. Malo–Geneva line, in short, obscures greater differences than it illuminates in the early period and turns attention away from the rapid growth that soon followed in some southern departments. The area north of the St. Malo–Geneva line stands out far more clearly, however, in the proportion of communes without schools. Of the five departments that had a school in every commune at the earliest date, three—Hautes-Alpes, Ardèche, and Lozère—were south of the St. Malo–Geneva line; the others were Aisne and Seine. But of the thirty departments in which by 1850 only 3 percent or less of their communes lacked schools, eighteen were above that line. The departments of northeastern France established a school system earlier, a fact that may be related to influences from the Netherlands and Germany, to general prosperity, to the ease of communication in flat country, to the growth of industry, and to many other things. That advantage, especially to committed advocates of universal education, could have made a whole region seem a distinctive culture.

Thus, despite the long tradition of assessing the social history of *le bel hexagone* in terms of its geographical facets, it is worthwhile to look at statistical groupings of departments—we used a statistical program to create *k*-means clusters—and then compare the results. For selected points, we have calculated the relative reduction of variation in availability obtained for the following five different departmental groupings: (1) the fifteen ancient provinces described above; (2) the seventeen academies; (3) ten geographical units taken from another study of education; (4) a semirandom grouping of fifteen departments; and (5) *k*-means clusters that would create the least variation within fifteen groupings. The results are striking.[19]

First, the variance removed by all these groupings decreases over time, which reinforces earlier evidence of increasing national homogeneity. Second, if provincial boundaries are slightly more significant than academic ones early in the century, the reverse is true by midcentury, but neither grouping gives much evidence of anthropological or administrative determinism. Third, provincial and academic groupings are marginally—but only marginally—more unified than random but geographically based ones (group 4). Geographical contiguity implies a common denominator—one that incorporates economic, social, cultural, and administrative characteristics—but computers can combine departments to create far more homogeneous units of France than did kings or rectors. Whereas provincial groupings explain 58 percent of national variance in 1829 and 41 percent in 1863, academies 50 percent in 1829 and 47 percent in 1863, regional groupings 53 percent and 31 percent respectively, a k-means cluster analysis explains 97 percent of national variance in both years—a far greater gain over provincial and academic groupings than the latter over semirandom ones (table S.15).

The power of cluster analysis demonstrates the importance of establishing a general criterion for statistical groupings, one that would be fruitfully applicable to all departments but would also take into account change and rates of change in the course of the nineteenth century. One might, for example, focus on the number of communes without schools. It is interesting that when we mapped departments by this criterion (fig. 2), groups tended to be contiguous, suggesting the importance of geographic and cultural factors (and further explaining the regional reality on which theories of the St. Malo–Geneva line rest but which they tend to obscure).

Other maps constructed on the basis of these statisics would have pointed to the contrasting sources of the same result: departments that preferred large schools tended to be urban *or* in Brittany, where the combination of late development, a preference for Catholic schools, and parsimony may be as important as Brittany's urban agglomerations in accounting for the large number of students per school. Departments with small schools were likely to be mountainous, but those same departments tended to be ones in which availability changed more than in the nation as a whole. Departments that significantly changed their rank order or relationship to the national mean were also likely to be contiguous and either themselves to be, or to stand next door to, departments that ranked very high on availability. Departments with many schools may well have influenced their neighbours to compete with or copy from their example.

A principal disadvantage of this indicator, however, is that it quickly disappears. To analyze change through the entire period, we developed the concept of fulfillment. Assume that by 1906 France had all the schools that the numbers of school-age children required; in the nation as a whole some 85 percent of that goal was reached by 1876, at which time availability was essentially achieved and a third stage of institutional development was beginning. For each department it is possible to determine the date by which it achieved 85 percent of all the primary schools it would have before World War I, a point at which it had sufficiently fulfilled the need for schools to make universal schooling imminent (table S.7). The major concern of administrators would then become less the establishment of new schools than improvement in the quality of old ones.

The spread of departments that had reached this level of fulfillment can be mapped, and it presents a new configuration that deserves consideration.

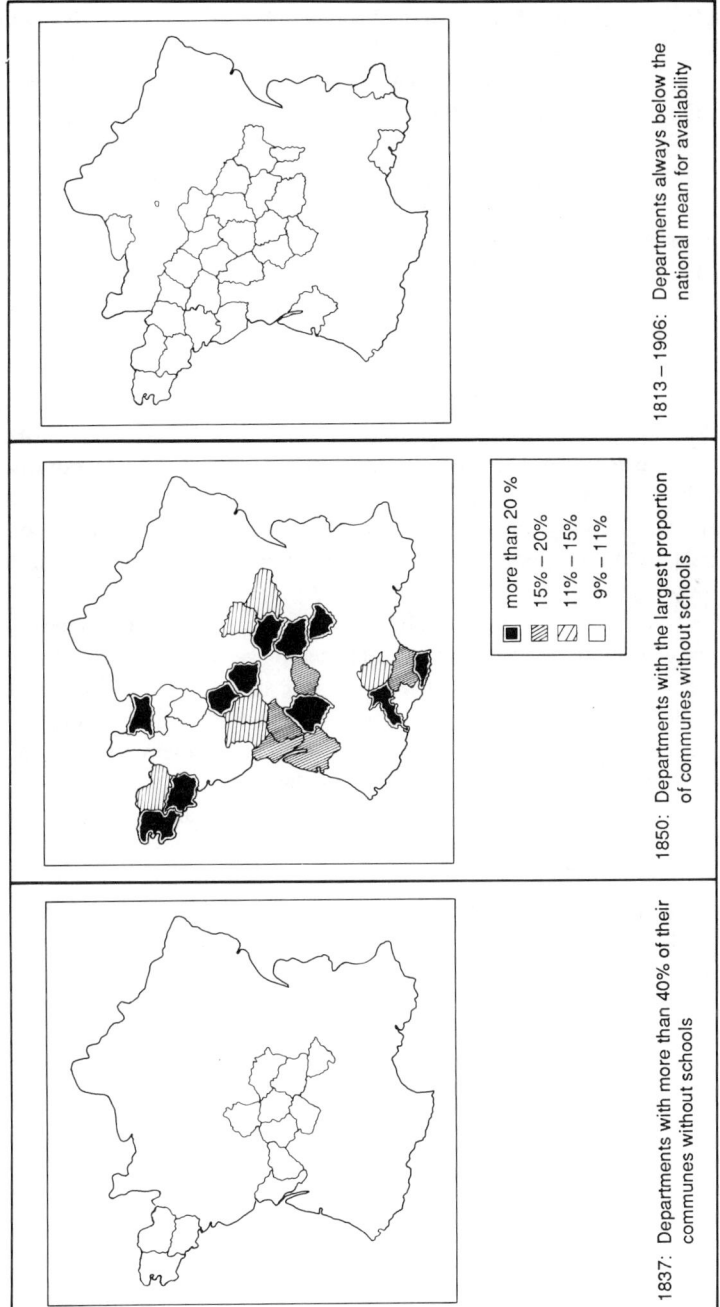

Fig. 2. The western wedge of fewer schools

By 1829, established school systems had spread across Moselle, Bas-Rhin, Meurthe, Nord, Pas-de-Calais, and Seine. With the data from 1837, the geographical pattern began to change with the addition of other urban departments, Gironde, Bouches-du-Rhône, and Rhône, as well as Hérault and Var on the Mediterranean and Doubs along the frontier. By 1850 and 1863, the map of all departments that had reached fulfillment recreates the commercial circle of France. It may well be that it was departments that felt the stimuli of frontiers, seaports, and foreign competition—departments enriched by commerce and industry but seeking more of both—that felt more strongly the importance of making universal education available to all. Certainly that is suggested by the map of the thirty-one departments that reached fulfillment fifteen years before half the nation as a whole would do so (fig. 3).[20]

The concept of fulfillment, and the maps based on it, emphasize the chronology of development and point to another cluster analysis as a way to study both the degree of similarity among departments (at each data point) and the relative similarities or smoothness of their shifts over time. Taking the measure of availability for all departments that existed across the entire period from 1821 to 1906, cluster analysis selected eight groups as statistically the best grouping.[21]

First, although they are purely statistical, these clusters reproduce geographically contiguous groupings; similarities of geography and culture did matter. Second, departments that moved most sharply against the national mean tended to be mountainous, reflecting the fact that the number of schools was greatly affected by a terrain that isolated small agglomerations of population but, in the case of the Basses Alpes and Hautes-Alpes especially, reflecting culture as well—the tradition of mountain literacy and of teaching as a seasonal industry. Third, despite the tendency of these clusters toward geographical contiguity, they consistently cut across the artificial administrative units of academies, usually include some departments from both above and below the St. Malo–Geneva line (finding consistent similarities among departments north and south, east and west), and nearly always absorb traditional provinces (when they are preserved at all) in larger groupings.

These clusters are like an educational geography seen from the infrared cameras of a passing satellite, an abstract and distant view. They contrast with the traditional regions, the persistence of which, in the age of railroads, struck nineteenth-century reformers as a kind of perverse intransigence. Both perspectives have their advantages.

Cluster 3, departments that changed little with regard to the national mean but usually remained just above it, constitutes the France of commercial shipping and the Paris basin. Cluster 1, departments that fluctuated around the mean, tending to be above the mean earlier and slowly moving below it, presents a triangle of sober, provincial education. From Coutances and Caen

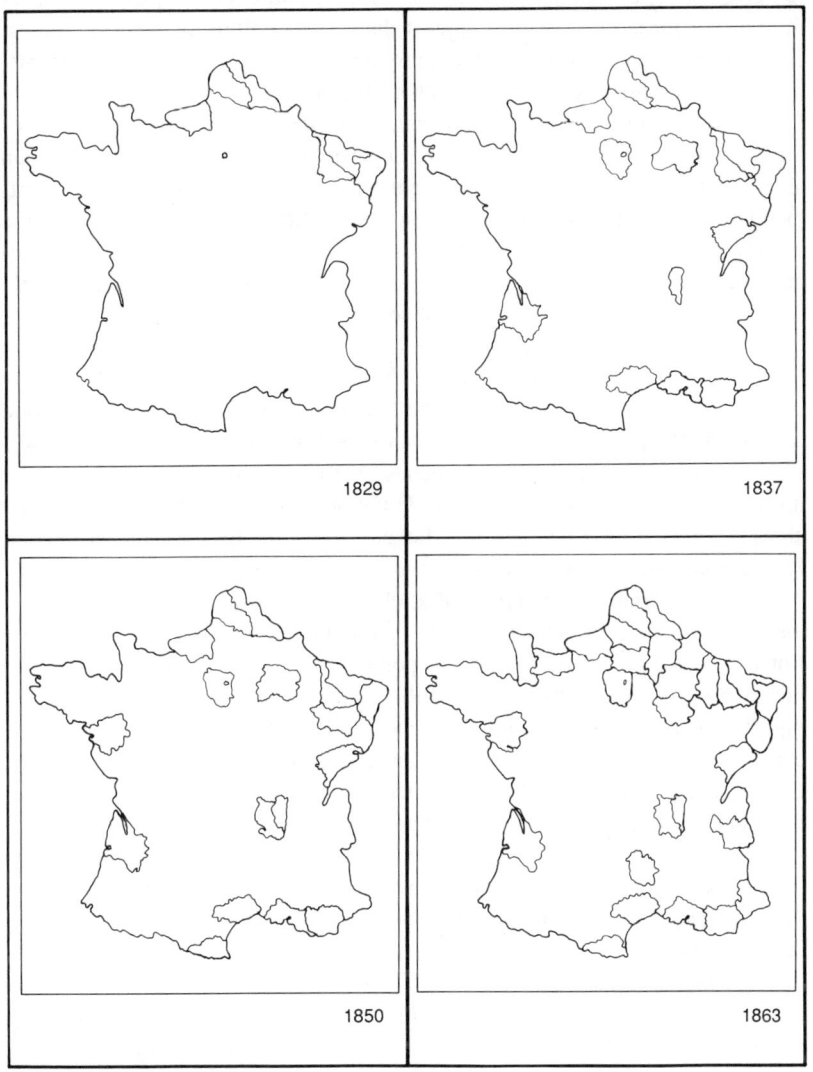

Fig. 3. The departments of France that achieved fulfillment by 1829, 1837, 1850, and 1863

to Périgueux and Toulouse, Clermont-Ferrand, and Grenoble, the *chief-lieux* of many of these departments suggest the serious culture of modest cities in close touch with the surrounding countryside. With one exception, the departments in one cluster touch those in the other to create the stable crescent of French education around the educationally less well-furnished center of France. Cluster 4 joins Hérault to five departments in the northeast as a group always just above the average, and cluster 7 joins five mountainous departments always well above the mean in availability, four of which are in the northeast. The wildly fluctuating departments of cluster 2, mountainous departments which eventually needed to have many schools and apparently acquired them in spurts, are then not so different from the Alpine exceptions of cluster 6 or the single outlyer of the Lozère. Cluster 5 reminds us again that the number of schools was low either where the population was heavily concentrated (thus the presence of the Seine and the Nord but also the Loire and maybe the Rhône) or where local governments were not eager to support more schools than they had to. Bouches-du-Rhône may have reflected something of both factors, but on the whole the departments that were strung just above a line from Quimper to Marseilles belong to the latter category, France's laggards in availability.

It is important to remember that change can occur in the denominator, too—in school-age population rather than in the number of schools. Gers and Lot lost a good deal of school-age population, which made them seem to increase in the standings for availability; Meuse and Haute-Saone also rank high because of this. Finistère, Bouches-du-Rhône, Seine, and Nord, however, consistently gained school-age population, which lowers their rankings. Cluster analysis of availability normalized by total population produces somewhat but not radically different configurations.

We have argued that primary education in France shows signs of having developed in a regular and systemic way. Although availability increased at each data point and at different rates within each department, few departments radically changed their rank among all the others. This systemic quality of the increase in availability made it possible to establish a periodization of national growth and then to apply a similar pattern to individual departments through the concept of fulfillment. The concept of fulfillment is useful not because of a single arbitrary date and percentage, however justified, but because even as lagging departments were catching up with leading ones in terms of availability, so the leading ones were continuing to expand. The concept contains a prediction that as most of the needed schools were established and most communes provided with one, the educational system continued to grow. Cluster analysis gave that sense of patterned development a geographical dimension.

To complete the argument, the impression of a predictable system needs to be demonstrated. One way, through regression analysis, is to identify for each data point, the other dates that produce the highest correlation between the number of schools and the number of students—that is, between availability and enrollment.

In table S.16 enrollment is the dependent variable. If there were merely a mutual association between schools and enrollment, regression analysis should select a variety of temporal points, but in every case in two-stage regression and in twenty-nine of thirty dates in three-stage regression, enrollment depends upon availability of schools at an earlier date. Remarkably, the year 1829 occurs for eight of the ten dates in three-stage regression and for six of them in two-stage regression and barely misses inclusion for every year. (That would have required a change in R^2 of only .01 or .02.) Availability before the Guizot Law appears to have been an indication of some critical qualities—perhaps commitment to and enthusiasm for education, necessary cultural values or habits, or institutional patterns—that universal education required. The level of enrollments (that is, the proportion of children in school, which reflects both the number attending and the number of years that their schooling continued) a generation or more later may thus reflect the continuation of these qualities in a more developed educational context.

Perhaps money was the key. The correlation between the absolute number of schools and ordinary expenditures, high at first, declines steadily. Increasingly, school systems were doing more than just maintaining a certain number of schools. The highest correlations between these variables at earlier and later dates, however, remain at about the same level—a sign of an essentially stable system of primary education in which the differences among France's departments in the relationship between their expenditures and the number of their schools tended to maintain established patterns even though actually expenditures markedly changed (table S.12). The correlation of ordinary expenditures to schools normalized by school-age population confirms these findings but adds something more (table S.13). The basic correlations are lower—simply maintaining schools was a major expense—and the declining correlations become negative after 1868, when much of the increased expenditure meant more money spent on improving quality. Here, too, a comparison of the highest correlation with availability before and after a given date shows the earlier correlation always to be higher. Rather than increased expenditures predicting the number of schools, the availability of schools launched a process of spending more on education. This retrospective quality provides an important hint that local demand for education often preceded pressure from the central state and that, once established, the schools drew money for their support.

One sign of local initiative can be seen in the proportion of schools that were actually housed in a building owned by the commune itself (table S.8).

This dignity and stability was enjoyed by a steadily increasing proportion of schools, from one-quarter in 1834 to 69 percent in 1906, and the drop in standard deviation indicates this increased uniformity. Yet the range between departments remained great, and the declining rate of growth suggests a kind of local contentment with the status quo. It is surprising that the commune's willingness to provide a building was more important to the number of schools earlier rather than later. The schools that served as the foundation upon which a universal, national system was built were not such informal and accidental creations as we sometimes assume. The more schools in a department in an early period, the higher the proportion of them that communes would come to own later. That, too, was part of the growth of a system, but schools added later (often in departments that had been slow to embrace universal schooling) were less likely to lead to a special school building owned by the commune.[22]

Early in the century, the establishment of a proper school was an important accomplishment in the villages of France, and many of them managed it. By the end of the century, although 65 percent of all primary schools in France were still taught in a single class—a modest decline from 72 percent at the beginning of the Third Republic—much educational energy had been channeled in other directions. This is shown not only in the numbers themselves, but in the kinds of data it was now thought necessary to collect. By the end of the century, statisticians had no interest in the number of communes without a school, but they collected data on the number of gymnasiums and the size of the gardens and on many different types and levels of education.

These new interests expressed a continuing belief in education and the evolutionary expansion of an established system. Small classes in multiclassroom schools, which presumably permitted more specialization by teachers and more individual attention to students, increased dramatically between 1896 and 1906—from 1,500 schools involving 90,000 students to 3,700 schools with 220,000 students. By the 1880s, schools were regularly giving a *certificat des études primaires* to those who completed the full course of study, and the number awarded in each department still showed some correlation with the availability of schooling in 1821 (table S.14).

In the Third Republic, school libraries came to be recognized as important resources, and the number of books in them increased fourfold from over 100,000 in 1881 to more than 400,000 in 1907. But one can see the unfolding of a system and the endurance of local preferences even in the statistics on school libraries. The differences among departments were great, but the correlation between the availability of schooling early in the century and the number of books later is significant. So is the fact of a higher correlation with availability in 1821 than in 1837 (before the state intervention of the Guizot Law) and with the number of books in 1881 (when libraries more clearly measured local effort) than in 1907. Of the ten departments where more than half of the schools had a library in 1876, nine had led in the establishment of schools a half century earlier. With the establishment of free, universal education, ordinary expenditure again became more a matter of local choice, which then correlated more strongly with the local decision to have a school sixty years earlier.[23]

Universal primary education in France, like any healthy and long-lived social institution, was deeply rooted in local circumstance and readily developed a momentum of its own, which historians can roughly measure. Intervention and pressure from the national government was also an important part of this system and of its expansion, and those who directed it from the center and who so insistently collected these statistics naturally used numbers to measure their own successes and to identify those who appeared resistant. But historians, especially with the friendly aid of a computer, need not be limited to the same optic.

It now appears that the national pattern of French elementary schools was established by the time of the Restoration and the July Monarchy and changed relatively little thereafter despite great growth. In the period from 1821 to 1837, the period of greatest growth in availability, the existence of schools predicted enrollment then and development later. In the period from 1837 to 1867, the slower growth in availability represented the spread of schools to sparsely populated areas. The most important changes from 1876 to 1906 had to do with the quality of schooling, and the departments that led in making these changes were likely to have been leaders in the availability of schooling in the earlier periods. A century later, we can more readily acknowledge the alacrity with which Frenchmen established schools and the systemic nature of their efforts.

Notes

1. Roger Chartier, Marie-Madeleine Compere, and Dominique Julia, *L'éducation en France du XVIe au XVIIIe siècle* (Paris, 1976), 293; Elizabeth Eisenstein, *The Printing Press as an Agent of Change* (New York, 1979); François Furet and Jacques Ozouf, *Lire et écrire: l'alphabétisation des français de Calvin à Jules Ferry*, 2 vols. (Paris, 1977); Marshall McLuhan, *Understanding Media* (New York, 1964).

2. Figures for the Restoration period are problematical. There was a general underreporting, especially of schools in isolated areas (see *Statistique de l'enseignement*, II: xix–xx, lii–lvii) and for girls schools (see Jean Perrel, "Les écoles de filles dans la France d'Ancien Régime," and Gerard Cholvy, "Une école des pauvres au début du 19e siècle: 'pieuse filles,' béates ou soeurs des campagnes," in *The Making of Frenchmen: Current Directions in the History of Education in France, 1679–1979*, ed. Donald N. Baker and Patrick J. Harrigan [Waterloo, Ont., 1980], 75–84, 135–44). For some dates, girls schools were not reported, only the boys in mixed schools were

counted, etc. We created estimates of the number of girls schools for 1833 (by linear adjustment from the data for 1832 and 1837), for 1829 (by comparing enrollment data for girls in 1829 and 1832 and assuming that enrollment:school ratios did not change between the two dates), for 1821 (by assuming that the ratio of girls schools to other schools was the same as in 1832), and for 1813 (by assuming that the 40 percent of the departments that did not report in 1813 had the same proportion of the nation's school as they had in 1821). We regard the totals prior to 1837 as minimums, but the schools not reported were probably the poorest and least stable and often privately run. The apparent growth between 1829 and 1832 is undoubtedly exaggerated (as the earnest compilers of the *Statistique de l'enseignement*, II:liii, remind us). Our adjustments are not entirely satisfactory, but they at least avoid the inconsistencies and misleading comparisons of totals for one type of school with those for another that creep in even to the summary table of the *Statistique* (II:liv) and have undoubtedly ever since affected the historiography that hails the impressive growth following the Guizot Law. The statistical evidence of slower growth in the last years of the Restoration fits with Maurice Gontard's picture of an educational reversal under the government of the Ultras, *L'enseignement primaire en France de la Révolution à la loi Guizot, 1789–1933* (Paris, 1959), 360–95.

3. Much of the apparent stagnation, in the period 1867–72, was due to the loss of some 3,400 schools in territories ceded to Germany after the Franco-Prussian War; during the same period, however, some growth was induced by the law of April, 1867, requiring communes of five hundred to eight hundred people to operate separate schools for girls. Few of those schools actually increased "availability."

4. For Gabriel Compayré, it worked magically—"thereafter all communes would have a school," *Histoire critique des doctrines de l'éducation en France depuis le seizième siècle* (Geneva, 1970; reprint of Paris, 1879), II:381; see also Robert Anderson, *Education in France, 1848–1870* (Oxford, 1975), 7; H. C. Barnard, *Education and the French Revolution* (Cambridge, 1969); Charles Fourrier, *L'enseignement français de 1789 à 1945* (Paris, 1965), 136; Gontard, *L'enseignement primaire*, 535–36; Pascale Gruson, *L'état enseignant* (Paris, 1978), 70; Antoine Prost, *Histoire de l'enseignement en France, 1800–1967* (Paris, 1968).

5. Felix Ponteil, for example, declared that France needed 33,398 additional schools in 1876, *Histoire de l'enseignement en France: les grandes étapes, 1789–1965* (Paris, 1966), 290.

6. The number of schools apparently declined during the revolutionary years of 1848 and 1849, for it was slightly lower in 1850 than in 1847, *Statistique de l'enseignement*, 1876–77, (Paris, 1878), I:liv.

7. The difference, for these data, between the two well-known measures of correlation deserves comment. The Spearman is a rank-order correlation used here to compare the rank order of all the departments of France on one variable at two different dates or on two variables at the same date. When many departments are closely grouped because of very similar measures on the variable in question, as in the case for most of our variables later in the nineteenth century, then changes that are really very slight can heavily affect rank order, producing lower correlations. The Pearson correlation, which measures the distance by least squares of each data point (in this case, each department on one measure at one date) from the regression line that represents a

perfect correlation, is particularly sensitive to a few extreme cases, which for these data are more likely to occur in earlier periods. We have generally taken both correlations for every variable but will report only the Pearson correlation unless there is an important difference between the two. Those few departments gained or lost by France within the period under study are automatically eliminated from consideration.

8. Correlations of the number of schools in 1906 with the number of schools at earlier dates (normalized by school-age population) are: 1813, .08; 1821, .23; 1829, .31; 1834, .47; 1837, .55; 1850, .67; 1863, .80; 1867, .84; 1876, .89; 1882, .89; 1886, .94; 1891, .97; 1896, .94; 1901, .99.

9. For "single-linkage cluster analysis" across time, a matrix is created by standardizing the departmental values for each temporal point. The columns of this matrix were the standardized values of departments at a particular point in time, while each row contained the values for a department across all time points. Clustering began by treating each time point as a cluster and ended with all columns in a single cluster. At each step in between, a time point was joined to the closest time point (straight line distance) to enlarge a previous cluster; once formed, a cluster could not be broken but only combined with others. The procedure is discussed in S. C. Johnson, "Hierarchical Clustering Schemes," *Psychometrika* 32 (1967): 241–54; P. H. A. Sneath, "The Application of Computers to Taxonomy," *Journal of General Microbiology* 17 (1957): 201–26. We lacked sufficient departmental data for the years 1813, 1840, 1843, and 1872 to include those data points; 1837 linked to 1850 in addition to 1821; the last data points linked were 1867 and 1876. For cluster analysis among departments (its findings to be discussed below), the same matrices applied, but rows rather than columns were clustered.

10. The correlation of the number of schools (per school-age population) with urban population (the percentage of departmental population living in agglomerations of more than two thousand people in 1865) is: 1813, .13; 1821, .02; 1829, .02; 1833, −.06; 1837, −.06; 1850, −.08; 1863, −.23; 1867, −.25; 1876, −.34; 1882, −.35; 1886, −.37; 1891, −.41; 1896, −.45; 1901, −.46; 1906, −.51. The correlation of the total number of schools in a department (per school-age population) with the percentage of its communes that have no school declines: 1837, −.62; 1850, −.43; 1863, −.18; 1876, −.10; 1882, −.09.

11. *Statistique de l'enseignement*, II:cil. Compare this with the pessimistic comments of Gontard, *L'enseignement primaire*, 535–36; Jean Rohr, *Victor Duruy, ministre de Napoléon III: essai sur la politique de l'instruction publique au temps de l'Empire Libéral* (Paris, 1967), 51; Ponteil, *Histoire*, 290; Roland Tartayre, *Histoire des institutions scolaires en France des origins à la fin de la IIIe république* (n.p., 1962), 223. William B. Cohen has found that urban schools were often flooded with students as soon as they were opened, from his work in progress on French cities.

12. If one ranks all the departments of France for each of the data points from 1821 to 1906 according to the availability of schools (i.e., the number of schools per school-age population) only fifteen departments shift their order in rank by more than half the length of the list over the entire eighty-five years: Haute-Alpes, Ariège, Aveyron, Cantal, Isère, Haute-Loire, Lozère, Nord, Pas-de-Calais, Bas-Rhin, and Yonne changed by more than fifty places; Hautes-Garonne, Hérault, Landes, and Tarn-et-Garonne between forty-five and fifty places.

But twenty-three departments (about 30 percent) stayed within the same quintile throughout the period, twelve of those always below the national mean: Allier, Cher, Côtes-du-Nord, Finistère, Ille-et-Vilaine, Indre, Mayenne, Morbihan, Nièvre, Saône-et-Loire, Vendée, and Haute-Vienne. The others were Aube, Aude, Calvados, Cher, Doubs, Haute-Marne, Meuse, Moselle, Hautes-Pyrénées, Savoie, and Meurthe. For schools by population, more than half the departments (forty-six) stayed either above or below the national mean.

13.

Number of Departments within Specific Ranges of Standard Deviation

	1	1–2	2–3	3–4	4+
1821–1906	41	34	9	3	1
1821–34	81	3[a]	1[b]	1[c]	0
1834–50	72	12[d]	1	0	1[e]
1850–76	84	5	1[f]	0	0
1876–82	87	1	0	0	0
1876–1901	79	8[g]	0	0	0

1821–34: [a] Hérault, Basses-Alpes, Ardèche; [b] Ardennes; [c] Hautes-Alpes. All but Hérault began below the mean and rose sharply above it.

1834–50: [d] seven of these remained above the mean, three moved from below to above, two remained below; [e] Lozère leaped from below to above the national mean in this period.

1850–76: [f] Hérault, the national leader, until passed in this period by Lozère, one of those that moved more than one s.d.

1876–1901: [g] For all but two of these departments (Ardèche, Haute Loire) their shift in rank is primarily a reflection of the movement of population.

14. Many departments fall in more than one province; in those cases, the data from a department were divided among provinces according to the proportion of its area in each province. It must be stressed that these produce only the roughest approximations of the old provinces. Some smaller provinces were joined with neighbors to reduce the total to fifteen "provinces" in all. Dauphiné, which ranked twelfth by the data for 1821 and 1829, is third in 1834, and first or second from 1837 on, when the data are better.

15. Conrad Malte-Brun, *Précis de la géographie universelle*, 4 vols. (Paris, 1810–29): H. Privat, *Tableau politique et religieux de la France* (Paris, 1830); Charles Dupin, *Forces productives et commerciales de la France* (Paris, 1827); André Michel Guérry, *Essai sur la statistique morale de la France* (Paris, 1833); Adolphe d'Angeville, *Essai sur la statistique de la population française* (Paris, 1836; reprinted 1969 with an introduction by Emmanuel Le Roy Ladurie); Pierre Marie Bigot de Morogues, *Recherche des causes de la richesse et de la misère des peuples civilisés* (Paris, 1834); Martin Doisy, *Dictionnaire d'économie charitable*, 4 vols. (Paris, 1855); Augustin Malarce, *La France morale* (Paris, 1860); Louis R. Villermé, *Tableau de l'état*

physique et moral des ouvriers employés dans les manufactures de coton, de laine et de soie, 2 vols. (Paris, 1840).

16. André Siegfried, *Tableau politique de la France de l'ouest sous la troisième république*, 2d ed. (Paris, 1964); Le Roy Ladurie and Michel Demonet, "Alphabétisation et stature," *Annales, S.E.C.* 35 (1980): 1320–33; Furet and Ozouf, *Lire et écrire*. For a superb analysis, see Bernard Lepetit, "Sur les dénivellations de l'espace économique en France, dans les années 1830," *Annales, S.E.C.* 41 (1986): 1243–72.

17. If the data are normalized by total population, the differences between north and south become a bit smaller (higher birth rates and thus a younger population was one of the problems with which the south had to contend) until the two regions are equal in 1896 and the south a bit ahead thereafter. Southern schools tended to be larger than northern ones in 1876 and 1886. The difference between north and south was greater in the proportion of schools in school buildings owned by the commune (because northern departments were wealthier or because they cared more about schooling?).

St. Malo–Geneva Line Schools by Communes and Number of Students Per School

Date	Percentage of Schools in School Buildings Owned by the Commune		Students Per School	
	Mean	Coefficient of Variation	Mean	Coefficient of Variation
1834	above 45%	.53	53.18	.20
	below 16%	.58	33.54	.38
1863	above 75%	.25	67.17	.24
	below 39%	.37	59.34	.24
1876	above 76%	.20	63.31	.36
	below 47%	.33	65.59	.25
1906	above 83%	.11	68.32	.54
	below 63%	.18	63.38	.33

18. In the period 1813–34, the ratio between the north and the south decreased from 2.5 to 1.7; in the period 1837–82, it fell from 1.4 to 1.2; in the period 1886–1906, the two were equal.

19. These variance tests determined the total variation among all departments in the usual way. R^2 (see table S.15) is the ratio of this variation that the groupings account for and was calculated by subtracting the sum of the within-group variation (the sum of the squares of the deviation of the departments within the group's mean) from the total variation. Obviously, the greater the number of groupings, the greater the proportion of deviation explained (i.e., in a grouping of eighty-seven, no department would have deviated from itself; the R^2 then would have been 100 percent). Because, as the number of groupings increase, the likelihood of variance decreases, the differential between provinces, academies, and regions has little significance. The

k-means procedure is discussed in John A. Hartigan, *Clustering Algorithms* (New York, 1975); the BMDP-79 Statistical Package, University of California Press, was used. The bias of the *k*-means procedure is its ability to create numerically unequal groupings, isolating deviant departments and thereby reducing deviation within groupings. These clusters of 1829 and 1863 linked enrollment with schools but produced separate variance tests for each. The ten geographical groups are those used in Harrigan, with Victor Neglia, *Lycéens et collégiens sous le Second Empire: étude statistique sur les fonctions sociales de l'enseignement secondaire public d'après l'enquête de Victor Duruy (1864–1865)* (Paris, 1979), 26.

20. Because of incomplete data from the 1829 census, some of the departments listed as reaching fulfillment in 1837 may have achieved it a decade earlier. Note, too, that a department (especially an urban one) could greatly increase enrollments by enlarging schools rather than adding new ones; fulfillment is an institutional concept that measures retrospectively from the number of schools in use after schooling has become universal.

21. Eight clusters (the best fit between fourteen and four clusters). Only departments extant throughout the period 1821–1906 are included, and they are listed generally in order of linkage; thus, the top and bottom of each tends to link.

> Cluster 1: Ain, Orne, Manche, Isère, Drome, Haute-Garonne, Lot-et-Garonne, Tarn-et-Garonne, Ardèche, Ariège, Tarn, Dordogne, Puy-de-Dôme, Haute-Loire
> Cluster 2: Aveyron, Cantal, Gers, Lot
> Cluster 3: Aisne, Somme, Eure-et-Loir, Eure, Basses-Pyrénées, Seine-et-Oise, Seine-et-Marne, Ardennes, Aude, Gard, Calvados, Vosges, Charente, Yonne, Charente-Inférieure, Deux-Sevres, Gironde, Var, Pyrénées-Orientales, Pas-de-Calais, Seine-Inférieure
> Cluster 4: Aube, Oise, Marne, Côte-D'Or, Doubs, Hérault
> Cluster 5: Allier, Cher, Indre, Nièvre, Vendée, Corréze, Creuse, Mayenne, Saône-et-Loire, Vienne, Indre-et-Loire, Maine-et-Loire, Bouches-du-Rhône, Rhône, Landes, Loiret, Loir-et-Cher, Sarthe, Vaucluse, Côtes-du-Nord, Ille-et-Vilaine, Haute-Vienne, Loire, Loire-Inférieure, Finistère, Morbihan, Nord, Seine
> Cluster 6: Basses-Alpes, Hautes-Alpes
> Cluster 7: Jura, Haute-Saone, Hautes-Pyrénées, Haute-Marne, Meuse
> Cluster 8: Lozère

22. The government worried about religious schools, but the major concern of the commune was that it have schools. When faced with the legal dissolution of the Marist Congregation that would lead to the closing of the municipality's only high schools in Annonay (Ardèche), the leftist and anticlerical town council informed the government that it would support the closing of this private school *provided that* the state would immediately open a public one. *Archives Nationales* F19/6256 (1880). The number of schools in a department in 1821 correlates with the percentage of school buildings owned by communes at a later date: 1840, .72; 1850, .72; 1863, .68; 1906, .59. But the relationship with the number of schools after 1821 becomes much weaker; some

later correlations of the number of schools (the first date) with the percentage of school buildings owned by communes (the second date) are the following: 1834/1834, $r = .43$; 1863/1906, $r = .3$; 1876/1876, $r = .28$; 1906/1906, $r = .2$.

23. The nine departments were Seine, Ardennes, Haute-Marne, Yonne, Aube, Marne, Seine-et-Marne, Meurthe-et-Moselle, and Eure-et-Loire; the exception was Deux-Sèvres, *Statistique de l'enseignement*, II: 50–53.

CHAPTER 3

French Students in School, 1829–1906

On most days of the year throughout the nineteenth century, millions of French boys and girls walked to school, and observers watched that great social movement closely, as if France were one great village. Generally encouraged as the clusters of children grew larger and their daily trek extended into more months of the year, they worried, however, about those who did not regularly participate in this great march. These observers—politicians, local notables, priests, social reformers—wrote with paternal intensity about the phenomenon before them; and above all, the officials among them collected numbers. They counted boys and girls and teachers, both lay and clerical; they noted students' ages and estimated the frequency and duration of their attendance; they recorded expenditures and estimated the quality of schools in a variety of ways, and the procedures for collecting all these data became more and more systematic. Eventually, these numbers were assembled, department by department, for the entire nation and published. Because effective analysis at an aggregate level of such varied and complex data requires the use of a computer and a powerful one (as well as a sizable investment of time and money), these data—rarely compared across time and place—have not been very intensively used.

A close look at the aggregate figures in these statistics reveals some important trends: the growth in the number of students was great but occurred at a rather steady pace, and the disparity among the departments of France, very large early in the century, continually decreased; yet these two large-scale patterns of change had remarkably little effect on the relative ranking of departments in terms of the amount of schooling their youth received— leading departments remained leaders, laggards continued to lag. Steady growth, increased homogeneity, and continuity in relative rank order all suggest a fairly well-established and quite extensive educational system with stable social roots. Most surprising of all, these numbers allege and in fact proclaim that this educational system was established earlier in the century and that more students attended school sooner than is conventionally assumed.

The growth in the number of students is incontrovertible. From 1837 to the end of the century, the number of students doubled, but it may have almost doubled once before in the eight years prior to 1837. The most rapid growth thus occurred in the years just before as well as just after the Guizot Law. From 1837 to 1847, it continued at an annual rate of increase of about 3 percent, then continued for another decade at about 2 percent a year after the shrinkage that followed the revolution of 1848.[1] From 1861 to 1886—after which the increase in enrollments ceased—the annual rate of increase was a steady 1 percent with only one slight exception just *preceding* the Ferry Laws of 1881–82. After 1837, then, the steadiness of the growth in enrollments (at a decelerating rate) becomes as noteworthy as the overall growth itself (table E.1).

When these national figures are broken down by sex and type of school, the impression of continuity and of a complex social fabric interwoven into these enrollment figures is confirmed. The differences in the schooling of boys and girls and in the development of Catholic and state schools, which deserves close analysis, will be treated in later chapters. But two points need to be noted here. First, the enrollment of girls, 41 percent of the total in 1837, reached 48 percent by 1863—on this dimension, too, the trend toward national uniformity is clear. Second, the proportion of students in *libre* (private or independent) schools after 1881 actually rose to about what it had been in the 1830s, when the national system of public schools had just begun its great expansion—cultural preferences for public or Catholic schools seemingly survived intact the establishment of universal schooling (tables E.2 and E.3). A further complication needs to be kept in mind. Because pupils were often younger than six or older than thirteen, because attendance was not always regular, and because enrollment was not the same as attendance, the numbers enrolled could be greater than the cohort of school-age children. Using the same numerator (enrollment) and denominator (school-age cohort), however, permits comparison across time and proves one consistent measure of growth and change.

Although local differences in enrollments remained, departments lagging in enrollment gained steadily on the leaders, and France rapidly approached homogeneity in the proportions of school-age population actually enrolled. There are a number of measures of this phenomenon. The coefficient of variation declined with each *enquête*, from 80 percent in 1829 to 8 percent in 1901. The median department approached the mean by 1863, and (most socially significant) the single department with the lowest proportion of school-age population enrolled drew ever closer to the department with the highest enrollment, even while enrollments in the latter increased. The ratio between the departments at these extremes, more than 20:1 in 1829, was less than 7:1 by 1840, 3:1 in 1863, just over 2:1 before the Ferry Laws, and 1.5:1 by the end of the century. While total enrollments in France increased fivefold, the distance between the first and last departments decreased nearly fifteenfold (table E.6).

Thus, three patterns of change occurred simultaneously: increased overall enrollments throughout France, more varied increases in individual departments (with those with lower enrollments initially increasing more rapidly), and demographic shifts that caused the population to grow in some areas and decline in others while changing the proportion of the total population that was of school age.[2] Add to this the well-known differences in topography, wealth, and culture among the departments of France and one might reasonably have expected these departments to vary wildly in relation to each other in the proportions of their school-age population enrolled in school during eighty years of change (1829–1906). Instead, they displayed remarkable historical continuity and relative stability. Calculation of the proportion of school-age population enrolled in each department at each data point reveals that in the period from 1829 to 1906, fourteen departments moved less than one standard deviation from the national mean, sixty-two moved less than two standard deviations, and eighty-three moved less than three.[3] We then tested this relative stability in another way. We ranked all the departments of France by their enrollments per school-age population in 1832 and divided them into quartiles. The mean ratio of enrollment per school-age population was then calculated for each of these fixed sets of departments (the quartiles of 1832) at each of the sixteen data points from 1829 to 1906. In all that time, only once and then very slightly did one of these quartiles (fixed as of 1832) ever move above or below its neighbor.[4]

Smaller groups of departments would be more sensitive to change; so we established octiles on the basis of school-age enrollment in 1832 and then calculated the mean for those eight groups of departments at every other data point. The results are easily graphed; there are no crossovers among these 128 data points before 1881, and by that date, the eight octiles of 1832 are so close together that there are many ties (fig. 4).[5] If a department maintained 100 percent of its school-age population (all children between their sixth and thirteenth birthdays) in school, then all would have to attend for seven years; six of the eight octiles of 1832 had means at or above that figure by 1872. They averaged more than eight years of primary schooling for everyone by 1881 and thereafter. Above all, this graph depicts a pattern of systemic growth, systemic in a double sense of development toward a national system but also in local growth such that, no matter what a department's starting point, more schools led to more students and to their attendance for more years.

It also marks that growth as having occurred surprisingly early. As benchmarks of enrollment, we have chosen three percentages: 50, 75, and 100

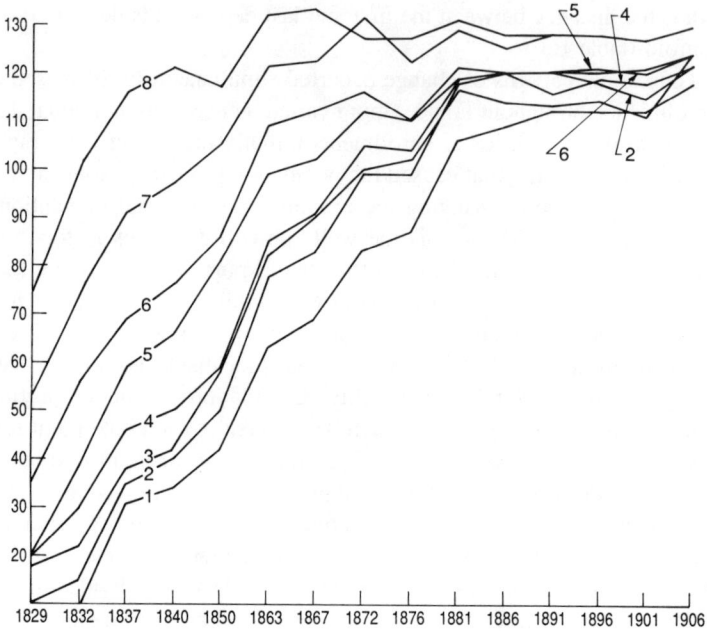

Fig. 4. Mean enrollment in departments grouped by octiles based on enrollment in 1832

percent. Statistically, a department could achieve an enrollment of 50 percent if all children between the ages of six and thirteen attended school for three and one-half years or half of those children attended for seven years. The reality, of course, was always somewhere in between, probably more often closer to the first pole, so that a figure of 50 percent enrollment can be taken to mean that a majority of school-age children attended school for several years.[6] Even that level, then, means that formal schooling had become an established and well-known norm, an important experience in the lives of most school-age children extending to six or seven years for a significant minority of them. Over half the departments of France passed this benchmark by 1837! Three-quarters of the departments passed it by 1850, all by 1876 (table E.14).

If an enrollment of 50 percent indicates that a national system had been established, an enrollment of 75 percent of the school-age population marks a quite different level. To achieve it, a department would have to have all school-age children enrolled for more than five years or three-quarters enrolled for seven. By then, children untouched by formal schooling or enrolled for only a couple of years had become identifiable exceptions. In 1837, when more than half of France's departments had reached the level of 50 percent, a little more than a quarter had reached that of 75 percent. Between 1850 and 1863, however, the number of departments at this higher level of enrollment doubled, increasing from two-fifths to four-fifths of the departments, all of which passed that level by 1881. The equivalent of 100 percent enrollment was achieved in more than one-fifth of the departments by 1850, in half by 1867, in three-quarters by the birth of the Third Republic, and in more than nine-tenths (93 percent) by 1881. No wonder that an English writer could declare in 1846 that "the statistics of this great and perfect system of French education offer a strange contrast to our own miserable and inefficient efforts,"[7] or that a few years later an American expert stated that "there is nothing in the history of modern civilization more truly sublime than the establishment of the present Law of primary instruction in France." While acknowledging "some imperfections and deficiencies," he asserted that "the [French] system went into immediate and successful operation, giving a powerful impulse to the progress of popular intelligence throughout the whole domain of France."[8]

Although these percentages are telling measures of the extent of the primary school system, the denominator from which they are calculated—the number of children between their sixth and thirteenth birthdays—is overly tidy. That age group was consistently used in later *enquêtes* (because those were the ages for which education was made compulsory by the Ferry Laws), but the choice of those ages reflects long-standing goals and later achievements rather than the looser practice of children and parents as they gradually became accustomed to many years of schooling. In fact, some children started school early, some late; some who dropped out returned, some eventually attended *cours d'adultes*, and many primary school students were older than thirteen.[9]

We have therefore also calculated enrollment as a percentage of all children five to fifteen years of age.[10] Even this indicator is remarkably high. Precisely half the departments had the equivalent of half their five- to fifteen-year-olds enrolled before the Second Empire, and all had achieved that before the Ferry Laws. As for the equivalent of six years of schooling for this larger cohort, nearly a third of France's departments reached that level by 1850, 90 percent by the beginning of the Third Republic. Thus, these figures, too, repeat the now familiar pattern: a surprisingly strong early start, a burst of growth nearly doubling enrollments in the first decade of the Second Empire, steady growth thereafter. By 1881, 98 percent of France's departments had the equivalent of everyone between five and fifteen in school for at least six years (table E.9).

At the equivalent of seven years of schooling (the official expectation in Republican France), the pattern for those five to fifteen years of age changes somewhat. This target was clearly beyond the earlier practices and goals of most departments. Yet more than half reached it prior to the Third Republic, the subsequent great bursts of growth at this level coming between 1867 and 1872 and again between 1876 and 1881. On the eve of the Ferry Laws, 93 percent of the departments of France had reached that goal. At a still higher level, equivalent to eight years of schooling for all, the proportions are lower; but two-thirds of the departments accomplished it by 1881, and the most rapid leap came between 1872 and 1881. Nor should it be forgotten that these figures include both boys and girls in an era when many educational "reformers" designed shorter educational programs for girls.

These aggregate figures of primary school enrollment thus provide a double challenge, for they contravene the dominant impression in much of the recent historical literature and beg for further analysis. The picture these numbers firmly suggest is of a primary school system well established in much of France quite early in the century, of a system that had its most rapid growth early in the century—growth that was systemic and steady rather than haphazard and that led to increased educational homogeneity—and of a growing system with local roots so firm that development did not await the requirements of national legislation. All of this is thoroughly consonant with the history of the availability of schools themselves. Enrollments follow just after that necessary first step, which we have previously analyzed as having had its most rapid growth in the period 1821–37, having become nearly universal in the period 1837–67, and having expanded primarily in terms of quality in the period 1876–1906. This revised picture, however, rests on the national statistics. Before using them for a closer look at enrollments, it becomes imperative to consider their overall reliability.

I

Although questions about the general validity of these statistics, and our approach to them, were addressed in the opening chapter, enrollment presents particular problems that deserve attention. The great strength of these figures is that there are so many of them, department by department and year by year, and that the totals are so large. Furthermore, the numbers forwarded by teachers, inspectors, and prefects were, so far as we can tell, carefully totaled and checked. Computer analysis reinforces the claims for taking them seriously: Columns add up, and patterns of consistency within departments and from one data point to another are quite remarkable.

Nevertheless, for most of the nineteenth century, the figures for enrollment must be taken to be a close and very useful approximation rather than a precise description of what enrollment has subsequently come to mean. In the first place, they were rarely if ever complete. Students not counted included those who received instruction at home or in informal, temporary, or so-called clandestine schools and those who attended classes offered by *béates*. Such ad hoc arrangements had ceased to matter by the Third Republic, and the need for them declined from the 1830s on. Still, it is important to remember that the enrollment counted here is an official measure of those registered in recognized elementary schools. That also means that there was another kind of omission: the figures omit all those who received primary instruction in institutions, officially recognized and maybe even prestigious, not part of this system and primarily devoted to another kind of instruction—schools for apprentices and *petites séminaires*, military schools, orphanages, and boarding schools. In addition, some students learned to read in *écoles maternelles*, in prisons, or in the army, and they are not counted in primary school enrollment. There is no reason to think that the total number of students in all these categories combined would significantly alter the analysis here. Where some figures are available, they are relatively small.[11] Nevertheless, it should be remembered that primary school enrollment did not include everyone receiving some elementary instruction and that this undercounting was greatest in the first half of the century.

Second, the official figures for primary school enrollment cannot be thought of as some form of absolute truth. The registers from which these numbers come were the work of thousands of different hands, compiled with differing degrees of precision and sometimes by somewhat diverse criteria. The numbers were not just invented (there were too many checks for that, which were especially effective where students paid tuition), but lists were often incomplete, particularly during the first half of the century, and before the 1880s at least many undoubtedly included the names of some who for one reason or another should have been struck from the rolls, students who no longer appeared in the classroom and some who may rarely ever have done so. The totals by department or for the nation are not such absolute descriptions of reality as the compilers of these statistics tried to make them (numbers were, for example, almost never rounded off). Nevertheless, the effort at accuracy was impressive, and it is not surprising that the most careful recent scholarly scrutiny of the national totals should have produced few and then only minor adjustments to the national totals.[12]

The enrollment figures are, then, a reasonably reliable measure of the number of students whose parents were sufficiently concerned with schooling to place their names on an official register. That is not quite the modern meaning of enrollment, but it is the measure of a socially significant act. There are some additional difficulties, however. The most striking of them results from the fact that the way of counting enrollment changed. Prior to 1850, enrollment figures included both students formally registered and those attending in the winter. From 1861 to 1872, enrollment figures were based on annual registration (a more formal count but one not necessarily attentive to actual attendance) during the civil or calendar year rather than the school year. In the Third Republic, enrollment was supposed to be based on registration during the academic year, but that change was probably not complete and therefore not fully reflected even in the totals for 1875–76, which were based on the academic year. If the calendar year register included every name entered at any time during that year, then enrollment totals would include students who had left school in the previous academic year. Thus, enrollment figures for the period from 1861 through 1875–76 may be inflated compared to the figures before and after. But by how much? On some registers from this period, the names of those not attending regularly were struck out, and figures for school-year enrollment in the 1870s were also based on annual registration rather than actual attendance. Both practices (as well as the failure of some schools to make the switch) would lessen the difference between the two systems. Although only meticulous local studies would give a precise measure of the change, there are other indicators of its dimensions nationally.

The rectors of France's academies were asked to present figures for enrollment in the calendar years of 1876 and 1877 using the old system, which could then be compared to the official figure for enrollment in the 1876–77 school year under the new system. The figures for the calendar year were 4 percent higher.[13] Thus, there was not, the compilers of the *Statistique* were concerned to point out, a drop in enrollment between 1875 and 1876–77. For the analysis here, however, the important point is that this adjustment has only a modest effect on the overall pattern of growth. Table E.1 gives a compound annual growth rate of 1 percent for the period from 1866 to 1876 and of 2 percent for the period from 1876 to 1882. These are, as they should be, rounded percentages, describing a steady, established growth rate maintained in the first years of the Third Republic and then doubled in the five years preceding the Ferry Laws. The growth in enrollment during the first decade of the Third Republic was probably greater than the official figures indicate,[14] but the overall picture is little altered by the changed method of counting. Using the absolute figure for the 1876–77 school year without taking into account the change in counting would produce an annual growth rate in the ten years before 1876 of .4 percent (lowering all the prior figures, a more logical approach, would leave growth about the same) and an annual growth rate in the five years after 1876 of 2.5 percent. The percentages of change, especially in this period, remain useful approximations.[15]

Comparison with other indicators further suggests that the hidden distortions are probably modest. From 1863 to 1882, there was a 23 percent increase in the number of students enrolled and a 26 percent increase in the number of teachers, the latter a figure little affected by the switch from the calendar year to the school year.[16] Enrollment apparently increased by 50 percent from 1840 to 1863, and it is doubtful that the increase could have been much less when the number of teachers increased by 72 percent and the annual increase in expenditures on elementary education was the highest ever in the period from 1850 to 1861. Many other indicators show that this was the period of greatest growth in girls enrollment, as contemporaries believed. The counting itself was also undoubtedly more complete than it had been in most of the preceding period.[17] In absolute terms, then, enrollment may have grown less between 1850 and 1863 and more in the early years of the Third Republic than the figures indicate, but overall patterns remain much the same. Absolute numbers, however, are not necessarily the most meaningful. Correlations are more telling and less likely to register changes between dates in the ways of counting enrollment; if in some years procedures were not uniform, that in fact would tend to reduce the correlations.[18] Enrollment figures became more and more precise in the Third Republic (which required that registration figures reflect the academic year, then that records be kept month by month, and subsequently also took attendance on specific days).[19] What those figures meant, as expectations rose, changed even more than what they counted. In analyzing such data, comparison can tell more than raw numbers and can do so without requiring absolute precision. That is the purpose of analyzing in terms of when departments reached enrollments equal to 50, 75, or 100 percent of their school-age population. Such calculations do not reveal whether 50 percent enrollment meant that half of all school-age children went to school for seven years, all of them went for three-and-one-half, or something in between. But it does reflect a degree of engagement with schooling as a normal expectation. The patterns that emerge, for various groups of departments and for France as a whole, would not be significantly affected if such figures were read as 45, 70, and 95 percent of the school-age population. The proportions stand as an indicator of the spread of a general expectation and a common experience.

There are additional reasons for being careful with enrollment data, although none proves on investigation to be terribly troublesome. Students who registered in one school and moved to another during the calendar or school year would be counted more than once so long as enrollment rested on registration. This double counting, which was undoubtedly more of a factor in certain areas and at certain times, seems unlikely to have seriously inflated national figures. Such mobility presumably increased in the course of the century, and we have figures on multiple registration for 1896–97, when enrollment was universal and mobility probably about at its height. In that year, 217,264 students registered in more than one school, meaning that total enrollment (5,427,211) should be reduced by about 120,000 to allow for triple registration, a reduction of some 2 percent.[20] Furthermore, this is another of those uncertainties likely to reduce correlations over time, thus increasing rather than diminishing their significance.

Changes in population created a more serious complication. France's boundaries changed in these years, which obviously affected enrollment figures. Part of the gains in the 1860s result from the schools and students added with the annexation of three departments from Nice and Savoy. The growth in enrollment after 1870 was actually greater than it seems because totals thereafter omit Alsace and Lorraine, which had been areas of high enrollment. Normalizing these totals by the total population of France at the time or by the school-age population automatically corrects for that, so that it is not a statistical problem for our analysis. Changes in the age structure of the population (more important for some individual departments) are similarly compensated for, although only as a good approximation given the limited precision of demographic data and the inevitable inadequacies of census figures. Happily, the analysis of patterns of schooling requires nothing like the precision critical for demography, but Etienne van de Walle's careful reconstitution of the French census led him to estimate that official figures for French population were underreported by 1.7 percent (in 1851) for the nation as a whole with larger omissions in some departments.[21] Although errors of such magnitude do not affect the conclusions we reach, several of his other findings are also relevant: later censuses are not always better even though that is the trend, and there are systematic biases, the most important of which is the tendency to underreport the population under the age of fifteen. Thus, normalization by school-age population may well give estimates a few percentage points too high for the proportion of school-age children enrolled. Readers so inclined may therefore assume that enrollment normalized by population produces a ratio slightly inflated for the period from 1850 to 1881, but underreporting of enrollment may have been equally great, especially prior to the Third Republic. It would be unsound to juggle the normalized figures, and in any case, there is no reason to fear that shifts in the size or age of the population were enough greater than the census figures to significantly affect an analysis of patterns of enrollment normalized by school-age population.

For enrollment, then, as for all the figures on primary schooling in the nineteenth century, the essential caution lies elsewhere. The data are relatively good, and careful normalization makes them legitimately comparable—for the purpose of analyzing patterns of change. Correlations further avoid differences between data points. Even if official systems of counting had never changed, even if it could be assumed that every local *instituteur*, inspector, and prefect were always devoted to precision, the numbers would not mean the same thing for different schools and in different periods. Enrollment figures, especially, must not be taken as the description of a fixed reality. They say little of how regularly students attended school and nothing of what they learned. They can be safely used, however, to analyze patterns of relative change, and they are socially significant, representing the institutionalization of schooling if not the education received. To register was to accept the principal of primary instruction and, for much of the century, to pay for it as well. This combination of individual decisions, social attitudes, and institutionalization is, above all, what these statistics represent.[22]

II

The patterns and sequences that emerge from these statistics clearly suggest that the development of primary education should be understood as the growth of a system, that was not so much bureaucratically imposed from Paris as built upon habits and institutions rooted in local society and also increasingly connected to the departmental and national administrative apparatus. Enrollment, the registration of school-age children, followed quickly upon the establishment of schools. But the general trend to higher enrollment was composed of several, only partially distinguishable, changes. One of these was increasingly regular attendance, which affected enrollment figures wherever they were based on regular presence or monthly counts in addition to annual registration. Until 1886, the enrollment figures came from the *registres matricules* (kept by school and commune) and the *registres d'appel*, the teacher's roll, which was renewed each month to include the names of those children who could be expected to attend regularly during that month. In 1886, teachers were also required to submit the actual attendance records for a specific day in December and in June that had not been previously announced. Only about 10 percent of those enrolled in 1886 appear not to have been attending regularly throughout the main portion of the school year. That proportion had been 13–14 percent twenty years before and was undoubtedly higher early in the century. The discovery that on a given December day the number in attendance could fall some 20 percent below the total number enrolled in the course of the year, which greatly troubled educational statisticians of the Third Republic, would be less shocking to any twentieth-century administrator. The ratio of attendance to enrollment in France compares well to nineteenth-century England or progressive Massachusetts.[23] For the nation as a whole, matriculation meant an average attendance of eight months by the 1860s, with three-quarters of the students attending for at least six months.[24]

Larger enrollments also resulted from the tendency of those enrolled to spend more years in school. The national statistics for the first two-thirds of the century are not very clear in this regard, but the inquiry of 1833 shows a greater disparity from department to department in the number of years that students were expected to attend than in the proportion of school-age children expected to attend at all. This increase in the number of years of schooling that students received is somewhat obscured, however, by a further pattern, the growing social acceptance of the concept that there were very specific ages at which children should be in school. As enrollments went up, the number (and even more markedly, the proportion) of students younger than six or older than thirteen declined. Those enrolled were also more likely to take their schooling in consecutive years. Undoubtedly, there was a tendency to make the time at which students left school coincide with their first communion, although statistically that practice is less prominent than most descriptions suggest.[25] Nationally, about four-fifths of all boys from six to thirteen were enrolled in school by 1876, and the proportion of boys and girls from six to thirteen approached 100 percent thereafter. We use enrollment normalized by school-age population as a consistent indicator, but it was becoming increasingly descriptive (table E.8).

That change came gradually. Lorain's inquiry of 1833 indicated that students' ages varied considerably as they had in the eighteenth century.[26] Although a published ministerial report made clear in 1843 that the "real" school age was from six to thirteen, not until a decade after the foundation of the Third Republic did the Ministry of Public Instruction deem a six- to thirteen-year-old cohort to be a more accurate representation of pupils' ages than one of five- to fifteen-year-olds. In 1867, enrollment equalled 90 percent of the school-age population if all schools were counted (83 percent in primary schools alone). Some 27 percent of that enrollment, however, was of children under six or over thirteen, a proportion that fell to 18 percent by 1881. For boys, the age of peak attendance was between the ages of eight and twelve.[27]

Ultimately, universal schooling would bring altered definitions of the life cycle and a sharper sense of generations. The school-age child not in school would become the exception, identifiable as a kind of delinquent, the target of great social pressure to attend school, and counted by communes and ministers as evidence of failure that must be corrected. Where it remained common for students to return to school after having been absent for a year or more (as in much of France at midcentury), the reports of inspectors (and the statistics themselves) can easily be misread; for inspectors sometimes listed as tragically "privé" of instruction any school-age child not in school and decried premature departures whether or not the students later returned to primary school or enrolled in one of the new adult schools. Similarly, many of those denounced as having attended for only a few months were students who had returned only long enough to complete their primary schooling. There were areas in which it may not have been uncommon for a student, especially a boy, to take nine or ten years to complete the expected six years of schooling. In each department, the practice of attending school in consecutive years while of school age developed after some (often intermittent) attendance over at least a few years had become nearly universal.

A further aspect of growth had to do with the duration of the academic year. While more children enrolled in school, attended for more years, and increasingly did so while of "school age," officials sought to keep students in school for what was in effect an eleven-month academic year. And the mountain of statistics they gathered on "summer attendance" reflects the seriousness of their concern. Summer attendance was measured after 1886 by presence on a given day in June, before that usually by presence during that month.[28] Throughout the nineteenth century, however, the data on summer attendance roughly charts the continuing battle to get students to go to school for longer than seven or eight months and into the summer, establishing a very demanding academic year. At first glance, those efforts seem to have brought the steady increase that one might expect. As with enrollment itself, the rate of increase is higher earlier, especially in the 1830s, and the greatest leap comes in the Second Empire and first years of the Third Republic (table E.11). Neither the national median nor the maximums rise so high as for enrollment, however, and the variance among departments tends to be somewhat greater. A closer look at the percentages attained by individual departments confirms the impression that the progress of summer attendance was considerably slower than for overall enrollment. Eighty to ninety percent of France's departments reported the summer attendance during the Second Empire at a level equivalent to half of the school-age population. All but one, Morbihan, reached that level by 1876. By 1881, before the Ferry Laws, nearly all departments saw the equivalent of 70 percent of their school-age children attending school in the summer, but not quite half the departments won everyone to summer attendance even by 1906 (table E.15). Summer attendance as a percentage of winter enrollment began at a surprisingly high 60 percent and slowly rose[29] (table E.10), and there was certainly a strong positive correlation between summer attendance and winter enrollment.[30] Yet that correlation is weaker than one might expect. In short, summer attendance appears to have produced some of that resistance about which commentators so often complained, and in fact, much of the overall historical emphasis on resistant parents and poor attendance seems to have come from misunderstanding reports about summer attendance as describing attendance in general.

Although we are limited to statistics at the departmental level, it is possible to extract some indications of who was resistant and who more accepting of the long academic year. Correlations point to higher summer attendance in the more urban departments up to midcentury, a difference that disappears thereafter. They indicate, too, that students in Catholic schools were more likely to attend in the summer months and that, once universal winter enrollment was the norm, girls were somewhat more likely than boys to attend school during the summer.[31] An 1863 report on public school divided enrollment into the number of months in the year, giving the percentage of students in school for one month, two months, on up through twelve months. Between 15 and 19 percent of those enrolled attended for three months or less, between 12 and 18 percent for four to six months. About half of the students attended from ten to twelve months, with eleven months by far the single most common school year (between one-third and nearly one-half the students went to school for eleven months). In this period, attendance was believed to be more regular and to extend longer through the school year in public schools, especially Catholic public boys schools, than in independent schools.[32]

It is clear, however, that lower summer attendance was not simply an expression of ignorance and indifference. There is a quite strong negative correlation between literacy and the proportion of winter students who attended in the summer as well, and high overall enrollment was the single best predictor that the proportion of those who stayed on in the summer would be low.[33] Going to school in the summer months was a new and more alien discipline (and one that may not have been necessary for the acquisition of minimal skills). Where enrollment was low, the enthusiasts for education who did go to school were more ready to continue throughout the year. Where winter schooling reached deeper into the general population, it took longer for a comparable percentage of students to become accustomed to summer attendance as well.[34]

This impression of a social distinction between the majority of students willing to attend even in the summer (somewhat more likely to be girls, from urban areas, and later in the century, to attend private schools) and the large minority who resisted this demand on their time (more likely to be older boys who could work in the harvest or hold a job in a nearby town) is reinforced by the use of scattergrams, which suggest that where enrollment was far above the national mean for the period (bringing everyone into school) or had recently shown a sudden increase (bringing many children to school for the first time) the proportion who stayed through the summer was consistently lower.[35] Even aside from the possibility of summer work, many parents must have found it irresistible to save monthly tuition in the summer months, a measure of thrift probably acceptable to their children. Early in the century, many schools in all parts of France simply closed during the summer months, a custom maintained much later in some rural areas. Nevertheless, this long academic year was accepted by most. Thus, the greater resistance summer schooling faced is a reminder that most French families chose schooling (and more of it) before the law compelled them to. Significantly, the Ferry Laws brought a slight drop in the proportion of summer attendance. The official insistence on the longer school year, in contrast to the concept of universal schooling, is a clear instance of a requirement imposed from Paris that did for many run counter to local mores.[36]

These four patterns of growth, not always easily separable in statistics or reports, were fundamental. They required and stimulated the development of an extensive educational system marked by many changes. Some of these (such as the availability of schools, which we analyzed in the last chapter, and the preparation of teachers, the pattern of expenditures for primary schooling, and the extension of schooling before and after primary school, all of which will be treated later) are separable from enrollment. But reductions in tuition and the award of *certificats d'études* were so directly tied to expanding enrollment that they need to be seen as part of that process.

One of Ferry's laws declared all primary schooling free. That major step, like universal schooling itself, followed upon local trends. On the eve of that measure, there had been a marked increase in the number of French students paying reduced fees or exempt from them entirely (about half were by 1872) (table E.4). Indeed, enrollment increased more in the year after fees were abolished than it did in the year after attendance was made compulsory. Parents often did keep their children out of school when illness or work caused them to miss part of the month as long as fees were charged by the month, and the introduction in the 1860s of a system that allowed the annual fee to be paid in installments had apparently led to better attendance.[37]

By the Third Republic, most large cities charged no fees at all; neither did most Catholic schools. The poorer departments were exempting more and more families, and in principle the very poor had been excused from paying tuition throughout the century.[38] But this trend toward free schools can also be seen as part of the development of the educational system. The proportion of students on scholarship, which tended to be high where families were poor, produced a negative correlation with enrollment earlier in the century and none at all later. The fees do appear to have discouraged enrollment, though less perhaps than one might expect. Characteristically, departments with high enrollments early in the century tended to be among the leaders in reducing charges per student[39] (table E.17A). Thus, the democratization implied by increasingly free education was part of the changes in funding, administration, and quality that marked the more centralized and secularized schools of the Third Republic. And if the most visible aspect of those changes was the centralization and secularization imposed by the national state, the larger pattern of change should nevertheless be understood as evolving out of local society as well as republican politics. Preschool, too, would become more universal but later, when the mysteries of schooling were more firmly in the control of professional educators and a child's success in school was more widely believed to determine adult opportunities (table E.12).

The growing sense of the significance of primary education as a social and individual achievement is reflected in the granting of *certificats d'études* to those who passed a final examination at the completion of primary studies.

Such a measure had been discussed as early as the 1830s and introduced in some departments during the Second Empire, but apparently it was only when full national enrollment in primary schools had been achieved that conditions were ripe for the widespread institutionalization of such a practice. Then the completion of primary study came to be seen as an individual milestone to be marked, a requisite for further study to be certified, and a measure of educational accomplishment to be assessed by official examiners. The Vosges instituted the *certificat* in 1866; five more departments did so in 1867, and nine others in 1868. By 1870, twenty departments offered the *certificat*, and every department in France save three had instituted it by 1879. It became an official national matter as part of Ferry's legislation, which permitted holders of the certificate to be exempted from the requirement of compulsory attendance. By then, most departments offered the examination at a score of sites at times that varied from April to August, and most required candidates to be at least twelve years old, some thirteen, and one eleven.[40] This was clearly a measure that appealed to officials, and one can sense a growing bureaucracy in the speed with which the practice was adopted. The rapid growth in the number of candidates (and perhaps in the percentage who passed) suggests, however, that many families, too, thought the certificate valuable (table E.5). The awarding of these certificates was surrounded with ceremony, and the names of the victorious candidates were published in the local newspapers. By 1882, something close to one-fifth of the students in a graduating age group presented themselves for examination; by 1907, that proportion was about one-third. Yet, those fractions reflect the fact that this hurdle was not accessible to most, perhaps because the examination took place elsewhere, because its timing was awkward and its failure threatening, or simply because the previous years of study had not prepared students for that level of expertise or that level of ambition (table E.13).

To the officials of the Ministry of Education, the *certificat* was a highly desirable step, the best measure of the effects of education yet devised. Yet, in this as in other measures of educational activity, departments maintained a very stable relationship to each other in the degree to which they adopted the new practice.[41] A department's established institutions and customs largely determined the pace with which it embraced this test, but other factors then determined the proportion who actually took the examination. More certificates were awarded of course in departments with high enrollments, but more were also awarded in those with higher summer enrollments. Assiduity did count in this serious system. But the awarding of *certificats* in the various departments (and the establishment of *écoles maternelles*) was strongly related to their past. Until the end of the century, enrollment in 1829 or 1832 was correlated with the award of *certificats* in the 1860s, 1870s, and 1880s[42] (table E.18).

Education was debated in the nineteenth century as an instrument of change that foretold the future, but the education offered then as now was remarkable for its retrospective quality and its dependence upon its own history. Agricultural departments awarded a smaller proportion of *certificats*, urban ones a higher proportion, and of course their number varied with the number of students; but there was a higher correlation between *certificats* awarded and the literacy rate in 1851, a generation earlier. Although examiners were legitimately proud of the progress they had wrought, the students who stood before them were likely to be the children of parents who could read and write. One can thus understand the frustration of reformers who lamented the immalleability of the society they sought to transform. Historians of French education can take a larger view—sympathizing with the frustrations of dedicated inspectors and directors of nineteenth-century French schooling, acknowledging their efforts but recognizing the remarkable development of that educational system as an accomplishment of a whole society (table E.19).

III

Beginning with the important fact that early enrollment is a good predictor of later development, the patterns of enrollment are sufficiently clear to encourage further analysis. We have looked to see if certain social conditions seem to favor primary school enrollment and if geographical differences in enrollment prove revealing. We have looked to see whether there are definable stages through which most departments passed on the way to universal primary instruction and whether it is possible to establish a periodization for the history of enrollment in the nation as a whole.

There are three major constraints on what these data can reveal about the social factors associated with school enrollment. The first is that the data are aggregated at the departmental level, so that the rich and poor, urban and rural parts of any one department tend to average out what may be very significant differences. The second is that, in general, social data, even on such major matters as wealth or poverty, are far less reliable than the data on schooling. The third is that combining such data into useable indicators necessarily increases unreliability. We have therefore resisted the temptation to construct elaborate indicators based on the challenging and heterogeneous data in the French censuses.

Relatively simple cultural, economic, and demographic indicators, derived from those censuses, do give significant results, however, and in about that order (table E.20). Nearly all of these indicators produce higher correlations with enrollment earlier in the century and then much lower ones with enrollment late in the century. One of the goals of a national educational system was, after all, to override such social differences. Among these various factors, the level of literacy gives the highest (and always positive) correlation with the proportion of school-age children enrolled in school, at every date. Few other correlations are so consistently high, and the fact that this correlation is higher from enrollment to later literacy than from literacy to later enrollment implies that the schools did indeed foster some of the basic skills they were intended to impart. Believers in progress thus seem also to have been roughly right when they insisted that educated young people would become parents who valued education for their children.

The per capita wealth of a department also correlates with enrollment, a positive correlation higher when mass schooling was new and its funding almost entirely local. The virtual disappearance of this correlation (rough as these measures are) by the time of the Ferry Laws is an impressive achievement, a step toward educational equality that should not be forgotten.[43] When tested as a social factor, urbanization produced results difficult to interpret (the overall correlation of enrollment and urban population, which was very low, changed sign in 1863). For France, with its rural population and small towns, only in a few cases can figures for an entire department reflect the impact of cities.[44] We turned, therefore, to a different technique, creating quintiles of departments by the percentage of their total population that was urban (there is no escaping the fact that three-quarters of France's departments had less than 20 percent of their population in towns of more than two thousand people!). The most urban departments always had the highest rates of enrollment from 1829 through 1867; thereafter, as all the departments drew closer together, the least urban ones usually had the highest enrollment (table E.16). Clearly, French education was reaching deep into the countryside, but these figures probably also reflect higher averages for departments in which a more evenly dispersed population put children in easy reach of rural schools.[45] In any case, as measured by enrollments, the French school system would appear by the beginning of the Third Republic to have overcome some of the most basic social differences to a degree that might be the envy of any social planner.

Although statistics aggregated by department tend to dilute social indicators, they can convey a great deal of the regional differences so much a part of French historical consciousness (even though the departments themselves had been created to break up the political and cultural cohesion of the ancient provinces). Maps of *la belle hexagone*, with its crazy quilt of departments, remain the favorite illustration of French social history. For the historiography of education, by far the most famous (indeed vastly overused) division is along the imaginary line from St. Malo to Geneva. Enrollment statistics confirm the sharpness of that division through the 1870s, after which it ceased to matter (table E.7). The region north of that line consistently spent much more on education, relieved more students from tuition, and showed less favoritism for boys over girls. The area south of the line actually spent more per student in the period of rapid growth (1840–63), however, and there is little difference in summer attendance.[46] That demarcation clearly points to some fundamental regional differences, but, as argued in chapter 2, the comparison of thirty departments (including some of those educationally most advanced and the national capital) with all the rest of France also obscures important regional distinctions.

There are a number of other ways to explore the educational geography of France. Broad regions, the academies that served as the education ministry's administrative units, and a rough grouping of departments to approximate the provinces of the old regime all reveal some homogeneity in their enrollments. Provinces and academies, however, despite their historical associations, do not appear to have responded to the challenge of increasing enrollment any more coherently than would any reasonable grouping of contiguous departments. When departments are grouped by academy, they produce an association that is not significantly higher for the period when the academies functioned as administrative units than for the periods before they were formed or after they declined in importance. The association among provinces, considering the statistical approximations from which they were constructed, does suggest the continuation of historic contacts and cultures. Yet even those fifteen provinces are far behind the statistical octiles of 1829 or 1832 in consistent ranking across the century (fig. 5). In short, statistical constructs—octiles and k-means clusters—provide by far the greatest coherence, and these, too, can be mapped[47] (table E.21).

The map shown in figure 5, which essentially held valid throughout the century, shows the advanced northeast but differentiates it into three leading groups, two of which are joined by departments elsewhere in France. Similarly, the lowest three octiles form the familiar western wedge of lagging educational development;[48] but there, too, the breakup of that large area is foreseen: a circle in central France joins Finistère, Morbihan, and Loire-Inférieure as the departments of least schooling, and the next two octiles break up even more. Finally, the two middle octiles, the norm for France as a whole, do not constitute regions at all. Eighty percent of these departments do touch at least one other department in the same octile, but neither regional geography nor even topography determined the development of primary education, however influential (along with culture, politics, and the economy) they may have been.

When statistical clusters are established for any large period of time, they tend to produce one or two very large groups of departments: the national mean did have reality across the country. Nevertheless, the development of the educational system can be shown in a map of statistical clusters of departments, based on their enrollments from 1832 to 1881 and (after enrollment

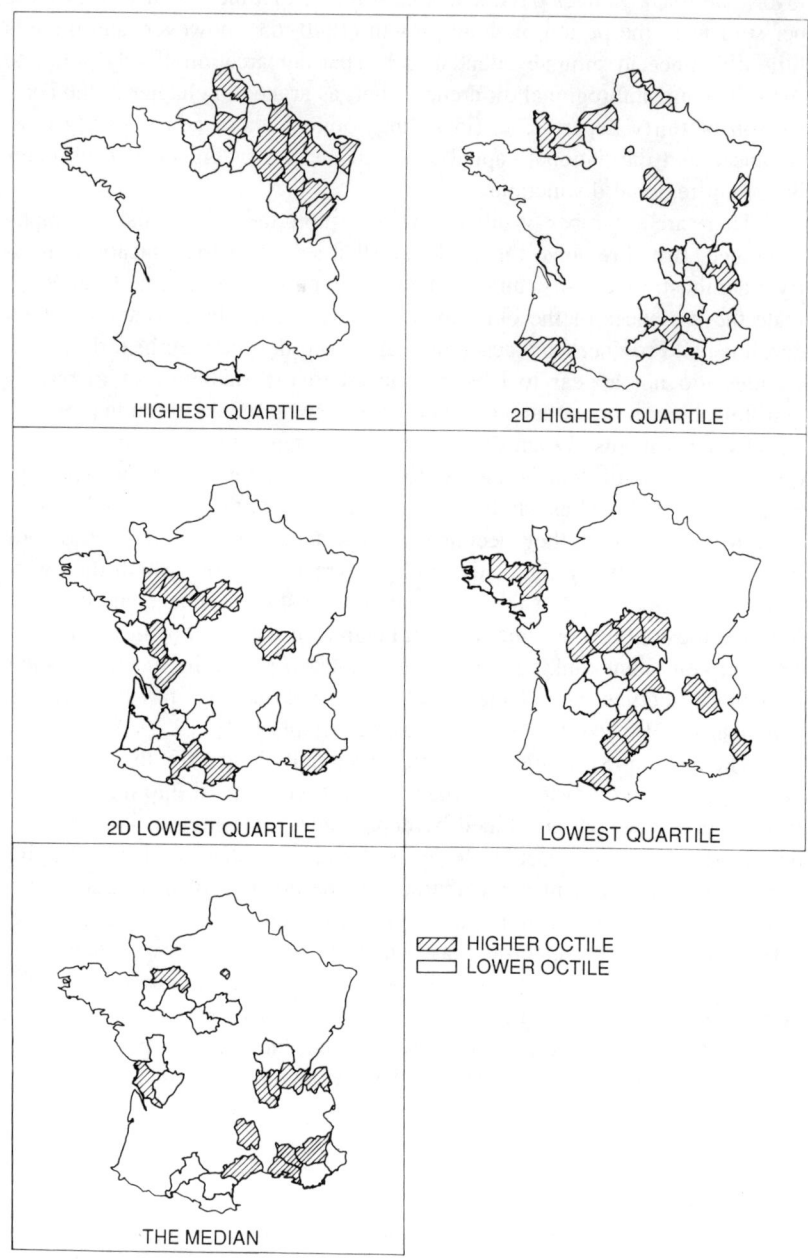

Fig. 5. Octiles and quartiles of departments in France based on 1832 enrollment

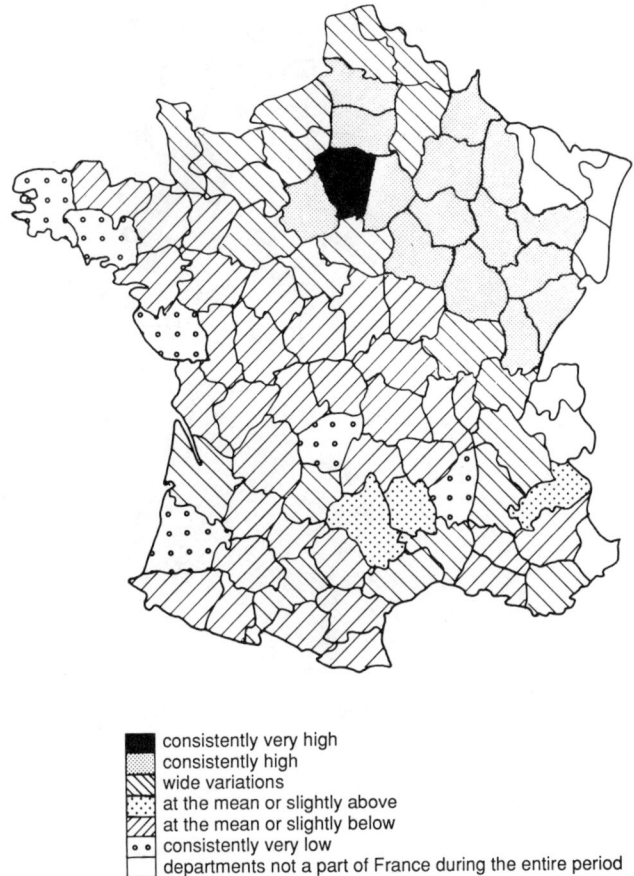

Fig. 6. Best cluster fit of departments based on enrollment 1832–81 and on *certificats d'études* 1882–1907

was universal) the number of *certificats d'études primaires* awarded from 1882 to 1907 (fig 6). Five clusters provide the best fit (60 percent), and the largest cluster can be divided into two parts. Inclusion of the *certificats* makes the Seine and Seine-et-Oise stand out, but the two groups that fluctuate near the national mean extend from the Nord to the Basses Pyrénées, from the Var to Côtes-du-Nord. This suggests the possibility of creating a still more revealing map of the evolution of the system of schooling, a map based on the statistical clusters of departments that combine four distinct (but closely related) variables: the number of schools in 1821, enrollment in 1837, summer attendance in 1876, and the number of *certificats* awarded in 1886 (fig. 7)— each date is one at which a distinct pattern for that variable was established

76   School, State, and Society

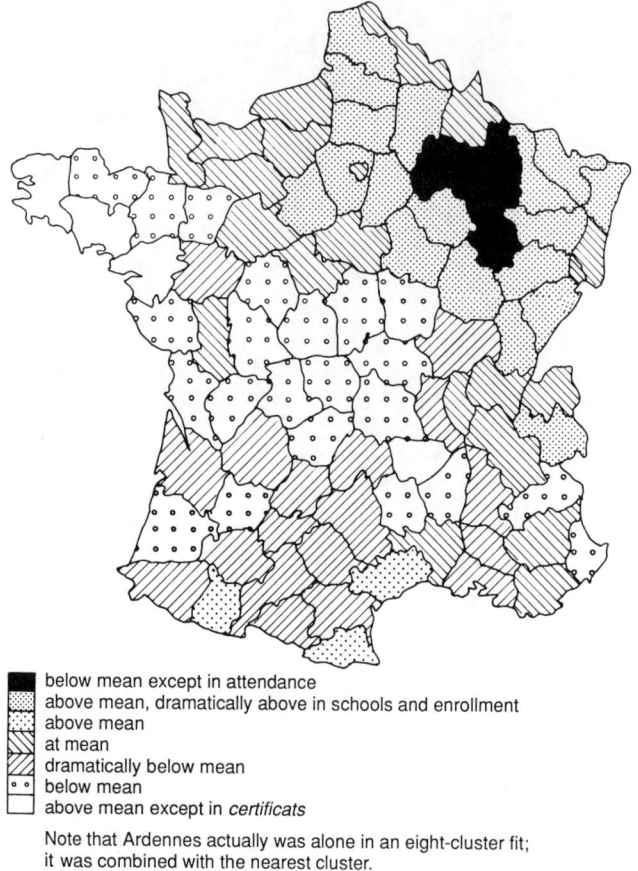

■ below mean except in attendance
▨ above mean, dramatically above in schools and enrollment
▦ above mean
◨ at mean
▨ dramatically below mean
∘∘ below mean
□ above mean except in *certificats*

Note that Ardennes actually was alone in an eight-cluster fit;
it was combined with the nearest cluster.

Fig. 7. Seven clusters based on schools in 1821, enrollment in 1837, summer attendance in 1876, and *certificats d'études* in 1886. Note that Ardennes actually was alone in an eight-cluster fit; it was combined with the nearest cluster.

among the departments of France (and each of the variables is normalized, of course, by the department's school-age population). A group of eight clusters provides the best fit, and when mapped these clusters provide a now familiar but rather more sophisticated picture of the evolution of France's system of primary schools. Most, but by no means all, of the northeast, joined by Savoy, maintained its lead in all variables. The departments of eastern Champagne drop a notch by these staggered measures. A large tier extending diagonally across France (just above and below the St. Malo–Geneva line) stays generally above the national median. A second tier lies just below the first, and the old western wedge breaks up to form a third tier (generally just at or below the national mean), a southern and Rhône valley bloc, and the familiar laggards. In these groups and in the remaining cluster along the Pyrénées, the special problems of mountainous regions and dispersed populations again stand out (as they had in the availability of schools early in the century). A variety of other clusters can be calculated in various ways (almost always with a weaker statistical fit), and these produce shifts in the affiliation of single departments (because most of the clusters are, at their extremes, very close to each other). But figure 7, with its layers of statistical clusters, provides a subtle and useful picture of the extent and pace of departmental response to the rising standings of primary schooling in nineteenth-century France.

Given these regional patterns in the development of a national system of primary education, is it possible to generalize about the stages through which the various departments passed, about the level at which growth was likely to be slow or rapid? Almost all departments experienced uneven growth (in enrollment, summer attendance, and primary certificates awarded), with each level followed by a slight decline and then a new high. Educational growth did not proceed mechanically but like a real social process. A few departments that in 1832 had enrollments of over 50 percent of the school-age population thereafter increased enrollments very slowly; a few that were below 20 percent in 1832 very rapidly caught up with the leaders. Growth in enrollments did not always follow from the establishment of a school system or even from the widespread practice of attending for a few years. Nevertheless, some patterns emerge.[49]

Generally, departments that had enrollments in 1832 of 20 percent or below proceeded toward 110 percent (the minimum final figures for all but three departments) at a pace slower than the national norm. Departments that in 1832 had more than 50 percent of their school-age population already enrolled climbed to over 110 percent more rapidly than the norm. About two-thirds of all departments experienced one or more periods of exceptionally rapid growth. These leaps occurred most commonly from 70 percent to some higher figure (90, 100, 110, or 120 percent—about one-third of all the rapid leaps). Once two-thirds of full enrollment was achieved, most of the rest quickly followed, which may have been a matter of getting some children into school for the first time or getting those already there to stay longer. Leaps from 10 percent to 30 percent (or more, even up to 60 percent) were the next most common, followed by those from 30 percent to 80 or 90 percent. The very frequency of these leaps in enrollment suggests a local society markedly receptive to schooling once the facilities were available and enrollment had become a well-known practice. There were two levels at which enrollment remained more or less constant across several data points: at 60 or 70 percent and above 100 percent of the school-age population. Local studies would be needed to determine whether the earlier plateau reflects the absence of certain social groups, resistance to longer schooling, or rural regions that lacked sufficient schools. As for the second plateau, some departments by the end of the century enrolled 120 to 140 percent of their school-age population, but that required a further extension of the school career (and presumably increased expenses for more teachers and larger facilities) that many departments did not adopt.

The importance of local preferences shows also in the figures for summer attendance, which was always lower than winter enrollment (for the modal department, by about 25 percent). But the relationship between the two figures varied enormously between departments and over time. Not only did summer attendance vary more among departments, but the gap between the two measures, which was smaller when enrollment was low, generally became greater when there was a sudden leap in enrollment. Thus, for the nation as a whole, summer attendance lagged more from the 1840s through the 1860s than either before or after, and in departments that achieved high enrollments relatively early in the century, summer attendance often continued to lag at a level achieved for winter enrollment a generation earlier. The weight of local custom, uneven growth, departmental variations, and sudden leaps (and therefore lags) all help to explain some of the anguish officials felt as their department fell behind its neighbor while the nation maintained an impressive growth in schooling.

That national growth does allow for some overall periodization. Less neat than the periodization we found for the availability of schools—1821–37, 1837–67, 1876–1906—it is also slightly different. Cluster analysis (of data points) supports two distinct periodizations: 1829–50, 1863–76, 1881–1906 or 1829–67, 1872–76, 1881–1906 (with the added possibility that the last period can be divided into two, 1881–91, 1896–1906).[50] The most natural break appears, depending upon the statistical method used, between 1850 and 1863, 1867 and 1872, and in the five years before or after 1886. By 1850, when three-quarters of France's departments had enrollments equal to 50 percent of the school-age population and one-half had enrollments equal to more than 60 percent, the principle of universal schooling if not its practice can be said to have been established. We suggest 1829–50 as the initial period of rapid growth in which the basis of a national system of primary schools was firmly founded. By 1876, especially as a result of extensive growth in the period after 1867, nearly all departments had enrollments equal to 75 percent of the school-age population and more than six-tenths had enrollments equal to population itself. By then, those departments with anything less than all school-age children enrolled for seven years stood out as laggards. We suggest 1850–76 as the period in which the practice of full enrollment became the accepted norm. This was actually achieved by over 90 percent of the departments in the 1880s. The decade 1876–86 thus saw the completion of the system of universal education, but at the same time the process of improvement in quality pushed ahead with new vigor, and the growth of *écoles maternelles*, the extension of the years of schooling, improved teacher training, and the award of more *certificats* marked the period from 1876 to 1906.[51]

Analysis of enrollment statistics also makes a number of other points, points more important than a particular periodization, and makes them more sharply. Throughout the period studied, much of France maintained a level of enrollment above national requirements. That effort, which rested on local commitment, developed into an expanding system in which some schools led to more, initial expenditures to larger ones, and a few years of schooling to a full course of studies, so that an early start in establishing schools predicted an early lead in enrollments, expenditures, and even the award of *certificats*. The systemic quality of this development permits mapping regional levels of educational growth that are valid for the period as a whole. Analysis of the enrollment statistics also suggests that the famous pieces of national legislation, important as they were, expressed (as in a representative government they should) goals widely shared and that in France the practice of universal education—like much else in history—spread from the bottom up as well as from the top down. It may thus be the failure to perceive this that now needs explanation. This analysis has, of course, combined enrollments in boys and girls schools and in Catholic and public schools. The exploration of those distinctions, around which so much conflict raged, may help to explain how the relatively rapid achievement in nineteenth-century France of one of the most demanding, complex, and expensive of liberal dreams has been so often overlooked or underestimated.

Notes

1. That decline was due not merely to the disruption of revolution but probably reflects the repression that followed (and was felt by teachers), in addition to the conservative distrust of secular schooling which contributed to the Falloux Law (Thier's "conversion" to Catholic schooling is a famous instance). A recent account of the success of repressive measures is Thomas Forstenzer, *French Provincial Police and the Fall of the Second Republic: Social Fear and Counter-revolution* (Princeton, 1981).

2. Demographic changes were of course generally less great in France than elsewhere in the nineteenth century and the rank ordering of departments by total population with school-age population produces high correlations (of .94 to .97) from 1821 to 1906. Early in the century, some departments merely estimated age groups, but by the 1870s compilers were describing considerable variety. In 1876, 15 percent of the population in Côtes-du-Nord was six–thirteen years old (the highest in France) while not quite 10 percent belonged to that age group in the Seine (the lowest), *Statistique de*

l'enseignement, 1876–77, I: 16. In 1886, the Seine remained the department with the lowest proportion of school-age population (still one in ten) when Landes, at nearly 17 percent, had the highest, ibid., 1886, lxxxviii.

3. Only five departments moved more than three standard deviations: Hautes-Alpes, Isère, Landes, Lozère, Haute-Marne. Twenty-one moved between two and three deviations: Ariège, Aube, Aude, Aveyron, Cantal, Charente, Corrèze, Corse, Drome, Gers, Gironde, Hérault, Lot, Manche, Marne, Meuse, Oise, Puy-de-Dôme, Basses-Pyrénées, Rhone, Seine-et-Oise.

4. 1832 was chosen as the first year in which enrollment figures included boys and girls. By 1886, the lowest two groups were 1 percentage point apart, and in 1891 the lowest one moved above the third (.84 and .83); they returned to their normal rankings (but still only 1 percentage point apart) in 1896 and 1901, tied (at .87) in 1906.

5. Twenty of the last 48 data points are shared by two or three octiles. Of the 9 points of crossover among the total of 128 data points, 6 are accounted for by the movement of the second octile above the third from 1881 on. We also looked at the departments with the largest increases or decreases in school-age population in the periods 1850–76, 1876–96, and 1881–1906; they scatter across the octiles, and all octiles include some of these departments that experienced the greatest demographic change, which suggests the stability of departmental rankings was overridden by other social and institutional factors.

6. The *enquête* of 1829 indicates that most children had attended some school, but only in a few, leading departments did they attend for six years or more. The reports for each arrondissement are in the Archives Nationales, F17/80ff.

7. Joseph Kay, *The Education of the Poor of England and Europe* (London, 1846), 73-74.

8. Henry Barnard, *National Education in Europe* (Hartford, 1854), 382, 390.

9. Reports submitted to Paris indicate that in the early 1830s, there was a wide variety within the same department as to the age at which children attended school. Even in the Marne, an advanced department, the age at first entry into school ranged from three to eleven, Archives Nationales, F17/125; see also note 24.

10. The question of school-age population is a crucial and complicated one that often confused nineteenth-century statisticians and not just in France; see E. G. West, *Education and the Industrial Revolution* (London, 1975), 8–10. In 1922, only 31 percent of fourteen-year-olds attended school in Great Britain. Yet Victor Cousin believed in 1831 that all children seven to fourteen attended school in Prussia, Kay, *Education of the Poor*, 77–78. The charts and maps in the most recent survey of French education (Françoise Mayeur, *L'éducation en France* [Paris, 1982], 328) are based on a five to fifteen school-age cohort, but the expectation was for six or seven years of schooling in the nineteenth century, never ten. As early as 1843, the published ministerial report indicated that 6 to 13 was the proper school age, Ministère de l'instruction publique, *Rapport au Roi sûr la situation de l'instruction primaire en 1843* (Paris, 1843), 32. But the five to fifteen cohort continued to be used in French statistics through 1876 to allow for the variety of ages at which children in fact attended (interestingly, the same cohort was used in Massachusetts and Ontario for the same reasons), Carl Kaestle and Maris Vinovskis, *Education and Social Change in*

Nineteenth-Century Massachusetts (New York, 1980), 13; R. D. Gidney, "Elementary Education in Upper Canada: A Reassessment," in *Education and Social Change: Themes from Ontario's Past*, ed. Paul Mattingly and Michael B. Katz (New York, 1975), 3–26. Jules Ferry noted with embarrassment that the number of students enrolled in 1881 exceeded the six to thirteen age cohort by more than 150,000, Ministère de l'instruction publique, *Statistique de l'enseignement primaire*, 1881–82 (Paris, 1884), III:lxxviii; ibid., 1886–87 (Paris, 1889), IV:lxxxvi. And the compilers of these statistics in the Third Republic noted the difficulty of collating birth dates, calendar years, and school years.

We have used six to thirteen as the school-age population throughout. These figures are given by the census for boys in 1821 and for all children after 1850. When necessary, we have adjusted figures for a five- to fifteen-year-old school-age population by the straightforward 7:10 ratio. To be sure, sophisticated demographic analysis would permit slight modifications of this ratio, differing a tiny bit in various periods, but such adjustments would make only very small changes in the percentages of school-age children enrolled (changes that would tend to yield marginally higher percentages). In addition, we have analyzed nearly all these data by total population as well, noting the few instances in which some discrepancy emerged and drawing attention on occasion to those departments with the greatest variation in demographic profile.

11. In 1901, 2,828 families in France were listed as teaching their children at home; the army and navy taught 25,000 illiterate recruits to read in the period from 1878 to 1882, the peak of that program.

12. The most detailed study is J.-P Briand, J.-M. Chapoulié, F. Huguet, J.-N. Luc, and A. Prost, *L'enseignement primaire et ses extensions: Annuaire statistique 19e–20e siècles* (Paris, 1987). Table 1, p. 115, provides totals for all the data points in our table E.1 from 1829 to 1872. For these thirteen data points, their figures are identical for eleven. They make two modifications of these totals: The data for 1847 is really for 1846, and the total they give for 1850 is 1,000 students higher than that in the printed *Statistique* (an increase of 0.03 percent). In addition, they note that a separate report to the king in 1840 gave a total of 15,000 fewer students (a drop of 0.5 percent) for that year and that another report, for 1850, gave a total of 13,200 more students than their figure (already 1,000 higher than that in the *Statistique*, an increase of 0.42 percent). They also provide a figure for 1868–69 (which, at 4,667,703 students, falls neatly between the figures for 1866 and 1872). They comment as well that the reports for some of these years, especially 1846, were considered defective at the time.

The same study, in table 2, pp. 119–20, continues with enrollment figures for each year from 1875–76 to 1945. That includes nine data points in our table E.1, with identical figures for all but one. Their total for 1886–87 gives a figure of 70,000 more students than the *Statistique* (1.5 percent more than the printed figure), a total higher than for any other year from 1829 to 1945.

13. Their figures were 4,903,926 enrolled in 1876 and 4,918,890 students enrolled in 1877; compared to 4,716,935 on the *régistres matricules* for the 1876–77 academic year, *Statistique de l'enseignement*, II:cxiii–cxiv.

14. Expenditures were also increasing then, although the growth in the number of schools had slowed to 1 percent a year. The number of teachers increased rapidly

between 1876 and 1882, at about 2 percent a year, but much of that resulted from the addition of lay teachers without displacing religious ones, which need not have accompanied comparably increased enrollment.

15. One report declared that for Paris in 1859 the count by calendar year inflated enrollment by 17 percent; Jean-Noël Luc, *La statistique de l'enseignement primaire, 19e–20e siècles: Politique et mode d'emploi* (Paris, 1985), 121, cites the Paris example in the course of a detailed account, pp. 104–56, of these uncertainties. A simple statistical experiment is revealing. Let us assume that enrollment figures were inflated by 17 percent from 1861 to 1876, reducing the totals for those years by that amount. The effect on the growth rate between 1863 and 1875 would be slight, leaving 1850–61 and 1876–81, the points of transition between methods of counting, as the moments in which real growth would have been greater or less than the enrollment figures indicate. The experiment requires reducing the official enrollment figures by 17 percent for each of the data points used in our analysis and recalculating the annual growth rate. The effect on annual growth rates would be as follows: 1850–61, .9 (instead of 2 percent as in E.1); 1861–63, .6 (1); 1863–65, 1.1 (1); 1865–66, 1.8 (2); 1866–72, .7 (1); 1872–75, .6 (1); 1875 to 1876–77, −1.9 (−2); 1876–77 to 1881, 5.8 (2).

16. And a 10 percent increase in the number of schools, a large increase compared to most periods, though not compared to the 14 percent increase from 1843 to 1863. Both figures are nicely consonant with the apparent increases in enrollment.

17. If the increase in enrollment between 1850 and 1863 was really only one-half of what the official figures show, then enrollment would have grown at the same rate (1 percent) as the number of schools (see tables S.1 and E.1 and, for teachers, T.1J) as it did from 1861 to 1863 but rarely at any other time. Expenditures, however, increased at an unusually high rate (16 percent annually, see table Ex.1), higher than any time other than the years before and during the Ferry Laws.

18. The same principle applies to the analysis of attendance later in this chapter.

19. *Statistique de l'enseignement*, III:lxxviii–lxxxiii; IV:lxix–lxx; (1891–92) (Paris, 1895), V:lxv–lxvii, and with much attention to the age of students. Note also the concern that figures from private school are less reliable, despite the contrary evidence of their test case, ibid., IV:lxxvn.

20. *Statistique de l'enseignement*, (1896–97) (Paris, 1900), VI:xcvii. Double enrollment was mentioned ten years earlier, ibid., IV:lxxiii, where the number of "mutations" and resultant double enrollments was said to have gone up in 1884–85 as an explanation of increased enrollment in that year and, more pointedly, of the apparent drop in enrollment in the subsequent years.

21. He estimates an underreporting of 1.2 percent, 1806–46; 1.7 percent in 1851; 1.4 percent in 1871; 1.2 percent in 1881; and less than 1 percent for the other censuses. Etienne Van de Walle, *The Female Population of France in the Nineteenth Century* (Princeton, 1974), 13–15, 123–25, 151, 156.

22. For a harsh criticism of our analysis, see Jean-Noël Luc, "La scolarisation en France au XIXe siècle: L'illusion statistique," *Annales, Economies, Sociétés, Civilisations* 41, no. 4 (July–August, 1986): 887–911; and our reply, "L'offuscation pédantesque, observations sur les préoccupations de J.-N. Luc," ibid., 913–22.

23. In 1886, 91 percent of those enrolled in public schools for the year were listed on the *registres d'appel* for December (the absent 9 percent included those who were

seriously ill or had moved away), but only 79 percent of those enrolled were in class on December 4, 80 percent on December 11. When private schools were included, the figures for the latter date rose to 82 percent, *Statistique de l'enseignement*, IV:lxxxvi–lxxxvii. National attendance in England, confirmed by recent local studies, seems to have ranged from 68 to 82 percent, W. E. Marsden, "Social Environment, School Attendance and Educational Achievement in a Merseyside Town, 1870–1900," in *Popular Education and Socialization in the Nineteenth Century*, ed. Philip McCann (London, 1977), 211–12. In Massachusetts, an enrollment of 90 percent during the summer produced only 75 percent daily attendance, Kaestle and Vinovskis, *Education in Massachusetts*, 239.

24. The inquiries conducted in 1863 and 1867 indicate that one child in seven attended less than three months in a school year but that many of these were older students "finishing up." The average attendance in 1867 was 8.1 months (8.5 months if those who attended less than three months are excluded; 14.5 percent of all students attended for three months or less, 75 percent for more than six months, 63.5 percent for more than eight months, 50 percent for ten or eleven months). Archives Nationales, F17/9351 (1863), F17*/3158 (for public schools in 1863), and the *Exposé* (1867), Ministre de l'instruction publique, *Exposé générale de la situation de l'instruction primaire au 1 janvier 1867*, 23ff. The ministry's *Etat de l'instruction publique* of 1864 and of 1869 mention the older students finishing up. The attendance of those enrolled was probably always somewhat higher in private schools than in public ones, but that may have been due to looser enrollment records within private schools. The detailed monthly statistics of attendance in the *Exposé* of 1867 sustain the impressionistic comments from inspectors that Catholic schools had a larger percentage enrolled for one or two months (to prepare for first communion) and a larger percentage who attended for the full academic year; the Frères had the reputation of demanding regular attendance. At the level of universities, too, Jacques Verger et al., *Histoire des universités en France* (Toulouse, 1986), 8, stresses that their history is independent of the "grandes doctrines officiellement revelées."

25. Octave Gréard, *L'enseignement primaire à Paris de 1867 à 1877* (Paris, 1878), mentions this custom, as does Robert Anderson, *Education in France* (Oxford, 1975), 33–34. Regardless of episcopal directives, children received first communion at a variety of ages and inspectors often noted that teenage boys left school for a job.

26. Paul Lorain, *Tableau de l'instruction primaire* (Paris, 1837), 13, 70.

27. The mean percentage of boys enrolled in a primary school was: six to seven, 78; seven to eight, 80; eight to nine, 86; nine to ten, 86; ten to eleven, 84; eleven to twelve, 82; twelve to thirteen, 67; thirteen to fourteen, 43; fourteen to fifteen, 25. The various age groups as a percentage of total enrollment (in primary schools and *écoles maternelles*) were:

	1881–82	1886–87
2–6 years old	18.4	17.9
6–11	57.4	56.7
11–13	15.8	17.8
13–16	8.4	7.6

The number of those under the age of six enrolled was:

	1881–82	1886–87	% Decline
boys	251,965	232,861	7.6
girls	290,747	264,328	9.1

The number of those over thirteen enrolled in primary school was:

	1881–82	1886–87	% Decline
boys	267,599	251,839	5.9
girls	233,777	266,044	3.3

Data from "Introduction," *Statistique de l'enseignement*, IV:lxxxvi–lxxxviii. These figures were confirmed by and undoubtedly derived from a host of earlier reports: *Rapport* (1843), Archives Nationales F17*/5160, *Exposé* (1867), *Annuaires* (Resumé des états de la situation de l'enseignement primaire), 1878ff. There were some 71,000 students under thirteen in *écoles primaires secondaires* and 30,000 in *écoles primaires supérieures* in 1886. The number of students enrolled in *cours d'adultes*, which stood at 115,164 in 1846, had risen to 829,555 in 1866. The report of 1843 confirms the 1876 statistics indicating a falloff in that period, too, in enrollment of children under six and over thirteen. The *cours d'adultes* are discussed in more detail in chapter 7.

28. Measuring attendance by students present on a given day produced lower results, which largely explains the drop between 1881 and 1886. Obligatory enrollment and the increasing secularization of a system in which Catholic schools had higher summer attendance than lay ones were additional but less significant factors. It is important to stress, however, that early in the century a six-month school year was common and that summer attendance is *not* an indicator of the regularity of attendance. A nine- or ten-month school year was as common in the 1870s as the eleven-month one. (Reports on the number of months each school was open are in the Archives Nationales, F17/9253ff.) The historiography is unclear on this point, often confusing summer attendance with day-to-day or regular attendance. J. Gavoille's study of Doubs appears to calculate absenteeism on the basis of an eleven-month school year, *L'école publique dans le département du Doubs (1870–1914)* (Paris, 1981), 47. Eugen Weber, *Peasants into Frenchmen: The Modernization of Rural France, 1870–1914 (Stanford, 1976)*, 303, and Gabriel Desert, "Alphabétisation et scolarisation dans le Grand-Ouest au 19e siècle," in Donald N. Baker and Paluch J. Harrigan, *Making of Frenchmen: Current Directions in the History of Education in France, 1679–1979* (Waterloo, Ont., 1980), 161–63, believe summer attendance increased. Antoine Prost says there was slow improvement, *Histoire de l'enseignement* (Paris, 1968), 99–101; Félix Ponteil confuses summer attendance in private and public schools, *Histoire de l'enseignement en France: Les grandes étapes, 1789–1965* (Paris, 1966), 290. In 1876, attendance was lower in October than in June, highest in January, *Statistique de l'enseignement*, 1876, I:150. Interestingly enough, an English school for which we have figures from forty years earlier (when enrollment and length of schooling were much lower) similarly found attendance worse in September than May or June, highest in the winter

(but not in January), Meryl Medoc-Jones, "Patterns of Attendance and their Social Significance: Mitcham National School, 1830–39," in McCann, *Popular Education*, 58–59.

29. The figures in table E.10 are slightly higher for the period 1829–76 than those in the summary table in the introduction to the *Statistique de l'enseignement*, 1876, II:cl, but are based on the fuller tables in the same volume. The summary table may be for public schools only.

30. The correlations of summer attendance to winter enrollment are:

	1829	1832	1837	1840	1850	1876
Spearman	.84	.87	.72	.65	.73	.81
Pearson	.69	.75	.68	.62	.67	.68

31. The correlation of the percentage of girls in the total enrollment with the percentage of all those enrolled attending in the summer is: 1837, .28; 1850, .2; 1876, .09; 1881, .23; 1886, .42; 1891, .39; 1896, .41; 1901, .35; 1906, .35.

32. Although the figures given suggest that attendance in girls lay public schools was very similar. The report, in Archives Nationales, F17*/3158, appears to have figures for all boys but less than half the girls in public schools. It gives percentages for each possible number of months; we have grouped them for convenience:

	Boys Lay	Boys Religious	Girls Lay	Girls Religious
1–3 months	19.1	15.0	14.5	16.8
4–6 months	16.9	13.0	12.5	17.8
7–9 months	18.8	16.3	16.0	21.1
10–12 months	45.0	55.5	56.0	44.2

33. The correlation of the percentage of summer attendance with literacy is:

	Literacy, 1851	Literacy, 1865
1819	−.48	−.44
1832	−.54	−.52
1833	−.53	−.53
1837	−.53	−.52
1840	−.45	−.43
1850	−.34	−.35
1876	−.28	−.27
1881	−.19	−.02
1886	−.25	−.24
1891	−.24	−.22
1901	−.05	−.02
1906	−.13	−.13

The regression of summer attendance as a percentage of enrollment against eight different enrollment and social factors at three dates always produced enrollment as the most significant factor: −6. for 1837; −.41 for 1840; and −.49 for 1876. The other factors in the multiple regression (urban population, enrollment, Catholic schools, the proportion of girls with indicators of wealth, and the proportion of the population employed in agriculture, industry, and commerce) added very little to the leading indicator, producing a multiple R of .74 in 1837, .67 in 1850, and .59 in 1876.

34. Graph 1 (of the octiles) establishes that leaders and laggards in enrollment maintained their relative positions throughout the century. In the seven departmental leaders in enrollment in 1832, summer attendance ranged from 26 to 44 percent of enrollment except for one, the Aube, where it reached 72 percent. In the seven lagging departments of 1832, summer attendance ranged from 66 to 88 percent of enrollment. The two groups were more similar in 1850 (with a range of 43 to 66 percent among the leaders of 1832), 41 to 77 percent among the laggards (except for 91 percent in Finistère). By 1891, the early leaders were also ahead in the percentage of summer attendance (in terms of means; the ranges were 63 to 71 percent for early leaders, 52 to 78 percent for the laggards).

35. In 1837, there were seventeen departments with enrollment at 90 percent or more of their school-age population; only two had a summer attendance of 50 percent of enrollment, and their proportion (below 60 percent) was about the national mean. In 1840, of twenty-six departments with more than 80 percent of the school-age population enrolled, only three were above the national mean in their percentage of summer attendance. From 1840 to 1850, of the fourteen departments with the largest increases in enrollment, nine have a decrease in the percentage of summer attendance (and in the four in which summer attendance went up, it increased less than did the national mean). In 1876, of the twenty-six departments with enrollments of less than 100 percent of the school-age population, all but two had a summer attendance of more than 78 percent of enrollment; of the eleven departments with an enrollment above 125 percent, only one had a summer attendance as high as 75 percent of enrollment.

36. Inspectors under Duruy (who were generally opposed to the elimination of primary school tuition) judged that an annual fee paid in installments (rather than a monthly fee) resulted in increased attendance during harvest or at school's end (the summer). Scattered reports suggest that poorer parents with many children sometimes started the younger ones later in the year and kept the older ones home, Archives Nationales, F17/9376. Inspectors also repeatedly suggested to Paris some adjustment of summer hours or setting vacation to coincide with harvest. They reported success with such local experiments but never convinced Paris. *Etat* (1864) I: 170, 616, 811, 833, 907; II: 47, 264, 336, 426, 770, 843; Archives Nationales, F17/9376 (1869). Prussian schools in the late eighteenth century allowed for no vacations and only shortened hours in the summer but had to retreat from so demanding a schedule, Anthony J. La Vopa, *Prussian Schoolteachers: Profession and Office, 1763–1848* (Chapel Hill, 1980), 12.

37. Archives Nationales, F17/9376 (summary for 1869); *Etat* (1864), I: 817, 833, 907; II: 47, 336, 426.

38. For an analysis of the historical tradition concerning free education in France, see R. R. Palmer, "Free Secondary Education in France before and after the Revolution," *History of Education Quarterly* 14 (1975): 437–52. That the government kept these statistics distinguishing the proportion of scholarship and tuition-paying students

reflects growing concern for primary schooling as a right of citizenship as well as budgetary neatness.

39. Girls received fewer than half the scholarships, but their enrollment was statistically more affected. The departments receiving the lowest tuition per student in 1850 included poor ones (such as Lozère, .9, and Morbihan, 1.0), urban ones (Seine, 1.1; Loire, 1.3; Rhône, 1.5), and the educationally most advanced (such as the Haut-Rhin, 1.3; Meurthe, 1.5; Bas-Rhin, 1.5). Revenue per student was highest in departments at or below the national mean of enrollment (Seine et Oise, 6.9; Charente, 6; Gers, 5.5; Indre-et-Loire, 4.9; Dordogne, 4.9; Lot-et-Garonne, 4.8; Charente-Inférieure, 4.7; Allier, 4.6; Cher, 4.5; Pyrénées Orientales, 4.5), i.e., with less developed educational system. (Nationally, tuition fees had a decreasing effect upon enrollment but undoubtedly remained important in specific places and for many individuals.)

40. Corse, Mayenne, and Tarn were the three. Haute Savoie required candidates to be only eleven. Some departments set a maximum age as well, most often fifteen, but ranging from twelve to seventeen.

41. *Statistique de l'enseignement primaire*, 1876, II:cli–clii. When all departments are ranked as to the number of certificates awarded from 1882 to 1907, thirty vary less than one standard deviation, forty-eight between one and two. The nine departments that shifted position more dramatically are primarily ones with high levels of enrollment that had lagged a bit in instituting the certificates.

42. Enrollment in 1832 and the availability of schools in 1821 are the best predictors of the number of *certificats* awarded in 1886, but pairing either with summer attendance in 1876 produces a modest gain:

	Simple R	Multiple R
1832 Enrollment	.62	.65
1876 Summer Attendance	.52	.68
1876 Number of Schools	.26	.71
1876 Enrollment	.49	.71
1821 Number of Schools	.56	.71
1852 Summer Attendance	.51	.71

43. Census figures also make it possible to assess the proportion of a department's wealth that came from industry, agriculture, and natural resources (primarily mining, lumber, and fishing). The correlations that then result are generally too low to be very indicative (although statistically significant) but serve as a reminder that the social and structural differences accompanying agriculture, industry, and commerce did affect enrollment. The correlation of departmental enrollments (from 1829 to 1906) with the proportion of their wealth from industry or agriculture (in 1863, the date for which such figures are available) produces very low correlations, ranging from −.23 to .18. From 1829 to 1867, enrollment always produces a positive correlation with the percentage of wealth from industry and a negative one with the percentage of wealth from agriculture. From 1876 to 1906, this pattern is reversed (with one slight exception): the correlations with industrial wealth are negative and those with agricultural wealth are

positive. The correlation of enrollment in 1829 with the percentage of wealth from natural resources, however, is much higher ($r = .53$), declines steadily to 1867 ($r = .44$), drops more sharply in 1872 and 1876 ($r - .3, .28$), and is nugatory thereafter (the highest being .16 in 1891 and all others less than .10). This may stem from the influence of port towns (fishing) and the educational strength of the northeast (mining) and mountain regions (lumber), or possibly it hints that education prospered especially when wealth came from older, stable forms of production (and ones that were easily taxed).

44. The figures may be further confused by the fact that much of the west, in which schooling was least developed, was, by French standards, relatively urban. We had hypothesized that enrollment might be highest in small cities, and, to test that, subtracted the census figures for rural population and for the population in cities over ten thousand from the total population of each department to arrive at the proportion living in smaller cities. Correlation of that figure with enrollment, however, was significantly negative. What this means is not clear. It could be that the remaining rural population (very large in most departments) was in departments with many smaller agglomerations more unevenly dispersed than in those with a lower proportion of their population in towns of one thousand to ten thousand people.

45. Early in the century rural departments spent more per student as a result of having more and smaller schools; later, higher costs per student reflected more optional attention to quality.

46. Ordinary expenses were over twice as much north of the line in the period 1837–50; 1.6 times as much, 1872–87; 1.7–1.9 times as much at all other dates. Ordinary expenditures per student, however, were twice as much below the line as above it in 1833, minimally larger in 1837–63, and slightly smaller thereafter. The region north of the line generally allotted about twice as much to scholarships. Mean enrollments of school-age boys were more than twice as high in the north in 1833, with the gap narrowing until it had nearly disappeared by 1881. Mean enrollment for girls was nearly three times as high in the north in 1837, with the difference narrowing until the departments above the line had a mean only about 10 percent higher from 1881 to 1901, less than 5 percent higher in 1906. The proportion of school-age children attending in the summer was markedly higher north of the line in 1833–63, slightly higher thereafter.

47. For shorter periods of time, a ranking of provinces produces high Spearman correlations (r: .89, 1829–39; .66, 1837–76; but .18, 1829–1901, and .27, 1837–1901). How provinces were approximated, the regions selected, and k-means clusters calculated is discussed in chapter 2. Only fourteen departments in Map 1 do not touch at least one other in their octile.

48. The western wedge appears in maps of uncleared wasteland and few agricultural societies in the nineteenth century as well as in those showing the relative absence of factories in the old regime, Keith Sutton, "Reclamation of Wasteland During the Eighteenth and Nineteenth Centuries," in *Themes in the Historical Geography of France*, ed. Hugh D. Clout (New York, 1977), 261, 268–69, 275, 279; Hugh D. Clout, "Agricultural Change in the Eighteenth and Nineteenth Centuries," ibid., 417; Hugh D. Clout, "Industrial Development in the Eighteenth and Nineteenth Cen-

turies," ibid., 460. Compare Bernard Lepetit, "Sur les dénivellations de l'espace économique en France, dans les années 1830," *Annáles, S.E.C.* 41 (1986): 1250–52.

49. These statements are based on a sample consisting of approximately one-third the departments, for which the date was recorded at which enrollment and summer attendance first reached 10, 20, 30, . . . 150 percent of the school-age population. Calculations were then made of the length of time (and the number of data points) passed before a 10 percent gain and of the leaps of more than 10 percent between any two data points. The results can only provide an impression for the data points are not evenly spaced, and the absence of data from 1850 to 1863, a period of important growth, creates an almost crippling silence. Extremely rapid growth was defined as a growth rate averaging 3 percent or more a year for at least five years; such a rate (uncompounded) would, for example, increase enrollment from 60 to 80 percent in a decade.

50. For the periodization of enrollment as for availability we used both the statistical analysis system (SAS) and k-means cluster analysis, with targets of three, four, and five clusters for all departments over all data points (we also tried these measures with the five most deviant departments removed). Each approach produces slightly different results. Using SAS, the best fit is four clusters: 1829–67, 1872–76, 1881–91, and 1891–1906 (three clusters combine the period 1872–76 and 1891–1906). The three k-means clusters are 1829–50, 1863–76, and 1881–1906; on this test the "clusters" are composed of noncontiguous data points if the number of clusters allowed is raised to five.

51. Cluster analysis of summer attendance rather than enrollment produces three periods very neatly: 1829–50, 1876–81, and 1886–1906, emphasizing the changes of the 1860s as a break. Note that this periodization is largely independent of any effects from the fact that enrollment was counted by calendar year in the period 1861–72.

CHAPTER 4

The Catholic Contribution to Universal Schooling

Catholics and anticlericals waged the most persistent and widespread conflict of modern French history. Skirmishes could take place over any number of issues and at every level of French life, but even at their bitterest, during the Third Republic, the preferred battlefield was education.[1] Both sides assumed that teachers could instill in students values that would last a lifetime, an assumption central to that faith in education that brought schools to every hamlet. The fight over education, long given a prominent place in French political history and often used as a revealing measure of the church's continuing (or declining) influence, is also important for the history of French schooling itself. Here, however, the drama of conflict should not—as it largely has—obscure another perspective: like the lay public schools they competed against, Catholic and private schools were part of the process that made elementary instruction universal.

To this point, our discussion of primary schooling, of the spread of schools and the increase in enrollment—which found this process to have begun early in the century and to have continued at a remarkably steady pace in a very systematic way rather independently of the famous pieces of national legislation associated with Guizot in 1833, Falloux in 1850, and Ferry in 1881–82—has combined all the different types of elementary school in France, public and private, lay and Catholic, schools for boys and schools for girls and "mixed" schools that enrolled them both. Finer discrimination is possible, although the limitations discussed before weigh more heavily as more distinctions are made. Some data points are missing for one or another of the variables that now become more central, and the aggregate figures are smaller. Large enough at the national level, they become more vulnerable to small inaccuracies when analyzed at the departmental level, and the data on private schools may well be less reliable than those for public ones.[2] In addition, these statistics force a relentlessly institutional and formal perspective. Schools were counted as Catholic (*écoles congrégationistes*) when their teachers belonged to a religious order. They were counted as lay if their teachers had not taken religious vows (however pious the teacher might be, however dominated by the local curé or Catholic notables, or, in a relatively few cases, however ostentatiously Protestant). Schools were called public if

91

formally funded by commune, department, and national government and would be considered Catholic or laic depending on who the teachers were. All other schools were *écoles libres*, private or independent schools, which were similarly considered Catholic or laic according to whether or not their teachers were clerics and not whether they taught Catholic doctrine, sang Catholic songs, had a Catholic chaplain, or placed a crucifix in the classroom.

Religion had an important place in the vast majority of schools, one in fact stipulated by the Guizot Law. In all of France there were few classes that did not begin each day with prayer and teach some history of the Church and the lives of saints. Many lay teachers included the catechism in their curriculum, and many a priest was happy to have this done, especially if the *instituteur* himself regularly attended mass and brought his pupils with him.[3] The distinction between Catholic and lay schools, then, was an institutional one important for the kind of educational system being established more than for immediate differences in content or tone. Locally, that formal difference could nevertheless be fundamental in shaping a school's connections to the society it served.

Although national legislation tended to follow local practice in the establishment of schools and enrollment of students, official policy very directly influenced whether the schools those students went to were taught by clerics or lay men and women. The Falloux Law of 1850, the Ferry Law of 1881–82, and subsequent restrictions on religious orders, 1901–6, were accompanied by clear shifts in the percentage of students enrolled in Catholic schools (although it needs to be quickly noted that even here the trends in question often began to appear before these measures were passed and that other legislation was important, too (fig. 8 and table C.1). Statistical analysis of the proportion of students in Catholic schools in all departments at all data points from 1850 to 1906 points to four chronological divisions: 1850, 1863–76, 1882–1901, and 1906.[4] This study will follow that periodization, which fits national trends even as it obscures local and regional patterns; different responses for girls and for boys; and different tendencies in rural areas, small towns, and cities. Locally and nationally, however, all these trends were constrained by cultural tenacity, institutionalization, and convenience, so that changes in the proportion of children attending public or private, Catholic or lay schools were limited, even while the number of students in school was steadily increasing.

I

National data that fully distinguished Catholic from lay schools both for France as a whole and for each department are first available for 1850 (fig. 8). By then, primary school enrollment was equivalent to more than 70 percent of

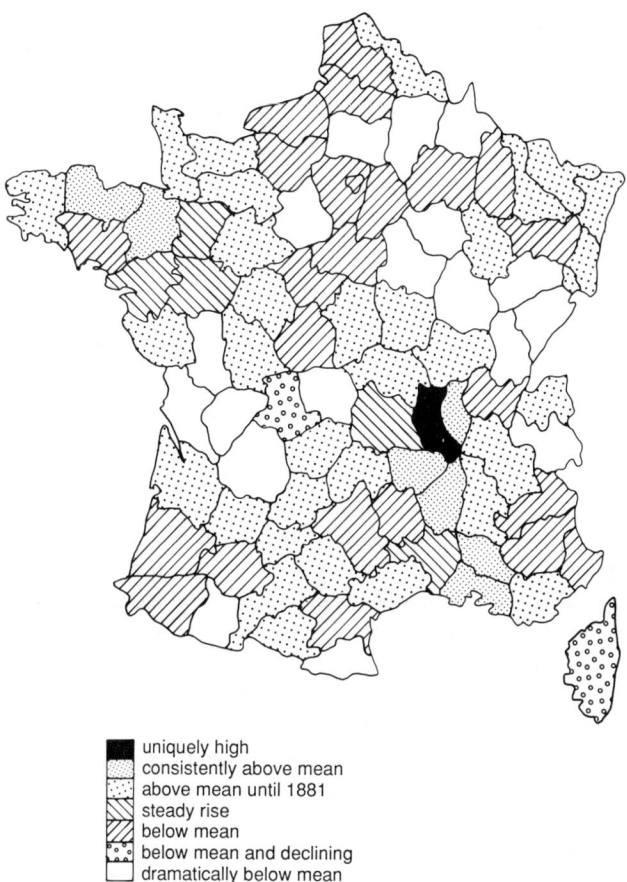

Fig. 8. Seven clusters based on the percentage of primary school pupils enrolled in Catholic schools, 1850–82

all school-age children (with important variation among departments: one-fifth had enrollments equal to 100 percent of their school-age children; two-fifths, 75 percent or more; three-quarters, at least 50). Within this system as it functioned in 1850, 29 percent of all students attended Catholic schools (both public and independent), 22 percent attended independent schools (both Catholic and lay, a proportion that had been slightly higher, 24 percent, in 1837). Catholic schools accounted for 40 percent of the enrollment in independent schools, 24 percent of the enrollment in public schools (table C.2). Every department had some schools of each of these types, although there remained rather a wide variation among departments, more so with regard to the proportion of students in independent schools than the proportion in Catholic schools.[5] By 1850, then, when a majority of French children received some elementary schooling, 53 percent of those students were in public schools taught by lay teachers, and there was a national norm for Catholic enrollments. In half of the departments of France, between one-fifth and one-third of all students enrolled in Catholic schools; in five-sixths of the departments, between 15 and 40 percent did so, anything more or less being clearly exceptional.[6]

Both Catholic and independent schools claimed a higher proportion of total school enrollment in departments that had many small cities (with populations of between one thousand and fifteen thousand people) and in departments in which total enrollment per school-age population was below the national mean (table C.10). In some five departments, half or more of all students were in Catholic schools, four of these departments in an area more or less along the Rhône (table C.9). Of these five, only Loire and Rhône approached having three-quarters of their school-age children in school. In the others universal schooling was not yet the social practice. All but the Loire, where a widespread Catholic public school system had been established, depended heavily on independent schools (which would maintain their importance only in Haute-Loire and Rhône, however). Most of these departments had been quick to achieve the number of elementary schools universal instruction would require; it was in enrollment that they lagged.[7]

In 1850, at the other extreme, seven departments had 15 percent or less of their total enrollment in Catholic schools, and these seven fall into three distinct regional groups: the area of the most advanced and established educational system in the northeast (Aisne, Aube, Haute-Saône, Seine-et-Marne); the area of the center west, a consistent laggard in educational development and well known for anticlericalism (Charente, Creuse); and the very mountainous area of the Pyrénées Orientales.[8] If one adds the fourteen departments that in 1850 had between 15 and 20 percent of their total enrollment in Catholic schools, the regional picture stays essentially the same.[9] Catholic schools and especially Catholic public schools played a less important part where the population was dispersed—as in mountainous regions in which communes could not support a "religious house"—where less emphasis on primary education was coupled with anticlericalism, and where a secular, public school system had already been established (in the fourteen departments that were at any point between 1832 and 1850 among those with the highest proportion of their children in school, only 21 percent of the students were enrolled in Catholic schools, eight points below the national average).

The role of Catholic teachers and independent schools could be expected to have changed in the period immediately following 1850, when enrollments experienced their greatest numerical growth. Could Catholic schools spread into areas where the populace was more dispersed? The desire for education had been shown to be widespread in French society, and there were signs of a steady movement toward universal schooling. In the relative prosperity of the 1850s, as educationally backward areas caught up with the national trend, the dominance of public laic schools would be likely to increase, Catholic and private schools to become relatively less important. Or would Catholic schooling maintain its hold on the teaching of girls, perhaps even increase it to the point that in France boys would receive a secular education while girls received a religious one?[10] Although local habits and preferences remained critical, the Second Empire did much to shape the answers to such questions with the passage of the Falloux Law, increased subsidies to the schools of poorer districts, and a more active Ministry of Public Instruction.

II

The law of March 15, 1850, the "Falloux Law," with its eighty-five articles, set the terms for a major reorganization of French education. Formally, it established clearer national standards and reformed the institution for maintaining them; encouraged girls schools, kindergartens, and adult courses; and provided for increased local options. In themselves these were important changes. Each department became an academy with its own rector and inspectors who were responsible to a departmental academic council that was required to meet quarterly, establish lists of approved teachers, supervise school budgets, and maintain a required curriculum. Every commune of more than eight hundred inhabitants was to maintain a school for girls (although the exception allowed for "poor" communes meant uneven enforcement). Communal councils were to hire *instituteurs* (whose minimum salary was fixed at eight hundred francs a year and who were now forbidden to accept additional employment without special dispensation). Poorer communes could be exempt from some of the requirements for a special education tax (and might expect some subsidy from the national government), and they could opt to use a licensed independent school rather than maintain a public one, provided they paid the tuition of the poor. One would expect provisions of this sort to have stimulated more attention to public schools, higher and more uniform standards, and a general expansion of elementary education—and that was one trend of the following period.

Far more famous, however, are a variety of other provisions that greatly increased the voice of the church in elementary education and encouraged the establishment of public schools taught by priests and nuns. The academic councils, like the national one over them, were composed primarily of officials (some ex officio and others named by the ministry) and were to include a rabbi, a Protestant minister, the Catholic bishop, and a priest named by him.

Instituteurs were required to have the *brevet* (a certificate awarded by the councils or the *écoles normales*), to have satisfactorily taught in a recognized school for three years, or to have a letter of obedience from a religious order. Thus, religious almost automatically qualified as teachers, and departments could even disband their *écoles normales* if they chose. Furthermore, although girls schools were required in principle, neither the pay nor the qualifications of *institutrices* were clearly specified, encouraging the choice of nuns to teach girls. Lay teachers who wished to maintain their standing had every reason not to offend municipal council, rector, or academic council, which was generally taken to mean good reason not to offend the local priest. And municipal councils could assign their obligation to maintain public schools to religious orders, confident of support from the educational authorities.[11]

Not surprisingly, the law of 1850, reinforced by the political compromises and social fears of the Second Empire, combined with a national enthusiasm for primary schooling to enlarge the role of Catholic teaching and increase the proportion of teachers who were priests or nuns. The number of departments in which enrollment equalled or passed the school-age population doubled between 1850 and 1863 (from 22 to 46 percent of the departments of France). Seventy-nine percent of the departments reached that goal by 1876 and 93 percent by 1881 (table E.14). Thus, the last spurt of growth in elementary school enrollment occurred in this period, essentially completing a far-flung system of universal primary instruction. The greatest change occurred, of course, where enrollment had been most limited, and enrollment increased primarily in Catholic schools, doubling between 1850 and 1863 and continuing to grow until 1876. Catholic schools, which had accounted for 29 percent of all elementary school enrollment in 1850, held 44 percent of the total in 1876, the highest proportion ever reached. Between 1850 and 1876, when Catholic enrollment increased by 117 percent, enrollment in laic schools grew by only 12 percent; Catholic schools accounted for 80 percent of all the growth in enrollment between 1850 and 1876 (tables C.2 and C.3). Even among departments that had been leaders in enrollment, Catholic schools experienced notable gains in the enrollment of both boys and girls.[12] The most important Catholic gains were in Catholic public schools, which received three-quarters of the one million more students attending Catholic schools.[13]

These changes continued the long-term trend toward greater homogeneity among departments. Not only did the proportion of school-age children in school become more similar from department to department, so did the proportion of students in Catholic schools. In half of all departments, between 27 and 43 percent of the students were in Catholic schools by 1863 (between 28 and 49 percent in 1876), and as the lowest percentages rose, the statistical measures of variation declined. The smooth distribution of Catholic schooling becomes clearer when all the departments of France are ranked by the percentage of total enrollment in Catholic schools. Only a few departments stand out—an important indication that the proportion of students in Catholic schools was by no means simply a reflection of regional custom or piety, for only multiple factors can produce such even and broad distributions.[14] One of these factors was the increasing Catholic dominance in independent schools; private school was coming to mean a school taught by *frères* or *soeurs* (table C.4). In nearly 90 percent of France's departments, three-quarters or more of all independent school enrollment was in Catholic schools by 1876 (it had been less than half in over 80 percent of the departments in 1850). A few lay private schools may have been elite affairs catering to more prosperous and ambitious parents, but most had been ad hoc adventures of self-proclaimed teachers, proportionally more important in poorer departments where enrollments were low and a public system not well established. The closer check on nonreligious private schools provided for in the law of 1850 was meant to eliminate the weakest of these schools and undoubtedly helped to do so. So, of course, did the expansion of the public system. Independent schools, to survive, had to have something special to offer. Where the public school was Catholic, not even a Catholic education was a distinction,[15] and independent schools gradually gave way (with only 28 percent of the national enrollment in 1837, 25 percent in 1850, and 18 percent in 1876) to the public sector (table C.2).

The great expansion in Catholic enrollments occurred between 1850 and 1863 (at an annual compound growth rate of 4.1 percent), and Catholic gains thereafter continued much more slowly, as overall enrollment increased but slightly. There were only 200,968 more students in 1876 than in 1867, but enrollment in public schools (which employed three-quarters of the new clerical teachers) increased by twice that number, reducing enrollment in independent schools and even in laic public schools (table C.4). The law of April 10, 1867, which permitted communes simply to assign an existing independent school to serve as the public school, must also have increased enrollment in clerical schools. Once Catholic orders were established in a local public school, it was unlikely that they would be removed, especially in the political system of the Second Empire and the political atmosphere of the Republic of the Dukes. Whenever a lay teacher left for another post or retired, the commune's need to choose a replacement gave advocates of Catholic schooling another chance to carry the day. Once a religious order held the teaching contract, however, there were fewer automatic occasions for reconsideration: not only were members of orders less likely to leave for other opportunities, but the order could if necessary simply replace them. So, overall Catholic enrollments declined only in the independent schools (presumably where the public school was Catholic). However the figures are manipulated, for the first time since the Ordinances of 1828 restricted clerical influence in the University, Catholics were not simply sharing in educational growth but actually taking students away from lay teachers.[16] Since the same phenomenon was occurring at the secondary level,[17] the sense of threat anticlericals so loudly expressed is understandable.

Analysis of those departments that stand out for the unusually low or high proportion of their enrollment in Catholic schools between 1850 and 1876 suggests the pattern for France as a whole.[18] Enrollment in schools taught by religious expanded primarily where the public system was not yet strong but also where there was a growing population.[19] Catholic teachers thus contributed significantly in the national system's effort to reach everyone.[20] The seven departments that most exceeded the national mean percentage for Catholic enrollment in 1850, 1876, and 1891 experienced an average growth (1850–91) of 77 percent in total enrollment. Catholic schools, then, played an increasing public and national role in French education—one in which regional differences became less important.

The Falloux Law opened new opportunities for the church in primary education, but the Catholic response was necessarily institutional and dependent on the teaching orders.[21] These developed impressively. By 1859, for example, France had more than four times as many monks and nuns per capita as did Austria, and the great majority of them were devoted to teaching. Instructing the young had become by far the principal activity of the soldiers of the church. They were concentrated in France's few large cities and well dispersed through smaller cities of from one thousand to fifteen thousand people, with the nuns more consistently spread through such towns than the brothers. The distribution of religious orders was much less even among the cities of intermediate size, and they were not able to staff the tiniest hamlets in proportion to the importance of such places in the total population of France[22] (table C.10).

Yet, there was astounding stability in the proportion of students in Catholic schools, just as there was in the development of the elementary system as a whole. The proportion of students enrolled in Catholic schools in 1881 followed, despite its increase, from the proportion in such schools in 1850 ($r = .84$; at no time between 1850 and 1901 did the correlation with 1876 fall below that figure). The expansion of Catholic enrollments (primarily in towns in laggard departments) was still largely the extension of patterns of Catholic schooling already established. And its contribution to the national picture can be shown in another way. There were eleven departments in both 1850 and 1876 in which the proportion of Catholic enrollment in public schools was 1.5 times the national mean.[23] None was among the early enrollment leaders, that quarter of departments that had essentially achieved universal schooling in a primarily lay system. Among these eleven departments, those that were above the national mean were primarily in the area along the Rhône that made an unusually heavy use of Catholic teachers. The others were mainly in Brittany. Catholic schools, then, were especially important in departments with more educational catching up to do (just above or well below the national mean), in two regions, in the largest cities, and in medium-size towns. At the same time, however, France's departments were becoming more similar in the proportion of students enrolled in Catholic schools (the coefficient of variation dropping from 42 to 27 percent), in part because of the increasing use of clerical teachers in schools and in part because of the spread of girls schooling.

Statistics cannot tell us what difference it made for the education of children or the social and political life of local communities when public schools were put in the hands of religious orders. But a number of trends in education were probably accelerated by the growth in Catholic schools. The most visible of these was the establishment of separate schools for girls. The availability of women teachers in religious orders made that more feasible, contributing in practical but probably also in psychological terms to the increasing enrollment of girls (table C.5). State inspectors, in any case, considered Catholic girls schools to have somewhat better physical facilities than lay girls schools and to offer instruction in reading and writing (but not arithmetic) comparable to that received in boys schools.[24] In addition, fewer of the Catholic girls schools charged tuition.[25] Catholic boys schools were generally larger than laic ones (Catholic girls schools were too, but not by so wide a margin), which reflected the requirement that several religious live together and the preference of religious orders for towns large enough to support several teachers. That experience with larger schools may have helped to set an example of schools with more than one classroom and of specialization among teachers.[26] Catholic schools may also have contributed to the drive for more consistent attendance over a longer school year. Independent schools, we know, claimed higher summer attendance than public ones, and Catholic public schools may have brought the practices of their independent schools to their public ones. At least it was often claimed that the priests and nuns were stricter in these matters, and the more prestigious Catholic public schools for boys did exact the long school year some twenty years before it was legislated for all schools.[27]

More important, the spread of Catholic schools probably accelerated the trend toward eliminating tuition charges, a step most public schools took before national legislation required them to. From 1850 until 1880 when Jules Ferry proposed that public primary schools be forbidden to charge tuition, a substantially higher percentage of students in Catholic schools than in laic schools had already been freed of that burden. Catholic schools were also reported to have accepted payment in kind or provided free soup at lunch.[28] In

1850 and again in 1876, (at the peak of Catholic enrollment) about two-thirds of the students in Catholic schools paid no tuition; that was true for only one-third of the students in laic schools in the 1860s and just over half of them in 1876 (table C.7). In general, the departments with the oldest and most widespread school systems were among the first to reduce tuition, but large Catholic enrollments tended to have a similar effect.[29] Where tuition costs were high, on the other hand, independent schools prospered, and officials were keenly aware of the advantage this gave the competition.[30] By the 1870s, any communal council eager for its public school to be laic understood the wisdom of eliminating a charge to parents.

Catholic schooling may also have encouraged the spread of kindergartens. There had been a few in France in the 1830s, and only about one in ten of four-to-six year olds was enrolled in a *salle d'asile* (or *école maternelle*) by 1850. That figure doubled by 1863 and rose to one in three by 1876. Overwhelmingly, they were enrolled in Catholic schools. This growth in *écoles maternelles*[31] occurred as the teaching nun became a familiar figure, a coincidence that suggests that in many a town parents may have felt a particular ease in consigning preschoolers to pious care. Although the importance of religious orders in shaping the culture's conception of the teacher's role cannot be studied quantitatively, that may nevertheless have been among the most important effects of the increasing use of teachers from religious orders. Many a militantly secular town council expected its *institutrice* to lead a life as cloistered as if she had taken the veil, and many an *instituteur* dressed in black must have been seen as "impressive and dignified—just like a curé."[32]

III. The Secularization of Public Schools, 1876–1901

In the Second Empire, religious teachers had come to hold a vital place in an expanding educational system, providing schools especially in regions that had been slower to develop them and offering a congenial means for establishing the desired separate school for girls. Catholic schools had grown most where communes wanted public schools and then chose religious to staff them. The Third Republic soon set about undoing that, and in the period from 1876 to 1901, the secularization of public schools was a major issue in French society and politics as well as education. The shift to lay teachers was often difficult, however, requiring a change in budgets, perhaps additional provisions for a schoolhouse and equipment, and the public selection of a teacher—steps resisted by the curé and leading lay Catholics, whose political pressure (seconded during the Second Empire by the Catholic bias of educational councils) was brought to bear in more public ways.

State inspectors, who now favored secular schools, increased in numbers and attentiveness (there were 385 in 1878, 428 in 1879, 455 in 1882), and a national political movement pushed for republican, secular schools (religious instruction was excluded from public schools by a law of 1882).[33] The proportion of French students in Catholic schools, which reached its peak in 1876 (at 44 percent), dropped dramatically in the next five years (to 33 percent) and slowly but steadily declined from 1881 to 1901 (fig. 8 and table C.1). Primary education, having become universal and largely public, became overwhelmingly secular.

In 1879, prefects had been given the power to order that teaching posts vacated by clerical teachers be filled by lay teachers, and a law of 1886—in remarkable testimony to the fact that laicization depended on a fully developed educational system—required that all new appointments go to lay teachers in departments that had maintained an appropriate *école normale* for at least four years. By then, most met that standard.[34] In any case, the law further required that all public boys schools have lay teachers within five years. As the conflict between secular and religious education grew more open and fiercely political, the battle lines hardened, and further gains for public, secular schools came in small percentages. In the ten years from 1879 to 1888, more than five thousand public schools (about 7 percent of all public schools and one-third of schools still taught by members of religious orders) replaced clerical teachers with lay ones. But in more than half these instances, involving 70 percent of the students affected, laicization of the public school was met by the establishment of a private Catholic school. When that happened, the new Catholic schools were likely to claim a little over half the students for which the two schools were competing. In 1890, for every three pupils attending a public school that had been laicized in the previous decade, there were two students enrolled in the newly established and competing Catholic school—thus, the proportion of students in Catholic schools remained higher in these districts than in the nation as a whole.

By 1891, enrollment in Catholic schools still accounted for 28 percent of all elementary school students, the pre-Falloux level of 1850, and Catholic schools had nearly 27 percent of total enrollment even in 1901. The gains for one side came largely at the expense of the other, for enrollments overall could grow only slightly. Conflicts, often intense, were experienced as local battles. The thousands of local political changes that followed the republican triumphs of 1875–76 did as much or more to secularize French public schooling as national legislation,[35] and the limited reduction in Catholic enrollment expressed a local and individual commitment to the Catholic alternative. Nor was the battle simply one-sided. As priests ceased to have an automatic voice in local education, efforts were made in some departments to elect them to the *commissions scolaires*. When that was prohibited, Catholics learned to apply all sorts of other pressures. The politicization of these issues and the mobilization of Catholic and anticlerical voters thus frequently overshadowed the more modest changes in who taught whom.

From the standpoint of the educational system, secularization was also part of the trend toward higher standards and professionalization. Having a choice of schools and the fact of competition between them stimulated local increases in enrollment,[36] and laicization often coincided with new quarters for a school, the replacement of aging and less formally trained clerical teachers with young graduates of *écoles normales*, and greater attention to examinations for the *certificat des études primaires*. When in a specific case the shift to lay schooling seemed to offer clear improvement, there were curés ready to acquiesce with grace just as many lay teachers went out of their way to cooperate with parish priests. Despite the rhetoric, crucifixes were often slow to disappear from classrooms.

The decline in Catholic enrollments was sharpest in public boys schools, where Catholic schooling had enjoyed recent gains. Between 1876 and 1881, the number of boys in public schools with clerical teachers was halved, dropping from 587,351 to 254,094, a figure reduced almost as much again by 1886. By 1891, less than 2 percent of French schoolboys were enrolled in Catholic public schools (table C.6). Many of the public schools that had been taught by Catholic sisters also shifted to *institutrices*, but they did so much more slowly. There were nearly twice as many girls as boys in Catholic public schools in 1876, but thirteen times as many in 1891 and fifteen times as many by 1901.

The dramatic reversal between 1876 and 1881 in the fortunes of Catholic education underscores what an exception the peak Catholic enrollment of 1876 had been. By every measure, the distribution of enrollment between Catholic and lay teachers in 1881 was more similar to that of 1867 than either was to 1876. If the period 1881–1901 saw a long war of attrition in which secular schools eroded Catholic enrollments, the first skirmish—during the decade ending in 1876, when total enrollments could not increase by much—had gone to Catholic public schools. The change between 1876 and 1881 can thus be seen as in large part an undoing of the most recent and exceptional Catholic gains.

The continuing secularization after 1881, which (like the preceding Catholic gains) was the result of national political policy and a subject of bitter contention, changed the social significance of Catholic education. Catholic schools became more important as alternatives and less important as supplements to laic schools. As the number of Catholic public schools shrank, private schooling expanded and became overwhelmingly more Catholic. Prior to 1850, the proportion of students in independent schools taught by religious was only slightly higher than in public schools. After the Falloux Law, the

Catholic share of private school enrollment rose to 55 percent in 1863, 59 percent in 1876, 82 percent in 1881, and 93 percent in 1901[37] (table C.2).

As private schools in France became more formally Catholic and more often directly subject to Church discipline, their share of total enrollment remained constant—modest in three-fourths of the departments, markedly higher in a quarter. More clearly than before, Catholic education expressed a local religious and political subculture. After 1881, some Catholic independent schools for girls still constituted a supplement to the official system, but the new significance of independent schools showed clearly in the enrollment of boys, which after 1880 increased at a rate that provided almost perfect compensation for the decline of Catholic public schools (table C.6). The expansion of Catholic teaching orders following 1850 had provided the personnel for the rapid development of Catholic independent schools as public ones were secularized.

Nationally, neither the number of public schools nor enrollment in them was much affected by the shift to lay teachers, a sign of how firmly the national public system had already been established. This was not so true of the *écoles maternelles*, in which clerical teachers taught 88 percent of the pupils by 1881 and the number of students enrolled initially declined from the high reached in 1876–81 until the secular system in turn reached and passed that level by 1896. Undoubtedly, kindergarten enrollment was determined primarily by the strength of the local commitment to universal instruction, but the availability of religious teachers seems also to have been important, for enrollments declined after each new restriction of religious orders.[38]

Because Catholic schools took on an altered political and social significance after 1876, it becomes all the more interesting to look closely at where Catholic schools were. Even in 1901, they were largely where they had been in 1850 and probably before. Nationally, the Catholic share of elementary school enrollment had risen and fallen, but any given department's place on a national scale at one date was likely to be very similar to its place at any other date in this half century of change. In fact, departmental rankings based on the proportions of students in Catholic schools were even more stable from year to year than rankings based on the proportion of school-age children in school, which were in themselves remarkably consistent. This consistency suggests, of course, the persistence in certain areas of a strong Catholic culture, an explanation stressed in the general literature ever since André Siegfried explored the overlapping geographies of religious and electoral practice.[39]

In earlier chapters, we have emphasized another quality, the tendency of primary education to develop into a system—local, regional, and national—marked by statistical viscosity. The best predictor of any department's pattern of schooling later in the century was its level of development early on (marked also by the level of its dependence on independent schools in 1850). Both secular and Catholic parts of this system tended to grow, with national pressures, which favored first one and then the other, affecting all departments. Because the educational system needed them or because the local culture demanded them, Catholic schools remained proportionally more prominent where the practice of enrolling all school-age children had been more limited. This was true in 1832, when only a minority of children went to any school, and—because Catholic schools remained where once established and departments then developed at rates that maintained their relative standing—it was true seventy years later. Cultural explanations stress the extent to which these departments tend to be poorer and more devout. Systemic ones note that Catholic schooling developed most after 1850 and did so in public schools; Catholic schools were thus more likely to be where the public system had not been strong in 1850. The multiple factors at play cannot be definitively sorted out, but there is good reason to combine both explanations. Although there was greater regional variation in religious practice than in Catholic enrollments, Catholic schools were more prominent in areas strong in priestly vocations: institutional and cultural factors were connected.[40]

Still, both systemic and cultural factors can be measured more closely. Let us look again at a familiar systemic indicator, the arrangement into octiles of all departments of France according to their enrollment (as a percentage of school-age population) in 1832, noting for each octile at each later data point the proportion of students in Catholic school (table C.8). One sees immediately the stability of these octiles and the persistently greater importance of Catholics where enrollments are lower. The larger Catholic presence in octile 5 reflects the presence in this octile of several of those departments along the Rhône that early established a widespread system of Catholic schools (and of the Seine), but note also the slight decline in the prominence of Catholic schooling in the lowest two octiles after 1876. The laggards in French education, these departments were also a little less inclined to keep their Catholic schools, perhaps because poverty and dispersed populations made it more difficult to sustain the competing schools or discouraged Catholics from trying so hard, or perhaps because in these departments people were simply less concerned about schooling.

A further point emerges when the percentage of enrollment in independent schools is listed according to those 1832 octiles: The rank order of departments by Catholic enrollment in 1876 is almost identical with that by enrollment in independent schools in 1901 ($r = .96$). The place of independent schools at the turn of the century reflected the conditions and the intransigence—systemic, cultural, political, developmental—that had favored Catholic schooling. The difference between the proportions of girls and of boys enrolled in Catholic schools tended to be wider in the lower octiles, consistently so from 1881 on. Although Catholic schools were more important among less developed educational systems and Catholic orders were particularly likely to provide girls schools, that did not overcome the educational lag in the lower octiles. The development of the educational system (and therefore of educational practice) determined who went to school more than whether the teachers were in Catholic orders or lay.

A closer look at the geography of Catholic schooling reveals a certain independence of departmental reputations for religious intensity. Take, for instance, the ten departments with the lowest and with the highest Catholic enrollments in 1886. Of the ten departments with the lowest Catholic enrollment (actually eleven departments because two tie for tenth place), seven or eight were mountainous (Pyrénées Orientales, Basses-Alpes, Hautes-Alpes, Ariège, Corse, Creuse, and Jura; Haute-Saône was partially mountainous, and Hautes-Pyrénées just missed inclusion in the top ten). Two of the above and two others (Seine-et-Marne and Yonne) were in the traditionally more advanced northeastern area. Some of this group were in regions that by other measures count as fairly Catholic; only four (Creuse, Charente, Seine-et-Marne, and Yonne) would be on everyone's list of the departments that were anticlerical, "de-Christianized," or low in the measures of Catholic practice, although the Midi and Languedoc certainly had strong anticlerical traditions.[41] As for the eleven departments with the highest Catholic enrollments in 1886, six are in a contiguous group more or less along the Rhône (Ardèche, Gard, Loire, Haute-Loire, Aveyron, Rhône) where Catholic schooling was entrenched early; five are in a contiguous block in the west (Côtes-du-Nord, Ille-et-Vilaine, Loire-Inférieure, Maine-et-Loire, and Mayenne), Catholic departments in a Catholic region but not necessarily the most Catholic ones of the west. The spread of schooling, and the form it took, seems to have had its own history, related to religious attitudes but not fully determined by them.

The larger pattern may be obscured, however, at a single date. Let us look at the statistical outliers in another way, selecting all departments that at any time between 1850 and 1906 were more than two standard deviations from the national mean in the percentage of total enrollment in Catholic schools. Thirteen departments achieved that distinction, only one of them (Creuse in 1876) by being two standard deviations *below* the mean.[42] Of the remaining twelve departments, all with high Catholic enrollments, five had been at least two standard deviations out of line as early as 1850. The Côtes-du-Nord, with a high percentage of its students in Catholic schools in 1850, maintained that level thereafter (while the national mean rose) and then saw it fall in the 1890s (although it fell less than the national mean). The Rhône remained more than two standard deviations above the mean from 1850 to 1867; its high proportion of students in Catholic schools rose still higher during the Second Empire but fell in the 1870s and after that was no longer so much above the national mean. The tradition of Catholic instruction showed great strength and tenacity in these departments; yet neither piety nor a tradition of Catholic schooling was a guarantee of such outstandingly high Catholic enrollments after 1876. Among these departments, only the Loire remained more than two standard deviations above the national mean for Catholic enrollment during the entire period from 1850 to 1901, and it was the only one of these departments consistently above the mean in total enrollment as well. In the others, Catholic schools, which had two-thirds or even three-quarters of the total enrollment in the 1860s and early 1870s, gave way before the pressures for secularization to keep some 30 or 40 percent of the students.[43]

Surprisingly, however, seven of the departments that ever stood so far above the national mean for Catholic enrollment did so *only* after 1876 (although all but two of them had been above the mean as early as 1850),[44] and they became statistically outstanding not so much because Catholic schools had claimed abnormally high proportions of their students but rather because in those departments Catholic schools tended to hang on to their share of students after Catholic enrollments nationally were falling. Furthermore, four of these departments were statistically exceptional only momentarily because there girls went overwhelmingly to Catholic schools toward the end of the century.[45] The other three departments at least two standard deviations above the mean (Ardèche and Ille-et-Vilaine from 1876 to 1901, Morbihan from 1881 to 1901) had—like Rhône and Haute-Loire—already had significantly high enrollments in independent schools at midcentury. Slow to develop a public system, these departments appear to have developed an earlier system of Catholic schools that maintained much of its appeal later on.[46]

Even so, the preference for Catholic instruction also had a marked geographical component. Some twenty-one departments of France, nearly a quarter of the whole, at some time enrolled half or more (to be exact, 49 percent or more) of their students in Catholic schools. Of these, eleven form a contiguous group around the Rhône,[47] seven are contiguous in the west,[48] and only three fall outside these two groups.[49] Nor did political change easily overcome established school systems; the geographical pattern of departments with large proportions of their students in Catholic schools was sustained over time, often despite or at least independent of political flux.[50] All but five of these twenty-one departments achieved their highest proportion of Catholic enrollment in the same year that Catholic enrollment in public schools was at its peak—they were building a public system, however Catholic.

When secularization occurred it did not destroy that system. Many families continued to send their children to the public school that had been laicized. Even where public schools had been the most Catholic—in Loire (80 percent in 1863 and 1867), Vaucluse (77 percent in 1867), Bouches-du-Rhône

(74 percent in 1863), Rhône (65 percent in 1863)—total enrollments continued for a time to rise slightly while the percentage of students who had clerical teachers began to decline.[51]

Political and cultural divisions were forming around the issue of education, but the connection between strong Catholic or anticlerical feeling and educational practice was far from absolute. The clearest measure of resistance to secularization is the number of private Catholic schools created as clerical teachers were removed from public schools and the percentage of students who then chose Catholic instruction. We have that data for the period 1879–89. In twelve departments, the new Catholic schools had larger enrollments than the laicized public schools at the end of the decade. Some of these departments had always had high proportions of students in Catholic schools, but several were on the whole exceptionally low in Catholic enrollments. At both extremes, the experience of strongly Catholic or strongly secular schools (possibly in an anticlerical environment) may have stimulated Catholic parents to confront the challenge of secularization by choosing a Catholic school. Elsewhere, the new Catholic schools did not necessarily prove so attractive even in some of the departments that had previously had unusually high or low Catholic enrollments. In most, the replacement of clerical teachers appears to have been as accepted as their presence may once have been convenient.[52]

Once more notable in departments that were poorer and less literate (even though more urban), Catholic schools now remained important where parents, determined on a religious education, turned to private schools. These were more clearly becoming a sign of the separate subculture republican educators had always feared them to be, and there were many indications that a separate Catholic educational system was developing.[53]

IV

Between 1901 and 1906, teachers in religious orders all but disappeared. This transformation of the French system of primary education fulfilled a particular vision. By 1906, the number of students in Catholic schools was only one-seventh of what it had been five years before (and less than 1 percent of public school enrollment). Over half the departments of France now had no teachers who wore religious habits, even in private schools. The lay public school had triumphed; schooling was universal, free, compulsory, and assuredly secular. The national system of public instruction that had been built over the past eighty years was to be firmly under the state's control. Even before the Third Republic, however, the government's role in schooling had become more direct and assertive, progressing from the requirement that communes establish schools to inspecting those schools in order to assure a certain standard, from setting the terms for the funding of schools to setting them for the training and certification of teachers and for the curriculum itself. During that process, public schools had been seen as an instrument of progress, as a means to increase civic virture, and (therefore) as a political weapon as well. In those terms, the drive to have an army of patriotic and lay *instituteurs* and *institutrices* take charge of schooling was not so different from the Second Empire's policy of encouraging communes to use clerical teachers.

Yet, this perspective is not the only one. The development of primary instruction was firmly fixed in local society, where it had its own rhythms and tone, and universal schooling had come about through a process of institutionalization that had its own momentum. Even the changes apparent in 1906 need to be understood in this light. Many lay *instituteurs* got along well with local curés, who in turn found the secularized public schools quite satisfactory. Nor were the changes always so great as they seemed. In a drastic move, the state banned religious orders from teaching, but in 1906, 18 percent of France's students still went to a private elementary school, where there was probably little change in the religious content of what was taught or in the religious atmosphere of the school itself when the teachers removed their clerical garb.[54] The dramatic assertiveness of a secular state in 1906 was an important turning point for many aspects of French life, but seen from within the history of French elementary education, the change was also an incremental one. And that explains why, to the surprise and disappointment of many Catholics, this further change proved generally acceptable and lasting. Public schooling with professionally trained teachers had won its place in French society, commune by commune and family by family, sustained by elaborate institutionalization.

The secularization of education stemmed from more than the battles between Church and State. As the campaign for universal, systematic schooling got under way in the 1820s and 1830s, the Church had played an important part in legitimizing and encouraging this new intrusion into village and family life.[55] Its role became more formal and visible with the Falloux Law, but—as intransigents like Louis Veuillot had warned at the time—so did the authority of the state as the sponsor and arbiter of education. Bishops and priests sat on the educational councils, gaining enormous influence which they used to further the expansion of clerical teaching, but the councils were instruments of the state. By participating in them, the Church in effect acknowledged the state's preeminent responsibility and concern. Catholic orders aided France's schools in their final push to make schooling universal and especially in establishing formal instruction (in separate schools) as the lot of girls as well as boys. At the same time, however, the orders acknowledged that they could not do it alone, could not reach into every hamlet as society demanded, could not sustain schools without public funds. So they cooperated enthusiastically with a sympathetic government in establishing a single system of universal elementary education, incidentally undermining the basis in theory or practice for a pluralistic system of the English or American kind.

When state policies changed, of course, Catholics reacted with the strength of their far-flung network of teachers; yet, they had contributed to the creation of a single, national educational system—the first step in secularization. That could only add to the sense of betrayal and outrage many Catholics felt, for the church had done much to help France achieve universal instruction. Not only had it given important general support to a remarkable nationwide effort, but Catholic orders had contributed in many specific ways—by working in educationally less developed areas, by encouraging the instruction of girls, by making schools free, by urging attendance in the summer months, and indirectly by helping to establish teaching as a distinct activity, a way of life and even a calling with its own standards of conduct and preparation.[56] In the process of doing all that, the Church in nineteenth-century France had made a commitment to and investment in education probably unequaled in Catholic history.

Yet, there were limits to the contribution of priests and nuns that in a sense foreshadowed secularization. Even in the 1860s, the proportion of enrollment in Catholic schools had begun to decline in some of the very departments where it had been most dominant, and the rapid decline of that proportion everywhere between 1876 and 1881 suggests something artificial or ad hoc about the previous decade's increased Catholic enrollments, which now gave way before new political pressures (and the removal of old ones) and, more important, in the face of the inexorable growth of an increasingly self-contained educational system. Even where Catholic schools had been most firmly established, their enrollments had not risen as rapidly toward universality as in departments with long-established secular systems.[57] Departments that had once achieved relatively high enrollments and then shifted toward a heavily Catholic system (there were a few instances of this, Manche is the best example) did not afterward keep pace with national growth. Even after 1881, areas with a high proportion of students in Catholic schools remained below the national mean for enrollment. Lack of funds and rules that required religious to live in communities were important inhibitions, and the clergy, regular as well as secular, who were missionaries for more than instruction, may have lacked some of the single-minded zeal of their lay competitors.

By the same token, the famous Ferry Laws need to be seen as more than the result of a republican political triumph. Significantly, they came just as a national instructional system had succeeded in becoming universal, reaching all of society and establishing common norms and practices. Seen from within the educational system, the dramatic institutionalization and professionalization of instruction[58] was but a step that followed on many others: the creation of schools, the establishment of norms for the length of the school day and school year and for the years of attendance, the creation of a recognized curriculum (followed by clerical and lay teachers alike), the development of teachers colleges and a system of inspection capped by the nationally administered *certificats d'études primaires*. The elaboration of a national system of public schools brought with it a demand for institutional autonomy and for professional teachers that was reinforced but not wholly caused by the politics of the Third Republic. Nor should this institutional development be seen simply as imposed from Paris. The standards and practices of these schools developed in some departments first and then spread throughout the nation, resulting from the efforts of hundreds of thousands of Frenchmen over several generations, of town councillors as well as inspectors, clergy as well as secular liberals. Only when the most laggard departments approached the national norm was it feasible to combine the established custom of sending all children to school—the practices of a national institution—with republican visions of secular instruction. By then, the greatest regional differences in patterns of schooling had already been overcome.

This, too, had been foreshadowed as lay public schooling steadily expanded and the position of Catholic schools slowly eroded from 1881 on. Catholic public schools lost ground rapidly, and Catholic independent schools could regain most but not all of that enrollment. With the divisive effects of secularization, private schools came to mean Catholic schools, a self-conscious, often militantly religious (and ideological) alternative rather than one among many choices. Thus, there were limits to the secular triumph, too. After twenty-five years of political pressure and Catholic retreat, the proportion of total enrollment in Catholic schools at the end of the century was only a little below what it had been in 1850 and higher than it had been in the fifty years before that. Even in 1906, twice as many girls as boys (and just over one-fifth of all the girls in France) selected that alternative (table C.5).

Catholic schools attracted the most students where an extensive and articulated Catholic system had been long established and where the pattern of sending girls to Catholic schools was strong, and only then when the Church was vigorous in other terms and Catholic concerns widely shared and deeply rooted. Of course, these conditions often overlapped, but not always and never exactly. French primary education, Catholic or independent, secular or public, had its own history, one marked by remarkable continuity. And that is the final point. That continuity was not broken from the 1820s on. The homogeneity achieved in 1906 had been presaged by the near universality achieved in 1876. The great transformation between 1901 and 1906 brought with it some decrease in the number of schools (there were 3,800 fewer schools in 1906), a consolidation that may have been a minor efficiency after a decline in school-age population. It was accompanied, as moves toward laicization had generally been, by one more slight increase in total enrollment.[59] Once universal education was established and lay teachers had been trained, secularization was possible—except, that is, for the firm and significant minority who insisted upon a Catholic education even if their teachers could not wear the habits of priests or nuns. For the broader history of primary instruction in France, the Church's participation had been an important phase whose rise and decline did not disrupt the larger outline.

Notes

1. For a recent survey of the ideological tensions surrounding education, see Emile Poulat, *Liberté, laïcité: La guerre des deux France et le principe de la modernité* (Paris, 1987), 228–65.

2. State inspectors had fewer checks on private schools and were sometimes refused entry to religious schools; the frequent claims that their enrollment figures were unreliable was also, it must be remembered, a weapon in the conflict over schooling. Ministre de l'instruction, *Rapports* [Paris, 1878–79], 500, and Archives Nationales F17/9279 [1852]. "Unrecognized" schools, such as those taught by the "dames de l'instruction de l'enfant Jesus," popularly known as the *béates*, were not included in the official statistics.

3. Christianne Marcilhacy, *Le diocèse d'Orléans sous l'épiscopat de Mgr. Dupanloup* (Paris, 1962), 253–55; Bernard Ménager, *La laïcization des écoles communales dans le département du Nord (1879–99)* (Lille, 1971), 263–70.

4. These dates follow from cluster analysis of the changing proportion of total enrollment in Catholic schools (public and independent)—perhaps the best single measure of the role of Catholic schools in the larger system. These clusters were produced using the SAS system. Three clusters (statistically almost as good a fit as four clusters) would fall at 1850–76, 1881–1901, and 1906. Clusters based on the number of students enrolled in Catholic schools would be: 1850, 1863–67, 1876–1901, and 1906 (with four clusters) or 1850–67, 1876–1901, and 1906 (with three). A k-means cluster calling for three units produces the same result as the SAS cluster of three. The k-means cluster calling for four clusters is slightly different from the SAS "best fit" of four: 1850, 1863–76, 1881–1901, 1906. All point to a major break around 1876 and 1881. Note that the national statistics distinguish between public and private schools from 1837 on but not between Catholic and laic schools before 1850, forcing our analysis to begin from that date. Subsequent data points are 1863, 1867, 1872, 1876, 1881, 1886, 1891, 1896, 1901, and 1906; there are national totals but not departmental ones for other dates.

5. The coefficient of variation among departments was 54 percent for independent schools in 1850 and 59 percent in 1837. For Catholic schools, it was 42 percent in 1850. Variation would steadily decline over the next quarter century as disparity among departments lessened, producing a coefficient of variation of 47 percent for enrollment in independent schools and 27 percent for enrollment in Catholic schools by 1876.

6. In eleven departments, between 40 and 75 percent of the students were in

Catholic schools. In only five departments did Catholic enrollment fall below 15 percent of the total.

7. Bouches-du-Rhône, Hérault, and Rhône achieved "fulfillment" (defined, see chapter 2 and table S.7, as 85 percent of the number of schools in 1906) by 1837; Loire and Loire-Inférieure did so by 1850—clearly a reflection of the number of Catholic schools. In the one of these five departments that was outside the region, Côtes-du-Nord, the proportion of students in independent schools would decline after 1850 while that in Catholic schools would remain about the same.

8. The Creuse was the only department of France to deviate from the national mean by as much as two standard deviations in its proportion of Catholic enrollment and to do so by being below the national mean.

9. Northeast: Ardennes, Côte-D'Or, Doubs, Eure-et-Loir, Jura, Manche, Marne, Oise, Yonne; center west: Charente-Inférieure, Dordogne, Deux-Sèvres; mountainous: Hautes-Pyrénées and Hautes-Alpes. Note also the prominence of mountainous departments in the northeast as well as the inclusion there of Eure-et-Loir and Oise, which share many of the characteristics of the anticlerical center.

10. In 1850, the Catholic clergy taught only 15 percent of the boys in French schools but 45 percent of girls.

11. For particulars, see Henri Michel, *La loi Falloux* (Paris, 1926).

12. Between 1832 and 1850, fourteen departments had ranked among the top ten in the percentage of school-age children enrolled in school. Between 1850 and 1876 in those departments, the percentage of students in Catholic schools rose from 21 to 36. Boys provided only 18 percent of the enrollment in Catholic schools in these departments in 1850, 28 percent in 1876. Eleven of these departments actually had fewer boys in laic schools in 1876 than in 1850, despite an average increase throughout France of 15 percent for boys enrollment in laic schools during the same period (23 percent if the above fourteen departments and those lost or gained in 1870 are excluded).

13. Uniquely for 1876 the introduction to the *Statistique de l'enseignement*, vol. II, *Statistique comparée*, cxxxv–cxlvii, introduces a category of *écoles libres* "tenant lieu a l'école publique." They had a total enrollment of 142,134. This category is not maintained throughout the volume, so some subcategories in some tables do not balance with those in another.

14. Regression analysis of enrollment in Catholic schools as a percentage of total enrollment at three exemplary data points (1850, 1876, 1891), enrollment in 1832, and the relative enrollment of boys and girls with measures of wealth, urbanization, and literacy (as explained previously) yields a low R^2 of .38, .32, and .18

15. The crude division provided by the St. Malo–Geneva line reflects these trends. Independent schools were proportionally more important south of the line. The enrollment of boys in such schools declined and of girls increased (declining, however, as a proportion of all girls enrollment: independent schools had increased their enrollment of girls primarily where they provided the only girls school). The proportion of independent schools that were Catholic was greater south of the line, but all these differences across that invisible line tended to decline. The highest negative correlation with any statistics of total enrollment is with the percentage of enrollment in independent schools (r ranges between $-.4$ and $-.5$ for the period from 1837 to 1876).

16. The *Statistique de l'ensigenement*, II: lxxii–lxxiii, makes the point about Catholic schools remaining Catholic. As tables C.3 and C.4 show, Catholic schools gained. The drop of over 90,000 boys in lay public schools probably reflects Catholic gains—and those most troubling to anticlericals. Of course, aggregate statistics cancel out many more changes that may have been deeply felt locally. Catholic public enrollment increased by 477,291; about 100,000 clearly must have come from independent Catholic girls schools—the main effect of the law of 1867 and thus a rather artificial rise. Perhaps the 143,867 new girls went to Catholic public schools as did all of those who left lay independent schools. Even so, that would imply that the 57,101 new boys entering the system plus the 91,803 boys who left lay public schools all ended up in Catholic public schools. (For evidence of *concurrence* drawn from contemporaries' observations, see Françoise Mayeur, *Histoire générale de l'enseignement et de l'éducation en France*, ed. L.-H. Parias, vol. 3, *Histoire de l'enseignement en France*, [Paris, 1981], 344.)

17. Patrick J. Harrigan, "The Social Appeals of Catholic Secondary Education in France in the 1870s," *Journal of Social History* 8 (Spring, 1975): 122–41.

18. Of the twelve departments whose proportion of students in Catholic schools ever exceeded the national mean by more than two standard deviations, five did so before 1876 (Loire, Haute-Loire, Rhône, Vaucluse, Côtes-du-Nord), four of which had established something of a Catholic public school system.

19. The correlation between population growth in 1836–61 and the percentage of enrollment in Catholic schools in 1850 and in 1863 is .35.

20. Nevertheless, the proportion of departmental enrollment in Catholic schools continued to have a modest but significant negative correlation with the proportion of school-age children in school, even as Catholic enrollment increased both absolutely and proportionally.

21. The presence of Protestant schools may also have stimulated greater Catholic efforts. Protestants were a small minority in France and were concentrated in a few departments (only eight had a Protestant population of more than 10 percent), which generally had high enrollment. Factors other than religion were probably more important for the early establishment of universal schooling. Still, the percentage of Protestants correlates positively not only with total enrollment but with the proportion of total enrollment in Catholic schools. The Guizot Law provided that communes should fund public schools where there was a significant religious minority. If that provision was not always adhered to rigidly, there were many instances of national subsidy for this purpose. Rivalry rather than religious preference per se seems to have spurred both Protestants and Catholics to promote schools—François Furet and Jacques Ozouf, *Lire et écrire: L'alphabétisation des français de Calvin à Jules Ferry*, 2 vols. [Paris, 1977], 1:88–93; C. R. Day, "The Development of Protestant Primary Education in France under the Constitutional Monarchy, 1815–1848," *Canadian Journal of History* 16 (August, 1981): 215–36; Robert Gildea, *Education in Provincial France, 1800–1914* (London, 1983), 74, 75, 89, 94, 140; Leslie Moch, *Paths to the City: Migration in Nineteenth-Century France* (Beverly Hills, Calif., 1983), 41; Gabriel Desert, "Alphabétisation et scolarisation dans le Grand-Ouest au 19ème siècle," in *The Making of Frenchmen: Current Directions in the History of Education in France, 1679–1979*, ed. Donald Baker and Patrick J. Harrigan (Waterloo, Ont., 1980), 155–56. Desert argues

that not only religious rivalries but anticlerical/clerical rivalries led to more schools as each responded to initiatives by the other.

22. For every one million inhabitants, Austria had 633 men and women in orders; France, 2,892; Belgium, 3,373. Only about half of Belgium's clergy were devoted to teaching, as compared to 65 percent in France of the women in orders and 72 percent of the men, *Statistique de l'instruction*, 1861, xii, cxx; Claude Langlois, *Le Catholicisme au féminin: les congrégations françaises à supérieure générale au XIXe* (Paris, 1984). By 1861, the proportion of religious (especially nuns) in towns of 1,500–10,000 population appears to have increased and the relative proportion in towns of between 15,000 and 50,000 to have declined (although differences in the way the figures for 1851 and 1861 were assembled make it difficult to be certain). Male and female clerics were dispersed among communes of various sizes quite differently in 1851 ($r = .5$) and very similarly in 1861 ($r = .95$). The new effort to extend teaching orders farther into the countryside had begun with the Restoration, Pierre Zind, *Les nouvelles congregations de frères en France de 1800 à 1830*, vol. 1 (Saint-Genis-Laval, 1969). Regression analysis indicates the most important factor in predicting the Catholic share of enrollment to be the proportion of population living in towns of 2,000 to 10,000—ahead of all the other factors tested for 1850, 1876, and 1881: population in cities; proportion of Protestants; population density, literacy, wealth; and proportion of the population engaged in agriculture, industry, commerce, or the liberal professions.

23. They were Ardèche, Bouches-du-Rhône, Côtes-du-Nord, Gard, Ille-et-Vilaine, Loire, Loire-Inférieure, Mayenne, Morbihan, Rhône, and Vaucluse.

24. In 1863, 66 percent of the buildings housing congregational girls schools were judged "sufficient," but only 47 percent of the lay girls schools were given that rating, Archives Nationales, F17*/3159. The assessment of teaching in Catholic schools, equal to boys schools in reading and writing but decidely inferior in numeracy, is in ibid., F17*/3158. Physical facilities in Catholic schools may have benefited from the donations of French nobles eager to promote catechistic instruction and from the leadership they provided, David Higgs, *Nobles in Nineteenth-Century France* (Baltimore, 1987), 170.

25. A report of 1863 said that more than 20 percent of Catholic girls schools were free against only 10 percent of the laic girls schools, Archives Nationales, F17/9351.

26. The average size of congregational schools compared to that of all schools in France was: in 1850, 100:55; in 1863, 94:63; in 1867, 94:65; and of congregational schools in 1872 to all schools in 1876, 100:66. If Catholic enrollment and schools are factored out of data for all schools, it means that Catholic schools were about two-and-one-half times the size of the average lay school during this quarter century. Catholic boys schools (a gradually decreasing proportion of schools) had an average size of 208, 157, 152, and 232 students at these same data points. By 1881, when independent schooling had become predominantly Catholic, more than 60 percent of the independent schools had more than one class, while only 20 percent of public schools did. The great increase in multiclassroom schools generally occurred between 1896 and 1906, a trend probably reinforced by the elimination of competing schools.

27. A report on *fréquentation*, but only in public schools in 1863, found boys in school for more months in congregational public schools, girls in laic public schools, with 49 percent of the boys in Catholic public schools attending for at least eleven

months in contrast to 36 percent of the boys in lay public schools, Archives Nationales, F17*/3158:

Percentage of:

Months	Boys in Lay Public Schools	Boys in Catholic Public Schools	Girls in Lay Public Schools	Girls in Catholic Public Schools
1	4.8	2.9	3.3	4.0
2	6.9	4.4	5.8	5.6
3	7.4	7.7	5.4	7.2
4	5.3	4.2	4.2	5.9
5	5.7	4.3	4.4	5.6
6	5.9	4.5	4.9	6.3
7	5.7	4.4	5.0	7.3
8	6.8	7.2	5.4	7.2
9	6.3	4.7	5.6	6.6
10	8.1	6.7	7.0	8.4
11	33.6	47.9	47.3	34.7
12	3.3	.9	1.7	1.1
Total Students	1,667,479	386,258	423,053	26,465

Overall, girls summer attendance (mostly in Catholic schools) was a bit higher than boys. There is a very slight positive correlation for summer attendance as a percentage of winter attendance with both the percentage of students enrolled in Catholic schools and in independent schools as a percentage of all enrollment in both 1850 and 1876 (.15-.22). From 1881 onward, separate figures for public and private schools consistently reported private schools to have maintained summer attendance about 10 percent higher than public schools. A similar picture emerges in ibid., F17/9351, and Ministère de l'instruction publique, Exposé de 1867 [Paris, n.d.].

28. Archives Nationales, F17/3872; Gildea, Education, 261.

29. Among the eleven departments with the lowest tuition revenues per student, only three—Loire, Rhône, and Morbihan—stood out as not having higher than average enrollments; each had an unusually high proportion of its students in Catholic schools.

30. Ministers of public instruction during the Second Empire regarded tuition as a major issue. Gustave Rouland proposed in the 1850s that the Christian Brothers be required to charge tuition so as not to draw students away from lay public schools. A decade later, Victor Duruy tried unsuccessfully to eliminate tuition in all primary schools. There was both a steady positive correlation of tuition costs per student in a department's public schools with its percentage of enrollment in independent schools and a negative correlation with its percentage of enrollment in Catholic schools:

	1832	1850	1863	1867	1872	1876
Catholic	−.26	−.26	−.2	−.11	−.13	−.11
Independent	.36	.38	.45	.24	.19	.32

31. The subject is treated more fully in chapter 7.

32. Barnett Singer, "The Teacher as Notable in Brittany, 1880–1914," *French Historical Studies* 9, no. 4 (Fall, 1976): 635–59, especially 652.

33. *Statistique de l'enseignement*, IV:xxii–xxiii; Jean Bruhat, "Anticléricalisme et mouvement ouvrier," *Mouvement sociale*, no. 57 (October–December, 1966): 84–86.

34. Ferdinand Buisson reported in 1886 that eighty-two departments already met that standard for *instituteurs* and that all would by 1889. For *institutrices*, forty-two departments met the test in 1886 and all but nine would do so by 1890 (his eagerness to include a few departments that had no *école normale* of their own but that contributed to one in an adjacent department reflects the professional educator's intense campaign for a secular national system). The insistent and stringent application of these regulations—seeking to create vacancies wherever possible—is also shown in the *Arrêtés* and *Circulaires* that followed the law, *Rapport présenté par la Commission de Statistique à M. le ministre de l'instruction publique sur les résultats des laicisations scolaires* (Paris, 1891), 163–73; the statistical profile is taken from the summary tables, pp. 134–36, 150–51.

35. The legal basis for the 2,005 laicizations from 1886 to 1890 (following the strong law of 1886) is tabulated in ibid., 180–81. Forty percent of the public schools (808) that replaced clerical teachers did so as a result of the law; more than one-third (731) did so because of administrative pressure or decision; nearly a quarter (466) by communal choice. The figures recorded for 1887–88, Archives Nationales, F17/9192, for one year within the five-year period yield slightly different percentages but are consistent with the five-year trend. In the period before 1886, when many more public schools had replaced clerical with lay teachers, municipal decision had been the primary mechanism. This process is closely and ably studied for one department by Bérnard Ménager, *La laïcisation des écoles communales dans le département du Nord (1879–1899)* (Lille, 1971), 66-268.

36. The combined enrollment in the newly laicized public schools and the competing new Catholic private schools was 31 percent higher in 1890 than it had been in the Catholic public schools alone in 1879 (adding some 200,000 new students). Although the figures may be somewhat inflated (some students who switched schools in midyear were likely to have been counted twice, and a mere six departments accounted for one-third the total increase), there is no question that enrollment went up significantly more where there were competing schools than in the nation as a whole, a phenomenon commented on by E. Levasseur in *Rapport sur les résultats des laïcisations*, vii–viii. The percentage of laicized schools that did not face competition produces a negative correlation ($r = -.3$) with the percentage of increased enrollment from 1879 to 1889. See also Katherine Auspitz, *The Radical Bourgeoisie: Ligue de l'Enseignement and the Origins of the Third Republic, 1866–1885* (New York, 1982), 144–56; Gildea, *Education*, 107–9, 143–45.

37. Independent schools had accounted for 24 percent of total enrollment in 1837, 23 percent in 1843 (estimate in *Statistique de l'instruction*, II: cxxvi), 19 percent in 1876, 18 percent in 1881. The variation among departments in the percentage of enrollment in private schools declined somewhat after 1881 as these became more widespread, while the variation in Catholic enrollments increased. A very similar

movement occurred among secondary schools: public and ecclesiastical independent schools grew while independent lay schools declined, John W. Bush, "Education and Social Status: The Jesuit College in the Early Third Republic," *French Historical Studies* 8, no. 1 (Spring, 1975): 128; Françoise Mayeur, *L'éducation des filles en France au XIXe siècle* (Paris, 1979), 103, 105–6. A sudden shift occurred in the distribution of Catholic independent schooling between 1896 and 1901. The correlation between Catholic enrollment as a percentage of all enrollment in 1850 with Catholic enrollment in independent schools as a percentage of all enrollment in independent schools changed from .31 in 1896 to .67 in 1901, indicative of a shift back to traditional Catholic strength.

38. National legislation favored *écoles maternelles*, declaring in 1867 that communes where *écoles maternelles* existed should not permit children to enroll in the primary school before their seventh birthday. Nevertheless, there remained an association between the presence of Catholic teachers and enrollment in *écoles maternelles*. Of the ten departments that in 1901 had the lowest proportion of preschoolers in *écoles maternelles*, six had previously had unusually low Catholic elementary school enrollments; of the ten departments with the highest enrollments in *écoles maternelles* in 1901, four were markedly above the national mean (1.5 times) in the proportion of primary school students in Catholic schools. A comparison by year of enrollment in *écoles maternelles* per one hundred five- to six-year-olds with the Catholic share of that enrollment is given in table Sys.2.

39. André Siegfried, *Tableau politique de la France de l'ouest sous la Troisième République* (Paris, 1964).

40. The negative correlations between total enrollment (as a percentage of school-age population) and the percentage of that enrollment in Catholic schools, although consistent, are never very high, leaving room for many additional explanations. Not only were most areas of higher Catholic practice also poorer, but the Catholic west was relatively urban, which facilitated the establishment of Catholic schools. In the early period, it was independent rather than specifically Catholic schools that were likely to be established in poorer areas of high illiteracy. The later decline of private schools thus obscures statistical analysis. See C. Langlois, "Permanence, renouveau, et affrontements (1830–1880)," in François Lebrun, ed., *Histoire des Catholiques en France du XVe siècle à nos jours* (Toulouse, 1980), 312–13, 324–25.

41. The Hautes-Pyrénées, for example, ranked high in pilgrimages to Lourdes, Thomas A. Kselman, *Miracles and Prophecies in Nineteenth Century France* (New Brunswick, N.J., 1983), 201–3. René Rémond, *L'anticléricalisme en France de 1815 à nos jours* (Paris, 1976), 45–46, reminds us that anticlericalism was not indifferentism and could be found in Catholic areas.

42. Like most departments, Creuse had its highest enrollment of Catholics in 1876, but even then they constituted only 19 percent of the students.

43. Catholic enrollment in the Côtes-du-Nord was 55 percent in 1850, rising to 59 percent in 1872 and falling to 44 percent in 1891 and 1896. Catholic enrollment was 60 percent of the total in Vaucluse in 1850, 72–73 percent in 1863 and 1867, 44 percent in 1881, 41 percent in 1886, 39 percent in 1896, and 31 percent in 1901. In the Haute-Loire, the Catholic system was more tenacious, claiming 59 percent in 1850,

rising to 66 percent in 1867 and 1876, and still at 41 percent in 1896 and 40 percent in 1901 (although it had fallen to 39 percent in 1891). In the Rhône, the pattern was very similar: Catholic enrollment was 58 percent in 1850, rose to 66 percent in 1863 and 1867, began a slow decline (63 percent in 1876) that leveled off at 51 to 48 percent in 1881–96, and held at 44 percent in 1901. In the Loire, Catholic enrollment was 76 percent in 1850, rose to 79 percent in 1863 and 1867, and held at 50 percent in 1891 and 1896 and 47 percent in 1901.

44. Catholic schools had 30 percent of the enrollment in Aveyron and 25 percent in Loiret in 1850, when the national mean was 29 percent.

45. The four (and the dates at which they rose two standard deviations or more above the national mean) are Aveyron (1896), Maine-et-Loire (1886–1901), Loiret (1891, 1901), and Mayenne (1901). Girls accounted for 73 percent of Catholic enrollment in Aveyron, 80 percent in Maine-et-Loire, and 86 percent in Loiret and Mayenne. The latter two were not laggards in enrollment.

46. The point must be made with some care. Having a high proportion of students in independent schools in 1850 (more than one-third in twenty-five departments) does not predict high Catholic enrollment at the end of the century, but it does seem to have provided an institutional base on which a Catholic system could be built as public schools secularized. From that standpoint, having preserved the importance of independent Catholic schools during the Second Empire (as Morbihan and Ille-et-Vilaine did, among others) may be more significant than the percentage of students in private schools, which was higher in a number of other departments.

47. Those departments around the Rhône (and the highest percentage of total enrollment in Catholic schools they ever reached) were Loire (79 percent), Vaucluse (73), Ardèche (66), Haute-Loire (66), Rhône (66), Bouches-du-Rhône (63), Gard (59), Aveyron (56), Cantal (49), Lot (49), and Puy-de-Dôme (49). All reached their peaks in 1876 except Loire, Rhône, and Vaucluse (which did so in 1867).

48. Those in the west were Ille-et-Vilaine (71 percent), Morbihan (66), Côtes-du-Nord (59), Mayenne (57), Maine-et-Loire (56), Finistère (52), and Manche (49); each reached its peak in 1876.

49. Seine-Inférieure (53 percent), Nord (50), and Haute-Savoie (49) in 1876. It is suggestive to compare another list. In contemporary France, over half the inhabitants make their Easter duty in twenty-one departments, François-André Isambert and Jean Paul Terrenoire, *Atlas pratique religieuses des Catholiques en France* (Paris, 1980), 44–57. Fourteen of these departments also appear on the list of the twenty-one departments that in the nineteenth century ever had more than one-half of their students in Catholic schools: Aveyron, Cantal, Côtes-du-Nord, Gard, Ille-et-Vilaine, Loire, Haute-Loire, Lot, Maine-et-Loir, Manche, Mayenne, Morbihan, Rhône, Haute-Savoie. The seven departments on the contemporary list for Easter duty in which Catholic enrollments never claimed a majority are Doubs, Loire-Atlantique, Lozère, Pyrénées-Atlantique, Hautes-Pyrénées, Haute-Rhin, and Tarn—which suggests once more the difficulty Catholic schools had in reaching dispersed mountainous populations (Loire-Inférieure stood out on other measures of Catholic schooling, however). Departments that once had more than half of their students in Catholic schools but are not on this later list are Ardèche, Vaucluse, Bouches-du-Rhône, Puy-de-Dôme, Finistère, Nord, and Seine-Inférieure—which may hint that in some of these depart-

ments an earlier Catholic supplemental role was not later maintained by a Catholic subculture. Similarly, see Yves-Marie Hilaire, "Les contrastes géographiques et les phases de l'évolution religieuse du XIXe siècle à travers l'histoire quantitative de la pratique culturelle," in *Christianisation et déchristianisation. Actes de la neuvième rencontre d'histoire religieuse tenue à Fonteuraud les 3,4, et 5 octobre l985* (Angers, 1986), 199–207.

50. Although Catholics waged a successful political offensive in the 1850s in Aveyron, Ardèche, and Haute-Loire, only in Ardèche was there a dramatic increase in the percentage of children attending Catholic schools. P. M. Jones, *Politics and Rural Society: The Southern Massif Central, 1750–1850* (New York, 1985).

51. Total primary school enrollment in these departments declined somewhat at the end of the century, conceivably in part as a reaction to secularization. On the other hand, two (Gard and Ille-et-Vilaine) had their highest percentage of Catholic enrollment in 1881, even though the percentage in public schools declined.

52. Of the twelve departments in which new Catholic schools took over half the total enrollment, three (Aveyron, Ardèche, Loire-Inférieure) had always been among the top quarter of departments ranked by proportion of students in Catholic schools; one (Vendée) had recently moved into that group, to be joined by two others (Lozère and Tarn-et-Garonne) in the 1890s. One (Charente) had always been among the lowest in Catholic enrollment; one (Haute-Vienne) had steadily become so; and one other (Deux-Sèvres) had been so until recently. The others were Aude, Haute-Garonne, and Basses-Pyrénées. These calculations use the data, school by school, commune by commune, for all the departments of France in *Rapport sur les laïcisations*, 2–148. They cannot show the effect where a Catholic private school already existed or students went to a Catholic school in a neighboring commune. Of the twenty-three departments that between 1850 and 1881 ever had fewer than one-fifth of their students in Catholic schools, eleven were in the northeast and five or six of the others would be counted as mountainous. Only in the educationally backward flatlands (in departments like Charente, Charente-Inférieure, Creuse, or Deux-Sèvres) can the statistics confidently be said to indicate anticlericalism. In 1879, when petitions were gathered in favor of free (Catholic) higher education, thirteen departments collected the most signatures (30,000–100,000); ten of these were among the highest in the proportion of enrollment in Catholic elementary schools, although half of them were near the bottom of the highest range. Of the twenty-two departments that collected the fewest signatures (2,500–10,000), nine were among the twenty-two departments with the lowest Catholic enrollments; one of them (Cantal) had high Catholic enrollment. The figures for these signatures are from *Atlas historique de la France contemporaine, 1800-1965* (Paris, 1966), 153.

53. The negative correlation between the award of *certificats d'études* and the proportion of students in private schools increased: $-.12$ in 1881, $-.3$ in 1891, $-.41$ in 1896 (though this was, in part, a reflection of the predominance of girls in private schools). So did the negative correlation between the percentage of the school-age population enrolled in all schools and the percentage of students enrolled in Catholic schools. Variance among departments as to the Catholic share of enrollment also increased. The proportion of enrollment in independent schools became a clearer reflection of Catholic sentiment than the proportion in Catholic public schools. As

Catholic independent schools (usually, but not always, lacking communal support) were sometimes forced to charge tuition, there may also have been a shift in the clientele for Catholic instruction.

54. On the relation of curé and *instituteur*, see Gerard Cholvy, *Géographie réligieuse de l'Hérault* (Paris, 1968), 307–8, 314. Moods could also change; there was a resurgence of Catholic enrollment after both world wars (see Lucie Tanguy, "L'état et l'école privée en France," *Revue française de sociologie* 13 [1972]: 325–75).

55. For examples of the role of the clergy in making schooling acceptable, see the recent works by Gregor Dallas, *The Imperfect Peasant Economy: The Loire Country, 1800–1914* (New York, 1982), 88–93, which explores the differences and similarities in communes that favored Catholic or laic schools, and Laura S. Strumingher, *What Were Little Girls and Boys Made Of?* (Albany, N.Y., 1983), 40–46.

56. It should be noted that Catholic schools had also helped cope with population increases: of the six departments with the greatest growth in school-age population beteen 1850 and 1876, three were among those with high Catholic enrollments (Loire-Inférieure, Bouches-du-Rhône, Nord). Of the seven with the greatest growth in school-age population between 1881 and 1906, two had high Catholic enrollments (Bouches-du-Rhône, Finistère). Increased demand for schooling may also account for the tendency of Catholic schools in these departments not to keep pace.

57. Although many departments along the Rhône were early leaders in the number of schools, a high proportion of them were Catholic, and their early start did not make them early leaders in enrollment. Perhaps the schools lacked funds, were not ideally located, or did not recruit effectively enough or retain their students for as many years. Some parents may have resisted sending their children to the clerics. In any case, the growth in enrollment in these departments did not match that of the early secular system.

58. On the professionalization of teaching, see C. R. Day, "The Rustic Man: The Rural Schoolmaster in Nineteenth-Century France," *Comparative Studies in Society and History* 25, no. 1 (January, 1983): 26–49; Peter Meyers, "Professionalization and Social Change: Rural Teachers in Nineteenth Century France," *Journal of Social History* 4 (Summer, 1976): 542–48; Jacques Ozouf, *Nous les maîtres d'école: Autobiographies d'instituteurs de la belle époque* (Paris, 1967).

59. Enrollments dropped slightly among departments in the top two octiles (perhaps because of the loss of Catholic schools or because of the increasing tendency for students above or below elementary school age to enroll in different sorts of schools). Enrollments among departments in the bottom two octiles increased more markedly. In the *écoles maternelles* enrollments fell—another sign that these schools remained less well established and more dependent on clerical teachers.

CHAPTER 5

The Schooling of Girls

On the eve of the French Revolution, only one-quarter of the women of France could read and write—which was more than ever before. A century later, more than two-thirds of adult women were literate, and that figure was seen as disgracefully low. Until the July Monarchy, a majority of French children but more girls than boys probably received little or no formal schooling; by the Third Republic, girls were as regularly and universally enrolled as their brothers. The growth of elementary schooling must to a considerable extent have included girls, and so perhaps our statistical analysis can be extended to focus on girls instruction, revealing something of the pace and manner in which it came about. There are good reasons, however, for considering girls schooling in nineteenth-century France to have had its own, separate history. Illiteracy was higher among women than men, and only a few radicals favored coeducation. Although the national laws and regulations for girls schools were similar to those for boys schools, they were not the same, and they usually came later, often many years later. The official curriculum expected girls schools to be different, and girls were much more likely than boys to attend a Catholic school, increasing the chances that their experience of schooling was not the same. Even at the end of the century, educational reformers were complaining of the inadequacies of girls schools. No wonder, then, that historical writing on the subject of girls schooling tends to have a peculiarly ambivalent tone.

The current literature on girls education emphasizes social complexity and diversity. It is likely to reject the triumphalism of republican pedagogues (while accepting their confessions that success was slow and incomplete) and to stress the importance of social attitudes and of historical continuity reaching back into the old regime. It is also likely, given the nature of the accessible sources, to rest largely on the history of the relevant legislation and (like the famous nineteenth-century debates about girls schooling) to pay more attention to secondary than to primary education.[1]

We now know that the educational efforts of the ancien régime must be taken seriously, however limited they may have been, and that they included some remarkable networks of schools for girls. Like the spread of literacy, the development of schooling must be seen as part of a process that extended over several centuries. We are also aware that literacy is not the simple measure of schooling some once took it to be.[2] Thus, although it is true that the gap between the literacy of women and of men narrowed and was finally eliminated in the nineteenth century, it is also true that women's literacy had begun to rise before then, that it always lagged behind that of men, often by several generations,[3] and that the role of the school system in that achievement has been questioned. Furthermore, the modern historian, for whom it is obvious that opportunities for women should equal those for men, finds it hard to be very enthusiastic about a process of merely catching up, especially one extending through a century. More striking from this perspective are the promises unfulfilled, the many instances in which politicians and educators were silent about girls schooling, and the occasions that elicited from them disparaging comments about women's capacity. There may have been some admirable talk about instructing girls, particularly from the days of the July Monarchy on, but historians are bound to be sensitive to the limitations such declarations contained and to wonder in any case what real effect these proclamations had. Conservatives and progressives alike insisted upon separate schooling for girls and intended that it should not be entirely equal.[4] Their arguments about the necessity of instructing girls to be good homemakers, companions, and mothers (who, it was noted, would be the instructors of men) carefully maintained an emphasis upon traditional roles. So did the preference for entrusting girls instruction to Catholic schools. Among the upper classes, old-fashioned preferences for boarding schools (usually part of a secondary school) combined with the belief that primary schools for the people should give a great deal of attention to sewing (valuable both for future housewives and those who might need to work as seamstresses) similarly suggest that instruction was not meant to change women's lot.[5]

Nor is it certain that the politicians, even when they favored girls schools, actually accomplished very much. An ordinance of 1816 said classes for girls should meet at separate times, something less than requiring a system of schools for girls, and a requirement for girls schools was dropped from the Guizot Law of 1833 (with cost as the excuse). An ordinance of 1836 followed earlier instructions to prefects in calling for girls schools where communes had the means but provided no sanctions for communes that failed to do so, and many prefects reported by way of explanation that their department lacked the necessary teachers. Although some inspectors in the 1840s interested themselves in girls schools, it was not until the Falloux Law of 1850 that communes were required to establish girls schools—and then only in communes with more than eight hundred inhabitants (the Second Republic had favored a more stringent standard) and in a context that favored Catholic schools. Even so, an exception was soon allowed for "poor" communes, and not until 1867 were all communes with more than five hundred inhabitants required to have a girls school. All of this seems to justify the conclusion that before 1850 public primary instruction for girls did not really exist.[6]

The progress that followed remained less than ideal. Although the percentage of communes without any school at all was very low by 1850, more than one-third still had no girls school until the end of the century (table G.4), when one department (Corsica) had a difference of thirty points in the percentage of boys and of girls enrolled in school. We have criticized excessive use of the imaginary line drawn between St. Malo and Geneva to distinguish educationally advanced departments from more backward ones. Nevertheless, that crude measure provides a suggestive comparison of girls and boys enrollments—revealing that, whereas the difference above and below that line in boys enrollments had all but disappeared early in the Third Republic, the difference in girls enrollments above and below that line remained significant for much longer and that girls enrollment in the south lagged behind girls enrollment in the north by even more than boys enrollment did (table G.3). Indeed, there are signs that it may always have been a little harder for girls to go to school than it was for boys: fewer of them had scholarships to cover tuition,[7] and more than twice as many took their schooling in private or independent schools rather than public ones. To an impassioned believer in girls education like Jules Simon, who was convinced that the Catholic sisters offered inferior instruction, the schooling of girls in France on the eve of the Ferry Laws was almost a disaster, a principal reason that the literacy rate of women had not yet risen higher.[8] Although no longer so sure that schools cause literacy nor so convinced that girls must be taught separately from boys, historians have sensed much truth in the pained candor of nineteenth-century educators.

I

The picture changes, however, when one simply considers how many girls were enrolled in school, and rather different questions then emerge. Millions of French girls did in fact go to school and in impressively rising numbers, and the difference between the enrollment of girls and of boys steadily decreased—even in 1837 the number of girls registered for school was 70 percent the number of boys—until it became insignificant by the time of the Third Republic[9] (tables E.2, E.3, and G.2). Even in the period before 1850, French parents were fairly energetic in sending their daughters to school. Some 40 percent of the number of girls enrolled in 1906 were enrolled by 1837. And girls enrollment continued to grow faster than boys did, halving the difference between the sexes in the period from 1837 to 1850, when the state established a national policy in behalf of girls schools. In the thirteen years before 1850, more than thirty thousand additional girls enrolled in school each year, a figure that increased to forty thousand a year in the decade following the Falloux Law. In terms of these nationwide enrollments, that important step appears more as a measure facilitating a process already underway than as its beginning or cause. A nation with two million girls sitting in its classrooms is hardly unfamiliar with either the daily routine or the larger implications of girls elementary instruction.

What then was the proportion of girls enrolled in French schools? The number of girls enrolled was equal to half of the school-age girls in France by 1837 and to two-thirds by 1850, by which time the pattern, custom, and expectation of girls instruction was surely established (table G.2). Something of the weaknesses of girls schooling and its uneven distribution is also suggested by the much lower departmental minimums and maximums for the enrollment of girls than of boys. Even in departments with the most developed primary school systems, girls did not stay in school as long as their brothers, although nearly all of them appear to have been enrolled for the normal term. Still, a national mean indicating full enrollment for school-age girls at the beginning of the Third Republic is significant.

The growth in girls enrollment can be seen as having developed in stages, each of which precedes as well as follows the landmarks of national legislation. Two-thirds of the departments of France enrolled 50 percent or more of their school-age cohort of girls by 1850, three-quarters enrolled a number equal to at least 75 percent of their school-age girls by 1867, nine-tenths had enrollments at or above their population of school-age girls by 1881. By then, all but two departments had passed the 75 percent mark (table G.5). In the Third Republic, the struggle to make girls schools better and the battle over what should be taught and by whom reached deep into society because French parents were accustomed to sending their daughters to schools in a system already established.

That the development of girls enrollment had also been systemic—with a department's schools and enrollment early in the century predicting later growth—is revealed by once again arranging the departments of France into octiles, according to their ranking on the proportion of school-age population (boys and girls) enrolled in 1832.[10] Those eight groups of departments generally preserve their relative ranking in girls enrollment throughout the century, although less sharply for girls alone than for girls and boys (girls enrollment did not exactly follow boys) [table G.6]. More impressive still, these departments (grouped by total enrollment in 1832) achieved the full enrollment of girls in neat chronological sequence, a statistical staircase that is a picture of systemic growth.[11]

From a rather early date, the distribution of girls enrollment was thus remarkably even, usually behind that of boys but also usually only slightly so and without pockets of exclusion large enough to stand out statistically at the

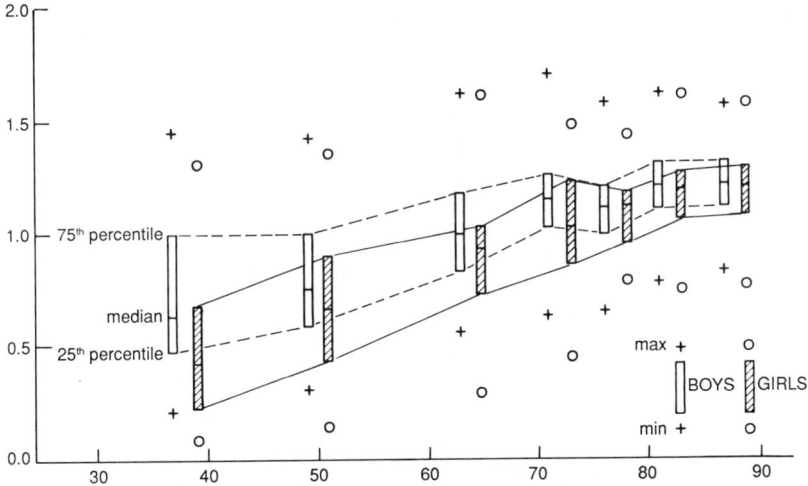

Fig. 9. Percentage of school-age girls and of school-age boys enrolled in primary school

departmental level. The patterns can be made somewhat clearer visually than mathematically, by looking at scattergrams of boy and girls enrollments in each department of France (fig. 9).[12] They look very much like the graphs of male and female literacy in the nineteenth century,[13] with some suggestive differences. The dominant pattern is of two narrowly separated lines, both rising but with the lower line (representing girls enrollment) rising slightly faster, so that the lines are farthest apart earlier in the century and move toward convergence, most often early in the Second Empire. Boys enrollment as a percentage of school-age boys was almost always higher than girls enrollment until the Third Republic and usually a little above thereafter.[14] Then it became less uncommon for the proportion of girls enrolled in a department to exceed the proportion of boys (as it did in about one-quarter of the departments by the 1890s), but that occurred where boys enrollment, too, was already universal. There were always some departments with a greater absolute number of girls than boys in primary school—only a few until the Third Republic, one-fifth by 1876, one-quarter by 1881, nearly 40 percent by the turn of the century, a figure that has held since 1911.[15] A majority of departments enrolled more boys than girls, but in only a few cases did boys enrollments continue for two or three decades to be markedly higher than those of girls. In those instances, boys enrollments were also low—these were laggard departments also weak in Catholic schools.[16] In one-quarter of France's departments, girls and boys enrollments remained extremely close

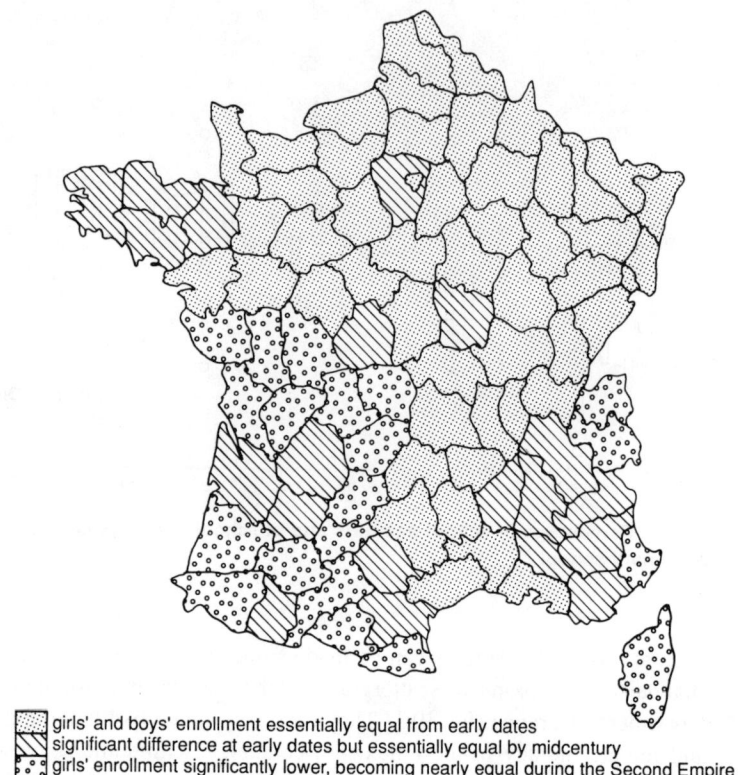

girls' and boys' enrollment essentially equal from early dates
significant difference at early dates but essentially equal by midcentury
girls' enrollment significantly lower, becoming nearly equal during the Second Empire

Fig. 10. Three clusters based on girls' enrollment compared to that of boys, 1837–76

from the 1840s on (fig. 10). In the south,[17] center,[18] east,[19] and west of France,[20] these departments include some noted for advanced schooling, some where schooling developed slowly but with a strong Catholic component, most urban ones, and those of the Loire valley. Their very diversity reflects the general lack of sharp differences in the enrollment of girls and boys. In all of France, there were no departments with high enrollments for one sex only.

When in the Third Republic educators established the *certificat d'études primaires* as their earnest system's crowning step, girls at first lagged behind the boys in applying for that test as they earlier had in enrollment. But in that too they quickly closed the gap. Less than one-tenth of all students who might have been eligible presented themselves for the examination in the period 1872–76, one-fifth did so in the 1880s, and more than one-third thereafter.[21]

Girls at first accounted for only about one-quarter of this more ambitious elite, and initially a smaller proportion of girls than boys passed the examination. But girls accounted for 45 percent of the applicants by the 1890s and by then had a higher rate of success than the boys (table E.5). However limited the standards may have been, that *certificat* represented the triumph of a now highly organized educational system. Although the disastrous spelling on a Breton girl's examination doomed her hopes and called into question the quality of the instruction she had received, her conviction that "s'est une honneur davoir son certificat d'etude" (sic) expressed the system's success in reaching young girls as well as boys. The heroine of Colette's autobiographical novel, *Claudine à l'école*, may have been considered a bit odd by the townsfolk but not (by 1900) for staying on a year at school in order to suffer the three-day examination for the *certificat* merely to please her father and bring honor to her school. Like her, a great many girls (in contrast to boys) did not seek employment, but for a sizable number of young women the *certificat* meant entry into the departmental *école normale*.[22] The increased schooling of girls created a need for more women teachers and encouraged more girls to think in terms of possible careers, especially in teaching. The *certificat d'etudes primaires* and girls normal schools were institutional aspects of these broader aspirations as well as the means whereby a growing system could both reproduce itself and expand.

II

How, then, did the republican reformers of public education who denounced the inadequacy of girls schooling apparently overlook the millions of girls daily taking their seats in school? They were looking from the top down and were looking less at the girls than at girls schools, which they believed should be separate, public rather than private, and—by the Third Republic—taught by professional, laic teachers rather than by members of religious orders. On all three counts girls schooling left much to be desired.

Mixed schools of boys and girls were such an embarrassment that the official statistics hid their number. Such schools had been officially opposed in the eighteenth century; and legislation, and public declarations and ministerial communications throughout the nineteenth century maintained the view, which was rarely challenged, that a distinct school for girls was essential. Churchmen strongly supported that view, and the competition between Catholic and laic schooling undoubtedly served to strengthen the assumption that girls could receive the most appropriate and effective instruction only in their own schools (and from female teachers). That conviction was not simply a Catholic prejudice; in the United States, where literacy and enrollment were generally higher for both sexes but especially so for girls, administrators were insistent before the Civil War on the importance of segregating the sexes.[23] Nor was the concern primarily one of curriculum (for all the emphasis upon sewing and the other domestic arts, required subjects were not very different for boys and girls).

The notion of separate schooling for girls attached to a whole ideology of women's domestic destiny and of feminine character, considered a treasure of tenderness and delicacy. Jules Simon felt no need to explain to his readers what he meant when he declared that the mixed school "is not a school for both sexes; it is a school for boys that receives girls."[24] With universal primary schooling established and its importance unchallenged, he would no longer concede the point made by Victor Cousin in 1833, who explained in the Chamber of Deputies that separate girls schools were "almost luxury schools" for which in small villages there was no reason.[25] If cultural values seemed to support Simon, local penury, resistant taxpayers, and a lack of teachers sustained the expedient of teaching the two sexes together. Even those who denounced teaching girls and boys together as immoral admitted that mixed schools were better than none.

It is difficult to reconstruct how common such schools were. The definition of a girls school may not always have required a separate location and teacher, although that appears to have been the usual standard. And the published statistical tables conceal the figures for mixed schools because they combine the figures for boys and mixed schools.[26] Clearly, the number of communes without a girls schools, figures always presented with a shudder of shame, must not be taken (as they sometimes have been) to mean communes in which girls could receive no schooling.[27] Fortunately, it is possible to break down the aggregate number of boys and mixed schools for certain years[28] (table S.1). Once separated into the three types of schools, the figures reveal that in 1837 there were more mixed schools than schools for either boys or girls alone, that from the 1860s on there were more schools exclusively for girls than for boys, and that the large number of mixed schools remained quite steady throughout the century despite all the efforts to replace them.[29]

Generally taught by men, mixed schools sometimes obscured the fact that a relatively high proportion of French girls regularly attended primary school.[30] In 1837, the number of mixed schools was about the same as the number of communes without girls schools, and it was always considerably higher thereafter. Although the communes with mixed schools do not coincide perfectly with those without girls schools, mixed schools provide the key to understanding how the enrollment of girls in France could have been as high as it was.[31] Some 40 percent of the schools listed as boys and mixed schools were in fact mixed (the percentage was even higher in the first half of the century). These mixed schools accounted for about one-third the enrollment in boys and mixed schools, and within the mixed schools, approximately 40 percent of the students were girls.[32]

Overwhelmingly, schools that taught both girls and boys were public ones, the sensible compromise of small communes with few students.[33] Viewed by administrators as a kind of stopgap, mixed schools were nevertheless often found in departments that by all other measures were educationally among the most advanced. In the 1830s, they constituted a majority of all public schools, often in departments with high enrollments.[34] No longer likely to be a majority of a department's schools by 1863, they still often accounted for a significant number of students and still often in departments with well-developed school systems.[35] By the time of the Ferry Laws, when official pronouncements associated mixed schools with backwardness, they remained more than one-quarter of all the public primary schools in some departments that had for years enjoyed essentially universal enrollment.[36]

Educators' chagrin at this dependence upon mixed schools has left a heavier imprint on the historical literature than the underlying fact: Throughout France, communes had found a less expensive way to provide for girls instruction. The inability of most communes to afford, or their unwillingness to pay for, more than one school had been only reluctantly admitted in a report to King Louis-Philippe in 1843.[37] When the ministry began to prepare for the law of 1867 (which required a separate, public girls school in all communes with over five hundred inhabitants), it knew that the central issue was the financial resources available to such small communities.[38] In the face of these practical considerations, the law of 1867 had only limited effect. Nationally, there were about eight hundred fewer mixed schools in 1876 than in 1863 (out of seventeen thousand, that is a drop of less than 5 percent), and the increase in the number of girls schools during that period was only a tiny bit higher than the increase in boys schools, although it was significant in some areas where girls schools had lagged notably.[39] The most common result of the 1867 law was probably the transformation of a local independent school for girls into the public girls school, an institutionally important step but not necessarily the sign of any significant change in the lives of young girls. In some areas, there were few communes with more than five hundred inhabitants that did not already have a public girls school, but in others, academies had to report that there was a reluctance to comply with the new law.[40] By 1876, small villages—one-quarter of France's communes had fewer than five hundred inhabitants—and local attitudes combined to leave 45 percent of the communes in France without a public girls school.[41]

The persistence of mixed schools may, on the other hand, have contributed to a new attitude expressed during the 1860s toward women teachers, an attitude undoubtedly fostered by the fact that so many women teachers were nuns. Foreshadowing the later feminization of primary school teaching, officials began to ask about the merits of having boys taught by women. Some prefects were very supportive, seeing in women teachers an extension of "public and private customs [and of] the 'spirit' of the family," while adding that "religious sentiment could only gain in a school directed by a woman." The generally positive response was reinforced for some who noted the double economy of having one school rather than two and of then hiring women, who received lower salaries than men. There were also some fears that "a woman may lack the firmness necessary to maintain discipline and to assure progress" and concern about contacts between women and boys of thirteen or fifteen (a danger obviated, it was noted, when the teacher was a nun). Only occasionally were there firm objections about the political risk of alienating previously loyal male teachers or about the threat to the values of an "éducation virile."[42] Mixed schools remained important, and women teachers were gaining acceptance.

For the promoters of universal public schooling, however, there were additional reasons to be dissatisfied with girls schools: they were too often private and Catholic and probably inferior. Although two-thirds of the girls in primary school went to public schools, until 1863 a majority of the schools for girls were private. Not until 1875 were more than two-thirds of France's girls schools public—a rapid and important shift (table G.1). The presence of a school was more visible than the size of enrollments, and this heavy dependence on private schools for the instruction of girls suggests that parental demand had outstripped communal supply. Indeed, French parents more often paid for the elementary education of their daughters than of their sons—a tangible monthly measure of their commitment—because private schools offered fewer scholarships. Inspectors may well have been correct, however, in their belief that the quality of private instruction was inferior, and Duruy's insistence on the right to inspect Catholic girls schools despite clerical resistance was part of the persistent pressure to raise their quality.[43]

The growth in public girls schools was, nevertheless, largely an achievement of the religious orders. Even by 1850, before the Falloux Law, a majority of the girls in public schools were taught by Catholic sisters, whose dominance of public girls schools then increased during the period of the greatest growth in those schools, from 1850 to 1875. By that time, the majority of the remaining independent girls schools were also Catholic. Throughout the century, a far greater proportion of girls than boys attended Catholic schools. Furthermore, the enrollment of girls in Catholic schools differed from that of boys in that it was both more uniform across the nation and more constant over time. From 1850 to 1901, the coefficient of variation in the proportion of girls enrolled in Catholic schools was much less (it ranged from 24 to 37 percent) than the variation among boys (which ranged from 41 to 72 percent). The education of girls was solidly in the hands of the Church, and the reversal of that trend, which began with the Third Republic, brought with it a further rise in Catholic private schools.

Statistical data can be used with far greater confidence to discern general patterns of behavior than to assess the reasons for that behavior. Nevertheless, an effort to assess the relative weight of major factors can be worthwhile, provided that precise-sounding percentages are understood to be only very imprecise and general measures. French girls went to Catholic schools because of their availability (institutional convenience), a cultural preference for having girls educated by nuns, and the commitment some families felt to religious instruction for all their children. In addition, Catholic enrollments were affected by national politics. It is possible in a general way to try to look at each of these elements separately.

When national policies favored Catholic schools, from 1850 to 1876, the percentage of girls enrolled in school who were in Catholic schools rose from 44 to 59 percent (table C.5). During the next twenty-five years of contrary pressures, the percentage of girls enrollment accounted for by Catholic schools fell to 38 percent. That increase and subsequent decline, of about one-third or some 21 percentage points, might be taken to represent the maximum effect to be attributed to political policies. (The change of only 13 percentage points in the percentage of boys enrollment in Catholic schools was relatively somewhat greater; Catholic schools had a lesser role in the instruction of boys but one that was more sensitive to political change).

During the period from 1850 to 1901, the *difference* between the percentage of enrolled girls and enrolled boys who were inscribed in Catholic schools remained remarkably constant: The proportion of girls in Catholic schools remained from 27 to 34 percentage points higher than the proportion of boys—a strong sign of a national, cultural preference. Furthermore, that range of difference between girls and boys was similar in departments with high overall enrollment in Catholic schools (there, girls enrollment in Catholic schools was 26 to 39 percentage points higher than boys) and in departments with overall Catholic enrollments below the national mean (where girls enrollment in Catholic schools was 19 to 38 percentage points higher than boys). The cultural preference that sent more girls than boys to Catholic schools affected enrollments both where Catholic schooling was generally strong and where it was relatively weak.

Comparing these figures in other ways can also provide some indication of the relative impact of Catholic commitment and institutional convenience. In departments with high overall Catholic enrollments, the percentage of schoolgirls in Catholic schools was 21 to 28 percentage points higher than for girls nationally. In departments that were early leaders in enrollment, where there was less need for clerical teachers, the percentage of enrolled girls who chose Catholic schools was 6 to 12 percentage points below the national mean. If such comparisons could actually separate these distinctive aspects of girls enrollment in Catholic schools (and of course they cannot), they would indicate that on the whole, cultural preference was the strongest factor, followed by local Catholic commitment, then by political pressures and policies, and finally by institutional convenience.

The declining enrollments in Catholic girls schools from 1876 to 1891 were an obvious result of political pressure and changing social attitudes. In the context of the national educational system, they can also be seen as a response to changing institutional needs that altered the meaning of Catholic schooling. The employment of Catholic sisters had for many communes represented an easy and readily accessible means of providing schools for girls when vigorous and concrete governmental support for such schools was often lacking. In addition, where girls schooling still seemed an innovation and in a world that saw girls primarily as future wives and mothers, nuns may also have offered comforting reassurance. Such factors mattered less with the passage of time and the acceptance of formal schooling as a universal necessity of childhood. An established and better funded public system was now able to turn to the laic *institutrices* graduating in increasing numbers from the *écoles normales*. The decline in dependence upon Catholic orders continued the trend toward increased professionalization, for quite aside from differences in formal training, nuns living in small groups were even more subject to other duties (in local hospitals and charities) than lay teachers. And arguments for and against laicization often turned on issues of the teacher's competence as well as cost.[44]

A process of change that was often loudly political presented parents with a conscious and bitterly contested choice. Not surprisingly, then, the leveling off in the 1890s in the percentage of girls taught by Catholic sisters was accompanied by the growth of independent Catholic schools. Both trends, which had begun in the 1880s, reflect increasingly explicit religious preferences. As religious choice became the primary consideration, private schools (now overwhelmingly Catholic) began to grow again. The laicization of public schools during the Third Republic affected far more girls than boys, but sending boys to Catholic school was a stronger sign of religious commitment than sending girls. Thus, the secularization of a Catholic public school was more likely to lead to the formation of a new, private Catholic school when the old public one had been a boys school.[45] And boys enrollment in private schools (which had been half that of girls) increased relatively more. Still, the different traditions for girls and for boys continued. Private schools attracted less than one-tenth of France's schoolboys, one third of the girls. Some 82 percent of boys enrolled attended public school even in 1837, more than 90 percent from 1863 on. The percentage of enrolled girls who chose public schools ranged between 65 and 72 percent from 1837 to 1901 (hitting its peak in 1886, following the great wave of laicization).

In many villages of France, it was the new *institutrice laïque* who represented the most threatening innovation, and she might find herself snubbed or sometimes stoned or spat upon even when she was careful to attend mass regularly. Yet, the historian must always be wary of easy assumptions about the strength of customary culture. In many public schools, girls enrollment increased after secularization; some parents may well not have wanted their daughters spending too many years with the nuns.[46] Important as Catholic schools had been in the establishment of universal primary education for girls, girls were even more important to the establishment of a Catholic system of schooling, accounting for three-quarters of its enrollment.[47] The Church, too, had an institutional interest in the battles over the laicization of girls schools.

III

Girls schools thus had a somewhat distinctive history, but one might well expect the pattern of girls enrollment to have been more different from and more independent of boys enrollment than it was. Nineteenth-century attitudes toward women and women's roles included corsetting restrictions that would seem to have valued girls schooling much less than boys. In a largely rural society like France, peasants (who are generally held to be suspicious of formal education) might well have resisted sacrificing cash and a daughter's household services in order to send her off to school. And in fact the enrollment of school-age girls in primary schools was lower than that of boys, even if not by much. Girls enrollments did lag behind boys enrollments—on average by about ten years—department by department. Yet, a nationwide custom of sending girls to school even one year less than boys would have produced a larger gender gap than the statistics reveal, although the tendency to send more boys than girls for an additional year of schooling does show in the departments with the highest enrollments.

The circumstances that favored the schooling of one gender generally favored the other, so much so that small differences become suggestive. Girls and boys were more likely to be enrolled where literacy was higher, an effect that declined for both sexes later in the century (as literacy became more universal), but the encouragement that adult literacy gave to the schooling of girls was somewhat stronger and more lasting. The same is true of per capita wealth (the parents of girls more often had to pay tuition). Where a high proportion of the population was engaged in agriculture, boys enrollments had at first been lower, with the correlation becoming slightly positive as schools were established everywhere. For girls, the negative effect of agricultural employment was stronger, and the positive one never emerged. An industrial and commercial population stimulated boys schooling until the 1870s but then led to relatively lower enrollments later when students were expected to stay in school for a full seven or eight years. The presence of these occupations, with their implication of job opportunities (primarily for men), had at first been even more encouraging for girls instruction than for that of boys and statistically never showed a dampening effect. Cities appear, at least for a while, to have favored girls schooling (perhaps by providing more schools or fewer opportunities outside school for girls), but smaller towns may have provided only slightly less stimulus (table G.8).

These differences emerge more clearly when one looks directly at the percentage of the student body composed of girls (table G.10). Literacy and wealth, industry and commerce were more favorable, an agricultural population more of a handicap, to girls enrollment than to that of boys. Of all these factors, agriculture was the most telling, although all of them together can acount for only one-quarter of girls enrollment. In fact, when two groups of departments are compared, those in which girls and boys enrollments were most similar in 1837 and those in which the enrollments of girls and boys were farthest apart, they are very similar in their relationship to these social factors—with the proportion of population employed in agriculture or in industry making the greatest difference—despite their sharp divergence in measures of schooling. Girls enrollments were also slightly more consistent in their relation to each other, department by department and from 1837 to 1906, than boys enrollments, but the correlation between the enrollment of girls and of boys is overwhelming (table G.9). Establishment of a school system, even when at first more boys than girls were drawn to it, predicted the imminent enrollment of girls.

There is little evidence in the enrollment statistics for all the departments of France of peculiar local responses toward girls education (fig. 11). Of the seventeen departments with the greatest difference between girls and boys enrollments in 1837 (more than 35 percentage points), a dozen were by national standards laggards in all aspects of schooling and would remain so even as enrollments for both sexes rose and drew closer together. The other five of these departments give a hint of two later patterns: general if not always steady growth, in the course of which girls enrollment caught up, or very advanced boys enrollments, which briefly left girls enrollment behind. The leading and lagging departments in girls enrollment in 1837 generally held that position in 1850, 1867, and 1876, and they generally led or lagged in boys enrollments as well. Only a few departments failed steadily to reduce the gap between girls and boys enrollments,[48] and in most cases, those with a large gap earlier in the century (particularly heavily concentrated in the southwest) rapidly closed it with unusual gains in girls enrollment.

Girls enrollments were highest in well-established, secular school systems. Where the system was newer and weaker, Catholic contributions were

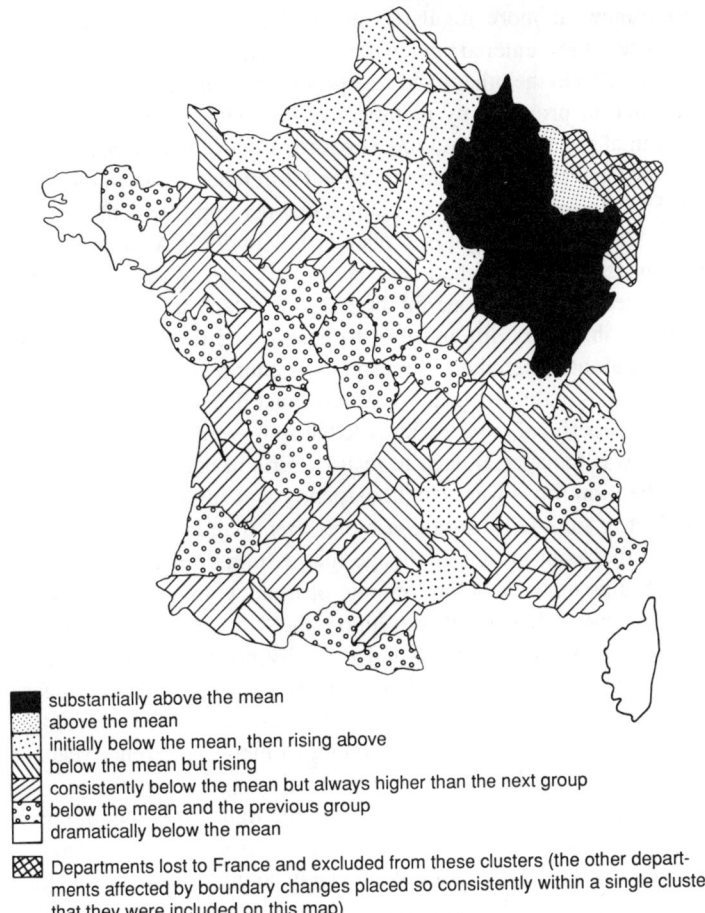

■ substantially above the mean
▦ above the mean
▨ initially below the mean, then rising above
▧ below the mean but rising
▨ consistently below the mean but always higher than the next group
▨ below the mean and the previous group
□ dramatically below the mean

▩ Departments lost to France and excluded from these clusters (the other departments affected by boundary changes placed so consistently within a single cluster that they were included on this map)

Fig. 11. Seven clusters based on the percentage of school-age girls enrolled in school, 1837–76

especially important in raising a department toward the mean but could not overcome a general pattern of less instruction.[49] Even in the period of greatest growth in the Catholic schooling of girls, from 1850 to 1876, Catholic schools were an essential part of that growth but not sufficiently independent of the larger process to have an autonomous effect on girls enrollments. Catholic schools, like private schools, supplemented public secular ones where those were insufficient. They may have made schooling more welcome and acceptable; they did not account for its expansion.

Enrollment, of course, tells little of the differences in the quality of schools and in the kind of instruction they provided. Girls do seem to have attended somewhat more regularly and to have been likely to be a little younger when they entered and when they left primary school than their brothers were.[50] On the other hand, the prominence of Catholic instruction for girls, instruction provided by members of charitable orders who often had rather minimal pedagogical training (or formal education of any sort), points to what may have been an important general difference between girls and boys schools. Still, those nuns were probably a distinct improvement over many of the mistresses who had taught in private girls schools.[51] As to the public girls schools, inspectors did sometimes report that they were inferior to boys schools but less often than one might expect.[52] Many inspectors seem not to have thought about any difference or to have found the two sorts of schools about the same, although there is reason to be cautious here, too: one positive report about the quality of girls instruction justified its praise by noting the absence of "superficial, useless knowledge that would be new food for frivolity."[53] It was the special need to instruct girls in needlework that received the most attention (boys were taught carpentry and surveying). Girls probably were subject to minimal instruction more often than boys, but our statistical data can neither confirm nor challenge that assumption.

That brings us back to the low rate of literacy among French women, a piece of evidence often cited to support the view that girls instruction in France was both slow to develop and woefully inadequate once established. Maggiolo's famous estimate was that only 66 percent of French brides signed their marriage registers in 1871–75, and the census of 1872 counted 59 percent as the national mean of literacy among women over twenty years of age. The impressive study by Furet and Ozouf gives good reason for accepting these figures as accurate.[54] At a time when the figures for school enrollment indicate that nearly all school-age girls were enrolled in school, such levels of literacy appear to cast a dark shadow on the meaning of that enrollment. Girls schools that did not produce minimally literate women are hardly a sign of a strong national interest in educating girls.

Still, if girls schools failed to produce the expected level of female literacy, boys schools did not have a significantly stronger effect; and by the end of the century, among the young, fewer women than men were illiterate.[55] In the 1870s, signatures on marriage registers were only eight percentage points higher for men than women, and the 1872 census listed male literacy as seven percentage points higher—differences quite comparable to the percentages of school-age boys and girls who had enrolled in school (table G.7). There is a further way indirectly to test the possibility that a high proportion of those who enrolled in girls schools did not learn to read and write. We have good estimates for the ages of the women who married in 1876; we can make much rougher ones for the proportion of women in each age group likely to have been enrolled in school. If all those enrolled learned to write their names (and other women did not), the percentage of women who signed the marriage register in the first years of the Third Republic would have been exactly what Maggiolo said it was.[56] A similar calculation can be made concerning all women, not just brides. Separating the population of women into age groups and multiplying each group by the mean percentage of girls in school when that group was of school age, produces a figure of 59 percent of the adult women of France in 1876 who would have been likely to have attended school, the same percentage the census gives as the literacy rate of adult women.[57] The point of these estimates, which necessarily contain a number of leaps of logic, is not to suggest how literacy was in fact achieved but rather to indicate that the often cited literacy rates do not really throw doubt on the efficacy of girls schooling nor on the data for girls enrollments. The literacy figures that so disappointed contemporaries reflected primarily the age distribution of the French population. In 1876, 43 percent of the women over twenty were fifty years old or older. A woman of fifty would have been unlikely to have attended any school not already established before 1842.

There are other indirect signs that school enrollment did relate to the literacy of women. One of these is the fact that more women than men and more girls than boys could read but not write (table G.7). That fits with the tendency of Catholic schools in particular (which were attended in higher numbers by girls than by boys) to introduce writing only after considerable time had been devoted to reading and with a general impression that girls went to school for fewer years than boys did. No such subtle explanation may be necessary, however. The difference between men and women on this measure is about the difference in their levels of enrollment. Correlations provide more suggestive evidence. The proportion of women in each department who could read and write in 1872 correlates more strongly with departmental enrollments before that date than after, more strongly with the ability to read but not write earlier in the century, and not at all with the presence of only such limited skills among younger women. Schools do seem to have had some of the effect expected of them.

It says something quite remarkable about nineteenth-century French society that, in a matter so complicated and sensitive as schooling, girls and boys were treated so similarly.[58] For girls, like boys, educational growth was steady, nationwide, and systemic: Some schools led to more, schools to higher enrollment, boys enrollment to girls enrollment, universal instruction to more public and secular schools, public schools to normal schools and inspectors (who promoted fuller enrollment and better trained teachers); and the cost of all this brought increased local, then departmental and national expenditures.

There are other points to be made. First, the leaders who advocated girls education during the nineteenth century represented their society well when they spoke about the importance of girls instruction and when they described its limited purpose. The lack of legislation on girls schooling is not evidence of hypocrisy—girls were going to school—but of a willingness to forgo nationally imposed standards for girls instruction in the interest of saving communes money. While politicians were candid about that, it is noteworthy how little resistance the universal primary instruction of girls encountered. Second, the great nineteenth-century thrust for education, and especially the push for the instruction of girls, did not come primarily from the state but more largely from society, from parents who on the whole were as willing to exert great effort and spend money for the elementary instruction of their daughters as of their sons. Third, the values and modest ambitions these efforts expressed spread more evenly over France than the social conditions (of urban life, secularization, workers' mobility, literacy itself) associated both with the advocacy of universal instruction and with the institutions expected to provide it.[59] Fourth, the universal primary instruction of girls was thus achieved through accommodation with the means available, mixed schools and Catholic nuns.

The great ideological and political conflicts over education, and especially girls education, that divided the French in the second half of the nineteenth century were as much the effect of universal education as about how or whether to achieve it. With the universal primary instruction of girls and boys established, the place of Catholic schooling then became a matter of religious and social choice evoking the culture's views of women. The limited linkages of primary to secondary instruction became a definition of social mobility and gender roles. It was at that higher level of education, which primarily affected the bourgeoisie, that woman's proper place became an issue.

In the battle over girls primary schooling, republicans were aided by the fact that their position most clearly addressed the quality of instruction and that girls schooling seemed a natural extension of the expanding system of instruction, recognized as one of the century's greatest achievements. Such success supported increased optimism about the effects of education and fed the illusion that in the right hands schools could reshape their pupils and thus society itself. These beliefs and these achievements made education an instrument worth fighting for and girls schooling one of the battle's highest prizes. That battle could be fought because most of French society—Catholics and anticlericals, republicans and monarchists, peasants and city dwellers, workers and members of the middle class—shared the conviction that girls should go to school.

Notes

1. This recent work also provides a valuable basis from which to look again at the educational statistics. Prominent examples include Linda L. Clark, "The Socialization of Girls in the Primary Schools of the Third Republic," *Journal of Social History* (Summer, 1982): 685–97, and "Primary Education of French Girls: Pedagogical Prescriptions and Social Realities," *History of Education Quarterly*, (Winter, 1981), 411–

28, as well as her book, *Schooling the Daughters of Marianne: Textbooks and the Socialization of Girls in Modern French Primary Schools* (Albany, 1984); Laura Strumingher, *What Were Little Girls and Boys Made Of?* (Albany, 1983); Gérard Cholvy, "Une école des pauvres au début du 19ème siècle; 'pieuses filles', béates ou soeurs des campagnes," in *The Making of Frenchmen: Current Directions in the History of Education in France, 1679-1979*, ed. Donald N. Baker and Patrick J. Harrigan (Waterloo, Ont., 1980), 135–41. Françoise Mayeur, *L'éducation des filles en France au XIXème siècle* (Paris, 1979), 9, explains that "il n'est pas étonnant que les efforts du XIXème siècle en matière d'éducation féminine soient moins perceptibles pour les filles du peuple que pour celles des classes plus favorisées. C'est donc à celles-ci surtout que s'interesses cette étude."

2. Roger Chartier, Marc-Marie Compère, and Dominique Julia, *L'éducation en France du XVIème au XVIIIème siècles* (Paris, 1976), is the most important study for the old regime. For special focus on girls, see Jean Perrel, "Les filles à l'école avant la révolution," *Révue d'Auvergne* 84, no. 3 (1982): 291–316, and "Les écoles des filles dans la France d'ancien régime," in Baker and Harrigan, eds., *Making of Frenchmen*, 75–83. Continuity in the growth of literacy and the reciprocal relationship of literacy and schools are among the major themes of François Furet and Jacques Ozouf, *Lire et écrire: L'alphabétisation des français de Calvin à Jules Ferry*, 2 vols. (Paris, 1977). We also discussed this connection a bit in our chapter on enrollment.

3. Furet and Ozouf, *Lire et écrire*, 1:44.

4. Some of the few advocates of coeducation are discussed in Georges Duveau, *La pensée ouvrière sur l'éducation pendant la Séconde République et le Sécond Empire* (Paris, 1948), 160–61, 216–17. On the commitment of the radicals to girls schooling in the Third Republic, see Katherine Auspitz, *The Radical Bourgeoisie: The Ligue de l'Enseignement and the Origins of the Third Republic, 1866–1885* (Cambridge, 1982), 15–19.

5. For a balanced summary of these views, see Mayeur, *L'éducation des filles*, 13–94.

6. Ibid., 78–91. Jules Simon, *L'école* (Paris, 1881), 123n, considered that early legislation merely a cry of distress.

7. In public schools from 1867 on, however, a slightly higher percentage of girls than boys had scholarships.

Percentage of Students with Scholarships

Date	Public and Private Schools		Public Schools	
	Boys	Girls	Boys	Girls
1833	24		29	
1837			27	29
1850	41	30	44	32
1863	36	34	37	34
1867	36	34	41	43
1872	52	46	54	54
1876			57	58

8. Simon, *L'école*, 121-80.

9. Some boys were enrolled in the elementary division of secondary schools or in *petits-seminairs*, neither of which girls could attend. Adding these would raise boys enrollment by about 2 percent nationally during the Second Empire and about 1 percent before and after.

10. The use of these octiles is more fully discussed in the chapter on enrollment.

11. A similar table of boys enrollment would show a somewhat less even progression toward full enrollment but a stronger tendency to even higher enrollments. In only one octile (number five) did girls enrollments pass 100 percent (1.00) before boys enrollment did; that octile, which included a number of urban departments with strong Catholic enrollments, is discussed in the chapter on Catholic schools.

12. We are indebted to J. B Whitney for making these scattergrams for every data point from 1837 to 1881.

13. See Furet and Ozouf, *Lire et écrire*, vol. 1, graph C, p. 8.

14. Only in Cantal, Maine-et-Loire, and Seine (where students from other departments may distort the ratio of girls enrolled to girls of school age) did the proportion of girls enrolled rise above the proportion of boys enrolled before 1872.

15. Two departments enrolled more girls than boys in 1837, seven in 1850, eleven in 1867, and eighteen by 1876. Pierre Chevallier, "L'évolution de l'enseignement en France 1850 à 1963," in *La scolarisation en France depuis un siècle*, ed. Pierre Chevallier, (Paris, 1974), 45, points out the continuing high enrollment of girls in primary schools and suggests that it may be due to the fact that girls enrolled in secondary schools less than boys (but only a small percentage of boys did so either before World War I). As a proportion of school-age population, seven departments enrolled a higher proportion of girls by 1871, sixteen more by 1891.

16. The one exception was Hautes-Alpes, where enrollment was well above the level of seven years of schooling for all boys of school age by 1850, when girls enrollment was just large enough to count as universal. Boys enrollments there then went higher still while girls enrollments increased more slowly. The other departments with scattergrams that show particularly large and lasting gaps between girls and boys enrollment were Charente, Charente-Inférieure, Corse, Pyrénées-Orientales, Deux-Sèvres, and Vienne.

17. Gironde, Aveyron, Hérault, Bouches-du-Rhône.

18. Loire, Rhône, Cher.

19. Ardennes, Meuse, Somme, Aube, Seine-et-Oise.

20. Finistère, Côtes-du-Nord, Morbihan, Ille-et-Vilaine, Maine-et-Loire, Mayenne, Sarthe, Manche, Calvados.

21. The C.E.P.is also discussed in chapters 3 and 7.

22. Barnett Singer, *Village Notables in Nineteenth-Century France: Priests, Mayors, and Schoolmasters* (Albany, 1983), 119-20; Colette, *Claudine à l'école*, trans. Antonia White (London, 1956). Of the students who took the C.E.P. at the turn of the century, 6 percent of the boys and 13 percent of the girls went on to normal school, 7 percent of the boys but only 2.5 percent of the girls went on to technical schools, and some 8 percent of the boys and 6 percent of the girls went on to other schools. More boys than girls took jobs (36 to 29 percent), and their jobs were generally more promising, but the greatest difference may have been between the 21

percent of the boys who returned to their families to launch a career and the 23 percent of the girls who returned to help "ménager," H. Vuibert, *Annuaire de la jeunesse pour l'année 1901* (Paris, 1901), 65–67.

23. Maris A. Vinovskis and Richard M. Bernard, "Beyond Catherine Beecher: Female Education in the Antebellum Period," *Signs* 3 (1978): 864–65. Even a Frenchmen who sympathized with coeducation and considered that separation of the sexes might be a source of inequality noted that "everyone agrees" that up to the age of fifteen it is better for girls to be taught by women, Henri Marion, *L'éducation des jeunes filles* (Paris, 1902), 47–55.

24. Simon, *L'école*, 124–25.

25. Cited in Mayeur, *L'éducation des filles*, 88; the history of the opposition to mixed schools is discussed throughout her book, see pp. 14, 28–33, 88–90. For a good review of the general values underlying girls education, see Clark, *Schooling the Daughters*, 26–80.

26. The three categories—boys, girls, and mixed schools—were distinct in the information requested by the ministry in 1835, Archives Nationales, F17/9352. The combining of boys and mixed schools was more than a device for hiding the prevalence of mixed instruction, for it reflected the preoccupation with making sure that communes met their obligation to provide schools of some sort as well as an assumption that mixed schools were a temporary measure that, once a school had been established, would lead to separate schools for boys and girls.

27. Simon said there were 3,308 communes without girls schools that did not admit girls to boys school, *L'école*, 128–35; but even many of those communes would have had private girls schools.

28. In some of the introductions to various volumes of the *Statistique de l'enseignement primaire*, a figure for the number of boys schools is given: vol. II, *Statistique comparée*, lxiii; III: xli; V: xxix. The missing figure for mixed schools can then be estimated by simple subtraction.

29. Simon gives a figure of 15,150 mixed schools (presumably in 1881), of which 12,490 were taught by laic *instituteurs*, 1,707 by laic *institutrices*, and 953 by nuns, *L'école*, 127n.

30. Of the 17,283 mixed public schools in 1863, 15,030 were directed by *instituteurs*, 1181 by *institutrices*, 1072 by nuns, Archives Nationales, F17*/3158–59. The proportions cited by Simon twenty years later were similar: see previous note.

31. The two highest among the octiles based on overall enrollment in 1832 consistently had the highest percentage of communes without schools, presumably because they included many communes long since accustomed to mixed schools. In fact, among all departments, the correlation between girls enrollment and the number of communes without girls schools is positive up to 1886! The two variables combine so many factors, however, that there is no way to know just what that means. It may not be evidence that girls in small villages were more likely to go school with their brothers, but it is a further sign that the lack of girls schools did not mean a lack of girls schooling.

32. Archives Nationales, F17*/3158–59, gives the figures for public schools in 1863: of 38,386 boys or mixed public schools, 17,283 were mixed, and these had 32 percent of the enrollment in that category. There were 2,399,293 students enrolled in

boys and mixed schools; 736,937 of them were in mixed schools taught by men, and 293,013 of those students were girls. Interestingly, the mixed public schools taught by women enrolled 17,721 girls and 17,587 boys. There is reason to suspect that enrollment data for boys before 1850 may sometimes have omitted those in mixed schools taught by women.

33. In 1901, 664,418 students were enrolled in public *écoles mixtes*, only 25,337 in private ones. The figures for 1906 were 708,873 in public mixed schools, 19,448 in private ones. As the last bastion of Catholic schooling, private schools remained reluctant to put girls and boys together. Summary reports in the Archives Nationales indicate a similar scarcity of mixed schools among those that were independent, F17/9352 for 1835–36, F17/9376 for 1869, F17/10724 for 1880–81. Mixed schools remained almost exclusively one classroom schools, smaller than most schools and only rarely employing even an *adjoint*; some figures for 1899–1900 and 1903–4 are in Archives Nationales, F17/14260 and 10733. Mixed schools taught by nuns were more frequent in Hautes-Alpes, Côtes-du-Nord, Finistère, Manche, and Morbihan, Archives Nationales, F17/10724–33, the same places where "clandestine" schools taught by "béates" had been familiar, Archives Nationales, F17/9279, and Ministre de l'Instruction, *Rapports* (1878–79): 500.

34. In 1835–36, they constituted a majority of the primary schools in Aube, Eure-et-Loir, Marne, Seine-et-Marne, Basses-Pyrénées, Haute-Pyrénées, Deux-Sèvres, Ariège, Haute-Garonne, Aude, Meurthe, Vosges, Loiret, and nearly so in Meuse. They were uncommon in Charente-Inférieure, Pyrénées-Orientales, Lozère, Corse, Bouches-du-Rhône, Mayenne, and Haute-Vienne, and Archives Nationales, F17/9352.

35. Those with large numbers of students in mixed schools in 1863 included: Pas-de-Calais, 36,892; Aisne, 31,081; Oise, 25,783; Somme, 25,852; Côte-d'Or, 22,757; Bas-Rhin, 22,337; Yonne, 22,863; Moselle, 21,386; Seine-et-Marne, 21,103; Seine-et-Oise, 20,976; Ardennes, 19,508; Vosges, 18,261; Marne, 18,154; Eure-et-Loir, 17,971; Aube, 17,786; Nord, 16,441; Seine-Inférieure, 15,597. The departments with the lowest enrollments in mixed schools included some with weak school systems as well as urban and Catholic departments: Seine, 611; Alpes-Maritimes, 602; Finistère, 448; Lot, 425; Mayenne, 382; Haute-Loire, 330; Vaucluse, 315; Rhône, 220; Var, 159; Côtes-du-Nord, 143; Aveyron, 98; Bouches-du-Rhône, 89. Seven departments listed no public mixed schools at all: Hautes-Alpes, Cantal, Gironde, Loire-Inférieure, Manche, Morbihan, Pyrénées Orientales. These figures are in Archives Nationales, F17*/3158–59.

36. There were, of course, many mixed schools in such departments as Calvados, Charente, or Corse, but they remained numerous (and a high percentage of the total number of schools) in departments such as Eure, with 349 mixed schools (which were 43 percent of all its public schools); Oise, 453 (38 percent); Marne, 415 (36); Orne, 327 (33.5); Meuse, 262 (25.5); and Doubs (25), Archives Nationales, F17/10724.

37. By François Villemain, cited in *Statistique de l'enseignement*, II:lxic–lxv.

38. That was the question to which each department was asked to respond in 1865, Archives Nationales, F17/10830.

39. Gabriel Desert, "Alphabétisation et scolarisation dans le Grand-Ouest au 19e siècle," in Baker and Harrigan, eds., *Making of Frenchmen*, 150; Roger Thabault,

Education and Change in a Village Community: Mazières-en-Gâtine (New York, 1971). As in other respects, in this one, too, legislation did not transform the system but served to push laggards toward the national norm.

40. The presence of an adequate private school or the claim that no woman teacher was available were among the reasons given, in addition to the more frequent explanations about limited resources in tiny towns. Academies that could boast of large numbers of new girls schools were likely to be ones in which there were comparable numbers of new schools for boys or even new mixed schools; reports for 1869 and 1870 in Archives Nationales, F17/9376, and for 1872 in F17/10358. The resistance had been similar if more widespread forty years earlier, in 1837, Mayeur, *L'éducation des filles*, 59.

41. *Statistique de l'enseignement*, II: lxv.

42. These comments came in reply to confidential circulars of February 16 and March 4, 1869, asking prefects to consult rectors and inspectors. The longer quotations above are from the prefect of the Ain. The prefect of Basses-Alpes, who made the point about economies, favored the use of women teachers in mixed schools only for the smallest communes. The reports from Lozère and Corse said such a policy might do for advanced departments but were not for them, where there were few qualified women. Some fairly imaginative responses are a reminder that universal schooling was still fairly new. The report from Ille-et-Vilaine thought local mothers would be more willing to send older girls to school if the teachers (in mixed schools) were women; the reply from Eure favored hiring women teachers for mixed schools but assumed that public schools were only a temporary measure that would no longer be needed in future generations when educated parents could teach their children at home. In Archives Nationales, F17/10927.

43. His circular of February, 1866, was part of a larger campaign, Sandra Horvath-Peterson, *Victor Duruy and French Education: Liberal Reform in the Second Empire* (Baton Rouge, 1984), 68. Jean Rohr, *Victor Duruy, Ministre de Napoléon III: Essai sur la politique de l'instruction publique au temps de l'empire libéral* (Paris, 1967), 145; see also the text of the law, pp. 204–8, and note the ban (article 207) on allowing teachers in independent schools to have pupils of the opposite sex. Hyppolyte Fortoul, who had also insisted on inspection of Catholic schools, settled for allowing priests to serve as their inspectors. Teachers in independent girls schools were much less likely to have the *brevet* than teachers, including nuns, in public schools; the *brevet* is discussed in the next chapter.

44. Bernard Ménager, *La laicization des écoles communales dans le département du Nord (1879–1899)* (Lille, 1971), 85–93.

45. This is further discussed in the chapter on Catholic schooling. Although more public schools were secularized before 1879, we have detailed data for the period 1879–89, *Rapport présenté par la Commission de Statistique à M. le Ministre de l'Instruction Publique sur les résultats de laicisations scolaires* (Paris, 1891). Some 5,063 individual public schools were laicized in this period, 57 percent of them girls schools, 25 percent boys schools, 5 percent mixed schools, and 13 percent *écoles maternelles*. New competing Catholic schools were established in 55 percent of the cases affecting girls schools, 62 percent of those affecting boys schools, 24 percent of those involving mixed schools, and 37 percent of those involving *écoles maternelles*.

46. See Ménager, *La laicization*, and Mayeur, *L'éducation des filles*.

47. Girls provided all of the Catholic enrollment in a few departments and over half of it everywhere after 1881.

48. Corse, Creuse, Deux-Sèvres, Haute-Loire, and Pyrénées-Orientales—consistent laggards on all measures—as well as Ariège and Drôme, both below the national mean. For the ranking of these departments, see chapter 3.

49. Patterns of high or low enrollments of girls, which correlated closely with boys enrollments, did so only faintly (and then negatively, if at all) with the percentage of school-age girls in Catholic schools.

50. *Statistique de l'enseignement*, II:cl; Archives Nationales, F17/9351 (1863) for Catholic schools. More regular attendance by girls apparently obtained in the eighteenth century as well, Perrel, "Les filles à l'école," 298; J. Queniart, *Culture et société urbaine dans la France au 18ème siècle* (Lille, 1977), I:200; Chartier, Compère, and Julia, *L'éducation en France*, 280–81. Girls also attended more regularly during the summer months, so that summer attendance had a positive correlation with the percentage of girls in a department's total enrollment both early and late in the century: $r = .28$ (1837), .1 (1850), .09 (1876), .23 (1881), .42 (1886), .39 (1891), .41 (1896), .35 (1901).

51. Strumingher, *Boys and Girls*, 8; Robert Gildea, *Education in Provincial France, 1800–1914* (Oxford, 1983), 102; Chartier, Compère, and Julia, *L'éducation en France*, 237; Desert, "Alphabétisation et scolarisation," 146–48; Ministre de l'instruction, *Rapports* (1878–79), I:500; Archives Nationales, F17/9279.

52. The inferiority of girls schools is mentioned in Ministre de l'instruction, *Rapports* (1878–79), I:500; II: 328, 423, 540. In 1869, a report from Creuse said that arithmetic was more poorly taught in girls schools; one from Seine-Inférieure cited both writing and arithmetic; the inspector for the Academy of Douai thought the tendency to overdo memorization was especially strong in girls schools, Archives Nationales, F17/9376.

53. The quotation is from the Academy of Caen; reports from Landes said girls schools were like boys schools and from Allier, Cantal, Corse, Eure, Manche, etc., simply made no distinction, ibid. Additional reports for the 1860s in Archives Nationales, F17/10408, give a similar impression.

54. M. Fleury and P. Valmary, "Les progès de l'instruction élémentaire de Louis XIV à Napoléon III d'après l'enquête de L. Maggiolo (1877–79)," *Population* (1957): 89; Furet and Ozouf, *Lire et écrire*, 13–44. These figures are consonant with those cited by Robert Anderson, *Education in France, 1848–1970* (Oxford, 1975), 159, which would have 54 percent of French women literate in 1854, 66 percent in 1865, 72 percent by 1880, with steady (slightly declining) increases throughout the period.

55. Desert, "Alphabétisation et scolarisation," 147–58.

56. The idea that the proportion of school-age enrollment predicts the proportion of that age cohort who were literate assumes that the percentage of school-age girls enrolled is the same as the percentage that attended school at all (i.e., that this percentage attended for seven years, when in fact a figure of 60 percent, for example, might mean that all school-age girls attended for four years). The proportion of each cohort married in 1876 is taken from the estimates in Etienne van de Walle, *The Female Population in France* (Princeton, 1974), 126–27, dividing figures in table 5.4 by those in table 5.3. The estimates of enrollments are loose interpolations (based on

enrollment figures for the available data points) for the twelve years during which the members of each five-year cohort were between the ages of six and thirteen and might therefore be expected to have been in school. The estimate of the percentage of brides who should have been literate was arrived at as follows:

	Age Cohort				
	15–19	20–24	25–29	30–34	35–39
a) Percentage of married women in 1876	6.3	37.8	61.4	71.1	75.2
b) Percentage of this cohort married five years earlier		5.6	35.2	59.8	73.1
c) Percentage first married 1871–76 (a–c)	6.3	32.2	26.2	11.3	2.1
d) Percentage of age cohort enrolled in school	97	90	82	73	57
Percentage of brides likely to be literate (d × c)	6.1	29	21.5	8.2	1.2

Total percentage of brides likely to be literate = 66.
Maggiolo's figure was also 66 percent.

57. This heuristic game contains many undoubtedly inaccurate assumptions—for example, that the enrollment rate at one time equals the percentage of girls who ever attended school or that enrollment should equal literacy—and the calculations require some broad groupings and crude interpolations. First, the mean enrollment of each cohort when it was of school age is calculated. Women over fifty-five, actually an age group of those fifty-five to ninety-nine, would have been of school age during the years from 1792 (when those now ninety-nine years old had been six) to 1821 (when those now fifty-five were thirteen); we estimated girls mean enrollments in that period at a high 33 percent. Figures for younger cohorts are more reliable. Then the number of women within each cohort in 1876 is multiplied by the percentage of them who were enrolled in school to arrive at the number of them that should be literate. The figures are then added as in the table below:

Age Group	Percentage Enrolled when of School Age	As a Proportion of Women Living in 1876
Over 55	33	1,006,665
45–54	48	1,030,080
40–44	58	698,548
30–39	69	1,848,648
25–29	83	1,171,047
20–24	92	1,342,740
Women over 19 expected to be literate:		7,097,728

That is, 59 percent of living women over that age.

The population distribution is taken from Van de Walle, *Female Population*, 126. The census of 1872 (when there were some 206,300 fewer women over nineteen in France) put the percentage of adult women who were literate at 59. The linear regression model constructed by James B. Whitney, our statistical adviser, provides "bounds" of 2 to 3 percentage points for all of these age groups. For each group, the percentages listed above fall within those bounds.

58. Girls enrollment equalled or exceeded that of boys in some other countries as well; in Canada, for example, by 1870, Patrick J. Harrigan, "The Schooling of Boys and Girls in Canada," *Journal of Social History* 23 (July, 1990): 803–16.

59. Clark, *Schooling the Daughters*, chapter 2, notes that the difference in girls schooling was less a difference of values than expectations.

CHAPTER 6

Instituteurs and *Institutrices*

The elementary school teacher holds a prominent place in the political and social history of nineteenth-century France. From the time of the July Monarchy to the end of the century, thousands of people—members of town councils, newspaper writers, religious leaders, and politicians—worried about what kind of people would make up the growing cadre of public school teachers. Historians since have ratified this concern by using government policy toward teachers as a marker of the political climate—the conservatism of the 1850s indicated by official favoritism toward teachers in religious orders, the Liberal Empire reflected in the expansion and professionalization of teaching under Duruy, and the republican triumph signified by a corps of teachers who are said to have indoctrinated their students with patriotism, liberalism, and faith in progress. As for the spread of schooling, few doubt that the establishment of universal instruction was one of modern history's major social changes. And discussions of its political and social impact have understandably tended to focus on the special character and public role of the French *instituteur*. Celebrated in song, poetry, fiction, journalism, and political speeches, he and later she are still warmly recalled as a kind of cultural army that served the Republic much as the Jesuits had served the Catholic church. The activities of *instituteurs* and the values they held are thus important and fascinating subjects already much written about.[1] Our quantitative analysis of French primary schooling in the nineteenth century can add little to that, but it can say something about the process by which such a remarkable corps came to be.

I

Primary school teaching in France was marked, from early in the nineteenth century, by attributes of professionalism that became more formal with the passage of time. We cannot know, of course, how many men and women taught groups of children in unofficial or clandestine classes, but we can be sure that their numbers shrank and that the official statistics therefore increasingly reflect the national experience of what a teacher was. Some 29,333 men not in religious orders taught in French public schools in 1837. Nearly all of them were known as *instituteurs*,[2] a title whose Napoleonic ring had been meant to indicate a special cadre. By 1906, 56,151 men taught in public schools. Their number had not quite doubled in seventy years and the number of these who were *titulaires*—the established teachers who exemplified the *instituteur*—increased by only one-fourth to 36,165. This growth occurred within an essentially stable national population, which means that the numbers also describe an increased prominence of teaching as an occupation. Furthermore, the *instituteurs* of 1837 constituted nearly half of all the people (men and women, lay and religious) then teaching in public and private primary schools (table T.1). They set the tone for an occupation that would become increasingly visible and well defined during the course of the century.

Thus, the proportion of teachers who were *instituteurs* is an indicator of what teachers (and schools) were expected to be. That proportion varied across departments, but departmental preferences were notably stable despite all the other changes during the century.[3] Throughout the century, the percentage of teachers who were male, lay, public school teachers correlated significantly with three factors: early enrollment (a positive correlation which predicted the continued prominence of *instituteurs*), the strength of Catholic schools (a negative correlation), and the proportion of the population that was urban (a negative correlation; there, other ranks and kinds of teachers were more common). The *instituteur's* cultural prominence in the villages of France had a numerical base, and the lines of conflict among competing conceptions of what a teacher should be were established early on. Increased enrollment, the expansion of Catholic schooling, and subsequent secularization altered only slightly the place of the *instituteur* among primary school teachers.[4]

The beginning was modest enough. By later standards, many of these men were hardly qualified to teach; most depended upon at least one other job in order to earn enough to live on, and many of those jobs hardly added to the prestige of teaching (in Hérault in 1833 one *instituteur* in ten also served as barber).[5] The supplementary positions that *instituteurs* most commonly filled (over the next forty years) were as secretary to the town council and as assistant to the parish priest. Even by 1863, about half of all *instituteurs* held one of these positions and about half the other (these halves overlapped, for many held both posts). By the Third Republic, few *instituteurs* would accept such subordination to the clergy (in 1882, they were forbidden to serve as cantors), and many began to find additional service of any kind undignified and unsuitable. Still, these positions may tell us something of how the *instituteur* had been introduced into village life. A *clerc-laïc* had canonical standards to meet and was often bell ringer, cantor, and beadle to the parish, making him almost wholly dependent upon the priest's favor. Nearly all *instituteurs* were at least nominally Catholic (pious behavior being a common requirement), and their connection to the church gave legitimacy to the demands they made of families and pupils. Similarly, the council's secretary knew many village secrets and observed local politics from their center. In the northeastern part of France, which had been the first to achieve high primary school enrollments, the majority of *instituteurs* held both jobs. Elsewhere, by late in the Second Empire, the political connection was far more common than the clerical one. By then, the state acknowledged that it had a stake in seeing that teachers lived with "dignity."[6] Part of that dignity came from the *instituteur's* integration into village life, so that he was likely to prefer the practical subjects his pupils would put to immediate use and to take pleasure in having tastes his neighbors shared. Still, pride in his garden and his influence on local affairs did not lessen the *instituteur's* belief that as a professional person he should have a better salary and greater autonomy.[7]

In 1837, two-thirds of those teaching in primary schools of all types were men, but by 1863, more than half (54 percent) of France's primary teachers were *institutrices*, a figure that rose (after a slight dip) to 56–57 percent at the end of the century. The increasing place for women within the teaching corps was one of the important trends of the period. The fact that teaching became a predominantly secular occupation was a separate and subsequent development once the position of women teachers was established. Until the Third Republic, two-thirds of the women teaching in public and private schools were nuns (who in 1863 constituted more than one-third of all elementary teachers in France [tables T.2 and T.3]). Religious orders had long provided women their major access to a "profession," and the prominence of teachers in religious habit undoubtedly helped to set cultural expectations of what teachers and especially female teachers should be like.[8] In this and other respects, the situation of lay women teachers was fundamentally different from that of their male colleagues. Not until 1872 were more women teaching in public primary schools than in independent ones; only in 1891 did the number of lay women teachers in all schools exceed (slightly) the number of religious ones; and only in 1901 were lay, women public school teachers half of all the women teaching in primary school in France.

Lay women teachers had some basis on which to build a sense of professionalism. As early as 1863, one-third of them were graduates of an *école normale*, five out of six served as *titulaires* (in contrast to nuns, who rarely worked singly and more of whom were *adjointes* than *institutrices*), and four-fifths of the lay women who taught in public schools were (like nuns) unmarried.[9] Although the Falloux Law exempted members of religious orders from the requirement for the *brevet*, women nevertheless continued to present themselves for that certification. But it was primarily lay women who did so, even during the 1860s when two-thirds of the women teachers were nuns and lay women accounted for only about one-fifth of France's elementary school teachers.[10]

These public school teachers, male and female, lay and religious, were seen by the government as agents of the nation. Information gathered during the Second Empire by the ministry in Paris indicated that in 1863 of all the men and women teaching in the public elementary schools of France, only 72 taught in patois although another 3,438 used both patois and French. One of the teaching corps' central functions is captured in the simple notation that 65,338 instructors taught exclusively in French.[11]

For all their importance, they were not well paid. The state set the minimum salary (a mere 200 francs in 1833), slowly increasing it over the years and establishing somewhat higher scales for those with experience and more demanding certification. Actual income was a bit better, however. Much of it came from tuition fees (providing a strong incentive for teachers to resist any expansion of the commune's list of poor children exempt from paying). Some communes chose to pay more than the minimum, and teachers could often expect other modest gifts and benefits in addition to the possibility of one or more additional jobs. By 1846–47, three-quarters of rural teachers averaged 500–550 francs in direct payment, and a few received more. By 1863, most salaries were 800–900 francs. Those in towns did better, between 900 and 1,200 francs in 1847, a figure that slowly rose thereafter.[12]

II

The *instituteur* had a direct connection to the French state (even before the national government replaced the communes as paymaster in 1889), and the special status acquired by the teaching corps in France was sustained by a remarkable array of institutional support. National laws and ministerial policies identified teachers as a distinctive group; departmental councils, prefects, and inspectors had a major role in the selection, training, and promotion of teachers; and communal councils worked closely with them in a variety of ways and provided most of their salary until late in the century. Thus, the appointment of an *instituteur* often generated local political conflict, even early in the century.[13]

The institution that was intended to prepare the nation's teachers and mark them as a special corps was the *école normale*. Despite hesitance about its cost and the competing pedagogies of mutual instruction and religious orders, the departmental normal school for boys caught on rather quickly. There were fourteen of them by 1830 and thirty-six before the Guizot Law required each department to maintain one on its own or in cooperation with a neighbor. Some sixty-five of the normal schools established by 1837 lasted throughout the century, and thirteen more had been added by 1875.[14] There were eighty-five boys normal schools by 1886. In their last year at the *école*, students did some practice teaching, but these schools initially concentrated on the elementary subjects their graduates were destined to teach, adding some surveying, drawing, music, French history, and geography to the curricular core of reading, writing, and weights and measures. If the July Monarchy and the Third Republic placed great confidence in the normal schools, the Second Empire at first viewed them with considerable suspicion; yet despite changes in style and content, they continued—apparently essential to public schooling and beneficiaries of the inertial energy that marks established institutions.

From 1837 to 1863, the annual number of graduates from the boys normal schools was quite steady, growing from 860 to 875 a year—a total of some 23,400 graduates. About 70 percent of that number were in fact active teachers in 1863, evidence of the effectiveness of these schools. By then, almost one-half of France's *instituteurs* were graduates of a normal school (twenty years earlier, nearly one-quarter of them were normal school graduates).[15] The number of students in normal school then began a steady rise in the 1860s, with 1,100 and then 1,300 graduating each year, a figure that peaked at 1,700 in 1885–87; more than 28,000 young men graduated between 1863 and 1886 (table T.5). Thus, for fifty years, the boys normal schools annually sent forth a number of new teachers equal to about 3 percent of the men teaching in French primary schools (that percentage was highest in 1837 at 3.7 and 1886 at 3.4). This steady production was never enough to provide all the teachers an expanding system required, especially given a significant turnover rate, which was particularly high in some departments. Teachers had to be trained by additional means, but normal school training remained the model. Considered something of an elite, the *normaliens* could expect to receive the better posts. After 1887, the number of them graduating each year began to decline, a trend that continued through the 1890s (staying at 1,270–1,370 a year) until it rose again in 1903 (reaching 1,583 in 1906). In effect, the *écoles normales* had enlarged as the teaching corps was expanding and then contracted somewhat from the mid-1880s onward. As fewer new teaching positions (especially for *titulaires*) were created, the annual number of *normaliens* graduated declined and then leveled off.[16]

These schools, intended to place a special stamp on the *instituteur*, were one of the system's distinctive achievements and one that required a remarkable effort. Often located in small towns, they had their own facilities and their own staff. Most of the schools remained quite small (the majority had between one hundred and three hundred students in 1876), and they were relatively expensive to operate. Even in 1837, about 90 percent of the young men in normal schools were provided with scholarships, a proportion that was sustained and even rose slightly in the course of the century. All together, these schools had more than five hundred teachers in 1837 (professors and *adjoints*) and more than twice that number in the 1880s (including directors, professors, and part-time teachers ranked in five categories), when they were at their largest. Thus, as a national average, there were usually only four or five students for every teacher.[17] The cost per student, calculated at six hundred francs in 1837, slowly rose through the Second Empire and leaped to twice that much early in the Third Republic—consistently more than the amount set by law as the minimum pay for an *instituteur*![18] The global sums were equally impressive: over one million francs in 1837, twice that by 1863, over three million francs by 1876, and climbing to more than nine million by 1887 before leveling off at a figure just below that. About three-quarters of this cost was paid from departmental taxes with communes adding more than the state until 1889, when a reallocation placed the burden on the national government for everything but the maintenance of the normal school's facilities.[19]

Normal schools became increasingly serious institutions in the Third Republic, and the state's heightened involvement brought greater prestige as well as regulations. Attentive ministers, inspectors, and rectors stressed the schools' place in a national scheme, while directors were encouraged to add special activities and guest lectures to a curriculum that now sought to build a deeper and broader foundation in the liberal arts while constantly emphasizing the teacher's special sense of calling. Impressive institutions famed for their almost penal discipline and the heavy demands they made on their uniformed students, the normal schools sought to build an esprit as solid as their somber buildings. Like the model primary school usually attached to them, the normal schools exerted an influence that reached beyond their own students.[20] As their ambitions grew, their attrition rates generally declined (that rate was probably about 10 percent in the 1880s), and the accomplishments of their graduates rose. Through the 1870s, as many as one-third of the students in their final year did not receive the *brevet* on graduation (although most of these took the examination soon after), but that was true of less than 3 percent five years later.[21] By the 1890s, two-thirds received the *brevet supérieur*, a proportion that steadily increased as this higher goal became the purpose of normal school (table T.4). In fact, the expected standard came to be for students to have the elementary *brevet* upon admission (having prepared for it in special courses or *écoles primaires supérieures*) and to receive the *brevet supérieur* at the end of the second year of normal school, preparatory to a final year largely devoted to practice teaching.

In this expanding, stable system, the contrasting development of women teachers stands out all the more sharply. By 1837, only two departments (Marne and Aveyron) had 85 percent of the number of lay *institutrices* in public schools that they would have at the end of the century. And that level of fulfillment (of ultimate needs) was not met in other departments until the Third Republic and by only fifteen departments in all by 1886. At first, far more lay women served as *institutrices* in independent schools than in public ones (their numbers reached parity in the 1860s). By the time that the lay, public school *institutrice* was becoming a well-established figure, her position was overshadowed by development in another direction. In the period of greatest increase in the number of women teachers, during the Second Empire, religious orders provided more than half the number of new teachers that girls schools required. Thus, with the switch to secular schools in the 1880s, there was a sudden demand for lay women teachers, and it strained the educational system as well as politics. Yet, within ten years, four-fifths of France's departments had hired 85 percent of the *institutrices* they would eventually need.

For most of the century, women's normal schools had been much less prominent than men's normal schools. Even by 1877 only about 200 girls graduated from normal schools each year. Ten years later, that figure rose to nearly 1,000; and it increased to more than 1,200 in the 1890s and more than 1,600 in 1906. In 1901, for the first time, more women than men graduated from normal school, but society had been slow to provide such schools for women. There were only ten in 1850, seven of them run by nuns. Of the seventeen normal schools for girls in 1875, eight were founded after 1872.[22] By 1881–82 there were forty-one, with eighty-one five years later, and eighty-seven by 1890. Only then, in the 1890s, does there begin to be a high correlation among the departments of France between the number of men and the number of women graduating from normal school.

The girls normal schools were less expensive to run than those for boys (about three-quarters as much per student in 1876). The student-teacher ratio was somewhat less favorable (usually about six to one), and their professors, like women teachers at every rank, were paid less than their male counterparts. During the Second Empire, just over 70 percent of the girls in normal school received scholarships, a proportion that reached 85 percent by 1876. Interestingly, a higher proportion of these scholarships were provided by the communes in girls than in boys normal schools, a sign of local interest in the preparation of *institutrices*. Once established, the *écoles normales* for women achieved attrition rates that were often somewhat lower than at boys schools, and by the 1890s the proportion of women graduates who received the *brevet supérieur* was slightly higher than among male graduates.

By then, the normal schools for girls, with a faculty of more than eight hundred instructors, were producing almost as many new teachers as those for boys and within a few years were graduating somewhat more. While the ratio of normal school graduates to lay teachers increased only slightly for men, it leaped for women from less than 2 percent the number of lay *titulaires* to 5 percent in the period from 1891 to 1906, more than enough to fill the newly created positions.[23] Thus, within the lay system, the rate at which *écoles normales* were producing new *institutrices* (the number of women graduates as a proportion of women lay teachers) increased from about two-thirds the rate for men in 1863 to an equal rate by 1886–87 and to one higher for women than for men thereafter. And, although the variation among departments was always greater for women than for men (and for *écoles normales* generally than for other aspects of the system), the trend toward greater national uniformity was unmistakable.

That represents an extraordinary effort on the part of politicians passing new laws, departments raising new funds, and hundreds of young women who were attracted by the brightening prospects for a career as lay schoolmistress. These efforts made it possible to target Catholic sisters for replacement by lay *institutrices*, and, beginning in 1891, there is some correlation between the proportion of Catholic enrollment in a department and the size of the classes graduating from its girls normal school.[24] Although never fully achieving it in the nineteenth century, France was headed toward a self-sustaining system in which *écoles normales* would produce the teachers needed by secular public schools, and the system's solidity was further assured by the creation of two *écoles normales supérieures* to train the women (in 1880) and men (in 1882) who would become professors in the teachers schools (and in the *écoles primaires supérieures*).

The students in these schools were in large part the sons and daughters of peasants and artisans (groups that also supplied most of the parish clergy and religious orders), for whom a career as teacher offered attractive social mobility and security, and the children of teachers (whose presence must have reinforced a sense of corporate distinctiveness).[25] Such students could be so numerous because access to normal school was not primarily a matter of money (cost of clothing was for most students their primary expense). The government, concerned that these schools create a loyal cadre of teachers, also made sure that its investment was not wasted: Graduates were expected to accept the position offered them (as stated in a decree of 1835–36) and men were exempt from military service if they taught in public schools for ten years.[26] The normal schools provided the most prestigious avenue to a teaching career and helped to establish elementary teaching as a distinct profession. Yet, entrance requirements and curriculum established normal schools as markedly below a *college* or *lycée*, a status reinforced by their recruitment from lower social strata. They retained something of the atmosphere of the cloister, and until the Third Republic, religious duties were stressed in boys as well as girls schools. By then, social origins and training, as well as republican ideology, set the stage for their competition with clerical teachers.

Girls normal schools could not produce enough graduates to replace all the Catholic sisters teaching in public schools, but girls could prepare for the *brevet* in other ways. As they did so, their hopes for a teaching career largely depended upon, and must have been added pressure for, a sizable reduction in the dependence on nuns to teach girls. Among the alternative paths to the *brevet*, the *cours normaux*, two-year programs usually attached to independent schools, were especially important for women. With little basis in statute, they rested on local efforts to meet local needs—and they appear rather sketchily in the official *Statistique*.[27] There were thirty-two of these *cours* in 1850 (with 543 students), some sixty in 1863 (teaching 188 boys and 812 girls), and seventy by 1876. Of these, there were eight *cours normaux* for boys (with 278 students), five of which were Protestant schools (three had been established in the 1840s, one in 1858, and one in 1872).[28] Of the sixty-two girls *cours normaux*, twenty-two were taught by lay instructors (but six of those were Protestant) and forty by nuns. Thus, early in the Third Republic, teachers training for women relied heavily on these schools. In the 1870s, with 1,385 girls enrolled, these two-year programs could graduate more than three times as many new teachers each year as the girls normal schools. Over half the boys in these schools received scholarships (most offered by departments) but only one girl in six in *cours normaux* had a scholarship (most of which were paid for by the state). With costs per student often less than half those of the *écoles normales*, these programs were obviously economical. For the educational reformers of the Third Republic, however, they must have seemed at best a stopgap and at worst a threat, with their heavily clerical and independent taint. By the 1880s, they disappear from the *Statistique*—giving way, like the employment of religious in public schools, before policies that favored the secularization of a national public school system directed by the state.

III

The official guarantee that teachers were qualified, whatever their training, rested on the *brevet de capacité*. The need to examine prospective teachers had been recognized in laws of 1792 and 1808, and a law of 1816 (applied to women in 1820) provided for the award of the *brevet* in three degrees by an inspector or some other *fonctionnaire*, but the formal standards were minimal, most teachers settled for the lowest of the three degrees, and the required certificate of good conduct from priest and mayor may often have been more demanding. An additional certificate of religious instruction became mandatory in 1828 and was dropped in 1831. Under the July Monarchy (1833–34 for men, 1836 for women), the procedures for examination were made more formal. The standards for the *brevet* then began to rise and became more uniform, changes demanded by further regulations in the 1860s and the policies of the Third Republic. Most departments started regular examinations for men in 1833 and for women in 1836, with all but a score of departments doing so in the next few years. The number that did not then steadily diminished, and from 1855 on all departments awarded *brevets* every year. "The profession of *instituteur de la jeunesse*," the law of 1833 declared, "is in certain respects an industry and on that score should be completely free; but, like the profession of medicine or law, it is not just an industry, it is a delicate function from which it is necessary to require some guarantees."[29] Although the *brevet* would seem to have been less essential in the Second Empire, the pride in professional standards remained. The Falloux Law allowed a number of substitutions for the *brevet*, including three years of experience or a letter of obedience from a religious order (which had been sufficient in the Restoration, too, from 1822 to 1831), but the *brevet* continued to be issued, and those examined in subjects not required made sure that their extra effort was recorded. Further gradations were added to the *brevet* in the 1880s.

Between 1837 and 1876, the number of men teaching (lay and religious) increased by nearly twelve thousand while more than eighty thousand men received the *brevet* (tables T.1 and T.4). About half the men receiving the *brevet* in 1837 were graduates of a normal school, but the relationship between normal school enrollment and *brevets* awarded in the same year declined to insignificance as the *brevet* became more popular. There was some connection, nevertheless. The number of departments' normal school graduates in 1837 correlates positively with the number of *brevets* awarded through 1896; the environment that favored the *brevet* toward the end of the century was likely to be one that had encouraged normal schools sixty years earlier. Raw numbers are an important reminder of two other points: The number of men who earned the *brevet* in a single department in any year was always small enough to stand as an individual achievement, and departments maintained a remarkably steady output of potential new teachers. Counting all the departments in each year from 1837 to 1906, in less than 7 percent of the cases—on only seventy-nine occasions—did a department award fewer than five *brevets*, and on only seventy occasions (more than half of them in 1882) did a department award more than twenty.

Although the number of *brevets* awarded in individual departments often fluctuated sharply from year to year, some overall patterns emerge. For the period between 1837 and 1882, correlations among departments by the raw number of *brevets* granted are weak or insignificant. They are higher, however, between 1833 and all dates after 1882: Persistent local factors, reinforced by the early establishment of an educational system, influenced departmental interest in the *brevet*.[30] An exceptionally large number of *brevets* were awarded to men between 1881 and 1885, some forty-one thousand (half the total for the previous forty years). About 15 percent of these went to clerics who presumably had already been teaching and were now meeting the legal requirement that teachers have the *brevet*.[31] Many of the lay men who sought a *brevet* in these years may well have anticipated that the Ferry Laws and the laicization of public schools would bring bright prospects for a teaching career.[32] If so, most must have been disappointed, for only 5,700 new public school posts for men were added between 1882 and 1886 (and only 1,600 of those were for *titulaires*).

Clearly, the number of *brevets* a department awarded was related to its capacity to increase the number of certified teachers and to replace established (and probably less qualified) teachers. As a general indicator of this capacity, we considered the number of *brevets élémentaires* granted to men as a percentage of male, lay teachers currently employed.[33] In the five-year period centered on 1837, more than one-quarter of France's departments awarded *brevets* at an annual rate between 4.4 and 6.4 percent of the number of lay men teaching, and only five departments awarded them at a rate of more than 10 percent. Given resignations and the growing number of openings for teachers in those years, most departments could probably have used more *instituteurs* than they officially qualified. In the 1840s, departments awarding *brevets* drew closer to the annual mean among them of just under 5 percent. By 1850, when there were more *instituteurs* and seventy departments issuing *brevets*, fifty of them issued *brevets* at a rate above 4 percent and more than a score of departments at a rate above 6 percent. Six percent was the mean rate for all departments in 1863, when France already had three-quarters of the number of male, lay teachers it would have at the end of the century (table T.12). The number of *brevets* had come to imply an improvement in qualifications and increased competition for posts as well as steady expansion.

The variation among departments in the number of *brevets* awarded (as a proportion either of lay, male teachers or of boys enrolled in school) was lowest in the 1860s and 1870s; and that, too, is suggestive. This may well have been the time when the number of *brevets* awarded was most closely related to the needs of the system as a whole. Before that, fewer young men were likely to receive *brevets* than were needed to teach; afterward, many more received the *brevet* than could be employed. During the boom of the early 1880s, the mean rate for the award of *brevets* equalled 17 percent of the men teaching (and only three departments issued *brevets* at a rate below 10 percent). The number of *brevets* granted to men declined sharply in 1886 both in absolute numbers (from over nine thousand to under three thousand) and as a proportion of men teaching. Yet, from 1886 to 1906, while the number of men teaching stayed about the same, the ratio of *brevets* award to men teaching hovered between 6 and 9 percent—higher than it had been when the school system was expanding. Nearly half the departments of France awarded *brevets* in this period at a rate that was probably well above the number of jobs available there or in adjacent departments (a dozen departments maintained a level above 10 percent, eleven more above 8 percent, nineteen more above 7 percent). Although it had become a mark of status or educational accomplishment, the *brevet* was no assurance of a job.

Characteristically, a department that in one period granted proportionally many (or few) *brevets* was likely to do so in other periods as well. Although the actual ratios fluctuated markedly across the century, correlations of departmental rankings (using five-year averages) are highly significant (.9 to .63) for a first period, 1837–63, and a later period, 1882–1906 (.8 to .54), marginal in the intervening period of transition. Although there was in these terms a broad national pattern in the number of *brevets* awarded to men, the variations in individual departments from year to year suggest that local needs and special circumstances remained critical. Many departments in the educationally advanced northeast produced a low ratio of newly certified teachers to the number currently teaching, perhaps because they already had so many. Some other departments, such as Basses-Alpes and Ille-et-Vilaine, stand out as consistently strong producers of teachers.[34]

The indication that the *brevet* was increasingly sought more as a certificate of study than with the expectation of actually teaching can be investigated somewhat by comparing the number of *brevets* awarded to men to the number of boys enrolled in school. Always low, that ratio rose from 1896 to 1906, when the number of openings for new teachers must have been shrinking (only increased resignations could help to compensate for the fact that the total number of men teaching in primary school, which had long stayed about the same, now declined slightly). By the end of the century, at least, the award of the *brevet* and the desire to have it were not closely tied to prospects for a teaching job. There may have been more connection earlier as schooling expanded, for a higher proportion of students received the *brevet* in the period from 1837 to the mid-1860s than in the next thirty years. It may also be true that those who attended school in the earlier period were more likely to be inclined toward teaching (just as they had been more assiduous in summer attendance). There was also some sign of persistent local traditions that encouraged men to seek the *brevet* and, presumably, a teaching position somewhere.[35] Thinking that the relative popularity of the *brevet* may reflect a local culture in which education was particularly admired or thought useful, we also considered the number of *brevets* in proportion to school-age population. That emphasis on the proportion of school-age boys who chose to seek the *brevet* and passed the examination produces a distinct order in which the departments of the northeast (or above the St. Malo–Geneva line) are prominently in the top quarter. For those departments, however, this interest in teaching could also be explained as a by-product of having had so many boys in school for so long; for some boys, familiarity with teachers may have bred imitation.

There are high correlations among these three measures despite differences in the rankings of individual departments. To normalize the number of *brevets* by the number of teachers or the number of students is to emphasize those in the school system (and the two rankings correlate strongly at the same date, especially in the later years). When *brevets* are normalized by school-age population, the whole society is included. These similar patterns indicate some continuity across the century, suggesting the possibility that older traditions, which favored teaching as an occupation, remained influential in the Third Republic, notably in Hérault, Lozère, Hautes-Pyrénées, and Basses-Alpes. They also show a greater interest in the *brevet* in urban departments and, in the later years, in some of those departments that had lagged in schooling and were now catching up.[36] They also mark four distinct periods: from 1837 to 1850 or 1863, from 1863 to 1876, and from 1886 to 1906, with 1882 an aberrant moment.

The *brevet* always had a somewhat different significance for women than for men. Departments were somewhat slower to establish the practice of systematically assessing the qualifications of young girls who might wish to teach. Only about one-third did so in 1836–37, but the number soon rose to two-thirds, and by the mid-1840s about three-quarters of the departments awarded *brevets* to women. Only five did not do so in 1851; from 1855 on, with rare exceptions, every department awarded some *brevets* to women each year.[37] In this respect, then, there was an institutional lag of perhaps a decade or more in the certification of women. The contemporary criticisms that questioned the wisdom of subjecting girls to these examinations came primarily from the advocates of Catholic schools, but the concerns these critics expressed, about emotional strain and threats to feminine modesty, do imply some general cultural resistance.

In the 1830s, the number of women receiving the *brevet* was less than one-third the number of men; by the 1840s, the proportion had risen to one-half, and it approached equality by the early 1850s. This path to parity was facilitated by a decline in the number of men receiving the *brevet* in this period,[38] but from 1864 on, the number of women awarded the *brevet* was larger than the number of men, becoming more than twice as great after 1873. Between 1873 and 1876, the number of *institutrices* had increased by more than thirty-eight thousand (almost three times the increase in *instituteurs*). By 1876, nearly eighty-seven thousand women had received the *brevet* (a number only about 8 percent higher than the figure for men), one-quarter of them in the last four years.[39] Although women were rumored to seek the *brevet* primarily as evidence of their additional schooling, in fact their chances of finding a teaching job had until the Third Republic been distinctly better than that of the young men who passed the tests for certification.

Because far fewer lay women than lay men were already teaching, the ratio of *brevets* awarded to the number of lay teachers was considerably higher for women from 1850 on. That ratio rose to be two or three times higher by the end of the century, before becoming about the same for both sexes in 1906. The distinction of having the *brevet* (and the prospect of becoming a teacher) had come to hold a more prominent place in the aspirations of girls. Indeed, the *brevet* became a mark of an educated woman in the middle class. It was fashionable in Paris and a source of pride for parents in small towns, whose newspapers published the names of successful aspirants.[40] The proportion of students who received the *brevet* was always small. A rough estimate of the number of students in their last year of primary school suggests that less than 1 percent of the boys would receive the *brevet* throughout most of the century. That proportion had been similar for girls but rose in the Third Republic to 2 and then 3 percent (table T.11). Before 1876, there was only a slight correlation among departments in the proportion of *brevets* awarded to men and to women, but that correlation became a strong one in the Third Republic, despite the greater number of women taking the examinations. Departments had developed consistent patterns and traditions regarding the *brevet* that lasted a generation and, by the Third Republic, affected girls and boys alike. Thus, the proportion of students earning the *brevet* in a department at one date tended statistically to predict the proportion who would do so in the next few decades.[41] Among girls, even during the Third Republic, the proportion seeking the *brevet* was often high in departments where Catholic girls schools had been strong. Perhaps the nuns had left an impression of teaching as a calling especially suited to women or perhaps the rapid secularization of schools in these departments had established lasting confidence in the opportunities for lay teachers. Apparently, some departments had also long served as regional centers, certifying more teachers than they could employ while adjacent departments awarded relatively few *brevets*, and some that granted a relatively high number of *brevets*—like the Seine, Bouches-du-Rhône, or the Territory of Belfort—seem to have attracted candidates of both sexes from other departments and to have trained them for the teacher's examination.

Did some departments consistently pass a larger or smaller percentage of their candidates for the *brevet*? Local examiners undoubtedly varied in the standards they set, and comments pointing to the written essay as the most frequent source of failure are a reminder that the *brevet élémentaire* was not a terribly demanding test. Concern for national norms is reflected in the fact that the *Statistique* carefully recorded each department's success rate from 1882 on. These data do show some correlation among departments over time, but no department stands out as consistently high or low. The larger pattern is one of great variation from year to year, and the signs of consistent local tendencies are weak. In 1882, over half the departments passed between one-third and one-half their candidates (nineteen departments passed fewer, eleven more, but only two passed less than one-fifth and only one more than two-thirds of those who took the examination). By 1906, a quarter of the departments passed between 50 and 60 percent of their candidates (and only seven departments less than one-third)—the success rate had gone up a notch but standards probably had as well. Still, throughout that period more than half the candidates failed, an experience stringent enough to accord some social significance to possession of that certificate. Furthermore, among all candidates a somewhat higher proportion of women than men passed the examination (table T.17).

By the 1880s, the more demanding test for the *brevet supérieur* had become the desired standard (and it came to be called the *brevet complet*), the professional examination for which candidates systematically prepared in special programs. Usually already holders of the *brevet élémentaire*[42] (which came to be called the *brevet simple*), candidates for this examination saw higher certification as a means of advancement. A rising standard reinforced the teachers' increasingly professional view of themselves (table T.6). From 1833 to 1847, between 9 and 14 percent of those receiving a *brevet* had earned this higher form, with the peak years being 1834-37 and 1841-42. Fewer than 200 a year were granted to men in most years before the Third Republic, double that in the 1870s; the number quadrupled again in the 1880s (to more than 1,600 a year), dropped somewhat in the 1890s (to around 1,200), but by 1906 was over 3,000—more than one-third of the *brevets* awarded to men. For women, receipt of the *brevet supérieur* rose even more impressively. More women than men received that higher certification from 1867 on, sometimes twice as many in the 1870s and 1890s (although the proportion of women receiving what was now called the *brevet simple* or *obligatoire* was higher still). In some departments, having women sit for this *brevet* must have seemed a direct challenge to the nuns. More than one-third of the departments awarded the *brevet supérieur* to women from the 1830s to the 1850s, two-thirds in the 1860s; but fifteen departments still did not in 1872, although eight more did the following year. Those that were late to offer the examination and that generally had very few candidates were on the whole the same departments that had been slower in previous years to offer the *brevet simple* to women.

In the national system of universal public education established by the Third Republic, the *brevet supérieur* had come to account for a larger fraction of all *brevets* awarded (nationally about one-quarter to one-third of the total from 1886 on) as a result of official and competitive pressure for higher standards.[43] It was the *brevet simple*, however, that had established the principle of state certification. Its statistical history is one measure of the acceptance of certification and an indicator of rising standards.

That history is a reminder, too, of what a complex and difficult task it was to construct such a system for it was a long time before the number of *brevets* awarded was sufficient to meet the system's needs. If one takes into account both the increase in the number of teachers and the need to replace a great many others, there were probably not enough properly certified men to fill all the available positions until the Second Empire, and there were certainly not enough newly certified women until the 1870s.[44] By the first years of the Third Republic, all male *titulaires* in public schools had the *brevet* as did nearly all lay *instituteurs* in independent schools, and that standard was spreading rapidly to their underlings, the *adjoints*. A vast majority of lay, female *titulaires* also held the *brevet*, and the fact that a much smaller proportion of clerical teachers had this certification was used to argue that reforms were needed. A law of 1881 declared that all *instituteurs* and *institutrices* must have the *brevet* by 1884. At a time when nearly 45 percent of the staff in girls independent schools were *adjoints* without the *brevet*, that was a significant requirement[45] (table T.7).

Normal schools and the establishment of more than one level of *brevet* did more than set a national standard. Such measures contributed to the professional identity of teachers by emphasizing the special formation they required and establishing an environment of competitive selection. The arrival of *instituteurs* armed with the *brevet* had, even in the 1830s and 1840s, helped push those already teaching to take summer courses (by 1843, one-fifth of those teaching had attended at least one summer session at a normal school). Older teachers were likely to feel some pressure to take examinations for a higher *brevet* in face of younger competition, and teachers everywhere had to be concerned to maintain the local ties that would secure their positions. In the early years when the *instituteur* had needed to undermine the competition from informal classes maintained by local figures, the regulations decreed by the state and the inspectors it sent out were the *instituteurs'* formidable ally. Inspectors were outspoken about the inadequacies of older teachers.[46] By 1877, when 21,666 men and 34,398 women took the examination for the *brevet*, standards were high enough that nearly two-thirds of the men and almost one-half the women failed. The failure rate then steadily declined to about half the candidates by 1891.[47] By then, some communes would hire only those who had the *brevet supérieur*. Certified teachers competed with each other for the more desirable posts, and not surprisingly, normal school graduates were more numerous in towns than in rural schools.

Thus, the famous competition between clerical and secular teachers was part of a broader competition, between normal school graduates and others, between those with the *brevet simple* or *brevet complet*, between *titulaires* and *adjoints*, and among all of them for the best positions. Conditioned by professional experience as well as local politics, France's teaching corps was in this sense prepared for the conflicts of national anticlerical campaigns. Already accustomed to the benefits of close association with the state, *instituteurs* lived in an ethos of competition that must in turn have enhanced their attractiveness for the politicians of the Third Republic. That competitive atmosphere had been established at the beginning of their careers. Entrance into both the two-year course for teachers in the *école primaire supérieure* and into the three-year program of normal schools was selective, and many who entered did not graduate. Although their pay was hardly grand and they often lived in isolation, French teachers could think of themselves as something of an elite who had succeeded in a career many desired. The basis was laid in experience and ideology, as even their expressions of disillusionment reveal, for a professional *esprit de corps*.

IV

In earlier chapters, we have shown how more schools and increased enrollments developed in a systemic way, building from local experience and incorporating the available resources of Catholic and independent schools. While becoming increasingly interrelated, this educational system was prodded, regulated, and shaped by state policies. Locally and nationally, public attention and conflict focused heavily on teachers. The need to provide a sufficient number of competent teachers in a relatively short time presented a difficult and complex challenge to French society. Decisions about how to do so were politically sensitive and institutionally taxing.

From 1837 to 1901, the total number of teachers in primary school increased two and one-half times, but this growth was not uniform. The number of male teachers increased by 69 percent, and the number of female teachers increased by 334 percent (table T.1J). While the number of lay men who served as *titulaires*—the title given to those independently in charge of class or school—increased (from 1850 to 1901) by only 12 percent in public schools and by less than 2 percent in all schools, the number of lay female *titulaires* in public schools increased by 630 percent and in all schools by 110 percent.[48] An institutional pattern was established early. In 1837, the mean number of teachers in the departments of France was seven hundred, enough to make the *instituteur* a familiar figure,[49] and 81 percent of all teachers were lay. That would change over the course of the century, primarily because the increased number of women teachers came largely from Catholic orders. As the need for more teachers (especially female teachers) slowed, the stage was set for a great battle over whether or not teachers should be members of religious orders. Growth of the teaching corps was also integrally related to three other long-term trends: the process of professionalization (in which standards became higher and more uniform and training more institutionalized [tables T.7 and T.6]), the secularization of schools, and the growing importance of women in the teaching corps.

Earlier, in discussing the establishment of primary schools, we introduced the concept of "fulfillment," the date at which a department had 85 percent of the number of schools it would have in 1901. Suppose we now take the date at which a department had 85 percent of the total number of teachers it would have in 1901 as a measure of the fulfillment of the need for teachers (remembering of course that teachers, unlike schools, resign and need to be replaced). Three patterns emerge. As one would expect, the two measures are often closely related: Over half the departments of France reached these two measures in the same year or within ten years of each other. More than one-quarter, however, achieved fulfillment in schools more than ten years (a few more than forty years) before reaching fulfillment in the number of teachers. These tended to be earlier leaders and/or urban departments, where classes grew large before more teachers were added. Just under one-quarter of the departments reached this measure of fulfillment in the number of teachers well before achieving it in the number of schools; these included both laggards and leaders but were most likely to be departments with both a strong proportion of Catholic schools (which more often used several teachers) and mountainous regions in which the needed number of small rural schools was more slowly reached. Even as the school system became more uniform, the ways in which it developed and the stress that accompanied growth varied with local circumstance (fig. 4).

Throughout the century, the standards of competence for teachers of every sort had also been rising. That applied in the first part of this period especially to men as newly certified young teachers in effect replaced the older and less qualified *instituteurs*. Unfortunately, we do not know, for the nation as a whole, the rate at which *instituteurs* resigned or were replaced. Some departments left a sizable fraction of their schools in the hands of teachers who were not granted the title of *titulaire*. A few of these had developed their school system very early, most were departments that had done so slowly and from a small base.[50] Scattered data make it clear, however, that despite great variations among departments and at different dates, there was a general and unsurprising pattern: Replacement rates were much higher in the 1830s and 1840s (apparently reaching over 20 percent in a single year in one department) but seem generally to have settled down by the 1860s to about 6 or 7 percent a year. Moreover, most normal school graduates did in fact become teachers and tended to continue teaching for some time.[51]

Add the fact that the total number of male teachers increased so little, and it seems clear that some cramping of opportunities was quickly built into the system. By 1837, five departments already had 85 percent of the total number of male teachers they would have in 1901 (generally the peak year). Twelve departments by that early date had 85 percent of the number of lay *instituteurs* in public schools that they would ever have, and that proportion was reached by one-quarter of France's departments by 1850 (table T.16). In such departments, generally those that already had the highest enrollments, the young man who had just won his *brevet* had to snatch whatever post was available. New openings were likely to be in either remote villages or established schools that already had one or more teachers and where the new *adjoint* would be subordinate to his older peers. Whereas the number of schools increased by 50 percent between 1837 and 1906, the number of teachers increased nearly 150 percent and the number of *adjoints* much more than the number of *titulaires*. When nearly all schools had but one teacher[52] and inspectors were few, the *instituteur* was the ruler of his classroom however subordinate to priest or mayor. As a teaching career became more proudly professional, it was also more subject to bureaucracy and hierarchy.[53]

Adjoint was always meant to be a kind of secondary rank, although it was applied to a number of different kinds of positions. In principle, *adjoints* were usually hired by the *titulaire*, but the term came to be used for teachers (also called *suppléants*) who were not granted full title to teach a school and who in consequence were given less secure tenure and lower pay. As of 1853, *titulaires* were expected to have had three years experience, which would normally be as *adjoints*. A much higher proportion of *adjoints* than of other teachers lacked the *brevet*, and that was true in every category, male and female, lay and Catholic. A department with a high proportion of *adjoints* was presumably putting more of its students in the hands of less qualified teachers. Not surprisingly, then, when departments are divided into octiles based on enrollment, the proportion of teachers who are *adjoints* is lowest among the top departments and rises steadily with each octile to be the highest among those departments with the lowest proportion of their children in school, the octiles that were also later in achieving full enrollment (table T.13). These octiles, which have proved to be good general measures of the development of schooling, in this case strongly suggest that it was the departments with less well-established school systems, departments still reaching out to part of their population, that made the most use of *adjoints*.

The octiles also reveal a second development, however: in each octile from 1863 to 1901 the proportion of *adjoints* increased (before dropping a tiny bit in 1906). As the educational system improved, it employed more *adjoints* but used them now to reduce class size by increasing the number of classes (table T.15). The additional teacher in a given school (and most of France's schools continued to have a single teacher) was usually considered an *adjoint*, distinct from the *stagaire*, the beginner on probationary appointment. The term came to mean a lower rank but not necessarily inferior preparation,[54] and it indicated an institutionalization that brought smaller classes and a hierarchy of rank among certified teachers based primarily on their experience.[55]

Despite this shift in the significance of the *adjoints*, there is notable stability among departments in the extent to which *adjoints* were employed. Correlations among departments over forty years according to the proportion of *adjoints* among their teachers are extremely high.[56] This stability reflects demographic continuity—dispersed populations required many small schools with a single class—but something else as well, the tendency of educational systems to institutionalize their early practice. Those accustomed to employing *adjoints* were more likely to hire more as they sought to reduce class size; where they had been less common, the tendency was rather to increase the number of *titulaires*.

Thus, Catholic schools, especially girls schools, made heavier use of *adjoints* than lay schools because religious communities provided an extra hand to help with classes, and many sisters had to be *adjoints* because they lacked the *brevet*, not having taken the required examination (and sometimes refusing to do so out of principled opposition to state interference as well as fear they might not pass). Even as the public school system was secularized, however, schools that had previously used *adjoints* continued to do so. The proportion of departmental enrollment in Catholic schools in 1850 predicts ($r = .52$) something of the proportional use of *adjoints* in secular schools in 1901.[57] Catholic schools, of course, were also strongest in urban departments, which would be expected to use *adjoints* most heavily, but not until 1891 does a department's current urban population outweigh its earlier history of Catholic schooling in predicting the use of *adjoints*.[58] In this as in so much else, the sense of what a school should be like and how it should be operated reflected its earlier history. Institutionalization of the past was part of the process of the growth of French primary schooling.

Within this larger pattern of stability, an important shift took place. In the period before the 1860s, student:teacher ratios were higher in the leading departments (those that had more schools in 1821 and higher enrollments in 1837). For those departments, that ratio began to decline as enrollment, having become essentially universal, stayed steady while more teachers were added. In the 1860s and 1870s student:teacher ratios were highest in departments that had experienced recent increases in enrollment. After that, these ratios tended to be lowest in those departments that had been early leaders and highest among the laggards[59] (table T.14). The student:teacher ratio had become another indicator of quality, likely to be lower in those same departments that led in other measures of quality such as libraries and the granting of *certificats d'études primaires*, the departments that had led in schooling and had high rates of literacy.[60] This change required the employment of more teachers nearly everywhere, which in turn reveals the divergent preferences as to whether these new teachers should be *adjoints* or *titulaires*, in part a matter of local custom and continuing concern for the formal measures of quality.

The primary school system was also remarkably stable in terms of classroom size, with the result that teachers probably shared a fairly uniform sense of what constituted an unusually large or small class in contrast to an average one. The mean number of students per teacher was forty-three in 1837 (rising to forty-five in 1840, the highest ever) and thirty-six in 1906 (having fallen to thirty-four in 1901, the lowest ever). The maximum mean for one department in 1840, however, was an appalling eighty-two students per teacher (a ministerial order of 1843 called for the hiring of an *adjoint* when there were more than sixty students). That maximum fell to sixty-two by 1863 and steadily declined to fifty-one by 1906; *adjoints* really were important in reducing the class size of urban schools. The minimum mean size for a single department, however, remained between twenty-one and thirty-one throughout the period; where the population was scattered and before the age of busing, there was a natural limit to how large classes could be (table T.8). The general trend toward smaller classroom size (a trend made possible by the availability of teachers) was part of the effort to improve the quality of schools, and after 1872, the departments with the fewest students per teacher tended to be the same ones that throughout the century led on most measures of educational development (and preferred to hire additional *titulaires* rather than *adjoints*).

A similar systemic stability is reflected in the relative prominence of male, lay, public school teachers, already discussed. For the departments of France in 1882, the proportion of all teachers (male and female, lay and clerical, public and private) who were lay, public *instituteurs* correlates strongly with a department's enrollment in 1832 combined with the percentage of its students in Catholic schools in 1850 and the percentage of its population in cities and towns in 1876 (these last two, of course, negative correlations).[61] The local system's earlier history remained important.

That institutional inertia characteristic of systemic development included, of course, the increasingly elaborate tables of pay in which teachers in cities generally did better than those in the country, *titulaires* better than *adjoints*, those with the *brevet complet* better than those with the *brevet simple* and both better than those without any *brevet* at all, those who had had refresher courses better than those who had not, and those with seniority better (in several steps) than those just beginning. They were indeed a corps, one with real incentives to seek the highest certification they could earn, to get along with the communal council, and to stay on the job. With the supplementary income available to them, by midcentury *instituteurs* even in rural communes had total revenues similar to those of skilled workers.[62] Thus, the widespread acknowledgment that teachers should receive higher pay implied recognition, however unsatisfactory, of their importance. As they read special journals;[63] met in local teachers conferences; were given a part in international expositions; subscribed to a mutual aid fund for teachers; joined alumni associations, *amicales*, or *unions pédagogiques*; and competed for medals of honor,[64] they could feel resonably secure of their professional status and its many institutional supports, whatever their economic, political, and personal problems. That was another reason to believe that their situation ought to be a good deal better than local conditions and low pay left it.

The tendency of this system was, like water seeking its level, to make primary schooling more equal and teachers more similar throughout France. It did that of course through growth and increasingly universal standards, but it did it in subtler and more complicated ways as well. We know how many male normal school graduates were teaching in 1863, and that data can tell us a great deal. Of the thirty departments that employed the largest number of *normaliens*, twenty-four were above the St. Malo–Geneva line and, except for the Seine, all the departments above that line were among the thirty-five with the most *normaliens* as teachers. Bas-Rhin, where 480 *instituteurs* were normal school graduates, had more teachers with such training than any other department; that early normal school in Strasbourg, the first in France, had made a difference.[65] But on the whole, normal school graduates were remarkably well distributed among the departments of France. There were twenty-five departments in which more than 250 *normaliens* were teaching (Bas Rhin and Meurthe, with 418, were the only ones with more than 400). Thirty-one departments had between 150 and 250, certainly enough to set a standard, and only thirteen departments had fewer than 100 (three of those, not surprisingly, were the ones recently annexed from Piedmont, three more were adjacent ones in the southeast, and three were in Catholic Brittany).[66] Most of these thirteen departments did not have their own normal schools before 1860,[67] and that, like the surprising presence of the Seine among the departments with the fewest *instituteurs* who were normal school graduates, is a reminder of how closely tied to their own departments these normal schools were (the Seine established its normal school in 1872, the school founded at Versailles by Louis-Philippe in 1831 having had a broader function).

The graduates of the boys *écoles normales* had never been sufficiently numerous to fill all the vacant posts in a department.[68] Thus, departments that led in enrollment and in the establishment of a school system as well as those that lagged in both had to employ teachers who had not been to normal school. The chronology of development therefore contributed to a more even distribution of *normaliens*. In the generation of the 1830s through 1850s, when many leading departments achieved universal enrollment, there were not many *normaliens* to fill their new positions. So those departments employed the best men available (and often sent them to summer courses). When one looks at the departments that in 1863 had the highest *percentage* of *instituteurs* who were normal school graduates, the departments that had been educational leaders are not prominent. Only four of them (Manche, where 81 percent of the *instituteurs* were *normaliens*; Orne, with 74 percent; Bas Rhin, 67 percent; and Eure-et-Loir, 64 percent) are among the twenty highest departments. Rather, *normaliens* were more likely to constitute two-thirds or more of the *instituteurs* in departments that had lagged in schooling or where Catholic teachers had once dominated and where the number of teachers had notably and recently increased.[69] And that helps to explain why there were only seven departments in which less than one-third of the *instituteurs* were *normaliens* but forty-nine departments where between 40 and 60 percent of the *instituteurs* were normal school graduates. Their training and the professional aura it carried quickly became a national standard. Something similar must have happened somewhat later to the girls who graduated from the rapidly expanding *écoles normales* of the Third Republic. Particularly large numbers of them would have found themselves employed in departments where there had been relatively few lay *institutrices* before but where the departing nuns were now being rapidly replaced.[70]

There may have been some statistical basis, then, for the familiar tales of dedicated *instituteurs* and *institutrices* formed in the isolation of the *écoles normales* who subsequently found themselves to be pioneers battling on the frontiers of ignorance in some distant village. Such tales would reflect, however, not just the condition of the countryside but the effective operation of an established system—one that trained teachers to have a particular sense of self, injected them into village life, defined and supported them with a variety of institutional arrangements, and distributed them throughout the nation.

Notes

1. Among recent treatments are Jacques Ozouf, *Nous les maîtres d'écoles: Autobiographies d'instituteurs de la belle époque* (Paris, 1967); Barnett Singer, "The Teacher as Notable in Brittany, 1880–1914," *French Historical Studies* 9 (1976): 635–59; the section "Teachers and Administrators" in *The Making of Frenchmen: Current Directions in the History of Education in France, 1679–1979*, ed. Donald N. Baker and Patrick J. Harrigan (Waterloo, Can., 1980), 443–520; Francine Muel-Dreyfus, *Le métier d'éducateur* (Paris, 1983); Philippe Lejeune, "Les instituteurs du XIXème siècle racontent leur vie," *Histoire de l'éducation* 25 (January, 1985): 53–82; Fabienne Reboul-Scherrer, *La vie quotidienne des premiers instituteurs, 1833-1882* (Paris, 1989); and Jo Burr Margadant, *Madame le Professeur: Women Educators in the Third Republic* (Princeton, 1990).

2. The figures for this early period are not entirely clear (nor exact); perhaps as many as two thousand of these teachers may have been *adjoints*, assistants in larger schools, and those of this group who were not in charge of a class were probably not

considered *instituteurs*. The compilers of the *Statistique* note that "le nombre total des maîtres est un de ceux dont l'exactitude laisse le plus à désirer . . ." and thus simultaneously warn the reader and explain how there could have been so large a number of *instituteurs* even before the Third Republic, Ministère de l'instruction publique et des beaux-arts, *Statistique de l'enseignement primaire*, vol. II (Paris, 1880), lxxx. There clearly was confusion as to what school employees to count as teachers, ibid., lxxxi–lxxxii, cxiii.

3. The Pearson correlation of departments according to the percentage of all teachers who were public school *instituteurs* in 1837 and in 1906 is .7 and slightly above that at all data points in between. The data points from 1863 to 1896 yield correlations from .96 to .88 with the percentage in 1837.

4. Enrollment in 1832, Catholic enrollment in 1850, and urban population in 1876, taken in combination, correlate at a consistently high level with the proportion of male, lay public school teachers: in 1840, $R^2 = .68$; in 1882, $R^2 = .69$. These three factors obviously overlap, and little change is produced by taking them one at a time through stepwise correlations or by adding other indicators. For France as a whole, male, lay public school teachers were 49 and 50 percent of all primary school teachers in 1837 and 1840, a proportion that fell to 35 percent in 1863 and rose slightly in the Third Republic to stay at about 37 percent. The proportion was always significantly higher (10 percentage points or more) in the quarter of the departments that had had the highest enrollment in 1832.

5. *Instituteurs* earned additonal income in any number of other occupations, including those of merchant, tavern keeper, or (more appropriately) surveyors. Jean Vial, *Les instituteurs: Douze siècles d'histoire* (Paris, 1980), 104–7; Daniel Dayen, *L'enseignement primaire dans la Creuse, 1833–1914* (Clermont-Ferrand, 1984), 33–36; Peter V. Meyers, "The French *Instituteur* 1830–1914: A Study of Professional Formation" (Ph.D. diss., Rutgers University, 1972), 86.

6. Figures in Archives Nationales, F17*/3159, list the religion of lay *instituteurs*: Catholic, 34,715; Protestant, 951; Jewish, 67 (which would leave 642 *instituteurs* unaccounted for, if the additional 5,120 lay, male "personnel enseignant" are excluded; perhaps no religion was listed for them, a category not reported). A report on twenty-six departments with 10,076 *instituteurs* in 1863–64, Archives Nationales, F17/10397–405, lists 5,770 as *clercs-laïcs* and 5,766 as *secrétaires*. In Marne, 98 percent of the *instituteurs* were *clercs-laïcs*, 97 percent *secrétaires*; the percentages in some nearby departments were: Haut-Marne 97/86; Meurthe 92/69; Meuse 90/60; Ardennes 89/78; Somme 89/62; Bas-Rhin 88/39; Basses-Alpes 88/74. In most of the other departments listed in this report, about one-third of the *instituteurs* were *secrétaires* and very few *clercs-laïcs*. Meyers estimates that between one-half and two-thirds of the *instituteurs* were either *chantres* or *secrétaires*, "The French *Instituteur*," 239. He quotes Duruy as wanting to build model homes for teachers to "add to their dignity," ibid., 238.

7. C. R. Day, "The Rustic Man: The Rural Schoolmaster in Nineteenth-Century France," *Comparative Studies in Society and History* 25, no.1 (January, 1983): 37–49. The favorite subjects in 1875–77 for the "examens facultatifs" which the *brevet* allowed were gymnastique, agriculture, industrie, hygiene, and chant. History and geography, required before 1850, was the eighth choice out of ten.

8. In 1863, 38,078 women in orders were teaching as compared to 36,457 lay men; the two groups were equal in 1872.

9. Archives Nationales, F17*/3159, gives the slightly incomplete totals, listing 1,986 of 5,998 lay women teachers as graduates of *écoles normales*, 4,721 of them as unmarried, 143 as widows, and 1,134 as married (it is suggestive that of the few women who headed mixed schools, 1,581 as against 33,767 directed by men, nearly 85 percent were married). There are a number of archival references to married couples as "teams" in which the husband taught the boys school and the wife the girls (sometimes in the same building), and such arrangements were officially favored in the Third Republic. The nuns who were *institutrices* may also have tended to be older; 493 of them were over sixty compared to only 138 lay institutrices that old.

10. Ninety-five percent of the women who received the *brevet* in 1863 were lay women, Archives Nationales, F17*/5160.

11. Archives Nationales, F17*/5160; these figures leave 1,593 teachers unaccounted for among the total "personnel enseignant" in public schools in 1863.

12. Meyers, "The French *Instituteur*," 38, 85–86, 104–6.

13. For example, André Thullier, *Economie et société nivernaises au début du $xix^{ème}$ siècle* (Paris, 1974), 165–68.

14. One in 1849 and another in 1857, seven in the period 1861–63, and four more between 1872 and 1875. The seven added from 1883 to 1886 were generally in areas that had been slow to develop a strong public school system, Morbihan, Pas de Calais, Oise, Charente, Côtes du Nord, Lot, and Haute Savoie.

15. Meyer, "The French *Instituteurs*," 17, gives figures for 1847 and 1861 (when, he says, 48 percent of the *titulaires* were normal school graduates). The data on active teachers (in public schools) in 1863 is from Archives Nationales, F17*/3158. The figures given here for the number of male teachers in public schools differ from those in the *Statistique* by small amounts (from four to seven in each column, giving an overall total larger by 21 out of nearly 42,800 teachers). Of these, 16,515 are said to be *école normale* graduates: 49 percent of the lay *instituteurs* and 39 percent of all male teachers, *instituteurs* and *adjoints*, lay and religious.

16. The maximum proportion of older teachers replaced by normal school graduates can be estimated by adding the total number of graduates between two data points, subtracting the number of new public school positions added in that period, and dividing the remainder into the number already teaching. By this abstract measure, the proportion of *instituteurs* who could have been replaced by *normaliens* was: 1863–71, 2.4 percent; 1872–75, 1.6; 1876–81, .9; 1882–85, .2; 1886–90, 2.8; 1891–95, 2.1; 1896–1900, 2.1; 1901–6, 2.1—a fairly stable figure except for the period of expansion in 1872–86 and probably never enough to fill all vacancies. Correlations among departments according to their normal school enrollments are not very high prior to the 1880s. The numbers per department were small, and class size often varied from year to year.

17. That ratio was 5:1 in 1837, over 7:1 in 1863, just over 4:1 in 1876, a bit over 5:1 in the 1880s; and over 4:1 thereafter until rising to a little more than 6:1 in 1906.

18. The *Statistique*, II:185, lists per student cost for 1837 at 597 francs; 1850, 668; 1863, 669; 1876–77, 956. When one divides total expenditure (of departments, communes, and the state) by the number of students, however, the result is slightly

lower; the mean per capita expenditure of departments presents a considerably lower figure, about three-quarters as high as those given above (because most departments, including many with small normal schools, spent less than this).

19. The figures on cost, carefully calculated by the compilers of the *Statistique*, usually combine figures for men's and women's normal schools.

20. Gilles Laprévote, *Splendeurs et misères de la formation des maîtres: Les écoles normales primaires en France, 1879-1979* (Lyon, 1984), 17-39.

21. The *Statistique* lists the number of students in each class as well as the number who received the various types of *brevet*.

22. The nuns still directed seven; at that time, religious directed three of the men's normal schools.

23. It is helpful to consider the number of *école normale* graduates in relationship to the number of lay teachers already employed and particularly in terms of the number of *titulaires*, those whom the new graduates could ultimately replace. These ratios are not a real replacement rate, which would have been affected by many other factors: Active teachers did not always finish out their careers; not all graduates made teaching their lifelong occupation; and new teaching positions were being created. In addition, even normal school graduates were more and more likely not to begin as *titulaires* but as *stagaires* or *adjoints* (a rank made especially familiar among women teachers by the practice of Catholic schools).

Normal school graduates as a mean percentage of lay *titulaires* in public schools (and in parentheses as a percentage of all lay, public school teachers):

	1863	1877	1882	1886	1891
Men	2.9(2.6)	3.4(3.0)	3.7(3.0)	4.5(3.9)	3.4(2.5)
Women	1.6	1.9(1.6)	2.2(1.8)	4.7(3.6)	5.6(4.0)

	1896	1901	1906
Men	3.3(2.4)	3.3(2.2)	4.4(2.9)
Women	5.2(3.5)	5.0(3.3)	5.4(3.2)

The number of women graduating from normal schools exceeded the number of new positions in lay public schools only in the period 1886-1901 and was large enough to have filled all new positions and replaced as much as 1 percent of the women currently teaching in public schools only in the period 1896-1901.

24. Pearson correlations of departments by the size of classes graduating from girls normal school and the proportion of elementary school students taught by members of religious orders are: $r = .30$ (1891), .39 (1896), and .34 (1901). There was also a significant correlation from 1886 on ($r = .56$ or higher) between the numbers of men and women graduating from a department's normal schools, a sign that similar factors were shaping both.

25. Antoine Prost, *L'enseignement en France, 1800-1967* (Paris, 1968), 380, suggests just over half the students in the normal schools in the 1880s were the children of peasants. Roger Martin, *Les instituteurs de l'entre-deux-guerres: idéologie et action syndicale* (Lyon, 1982), 11; Laprévote, *Les écoles normales primaires*, 61-62; Day, "Rural Schoolmaster," 26-33. The École Normale Superieure of course, drew stu-

dents from families of higher status, Robert Smith, *The École Normale Supérieure and the Third Republic* (Albany, N.Y., 1982), 34, 42; Victor Karady, "Normaliens et autres enseignants à la belle époque," *Révue française de sociologie* 13 (1972): 40–41.

26. This was reduced to exemption from a third year of service in 1889 and disappeared with the universal conscription law of 1905.

27. A decree of 1808 called for the establishment of *cours normaux* in *lycées* and *colleges* but seems to have had little effect as normal schools became the officially favored means of training teachers.

28. The other three were considered Catholic schools, although only one of them was taught by religious.

29. Cited in *Statistique de l'enseignement*, II:xcviii–xcix.

30. Any department not included in France during part of the period analyzed for that indicator was excluded. As indicated in the text, the means given in the following discussion are calculated for departments that awarded at least one *brevet*, which in the earlier part of the century also excludes some departments. The median, on the other hand, includes such departments as zero.

31. *Statistique de l'enseignement*, II:lxv.

32. Some thirty-five thousand *brevets* were awarded to men in the period 1879–82, but note that this period overlaps the one described in the text and occurs precisely at the time of the Ferry Laws.

33. It must not be assumed, however, that the number of *brevets* measures the number of people seeking a teaching position. Many did not, and some of those receiving the *brevet*, especially in the 1830s and 1840s, were already teaching. The *Statistique* gives the number of teachers in 1837, 1840, 1850, and 1863, and in every fifth year from 1872 on. For the first four dates, we calculated the average number of *brevets* annually awarded in the five years extending two years before and two years after that date; we then divided that average by the number of male, lay teachers at that date.

34. Departments with low enrollments were of course likely to stand out on this measure in the early years. The little Territory of Belfort would also rank high for all the years from 1872 on, the outstanding example of a regional center drawing candidates from beyond its borders. Ille-et-Vilaine, proportionally the leading producer of *brevets* in 1837 (at nearly 25 percent the number of male, lay teachers), remained a leader throughout the century, although that shows less clearly in terms of standard deviations than more direct measures. Interestingly, the proportion of *adjoints* without the *brevet* was higher there in 1876 than in France as a whole.

35. The following table lists all those departments that at more than one data point stood at more than 2 standard deviations above the national mean for men in the ratio of *brevets* awarded to students enrolled. The dates at which they did so come before the bar (|); the dates after it are ones at which that department was above the mean by between 1.5 and 2 standard deviations.

Ille-et-Vilaine: 1837, 1840, 1850
Corrèze: 1837, 1840, 1863
Indre: 1850, 1863, 1872

Corse: 1850, 1901
Basses-Alpes: 1837, 1863 | 1840, 1850, 1872, 1876, 1882
Hérault: 1882, 1886, 1891, 1896, 1901, 1906
Lozère: 1872, 1876, 1882, 1891
Hautes-Pyrénées: 1882, 1886, 1906
Seine: 1886, 1901

36. Generally, the number of *brevets* granted was a greater proportion of school-age population where enrollment was higher, even though in those same departments it was a lower proportion of total enrollment. Correlations on social measures such as literacy and wealth (which produced the highest correlations, in the .4 range) are not especially strong. The same is true of such systemic measures as enrollment in 1832, the number of schools in 1821, or enrollment in Catholic schools in 1850.

37. The *Statistique* gives no data on *brevets* for the three departments lost in 1871, except for the Territory of Belfort after that date and the new department of the Meurthe-et-Moselle, for which data are given from 1851 on (presumably combining results from what had been two departments). The last departments to award *brevets* regularly to women were Basses-Alpes, Charente-Inférieure, and the Gironde, all of which began to do so in 1855. Between 1851 and 1874, a few departments failed to grants any *brevets* to women in certain years: Ardèche (1851–56), Doubs (1856), Gers (1853–54 and 1871), Gironde (1871, 1874), Pyrénées-Orientales (1868), Deux-Sèvres (1853, 1856), and Var (1851). Alpes-Maritimes began to offer *brevets* to women in 1862, Savoie and Haute-Savoie in 1860. Up to the 1860s it was not uncommon, however, for a department to grant only one or two *brevets* to women in a given year.

38. The number of males granted *brevets* uniquely declined in the period 1851–56 from 2,283 to 1,171, a decline explained by the editors of the educational statistics as part of the reaction to 1848, *Statistique de l'enseignement*, II: cii–ciii, and as a consequence of the change in the law that permitted three years of teaching experience to substitute for the *brevet* (a change that, like other aspects of the law, probably most benefited clerical teachers).

39. Many of the women receiving *brevets* in the 1870s and 1880s were members of religious orders who were already teaching and now felt the need to meet state demands. Significant as a further sign of the increasing prestige and power of the state system, they were not numerous enough to account for more a part of the rise in *brevets* awarded to women. Their presence in the statistics, however, does add to the significance of the correlations that emerge despite this factor and are discussed below.

40. Margadant, *Madame le professeur*, 216. Although variations among departments were great, the minimum proportion for girls was almost always higher than for boys. These percentages are arrived at by dividing enrollment by seven, obviously an overestimate of the number in the last year of primary school, especially for girls. Furthermore, some of those presenting themselves for the *brevet* would have prepared in the elementary classes of a secondary school and in teacher training programs and some would have been out of school for some time. It must be remembered, too, that many of those getting the *brevet* never became teachers.

41. Some sixty correlations for female *brevets* as a percentage of enrollment consistently yield significant correlations with later data points.

42. A document of 1867 says only that most candidates for the higher *brevet* had the elementary one, Archives Nationales, F17/10358.

43. The proportion of *brevets* a department granted that were *brevets supérieurs* yields only a slight correlation with our established indicators of a department's early educational development—enrollment in 1832, the number of its schools in 1821, and the proportion of schoolboys who earned *brevets*. Around .3 for 1840 and 1850 and .2 for 1901 and 1906, the correlation largely disappears in the critical period of expansion in between. We found no correlation at all with a department's literacy rate, urbanization, or wealth.

44. The compilers of the *Statistique* estimated that new teachers were needed each year at the rate of about 6–7 percent of those currently teaching. Their most detailed example, Côtes-du-Nord 1875–79, comes to 5.6 percent; the needs of the Nord were about the same and of Eure-et-Loir much higher (from 6 to 9 percent for men, 13–17 percent for women), *Statistique de l'enseignement*, II:ci–cii.

45. By 1877, all *titulaires* in public schools had the *brevet* as did half of the *adjoints*, two-thirds of whom had it five years later. Among *institutrices*, some 56 percent had the *brevet* in 1877 and over 70 percent in 1881–82. In independent schools, only 2 percent of the male and less than 5 percent of the female teachers were without the *brevet*. Among clerical teachers, however, more than one-third of the men (37.5 percent) and more than half the women (54.9 percent) had not passed the state examinations, *Statistique de l'enseignement*, III:lviii; Archives Nationales, F17/10897.

46. Meyers, "The French *Instituteur*," 17–18, 24–25.

47. By 1906 in most departments more than two-thirds of the candidates for the *brevet supérieur* passed. Even in 1882 the success rate was higher among the better prepared candidates for this *brevet* than among the less select ones for the *brevet simple*.

48. The *Statistique* does not provide a figure for *titulaires* in 1837. Because nearly all teachers in schools with a single teacher were likely to be *titulaires* and few schools had more than one class, a reasonable estimate would be that 95 percent of those listed as "personnel enseignant" (*titulaires* plus *adjoints*) in 1837 were *titulaires*. On that assumption, the growth rates for *titulaires* in public schools from 1837 to 1901 would have been 23 percent for men and 91 percent for women.

49. The lowest number in any department was around 200, and that minimum changed far less (it was between 350 and 400 from 1886 on) than the maximum.

50. Haut-Rhin and Vosges were among the former. The latter, mainly in the south, included Lot, Aveyron, Lozère, Ardèche, Hérault, Gard, Hautes-Alpes, and Charente. In 1850, the only other departments in which more than 10 percent of the schools lacked a *titulaire* were Finistère and Côtes-du-Nord.

51. Meyers, "The French *Instituteur*," 232–35; he accepts the estimate for 1876 of 6 to 7 percent, suggested in the *Statistique de l'enseignement*, vol. II, but notes that the disciplining of many teachers (following the Paris Commune) must have briefly raised the rate of turnover. Meyers finds that of the nearly eight thousand normal school graduates between 1834 and 1843, 86 percent were teaching by the latter date; 92 percent of those who graduated between 1853 and 1863 were teaching in 1863.

52. The majority still did (table T.10). The mean number of teachers per school

was 1.15 in 1837 and 1.8 in 1906. Since many urban schools had several teachers, that still left a majority of France's primary schools with a single teacher at the turn of the century. By 1876, there were 1,800 more teachers than classes, primarily teachers in larger schools who had full-time administrative duties, *Statistique de l'enseignement*, I:xlii.

53. The change was even greater than the figures suggest for many of those listed as "teaching personnel" in the earlier period, especially in the independent schools, were really not teachers at all but aides, cooks, other members of a religious community, etc. By the end of the century, the requirement for a probationary period deepened the levels of hierarchy.

54. In 1886, *adjoints* were required to have the *brevet*, which by then most did. The relative number of the two kinds of *adjoints* can be estimated from the data for 1901 listing the number of classes as well as the number of schools. There were 72,420 teachers who were not *titulaires* and 63,128 classes likely to have been taught by *adjoints* (assuming that one class in each school was taught by a *titulaire*); that would allow for 9,292 *stagaires*. This can only be an estimate, however, because a small number of schools had more than one *titulaire*, and the categories were not precisely maintained.

55. Analysis by regressions against total enrollment, the early establishment of schools, the proportion of enrollment in Catholic schools, and estimates of literacy, wealth, and urban population establish the same point. A high number of students per teacher in 1837 not only correlates most strongly with enrollment in 1832 ($R^2=.44$) but including all these other factors adds nothing significant ($R^2=.48$). By 1863, a transition sets in, and these relationships become more random. The student:teacher ratio still correlates with enrollment but considerably more weakly ($R^2=.10$, and adding the other factors strengthens the relationship only slightly, $R^2=.19$, with the number of schools in 1821 the most telling factor). Where a sizable proportion of the schools eventually needed had been established early (1821), they were likely to grow in enrollment without adding teachers. By 1882, the strongest correlation with class size or student:teacher ratio is the negative one with literacy ($r = -.19$) at the nearest date (1865). Departments where education was most highly valued now tended to have more teachers and smaller classes—an indication of concern for quality. Martin, *Les instituteurs de l'entre-deux-guerres*, 16–17, notes the teachers' complaints of the increased weight of hierarchy on the eve of World War I as one of the sources of discontent.

56. The lowest correlation across nine data points between 1863 and 1906 is .73.

57. In the quarter of the departments of France with the highest enrollment in Catholic schools in 1850, nearly half the teachers in 1906 were *adjoints*; in the quarter that had had the lowest Catholic enrollment, just over one-third were *adjoints* in 1906. The correlations, using all departments, of the percentage of all students in Catholic schools in 1876 with the percentage of teachers who were *adjoints* show a consistent and only slowly declining relationship: 1863, .66; 1872, .61; 1876, .6; 1882, .62; 1886, .57; 1891, .55; 1896, .53; 1901, .52; 1906, .47. The correlations are almost identical with Catholic enrollment in 1850 (.62) and only slightly lower with Catholic enrollment in 1886, 40.

58. After 1891, the urban proportion of the population (it needs to be repeated

that this is, however, a crude measure) correlates with the proportion of *adjoints* more strongly than the proportion of students in Catholic schools in 1850. (The proportion of *adjoints* correlates with the proportion of total enrollment in Catholic schools in 1850 and with the proportion of the population that is urban as follows: R^2 = 1863: Catholics .44, urban .30 (combined, .57, with enrollment in 1832, .64); 1876: Catholics .43, urban .34 (combined, .57, including enrollment in 1832 brings it to .63 but including a still earlier indicator, the number of schools in 1821, results in a correlation of .68); 1891: Catholics .32, urban .50 (two factors, urban population and schools in 1821, are the strongest combination at .65; the Catholic factor is third and in combination produces a correlation of .72). The continued weight of the early establishment of schools underscores systemic elements; those early schools turned sooner to adding *adjoints*. The Seine is always the department with the highest proportion of them; those in the next ten departments include Loire, Bouches-du-Rhône, Rhône, and Nord (the next in order in 1863), urban departments as one might expect. In all, some fourteen departments remained in the top quarter of all departments in the proportion of their teachers who were *adjoints* for more than thirty-three years in the period 1863–1906. Of these fourteen, five were departments with the largest cities, nine were strongly Catholic and/or laggards in educational development, departments such as Finistère, Ille-et- Vilaine, Vendée, Var, and Vaucluse. Parallel results are obtained by taking the somewhat more artificial measure of the number of students per *adjoint* and correlating that with the proportion of students in Catholic schools.

59.

	1837	1840	1863	1872	1876	1882
Student-teacher ratio, leaders : laggards	53 : 36	54 : 41	43 : 39	43 : 46	39 : 48	37 : 50
Adjoints as % of all teachers, leaders : laggards			27 : 38	25 : 38	29 : 38	27 : 42

	1886	1891	1896	1901	1906
Student-teacher ratio, leaders : laggards	35 : 47	33 : 44	32 : 42	31 : 34	33 : 40
Adjoints as % of all teachers, leaders : laggards	28 : 42	31 : 44	32 : 44	33 : 46	32 : 45

"Leaders" is the mean of the fourteen departments that at any time between 1832 and 1850 were among the ten leading departments in enrollment as a proportion of school-age population; "laggards" is the mean of twelve departments that were among the bottom ten in enrollment in the same period. Or, to use another measure, there is a positive correlation across all departments between the student:teacher ratio and the number of schools in 1821 and between that ratio and enrollment in 1837 at the earlier dates (1837 and 1863) but a negative (although declining) correlation from 1876 on.

60. The correlation of student:teacher ratios in 1837 with enrollment in 1832 is telling. R^2 = .44, and adding such other factors as literacy, wealth, urban population, Catholic enrollment, etc., does not significantly strengthen the correlation (R^2 = .46). By 1863, the correlation of the student:teacher ratio with enrollment largely disappears but is higher with enrollment in 1832 (R^2 = .13) than at the same time. By 1882, student:teacher ratios correlate most strongly with literacy (R^2 = .59); classes were smallest where literacy was highest.

61. $R^2 = .69$, the multiple $r = .83$. Stepwise regression shows little difference in the separate weight of these factors; they overlap. What is impressive is their importance across time (the same factors produce an almost identical correlation with the percentage of all teachers who were male, public *instituteurs* in 1840), and adding additional factors (such as early schools, measures of wealth and literacy, etc.) strengthens the correlation only slightly.

62. Meyers, "The French *Instituteur*," 236–44, provides a good discussion and some useful tables on teachers' income.

63. There was an impressive number of these from the 1830s on. Vial, *Les instituteurs*, 113, lists many of them. *L'Echo des instituteurs* was founded in 1849. Four departmental *Bulletins scolaires* were established in the 1850s, forty-nine more in the period 1864–69 as called for in the law of September 14, 1865, and an additional thirty in the 1870s, *Statistique de l'enseignement*, II:cvii–cviii.

64. Two departments established teachers' mutual aid societies in the 1840s, twenty more had done so by 1863, forty-eight others by 1864–69, and five more did so in the 1870s, leaving only nine departments without such societies. Meyers, "The French *Instituteurs*," 143–45, indicates that about half the lay, male teachers belonged (45 percent of them in 1881 and 53 percent in 1902). He indicates that three-quarters of the male teachers belonged to alumni associations in 1907. Martin, *Les instituteurs de l'entre-deux-guerres*, 17ff, gives a good sense of the types of teachers' organizations in France as a whole as well as the Rhône. From the 1860s, on it became a custom to have a section on public schools that honored *instituteurs* at international expositions. The first Congrès international de l'enseignement primaire met at Havre in 1885. On the ideology that emphasized the importance of teachers, see Katherine Auspitz, *The Radical Bourgeoisie: The Ligue de l'Enseignement and the Origins of the Third Republic, 1866–1885* (Cambridge, 1982).

65. Those in the top thirty but below the St. Mâlo–Geneva line were: Saône-et-Loire, Ain, and Isère, extending in a line south of the leading group of departments; the Gironde, Basse-Pyrénées, and Hautes-Pyrénées.

66. The others were Indre-et-Loire, the Pyrénées Orientales, Haute-Vienne, and the Seine.

67. The effect is not automatic, however, for departments without normal schools could establish a cooperative arrangement with neighboring departments or otherwise compensate. Three departments that did not establish their own normal schools until the 1880s (Côtes-du-Nord, Oise, and Pas-de-Calais) nevertheless had between two and three hundred *normaliens* among their *instituteurs*.

68. We tested this proposition by creating a formula that assumed that between any two data points the vacancies in a department equalled the new posts created plus 5 or 6 percent of the established positions (we experimented with both figures, both of which certainly underestimate turnover for many departments in the early years and may be low as an overall figure); that number was then divided into 90 percent of the graduates of the departmental *école normale* in the same period (assuming that proportion to be teaching, a reasonable estimate at least for short periods). Even in the period 1882–86, when boys enrollments in public school experienced only limited growth, the production of the *écoles normales* never met all a department's needs for additional teachers, although it reached over 60 percent of that hypothetical need in departments

where schooling could no longer expand and classes in the *école normale* were already large. The proportion dipped to 20 percent in departments still significantly increasing their enrollments.

69. The others among the twenty departments with the highest percentage of *normaliens* were: Corrèze, 83 percent; Mayenne, 76; Creuse, 73; Ille-et-Vilaine, 72; Finistère, 69; Tarn-et-Garonne, 68; Allier, 68; Bouches-du-Rhône, 67; Loiret, 66; Indre and Rhône, 65; Tarn, 64; Loire, Cher, and Haut-Loire, 62; Pyrénées Orientales, 61.

70. Of the ten departments that in 1896 produced the largest number of *normaliennes* in proportion to the number of their *institutrices*, eight were in the region extending west of Paris—Mayenne, Eure, Indre-et-Loire, Ille-et-Vilaine, Maine-et-Loire, Eure-et-Loir, Loiret, and Côtes-du-Nord—and only two, Allier and Haut Marne, were in the traditionally advanced northeast.

CHAPTER 7

The System Circumscribed

For most of the nineteenth century, public schooling in France had steadily grown by every measure—evidence, we have argued, that schooling had widespread social acceptance and that growth had become a systemic process. An institutional inertia pushed the expanding system to reach ever more students, to raise its standards and make them more uniform, and to reduce differences in access to primary education, between boys and girls and between rural and urban areas. Thus, the question arises of whether and how far this process continued. Seen from our perspective a century later, the answer can seem deceptively clear. The practices that now provide more years of schooling for everyone and give more similar curricula to all resulted from twentieth-century changes that did not emerge directly from the process of growth described in this book. Rather, the expansion capped by the Ferry Laws slowed down after that, and the national norms established early in the Third Republic for the number of years that children should spend in school and the kinds of schools they could choose from changed relatively little until after World War I.

Conceivably, the outcome might have been quite different. Considering the efforts made and results achieved during the July Monarchy and the Second Empire, one could imagine expansion continuing as schools reached ever younger students, passed the graduates of primary schools on to secondary schools, and brought more and more former students back for still further schooling as adults. In reality, of course, many factors (including social constraints, restricted funds, and individual limitations) inhibited such expansive development. Among them, paradoxically, was the fact of having achieved a nationally organized system of elementary education. Its effects can be seen in the stunted growth of adult education and of kindergarten or preschool instruction. Both could be considered logical extensions of elementary schooling, a broadening of the concept of school age, and both might have developed quite naturally around the public elementary schools established in every hamlet.

The history of special courses for France's adults can be traced at least to the eighteenth century, and throughout the following century, such classes were praised as a source of progress and an important contribution to social order. Innumerable private associations dedicated to improving society sponsored adult courses from the Restoration on, and they were especially favored by secular reformers during the July Monarchy and by Catholic activists and labor groups during the Third Republic. It is thus noteworthy that most adult courses in France nevertheless came to be associated with the public elementary schools, a significant expression not only of their early prominence but of their broad social support.

Usually taught by the local *instituteur* and at night, these courses, intended primarily for men and boys, varied in length but normally lasted several months, following regulations set forth in 1836. By the end of the century, adult courses for men averaged about three months of classes meeting four or five hours a week. Their clientele could be quite mixed. Aimed especially at those "from the generations that did not enjoy the advantage" of the Guizot Law, "these courses were," Narcise Salvandy reported in 1847, "eagerly sought out by a notable part" of the population.[1] They also served former students who had left school early to take a job and now wanted to continue their elementary education, as well as some who discovered the need to review material they had been taught before. Rather different ambitions were met in adult courses designed for graduates of primary school who wanted to extend their education in courses that offered occupational or apprenticeship training or presented material rather like that provided in the *école primaire supérieure*.[2]

It is thus hard to know what enrollment figures for adult courses mean—either in terms of the kind, seriousness, or duration of the instruction offered or in terms of the personal ambitions and social purposes enrollment represented. That uncertainty, however, makes a point: Adult education *might* have developed in any number of ways. Certainly a great many, usually quite young, adults were attracted to it. The nearly 40,000 pupils of 1837 rose to over 100,000 in 1847 and more than 800,000 in 1866 and 1867; during the thirty years in which total primary school enrollments had become two-thirds greater, adult enrollments in public courses had increased twentyfold![3] Adult courses developed quite differently, however.

The growth in this case was not the steady, apparently socially driven, increase that marked enrollment in primary schools; rather, the popularity of adult courses proved to be highly sensitive to government policy. In 1837, twenty-six departments, almost one-third of France, offered no courses at all that were intended principally for adult males (primary school classes in such departments may well have included many older students, however). Highest enrollments occurred within departments that included or were near urban industrial centers, where they may well have attracted students hoping to work in the cities.[4] In 1850, although the number of departments offering some adult courses for men was greater than it had been ten years before, total enrollment in such courses was lower than before the revolution of 1848; and it had climbed only a bit above that level by 1863.[5]

The impressive expansion in 1866–67 was the direct result of new policies and regulations sponsored by Victor Duruy, a fact that makes the decline of adult enrollment in public classes after 1869 all the more interesting. From peak enrollments of nearly 750,000 men (in 1867) and more than 100,000 women (in 1869), the number of students in adult courses declined during the first years of the new regime but remained impressive (approximately 500,000 men and 100,000 women) in 1876 and 1881. By 1886, however, enrollments in adult courses had fallen precipitously, to about 150,000 men and 28,000 women.[6]

The immediate cause is clear: a sharp drop in the number of adult courses offered. In the early years of the Third Republic, more than half the communes of France[7] offered adult classes for men but only one-fourth that number did so for women. Departments with heavily Catholic school systems were likely to have small enrollments, but even departments with, proportionally, the fewest students in adult classes still had enrollments at the level of the leading departments in 1850. These leading departments included many in the Paris region but also many mountainous ones that were exporters of labor.[8] By 1886, only one-sixth of France's communes still offered courses for men (6,360) and just over a thousand communes (1,083) did so for women. A small increase in private classes could not begin to compensate.[9] This sharp decline was due, the editors of the *Statistique* explained, to the more rigorous requirements the state imposed for its subventions.

Educational authorities renewed their interest in adult education during the 1890s, however, stimulated by active associations (lay and religious, labor groups and chambers of commerce) and by pedagogical congresses. The ministry issued new regulations and assigned to adult instruction its own inspector, whose reports listing the departments with the most and the fewest adult courses were cited in the *Statistique* and featured at congresses and international exhibitions. These efforts bore fruit. Enrollments rose, and the statistics themselves became far more reliable (distinguishing now between the number enrolled and the approximately 60 percent of these registered students who faithfully attended their classes). The number of those who regularly pursued these public courses rose once again, to nearly 500,000 by the end of the decade and to 600,000 with the turn of the century. Although four departments offered no adult courses for women in 1895–96, all did so two years later.[10]

There were other changes, too. The monopoly the *cours d'État* had enjoyed was somewhat reduced from the 1880s on (the inspector responsible for adult instruction noted that some five thousand groups sponsored courses for adults).[11] These competing programs emphasized occupational training, and terminology shifted, with public courses often called *cours populaires* and the private ones, *cours professionels*. The twenty-five-year decline in enrollments that began in 1870 had marked a transition in public adult instruction. To be sure, the impressive figures at the end of the Second Empire had been loosely assembled (counting enrollment rather than attendance) and possibly exaggerated as well. There is no question, however, that adult education shrank in the 1870s and 1880s. As officials were quick to point out, there was now less need for remedial courses, and a regulation of 1882 formally distinguished that kind of course from the more advanced *cours complémentaires*.

The explanation seems somewhat suspect, however. That may have been the official view, for it is true that the state had paid instructors more for each adult they taught to read, write, and calculate than for each student in the more substantive courses.[12] Yet, even in 1876–77, less than 6 percent of the men and only about 8 percent of the women enrolled in adult courses were struggling with reading and writing. Even then the most popular course of study, for both men and women, had been history and geography, followed (for men) by geometry and surveying and then by bookkeeping and commercial arithmetic, which was second in popularity for women.[13] By 1886–87, three-quarters of the students in adult classes were in special or complementary rather than elementary courses (the proportion of women taking these higher courses was only slightly less, although, in contrast to men, nearly one-third of the women who did so were in private courses).[14] With the declining numbers in public courses for adults, the broader vision of adult education as a continuing exposure to high culture was often left in practice to a quite different institution, the more than 100,000 informal *conférences* that were open to the public.

For adult education, the powerful national system of primary instruction acted like a magnet, pulling adult courses within its curricular orbit as a complementary path to established educational goals, making such courses more solid and more uniform. At the same time, official policy pointed toward the world of work rather than secondary education. Three levels were now distinguished: *cours de réparation* (the very term assumed universal elementary education as a norm), *cours de révision* (even these, it was said, included material that went beyond elementary school), and *cours spéciaux* (which included modern languages, accounting, and applied courses in science, the arts, and the trades).[15] By 1907, more than thirty thousand adult courses were offered for men plus almost eighteen thousand for women, employing more than sixty-one thousand teachers and some eight thousand volunteer helpers as well.[16]

This attachment of adult education to the established educational system could be expected to have stimulated patterns of systemic growth similar to those so pronounced in elementary education. By the 1860s, regional differences were greatly reduced in men's adult education, but thereafter, the coefficient of variation stayed much the same for both men and women, with regional variation considerably greater than for the measures of elementary schooling.[17] Nevertheless, by 1863, all departments had some men and women receiving adult education, and the imbalance between the number of men and of women enrolled in adult education was greatly reduced. In 1843, there had been nearly twenty men enrolled in adult courses for every woman; that ratio, 6:1 at the end of the Second Empire, fell to 2:1 with the turn of the century.[18]

When departmental enrollments in adult courses are grouped by our octiles of departments based on total enrollment in 1832, something of the familiar pattern does emerge for males but primarily for the period 1850–72. That is, the groups of departments that had been high or low in adult enrollment in 1832 tended to hold a similar position twenty to forty years later. Although the fit is far from perfect (and utterly absent for adult enrollment at the first data point, 1837), arranging departments in these octile groupings reveals another and more significant pattern—the sensitivity of adult education to national policy despite the variety of local educational efforts. Enrollments in adult courses rose and fell from year to year, but in every year, the movement was in the same direction within nearly every octile.[19]

Enrollments in adult courses do not correlate strongly with measures of other aspects of the educational system or the social environment. That may result largely from the fact of smaller numbers less evenly spread across the nation, but it also suggests an important difference between adult courses and elementary schooling. The latter was both ubiquitous and firmly tied to local society; adult courses rested on the institutional base already created and the national policies affecting its use. The strongest correlations were between men's enrollment in adult education courses during the peak years of 1867 and 1869 and the number of public school *instituteurs* in 1863 or 1837 (ranging between .66 and .58). The *instituteurs* were clearly at the center of the expansion in adult education Duruy sponsored, and their early prominence in a department was telling, establishing a lasting tradition of adult courses.[20] There was a weaker but meaningful correlation between total enrollment in public adult education at later dates and primary school enrollments in 1832; adult enrollments were encouraged by an environment thoroughly familiar with formal education.

As one would expect, adult courses tended to attract more students in departments where more of the population was employed in commerce and lived in cities, fewer in departments where there was a high proportion of agricultural workers in 1850 and 1863. Even during its great expansion in the 1860s, adult education was most enthusiastically received in populated centers.[21] One other correlation stands out, and that is the consistently negative relationship between higher enrollments in Catholic elementary schools (both private and public) and public adult education, a negative correlation all the more surprising given the fact that Catholic enrollments tended to be higher in urban areas and that clerical teachers had been active in adult education. Adult classes, stimulated by urban demand and local initiatives, then drawn into the orbit of the public school system, had come largely to depend on national policy. At first largely remedial in intent, they had increasingly become an extension of schooling beyond the primary level and, potentially at least, an avenue of mobility. With other sources providing much of the apprenticeship training, the national system of public schooling, its costs rising, lost much of its interest in courses for adults.

The desire to reach children too young for primary school provided a very different challenge. They could not be expected to seek instruction on their own nor was it possible to limit them to odd hours when they might be offered the space and the teachers intended for primary school pupils. There were, nevertheless, important similarities between the development of adult education and of schools for preschoolers. Support for both efforts extended beyond professional educators and France's official institutions of learning. Both projects were motivated by a variety of social and pedagogical goals; and both, as they grew in size, became more and more closely attached to the primary school system, leading to higher and more uniform standards—with, in each case, results that strikingly circumscribed their venturesome reach.

The movement to create *salles d'asiles* (primarily for poor children whose mothers worked) became prominent in the 1820s and the July Monarchy, supported by leading social reformers and especially by Parisian social Catholics who were strongly influenced by the example of Protestant efforts in industrial England. The state's engagement, sought and won early on, was expressed in an ordinance of 1837, which defined the *asiles*, established a system of supervision including committees of "mothers" (usually the women of prominent, socially active families), and a commission to consider desirable methods of instruction. A combination of concerns pointed to the need for *asiles*. Social conservatives, especially, feared for the fate of abandoned waifs (ironically, these institutions, which were prompted by the belief that industrialization threatened the family because it led mothers to work outside the home, in practice made it easier for women to do so). Liberal reformers were eager to inculcate proper values among the poor and ignorant. Pedagogues, citing the theories of Jean-Jacques Rousseau and J. H. Pestalozzi, emphasized the need to prepare children for formal schooling. These mixed ambitions persisted throughout the century, with the early paternalistic emphasis on day care only partially giving way to the professional educator's vision of kindergarten as preparation for primary school. "The *salle d'asile*," the *Statistique* explained, "has a triple object: [to] keep children whose parents do not have the time to supervise them, inculcate in them the habits of order and cleanliness, and give them the first rudiments of instruction."[22] Something of this mixed purpose was implied in the evocative term *écoles maternelles*, the name employed by the Second Republic, frequently used after that (although officially abandoned in 1850), and formally adopted in 1881.

Embraced by the burgeoning national system of public schools, the *écoles maternelles* spread, and their enrollments rose at each data point from 1837 to 1886, with the greatest growth in the period between 1850 and 1886 (table Sys.1). At first glance, this looks much like the steady, systemic growth of elementary school enrollments; and contemporaries believed that, just as adult classes took some of the older students from primary schools, the presence of an *école maternelle* took some of the younger ones. But something quite different happened. Not only did preschool enrollment surprisingly cease to increase (and actually decline from 1886 to 1891 and again from 1901 to 1906), but variations among departments remained much greater than for ordinary elementary enrollment[23] (table E.12). Enrollment in *écoles maternelles* never really became universal for the country as a whole, nor did the system effectively establish just who was expected to enroll. Only a fraction of the communes of France had any *école maternelle* at all; where there were such schools, children between the ages of four and six were the principal target (but could stay until they were seven), and those between two and four were also accepted.[24] The problem, then, is to explain how the *écoles maternelles*, which had begun to spread much as primary schools had done, then stopped so far short of them.

The *écoles maternelles* did develop systemically. Enrollments in these schools in 1837 (which were miniscule, less than thirty thousand for the nation as a whole) nevertheless correlate significantly with their enrollments in 1850–76. Other measures also suggest that the *écoles maternelles* tended to flourish where elementary schools were strong, especially in the 1860s, but the relationship was not so close as might be expected and disappeared as elementary school enrollment became universal but enrollment in *écoles maternelles* did not. The correlations are actually stronger between enrollment in *écoles maternelles* in the last half of the century and elementary enrollment in 1832 (table Sys.3). At one time more closely tied, primary schools and the *écoles maternelles* developed differently before drawing slightly closer as the growth of *écoles maternelles* was cut off.

The octiles based on elementary school enrollment in 1832 confirm this impression. In the first four octiles—that half of the departments with the lowest elementary school enrollment—enrollments in *écoles maternelles* rise with few exceptions from octile to octile at each data point. Among the upper half of the departments, based on elementary school enrollment, enrollments in *écoles maternelles* do not follow the sequence of octiles at all, although in this upper group as a whole enrollments in *écoles maternelles* are much higher (table E.12). As in the case of adult education, the parallel movement in all octiles at the same dates, especially at moments of decline,[25] is a sign that the fall in enrollments was due to national policy. It also had to do with the important Catholic role in *écoles maternelles*.

The early history of the *asiles*, cultural attitudes, and state policy combined to place the *écoles maternelles* very largely in Catholic hands. That early history has already been alluded to, and there was a tendency to view these schools more as a place of charity and nurture than instruction. With very young children receiving motherly attention, it was permissible to put boys and girls in the same class (and in about equal numbers), and it was assumed that the teachers would always be women. Many of those women were members of the religious orders that proliferated in nineteenth-century France, ideally situated to fill a growing need. The 251 *asiles* in France in 1837 had increased, at a rate of more than one hundred a year, to 1,737 by 1850. With lay and religious teachers in both public and private *asiles*, by 1850 about 40 percent of them were women in orders. That changed with the Second Empire when the policies that so favored Catholic girls schools applied to kindergarten, too. By 1876, 80 percent of the 4,147 *asiles* were in Catholic hands. And enrollment was higher in the Catholic *asiles*, so that even by 1863, 85 percent of the kindergarteners had clerical teachers, a proportion that rose slightly until 1876.

Then the proportion with Catholic teachers began a steady decline of 1 or 2 percentage points a year. As late as 1901, however, just over half the enrollment in *écoles maternelles* was in Catholic schools; the trauma of separation reduced that to 7 percent in 1906 (table Sys.2). The elimination of Catholic *écoles maternelles* apparently accounts for the sharp drop in total enrollments after 1901. In 1881, the public *écoles maternelles* taught by religious had larger enrollments than all other public and independent *écoles maternelles* combined. By 1886, their enrollment had been pushed down, but independent religious schools gained still more, to become the largest category. Lay *écoles maternelles* became the largest category by 1891, and thereafter, as enrollment in public *écoles maternelles* taught by religious declined, enrollment in independent religious *écoles maternelles* increased by almost as much. In short, this competition was very much like (and a part of) the battle over Catholic elementary schools. Lay public *écoles maternelles* gained enormously in 1906 as Catholic public school enrollments were reduced to almost nothing (although many of the teachers in public *écoles maternelles* were undoubtedly former nuns whose orders had been dissolved), but total enrollment also fell by 100,000 as religious schools (primarily independent ones by then) disappeared[26] (table Sys.1).

If the dismissal of Catholic teachers directly explains some of the decline in *écoles maternelles* enrollments, especially after 1901, the presence of Catholic teachers is not so direct an explanation of the earlier growth. Catholic *écoles maternelles* tended to have a higher proportion of preschool enrollment in departments with less developed schooling (as shown when departments are arrayed in the octiles based on 1832 elementary school enrollment; departments in the lower octiles tended at all dates to have a higher percentage of their preschool children in Catholic schools than did departments in the upper octiles, which had higher overall enrollment in *écoles maternelles*). Nor was enrollment in Catholic *écoles maternelles* very directly related to the proportion of students in Catholic elementary schools. Convenience, or economy, or a feeling that it was natural to send preschoolers to the nuns was apparently more important than institutional piety in explaining the strong Catholic presence in these schools.[27]

Urban needs were a greater stimulus to *écoles maternelles*.[28] There were few of them anywhere else, and children were most likely to attend them, especially at the beginning and end of our period, if they lived in cities or towns where much of the population was engaged in industry or commerce. *Ecoles maternelles* were also more likely to be available where primary schools were well established and enjoyed high enrollments. Taken together, these elements of urbanization (and industry) and strong primary schools account for the departments that notably led or lagged in enrollment in the *écoles maternelles*, although the availability of nuns to serve as teachers was undoubtedly helpful.[29] The leading departments in *école maternelle* enrollment in 1867 were largely in the northeast, industrial and urban with strong schools and a tradition of Catholic instruction. By 1901, the leading departments, more widely spread across the map, met the same conditions. In fact, many of them had a significant proportion of their workers employed in textiles, a reminder of the early vision of day care for the children of working mothers.[30] The departments that lagged in *écoles maternelles*, on the other hand, were notably mountainous ones with dispersed populations, departments that had lagged in primary schooling and departments without a strong tradition of Catholic teachers.[31] During the period of expansion of the 1860s, the strength of the school system overall and possibly parents' attitudes toward schooling may have counted for more;[32] most of the time urban opportunity and need were more telling.

Even so, the factors that help to explain how the *écoles maternelles* developed, where they were, why Catholic schools long predominated and enrollments then fell in 1906 are not sufficient to account for the decline in enrollments after 1886, when there were more *écoles maternelles*, with more children in them, than at any time in the century. That more modest but still surprising decline has to do with policy and the national school system. The officials of the Third Republic looked kindly on the *écoles maternelles*, and a law of 1878, which was intended to encourage the building of new schools, was seen as a stimulus to new *écoles maternelles* as well.[33] With characteristic seriousness, statistics were gathered, pressures applied, and measures taken to assure their quality. By then, *écoles maternelles* tended to be large (averaging close to 125 children during most of the Third Republic), and so the distinction between *directrices* and *sous-directrices* was carefully maintained and closely watched. The rise in the number of *sous-directrices* in public *écoles maternelles* meant that classes were becoming smaller and the sexes could now more often be separated (a step officials favored but did not insist upon).[34] For some time schools taught by the sisters held an advantage in this more generous employment of personnel, but public and then public lay schools came to lead in that indicator of quality by the 1880s. As part of the educational system, teachers in the *écoles maternelles*, too, were now expected to have the *certificat de l'aptitude* or the *brevet*. In 1876, 92 percent of the lay teachers did; two-thirds of the Catholic sisters did not. Soon almost all teachers in public *écoles maternelles* would have the *brevet* and some even held the *brevet supérieur* (including some *sous-directrices*, as standards for younger teachers rose). By these measures, religious teachers continued to resist progress until the end of century, and the leaders of the Third Republic had broad visions of the civic and moral virtues that secular, public *écoles maternelles* might instill.[35]

In addition to uniform and high standards, however, the centralized national system was also drawn to efficiency and structural economies. In 1886, a law declared that only those communes with an agglomerated population of 1,500 and a total population of at least 2,000 inhabitants were obliged to support an *école maternelle* and thus entitled to a state subsidy. A variety of additional provisions were aimed at making this change acceptable. In communes too small to support an *école maternelle*, "classes enfantines" were to be established in public primary schools, and five-year-olds could be admitted to primary school in communes that offered no alternative. The effects were great. In 1886, 4,012 communes in France had *écoles maternelles*—even so, that was only about one out of every ten communes. By 1891, only 1,713 of them did. Although new schools continued to be added, they only reinforced the redefinition of the *école maternelle* as an urban, industrial service. There was a further, apparently unintended, effect. In those communes now too small to qualify for state funds and where the public *école maternelle* had been run by religious, there was a tendency for it simply to become an independent school. So the shift to independent schools (and the preservation of Catholic teachers in them) was actually encouraged. There were 5,882 *écoles maternelles* in France in 1886, 5,263 in 1891—a decline of only some six hundred. Now more concentrated in larger centers, nearly one thousand fewer of them were public schools, and three hundred more were independent.[36]

After having become an extension of the primary school system, the *écoles maternelles* were now turned in a different direction. Their greatest growth had come during the Second Empire, as it had for girls primary schools, and for both, it had come primarily in schools taught by Catholic sisters. Unlike the enrollment of girls in primary schools, however, the *écoles maternelles* did not continue their rapid growth. If society seemed to welcome them in urban areas, their necessity was less apparent in the rest of France, where dispersed populations would tend to make them more expensive. The needs of the primary school were central, and a national, universal system could absorb part of the functions of the *écoles maternelles* if parents and officials wished. Having been encouraged, sponsored, made more uniform, improved, and supervised by the educational administrators, the *écoles maternelles* could also be constricted by administrative policies and weakened by the conflict between anticlericals and Catholics. One of the achievements of France's primary school system had been to establish the universal expectation that all children between the ages of six and thirteen should go to (public) school. Indirectly, that achievement also included a shrinkage, as preschool and adult education became limited extensions of primary school rather than alternative and semiautonomous forms of education with purposes, publics, and even lives of their own.

II

Although France's *écoles élémentaires* came increasingly to concentrate on their central task, instructing the nation's boys and girls between the ages of six and thirteen, the existence of such a national network inevitably raised questions about how—or whether—these public primary schools should provide a path to higher levels of instruction. Secondary schools, *collèges* and *lycées*, were recognized and well established before the national system of primary schools had been created. There were public secondary schools (state-sponsored *lycées* and local *collèges*) and independent secondary schools (most often Catholic) that varied considerably in prestige and curriculum. The most selective often operated an attached primary school of their own from which most of their secondary students were recruited. Boarding schools were the most expensive, but for many students attendance at the nearest public secondary school might well require going some distance and renting a room. The most admired Catholic boarding schools enjoyed, like the *grands écoles* of Paris, their unique traditions and well-defined clientele. In catering to the well-drilled children of a national elite, these schools and the state's highly selective *lycées* already met the needs of those social groups most committed to the importance of secondary education. Within this segregated system, lesser schools could then accommodate the remaining demand.

Thus, elementary and secondary schools had been thought of more as distinct responses to different needs than as the lower and higher levels of a single system, and the practice of keeping those headed for secondary school out of ordinary public primary schools would have its defenders for a long time. On that basis, secondary schooling could develop into a system wholly separate from the *écoles primaires* intended for the people. The varied arguments for such a separation included, in the Third Republic, the danger that public secondary schools were likely to lose out to competing Catholic schools if not demonstrably different from primary schools in student body and function—a significant comment on the social ambitions of many parents.[37] Many educational leaders found such a system satisfactory, and an endless array of statements, from Guizot on, expressed the view that the masses had no need for the more demanding and abstract learning featured in secondary schools. Enrollment in France's secondary schools did in fact remain small, only about 3 percent of the number of students in primary schools during the later years of the Second Empire.

There is more to consider, however, The establishment of universal elementary instruction could conceivably create a growing demand for further schooling. That happened, of course, in the twentieth century, and it is significant that entrance into secondary schools from public elementary schools was always a possibility even in nineteenth-century France. The barriers of cost, custom, curriculum, snobbery, and the scarcity of schools were formidable enough, but they were not formal, legal barriers, and they were sometimes breached. Although fewer than 144,000 students were enrolled in secondary schools in 1865, more than one-third of that number were the sons of peasants, artisans, petit-bourgeois shopkeepers, and minor officials.[38] Many rectors did expect the public primary schools to send their best graduates to the public *lycée* or *collège* and were inclined to blame the local *instituteurs* if students were opting for Catholic secondary schools instead.[39] Thus there is reason, despite small secondary school enrollment, to look for statistical indications that the secondary school system aligned with the national primary system, as the latter came to concentrate almost exclusively on students between the ages of six and sixteen.

The connection remained indirect, as evidenced by data from the *enquête* of 1865, when secondary school enrollments had reached a level they would maintain through the century. When departments are arrayed by the percentage of their school-age population enrolled in secondary schools, the smooth distribution describes a national practice of sending only a few students to these schools.[40] Arranging these departments by octiles based on primary school enrollment in 1832 reveals that those in the bottom four octiles fall in the expected order for the proportion of students in secondary school, which is lower for them than any of the top four octiles. The upper octiles, however, do not fall in the expected order. General and early commitment to education was overridden by other factors. Chief of these was the presence of urban centers, followed by the proportion of population engaged in commerce and industry and by per capita wealth.[41] These overlapping measures underscore the importance of the city, with its concentrations of people and wealth, for the development of secondary schooling.

Generally, the factors that led to a strong primary school system did also favor secondary schools, but the connection was not strong. Most departments that had led in primary school enrollment did not have notably higher secondary school enrollments, and the cities in which secondary schools were most often located were not necessarily in areas that had been leaders in primary school enrollments. Similarly, departments in which the majority of secondary school students attended Catholic schools were as likely to include a major city as to have a pattern of unusually large enrollments in Catholic schools. Several of the departments with the highest proportion of students in secondary school were in the Paris region. Data on secondary school enrollments, in short, were often affected by the traditions or the national fame of specific institutions, a consideration without statistical significance for primary school enrollments. In practice, as well as in the minds of educational leaders, secondary schools remained distinct, although not entirely separate, from the national system of primary schooling—a distinctness most dramatically expressed in the assumption that secondary education was important primarily for boys, which persisted well after it was national practice for girls to attend primary school in about equal proportion to boys.

By the turn of the century, there were signs that secondary education was at a turning point, some sense even of crisis. The volumes of testimony assembled by the Ribot Commission and published in 1899 address questions of classical and modern curricula, the need (often expressed by parents and businessmen) for more practical training, the competition from Catholic schools, and the organizational structure of the public secondary system. Relatively little was said about access to such schooling. In its conclusions, the Commission accepted the estimate that perhaps 200,000 French families wanted their children to have the benefits of secondary schooling. That, they were confident, was a figure higher than it should be, diverting too much of the nation's energy and talent for artificial reasons that included a misplaced preference for government jobs. Secondary schools also needed to reform themselves to recapture "their *raison d'être* which is the preparation of a limited elite."[42]

There were other ways, however, by which a boy or girl could obtain some instruction beyond that offered in primary school classes. The most common of these were the one to three years of additional schooling provided in the *cours complémentaires* and the *écoles primaires supérieures* (e.p.s.) offered at many primary schools. Although some were attached to a *collège communale*, these e.p.s. generally grew up in close association with a primary school. The *Statistique* counted some fifty-one e.p.s. even in 1833, more than three hundred by 1837 (after the Guizot Law had required them in communes of more than six thousand inhabitants and in all *chef-lieux*), and over four hundred by 1840.[43] This rapid increase in the number of e.p.s., so similar to the growth of primary schools, suggests real local demand and an important possibility: the e.p.s. might have continued to grow along with elementary. Indeed, secondary school enrollment steadily rose, while remaining at a level that marked a major difference; enrollment in e.p.s. had grown to be a little over 27,000 by 1850, but that was less than 1 percent of the number of pupils in primary schools.[44]

Subsequently, the e.p.s. did not fair well. During the 1840s, more prestigious *collèges communaux* had begun to offer a similar program. The e.p.s., not mentioned in the Falloux Law, were officially ignored in the Second Empire as communes were quietly released from the legal obligation of maintaining them. Some primary schools where an e.p.s. had existed before nevertheless still offered a program beyond the required curriculum. More than half the e.p.s. of 1850 continued in this form into the 1860s, when some gave way to Duruy's program of *enseignement secondaire spécial*.[45] The promise of the e.p.s. remained unfilled. Neither individual demand (and it is noteworthy that 38 percent of e.p.s. enrollment in 1850 was in independent schools) nor the convenience of having such programs attached to primary schools had been sufficient to resist national policy.

Interest in postelementary education increased again in the 1870s, stimulating the creation of *écoles municipales* to provide it; and national policy changed.[46] In 1878, the government's budget for education even included a credit designed to encourage communities with the appropriate facilities to establish an e.p.s., with the state paying the initial cost of some professorships, scholarships, and special equipment. When Jules Ferry complained that, although "*l'enseignement primaire supérieur* is one of the clearest needs of our society, . . . it only exists as an exception," that extension of primary schooling was about to win a place in the 1881 measures for educational reform. It was to be given a special budget and regulated by the detailed provisions of a confident national bureaucracy requiring that an e.p.s was to have its own faculty and a program of at least two years of study; one-year courses attached to an elementary school would be called "cours complémentaires."[47]

This intermediate level of instruction would thus be carefully articulated with the national system of elementary instruction, a serious and relatively expensive set of schools (averaging approximately one teacher for every ten students). There was not only provision for a variety of levels and approaches (*cours*, e.p.s., and apprenticeship training, some of which was placed under the ministries of agriculture, commerce, and industry) but also an organizational structure that invited expansion in both numbers and quality. Soon the *cours* would be permitted to last two years, e.p.s. would be expected to have their own premises, and the standards for their faculties raised.[48] Part of the official system, these schools began again the steady growth that had seemed possible more than a generation earlier, apparently destined to recapitulate the earlier history of elementary schooling. By 1883, there were 567 e.p.s. and *cours* in France, including 172 for girls, with more *cours* than e.p.s. (at a ratio of 3:2), although the latter were larger and enrolled the majority of students. Echoing a familiar pattern, only a handful of the boys schools (32) were private, but more than one-quarter of those for girls (55) were independent, including nearly half of the most advanced three-year e.p.s.[49] By 1887, the number of these schools had risen to over 700.

Intermediate schools had become part of the national system of public education, and the e.p.s. had acquired sharper definition. Neither a very open conduit to secondary schooling nor a mere extension of primary school, the e.p.s. were to have a specially qualified faculty and a character of their own. The regulations and formal standards that guaranteed quality also made these schools relatively expensive and their spread to every commune with a primary school unlikely. As state schools, they were also to be secular, and so some of the e.p.s. operated by religious orders (particularly the Brothers of Christian Doctrine) transformed themselves into secondary schools. There had been three distinct periods in the history of the e.p.s. The growth before 1850 and after 1882 was interrupted by the Second Empire, and for a generation enrollment as a proportion of school-age population showed no significant increase. Within each of the two periods of growth, before 1850 and after 1882, there was a fairly consistent departmental pattern, with significant correlations from data point to data point in departmental enrollments (as a percentage of school-age population); between these periods, that correlation is very weak.[50] In the first period, growth occurred primarily in the departments that already led in e.p.s. enrollments (much as enrollment in primary school also tended to do at that time). In the second, the effects of national policy can be seen. Growth occured more evenly across departments, and those behind in e.p.s. enrollments drew closer to the mean. The continuity between these periods showed primarily at the extremes; those departments at the very bottom in primary school enrollment in 1832 remained well below the national average in e.p.s. enrollment from the 1880s to the end of the century.[51]

For intermediate schooling, too, the established national system may well have constrained further growth, through its centralization, more demanding standards, and narrow definition of the purpose of these schools. The e.p.s. were increasingly seen as centers of vocational training, preparing students for lower level positions in government offices and commerce. Their place within the national system was as a limited, special kind of school (almost one-third of the boys in e.p.s. enrolled in boarding schools, a portion that became about that high for girls only in 1906) serving a particular clientele. For a tiny fraction of French students, they were an avenue of some social mobility and a promise of job security.

Significantly, the looser *cours* spread more rapidly in the later period, reaching an equal number of boys and girls. Catholic schools were especially strong in *cours* for girls. Of the more than 1,800 schools of these two types at the turn of the century, five out of six were *cours*, over half of them for girls, and two-thirds of those Catholic.[52] One can see in this some evidence of popular pressures, pushing the system to create greater opportunities for girls and more schooling for all. If there was a rising demand for more schooling, the well-structured national system was now slow to meet it, and the restricted number of students reached by these schools reveals how severe the limitations were. The picture is complicated by some indeterminacy about what really constituted *cours complémentaires*, by the difficulty in obtaining precise figures from Catholic schools, and by the varied types of occupational or trade schools. There was a wide range of independent programs, from institutionalized apprenticeships to some that proudly called themselves professional schools, and there were other public trade and technical schools that reported to different authorities.[53]

By 1906, total enrollment in e.p.s. and *cours*, however, was still less than 2 percent of the enrollment in primary school (i.e., reaching at best only one student in every twelve to fifteen); expansion pointing toward universal intermediate schooling would not come until after World War I.[54] The two kinds of schools did not grow more where elementary education had first prospered (there is little fit with the octiles based on elementary school enrollment in 1832)[55] nor were departmental enrollments in these schools as closely correlated with other social factors as was secondary school enrollment.[56] Less dependent upon large cities than secondary schools, intermediate instruction was more widespread; yet, although a *certificat d'études primaires* was a requirement for admission, there was only a modest correlation between the number of *certificats* awarded and enrollments in these intermediate schools. In retrospect, then, there are statistical signs that the potential for a continuing growth in higher elementary schooling had been created by universal primary education and that it was finding a ready clientele, but before World War I, the e.p.s. and the *cours* did not become a common destiny even for the best prepared of primary school graduates.

Even so, some students continued to push for higher certification. The proportion of primary school graduates who acquired formal evidence of higher scholastic achievement (by earning *certificats d'études primaires* or *brevets* or by enrolling in an e.p.s. or a *cours*) doubled between 1882 and 1906.[57] As that number increased, the roots of desire for further instruction shifted. In 1882, the number of students seeking this higher certification remained connected with the institutional history of elementary schooling early in the century; by 1906, it was tied more to such social factors as urbanization, patterns of literacy, and wealth (table Sys.4). An extension of universal primary education, it was nevertheless becoming separated from the primary system. The quality of elementary schools may well have continued to reflect their early history and the local culture that supported schooling (as indicated, for example, by the size of school libraries [table Sys.5]), but that local commitment became less important as a prediction of whether primary school graduates would seek some higher scholastic accomplishment.

For many of that small proportion of boys and girls who graduated from an intermediate school, however, it was often an avenue to something more; and these schools may have been as important for the ambitions they seemed to legitimize as for the opportunities they actually opened. The officials who directed France's educational system were interested in what became of these graduates, and their incomplete reports for 1884 indicate that even then intermediate schooling could lead to higher schools as well as secure jobs.[58] One-quarter of the boys and two-thirds of the girls went home when they left an e.p.s., and we have no way of knowing for how long or with what added prestige or frustrated ambitions. For most of the rest, study in an e.p.s led to employment in industry, to a government post, or to further schooling. More than 40 percent of the boys but only about 11 percent of the girls took a job in the private sector (26 percent of the boys went into commerce, 16 percent into industry). The e.p.s. made its contribution to France's economic growth and provided the government with many of its lower level employees. Fourteen percent of the boys and girls leaving an e.p.s. went on the state's payroll, most as teachers (12 percent of the girls, 6 percent of the boys); the rest went to work in a post and telegraph office, government bureau (*ponts et chaussées*, customs, and other government offices), or the railroads (about 2 percent to each of these among the boys; girls went in that proportion only to the post and telegraph). Some 15 percent of the boys and 10 percent of the girls went on to other schools—the e.p.s. was something of a link among various levels of education, after all. The most popular choice was an *école normale*. About 8 percent of the girls and 6 percent of the boys went there, but *lycées* and *collèges* received 5 percent of the girls and 2 percent of the boys. Boys also went to the schools of *arts et métiers, beaux-arts,* mines, and veterinary medicine. With this interest in education, 5 percent of the boys and 6 percent of the girls took the *certificats d'études primaires*, 15 percent of the boys and 43 percent of the girls took a *brevet*.

If there is an important hint of social mobility in these figures, the state had contributed significantly to that. In the entire period from 1882 to 1906, only some 5 or 6 percent of the boys in e.p.s. were on scholarship and from 6 to more than 10 percent of the girls, but this small minority of students whose way was paid did rather well. Forty-three percent of the boys who left an e.p.s. with the *certificat d'études primaires* and 43 percent of the girls who took a *brevet* had gone to school on scholarship. Nearly one-quarter of the boys and 16 percent of the girls who went on to an *école normale* attended their e.p.s. on scholarship as had 10 percent of the girls and 7 percent of the boys who entered a *lycée* or *college*. Some scholarship holders went to work for the government (from 4 to 27 percent of those who chose state employment had held scholarships) and some went home or were even among the few boys who turned to agriculture—but none of the scholarship holders chose business.

For those leaving a *cours complémentaire*, the future was slightly different. Just under two-thirds of the girls went home and nearly one-third of the boys did so; this lesser program offered less assurance of a career. Only about 25 percent of the boys went into commerce and industry (15 and 10 percent, respectively), 10 percent of the girls. The proportion of those who went from a *cours* to work for the state was, however, about the same as for those leaving an e.p.s. (14 percent of the boys, 13 percent of the girls, 8 percent of each group to serve as teachers). A surprising 18 percent of the boys went on to other schools, including 8 percent to *écoles normales* and 7 percent to *lycées* and *collèges*; 11 percent of the girls continued their schooling, all in *écoles normales*. Thus, the less formal, less prestigious, less demanding, and less expensive *cours* (for which there were also far fewer scholarships—only about 1 percent of the students had them) also provided access to further education for boys and to a career in teaching for both boys and girls. The *cours* were much less likely than the e.p.s., however, to open an avenue into the lower levels of government bureaus, commerce, or industry.

Institutionally integrated into the national system of schools and socially linked to the opportunities for lower middle-class salaried employment, these intermediate schools did not have the kind of local roots that had fed the development of primary schools. If these schools did sometimes serve as links to further education, that resulted more from the ambition of students than the plans of officials.

A national system had extended elementary schools across all of France, reaching a highly dispersed, largely rural population. To a large extent, the efforts discussed in this chapter—efforts to reach adults, children before they were six, and primary school graduates—were aimed primarily at urban areas and the needs of industrial society. France's centralized system of public instruction followed her educational and political leaders in responding to these needs and offered some significant opportunities for modest social mobility, but it did so less confidently, generously, and spontaneously than the movement for primary schools had done and reached less deeply into the small towns and villages of France.

Notes

1. *Statistique de l'enseignement primaire*, II:cxl.
2. The official statistics included apprentices in the enrollment figures.
3. There was, of course, a certain overlap in that many students in "adult" courses were simply continuing at night a primary instruction they had abandoned in order to work, and the editors of the *Statistique* believed that elementary school enrollments went down a tiny bit where adult courses were established, ibid., II:cxxxix.
4. Adult education might also have helped to bridge the gap between the world of work and what was taught in school. There were also many factory workers who had not had the chance to complete their studies, Colin Heywood *Childhood in Nineteenth-Century France: Work, Health and Education among the "classes populaires"* (Cambridge, Eng., 1988), 207–9, 290–99. The Nord, for example, an early leader in the establishment of schools, was below average in the award of *certificats d'études primaires*. Of the ten departments with the highest proportional enrollment in adult classes in 1837, seven were west and south of Paris, and the other three were Moselle, Rhône, and Vaucluse. The departments with more than four adult students for every one thousand people were:

4.1 Seine	7.5 Rhône
4.2 Gironde	8.1 Orne
4.4 Pas-de-Calais	8.8 Indre-et-Loire
5.0 Gard	11.7 Moselle
5.2 Yonne	14.6 Sarthe
5.5 Vaucluse	18.6 Loir-et-Cher
6.1 Loiret	19.4 Seine-et-Oise

5. In 1850, only eight departments offered no adult classes for males (Basses-Alpes, Hautes-Alpes, Ardèche, Côte-d'Or, Creuse, Doubs, Gers, Lot). The ten departments that in 1850 had the highest proportion of their population in adult classes

enrolled a smaller proportion than the ten departments that led on that measure in 1837. These leaders in 1850 included some departments that had led in the past and some that would remain leaders in the future; they were Meuse (12.4 students per one thousand population), Rhône (7.8), Hautes-Pyrénées (7.5), Maine-et-Loire (7.0), Loiret (6.6), Gironе (6.6), Vienne (5.2), Seine-et-Oise (4.5), Ariège (4.2), Yonne (4.1).

6. The published statistics for 1891 omit data on adult education.

7. Some 20,919 communes gave courses for men in 1876, 21,084 in 1881–82; and the number offering courses for women rose by almost one thousand to over 5,600. (The peak number of communes offering adult courses for men had been 28,048 in 1866, when 5043 provided them for women, ibid., II:cxl–cli.) All but 2 percent of the courses were public, 94 percent of them taught by lay teachers. Clerical teachers did better in enrollments, with 40 percent of the adults in public courses in 1876–77, 23 percent in 1881–82, ibid., III: ci.

8. Those with lowest enrollments per one thousand population in 1881 were: Creuse (6.3), Finistère (6.8), Rhône (7.1—just below the level that had made it a leader in 1850 and 1837!), Cantal (8.1), Bouches-du-Rhône (8.3), Haute-Saône (8.4), Haute-Vienne (8.5), Saône-et-Loire (8.5), Gard (8.8), and Maine-et-Loire (9.8). The departments with the highest enrollments per one thousand population were: Hautes-Alpes (42.5), Ariège (33.8), Hautes-Pyrénées (32.9), Aisne (29.9), Lozère (27.8), Loire-et-Cher (26.9), Aube (26.3), Eure-et-Loir (26.1), Corrèze (25.8), and Seine-et-Oise (24.7).

9. *Statistique de l'enseignment*, IV:xci.

10. The four were Haute-Loire, Indre, Lozère, and Haut-Rhin, ibid., VI:cxi.

11. Ibid., VI:cx. In the 1860s, enrollment in private adult classes, at least as counted in the *Statistique*, had been well under 5 percent of the total, less than 2 percent by 1881.

12. Ibid., III:cii.

13. Some 8,079 men and 2,120 women left their adult courses still absolutely illiterate; 10,275 men and 3,424 women learned to read, 10,813 men and 3,161 women to read and write. Other enrollments were: history and geography, 91,869 men and 8,649 women; geometry and surveying, 76,627 men but only 574 women; book-keeping and commercial arithmetic, 36,295 men and 2,685 women; *dessin* enrolled 21,547 men and 566 women; physical sciences, 8,428 men and 566 women, ibid., I:lxix.

14. Ibid., IV:xcii.

15. Ibid., VI:cxi.

16. Ibid., VII:cxi.

17. The coefficient of variation among departmental enrollments of men in adult education courses (normalized by population) was over 100 percent in 1850, fell to 35 percent by 1867 and stayed in that range through 1881. The same coefficient for women's enrollment in adult education courses, 268 percent in 1850, was 113 percent in 1869 and 88 percent in 1881.

18. The number of men in adult courses for each women enrolled in one was: 1843, 19.6; 1850, 11; 1863, 13.4; 1866, 9.8; 1869, 6.3; 1872, 5.5; 1876–

77, 4.9; 1881–82, 4.7; 1886–87, 6.4; 1896–97, 4.9; 1897–98, 3.6; 1901–2, 2; 1906–7, 2.

19. Eight groups across seven data points provide fifty-six separate changes; in only five instances does one octile not move in the same direction as all the others, and in two of those instances it merely stays the same.

20. These correlations remained relatively important into the 1880s (the number of men enrolled in adult courses in 1881 correlates with the number of *instituteurs* in 1863 at .35); the correlation between men enrolled in adult education courses and boys enrolled in public primary schools is .56 in 1881 and above .4 with boys enrollment earlier or later.

21. The correlations are: enrollment in 1832 with adult enrollments in 1867, .43, and with adult enrollments in 1869, .41; the proportion of population in agriculture in 1866 with adult enrollments in 1850, −.33, and with adult enrollments in 1863, −.43; adult enrollments in 1863 with the proportion of the population in commerce (in 1866), .42, and with the proportion of the population in urban areas (as defined by the census, 1865), .48.

22. Ibid., II:cxxxvii. This long development and its conflicting goals are discussed in Jean-Nöel Luc, *La petite enfance à l'école, XIXe–XXe siècles* (Paris, 1982), 9–20.

23. The coefficient of variation for elementary school enrollment (normalized by school-age population) fell to 51 percent by 1837—a level of variation in *écoles maternelles* barely achieved at the end of the century—and declined to 8 percent by 1901. In 1863, the mean enrollment for *écoles normales* in the highest department was twenty-five times that for the lowest and by 1906 the highest mean was still ten times the lowest.

24. The national mean, calculated on the basis of the number of five-year-olds, reached almost 100 percent in 1886. That would be less than half of those four to six and less than one-quarter of those in the broader age group. In short, even in 1886, most children never enrolled in an *école maternelle*; in a few places, some attended for several years. In fact, even these estimates are slightly optimistic, for mortality rates among small children were high. In 1851, the proportion of the female population ten–fourteen was 3 percent smaller than the proportion which had been five to nine five years earlier (and, in a period of population growth, 6 percent smaller than the number five to nine in that same year). By 1901, the proportion of girls ten to fourteen was only 2 percent lower than the proportion five to nine, within the same cohort (and, in a period of stable or declining population, there were in 1901 actually more children in the older group than in the younger); see Etienne Van de Walle, *The Female Population of France in the Nineteenth Century* (Princeton, 1974), table 5.3, p. 125.

25. Only once, in 1891, does a single octile not decline with all the others.

26. As might be expected, boys tended to be a bit more numerous than girls in public, lay *écoles maternelles*, and there were more (often around 20 percent more) girls than boys in the independent, religious schools.

27. The correlations between the percentage of Catholic enrollment in the two types of schools rose to significance only toward the end of the century, when the pressure to have lay teachers in public schools was great enough to make the per-

sistence of Catholic schools the result of local, counterpressure. The correlations are: 1863, .10; 1867, .15; 1876, .19; 1881, .22; 1886, .24; 1891, .23; 1896, .31; 1901, .45; and 1906, .35. Correlations of the percentage of students in Catholic *écoles maternelles* with girls share of total primary school enrollment stayed at about .4 across this period, which suggests some relationship between the cultural attitude that put girls in school and put younger children of both sexes in *écoles maternelles*.

28. *Statistique de l'enseignement*, IV:xviii, notes (with a slightly self-exculpatory purpose, that these schools were never intended for rural communes).

29. Multiple regression on enrollment in *écoles maternelles* in 1863 against population density, urban population (1865), wealth, percentage enrollment in Catholic schools (1850), literacy (1865), and enrollment in 1832 produces a multiple r of .75; $R^2 = .56$. Eliminating all but primary school enrollment (in 1832) and urbanization (1865) still produces an impressive multiple r of .72; $R^2 = .52$. The same tests applied to 1891 enrollment in *écoles maternelles* gives still stronger results: multiple r of .87; $R^2 = .76$ including all factors; eliminating all of these but early enrollment and urbanization yields an r of .85; $R^2 = .73$. Urbanization steadily increases in importance from .49 in 1850 to .73 in 1891 and .78 in 1906. Early primary school enrollment, on the other hand, becomes less important, declining from its peak of .51 in 1881 to .33 in 1906.

30. Workers had experimented with many ad hoc solutions to this problem; see William M. Reddy, *The Rise of Market Culture: The Textile Trade and French Society, 1750–1900* (Cambridge, 1984), 165. In all these calculations, of course, enrollment in *écoles maternelles* is normalized by the population; we have used an estimate of the number of five-year-olds. The ten leading departments in 1867 were Meuse, Haut-Rhin, Bas-Rhin, Meurthe, Nord, Hérault, Seine-et-Marne, Seine-et-Oise, Maine-et-Loire, and Vosges. The first eight of these were also among the ten leaders in 1863; the last two were replaced by Var and Moselle. In 1901, the ten leading departments were Nord, Seine, Hérault, Var, Bouches-du-Rhône, Marne, Loire, Vaucluse, Rhône, and Gard. Nine of these had also been in the top ten in 1891, with Meurthe-et-Moselle in place of Vaucluse. Compare the map showing the proportion of workers in textiles in 1875 in *Atlas historique de la France contemporaine, 1800–1965* (Paris, 1966), 100.

31. The ten departments with the lowest enrollments in *écoles maternelles* in 1867 were Hautes-Alpes, Corrèze, Cantal, Creuse, Haute-Savoie, Eure, Tarn-et-Garonne, Deux-Sèvres, Haute-Vienne, and Sarthe. The first five of these were also among the ten with lowest enrollments in 1863; then, Dordogne, Lot, Landes, Corse, and Ariège replaced the second five. Those with the lowest enrollments in 1901 were Dordogne, Corrèze, Cantal, Creuse, Eure, Pyrénées-Orientales, Allier, Seine, and Corse. The first four of these were also among the ten lowest in 1891; the others were replaced by Lot, Haute-Savoie, Hautes-Alpes, Lozère, and Ariège. The volumes of the *Statistique de l'enseignement* from 1881 on regularly presented a list of leading departments based on the number of *écoles maternelles* per ten thousand children aged two to six. Using schools instead of enrollment produces some differences but is generally similar. Var was among these leaders from 1881 to 1906, Meuse from 1881 to 1901. The others are: Rhône, 1886–1906; Tarne-et-Garonne, Hérault, Seine-et-Oise, Maine-et-Loire, Gard, and Vaucluse, 1891–1906.

32. Except in the expansion years of 1863 and 1867 ($r = .46$ and $.48$), enrollment

in *écoles maternelles* did not correlate strongly with literacy (*r* ranged from .23 to .29 all other dates from 1850 to 1906 with literacy in 1865).

33. *Statistique de l'enseignement*, II:cxxxix.

34. A decree of 1887 formally confirmed that the two sexes could be together, ibid., IV:xxvii.

35. Luc, *La petite enfance*, 14–20.

36. The actual numbers were 994 and 315. *Statistique de l'enseignement*, IV: xxvii; V:xxiii–xxiv.

37. See, for example, the statement of the Rector of the Academy of Poitiers to the Ribot Commission, *Enquête sur l'enseignement secondaire*, vol. IV, *Réponses au questionnaire* (Paris, 1899), 262.

38. Patrick J. Harrigan, *Mobility, Elites, and Education in French Society of the Second Empire* (Waterloo, Ont., 1980), 13–23, on this and overall enrollment data.

39. See, for example, the reports of the Rectors of the Academies of Besançon and Poitiers, *Enquête sur l'enseignement secondaire*, vol. III, *Statistique et rapports des recteurs et des inspecteurs d'académie* (Paris, 1899), 255, 434.

40. For convenience, we have taken a department's secondary school enrollment as a percentage of its population of six to thirteen years old; these range in tiny increments from less than 2 percent to more than 10, with three departments as outliers above that range: Seine-et Oise, 11.9; Bouches-du-Rhône, 13; and Seine, 20.4. Figures adjusted to a more appropriate range of ages, say eight to fifteen years old, would give different percentages but essentially the same relationship among departments.

41. The proportion of school-age population in secondary school correlates with these other factors as follows: proportion of population in cities, .7; proportion of population engaged in commerce, .64; proportion of population in industry, .49; wealth, .43.

42. *Enquête sur l'enseignement secondaire*, vol. VI, *Rapport général*, 120–21.

43. Sandra Horvath-Peterson, *Victor Duruy and French Education: Liberal Reform in the Second Empire* (Baton Rouge, 1984), 129; *Statistique de l'enseignement primaire*, III:lxxxv. The breakdown of boys e.p.s. by type was:

Date	Public	Ind.	Total
1837	235	97	332
1840	268	191	459
1843	325*	78	403
1850	343	93	436

*includes 125 annexed to *collèges communaux*.

44. Ibid., III:lxxxv.

45. Horvath-Peterson, *Duruy and French Education*, 129.

46. A summary of this history and the statistics on e.p.s. since 1881 may be found in J.-P. Briand and J.-M. Chapoulie, "Statistiques des enseignements primaire supérieur et technique," J.-P. Briand et al., *L'enseignement primaire et ses extensions 19e–20e siècles* (Paris, 1987), 174–201.

47. Full-time *directeurs* and *adjoints* were distinguished from part-time teachers; of these, *professeurs spéciaux* would be paid more than *professeurs auxiliaires*, who

taught manual training or gymnastics. The state would continue to help with the cost of maps, books, and laboratory equipment, and a significant amount was earmarked for scholarships (with fixed sums for boarding students and less for those living at home). Students had to be at least twelve years old and hold the *certificat d'études primaires* or pass an equivalent examination. Ibid., III:lxxxv–lxxxix.

48. A law of 1887 added the further definition of these programs and made e.p.s. with three-year programs the norm, those "*de plein exercise*," ibid., IV:xl. A law of 1892 put the more applied e.p.s. under the Ministry of Commerce and Industry and renamed them (but left nearly fifty e.p.s. under dual ministries) and required that the head of a regular e.p.s. hold the *certificat d'aptitude* of a normal school professor. Officials were soon lamenting that many directors of girls *cours* held no more than the *brevet supérieur*, ibid., V:xxxvi–xxxix.

49. Ibid., III:lxxxviii gives the following figures:

	Boys		Girls	
	Pub.	Ind.	Pub.	Ind.
Cours	221	7	70	26
E.P.S., 2 years	79	4	23	62
E.P.S., 3 years	66	21	24	23

50. The correlation of e.p.s. enrollments in 1837 with those at later dates is .43 in 1840 and 1850 but never above .2 thereafter. The correlation of e.p.s. enrollments in 1882 with all later dates ranges between .56 and .82.

51. This can be simply demonstrated by treating the dozen departments with lowest primary school enrollments (per population) in 1832 as a separate group. In 1882, the rest of the departments of France had an average enrollment per population in e.p.s. that was 2.95 times that in the dozen traditional laggards. Although that ratio then drew closer (it was 2.7 in 1886, 1.7 in 1891), it remained at 1.6 in 1896.

52. Ibid., VII:xxxix:

	Boys		Girls	
	Pub.	Ind.	Pub.	Ind.
E.P.S.	204	3	94	1
Cours	539	147	283	555

53. Most notably, the *écoles d'arts et métiers*; see C. R. Day, *Education for the Industrial World: The ecoles d'arts et métiers and the Rise of French Industrial Engineering* (Cambridge, Mass., 1987).

54. One should be careful, however, not to apply anachronistic standards. These proportions were not particularly low by contemporary international standards; 2.5 percent of seventeen-year-olds graduated from high school in the United States in 1880, Maris A. Vinovskis, Immigrants and Schooling in the United States, unpublished paper, 1989, pp. 21–22.

55. The overall correlation with elementary enrollment in 1832 (.3 in 1840, somewhat lower in 1882) is still significant at all other data points.

56. The highest correlation (.54) was with the density of population (but much

lower with urbanization) in 1896. The next highest correlation (.47) was with the proportion of the population in commerce in 1882 (and correlation with that measure remained just below .4 throughout the second period).

57. The numbers are 5 percent in 1882 and 10 percent in 1906, but such combined figures are a very crude measure, valuable primarily as an indication of change. Many students are counted twice in these totals, which omit those in *Arts et Métiers* and other special schools. The differences in the proportion of girls (especially likely to seek the *brevet*) and boys earning one of these indications of achievement, which was never very great, tended to decline (the ratio of boys to girls was: 1.19 in 1882, 1.21 in 1886, 1.2 in 1891, 1.16 in 1896, 1.18 in 1901, and 1.07 in 1906).

58. Although the reports are very incomplete, information was obtained for about two-thirds of those who left intermediate schools in 1884. All the figures for career choices in 1884 are from *Statistique de l'enseignement primaire supérieur, situation au 31 décembre 1884*, 2d ed. (Paris, 1886), ii–iii, and tables 13–16, pp. 136–87. Less complete data for 1883 (showing roughly similar patterns overall, with those leaving Parisian schools less likely to enter an *école normale* and more inclined toward commerce) is in *Statistique de l'enseignement primaire*, III:xciii.

CHAPTER 8

The Balance Sheet

This study has set forth a series of arguments, chapter by chapter: That schools spread relatively rapidly in the 1820s and 1830s, enjoying significant local support and launching a process that would continue through the century. That the establishment of schools was consistently followed by a steady growth in enrollment, making that the critical first step and showing little evidence of large-scale resistance from ignorant or needy parents. That the development of schooling during most of the nineteenth century occurred in a remarkably systemic way, so that when schools were established and enrollment grew that in turn led to more regular attendance during more of the school year, to better qualified teachers, and to better facilities, and that this process was so regular that the rank order of France's departments on these measures was extraordinarily stable across this century of educational change. That the famous national laws that defined and did much to shape the French system of primary education recognized and codified developments already well under way (thus, the rate of increase in the number of schools rose sharply before the Guizot Law, Catholic schools were well established before the Falloux Law and were likely to have benefited from the subsequent growth of girls schools even without policies favoring teachers in religious orders, and universal enrollment was essentially achieved and tuition abolished in a majority of schools before the Ferry Laws). That the preference for Catholic instruction under Louis Napoleon made it easier for France to meet the difficult challenge of providing schools for all and especially for girls but with that accomplished also made it easier to compel secularization, having further concentrated primary instruction in the state's hands. That the schooling of girls lagged only a little behind the schooling of boys while differing in other ways. That the emphasis on teachers' training, which furthered a sense of professionalism and established *instituteurs* as a special cadre, also presented teaching as an attractive career for women and made preparation for teaching their most accessible and common form of certification. That together these developments, which were rooted in local attitudes and culture, increased state direction and resulted in a structured national system, extensive and centralized. That, as elementary schooling became complete, especially from the 1860s on, this self-contained system was also self-limiting, reducing the opportunities for further development of preschool programs, adult education, and links to a variety of secondary schooling. That these efforts considerably reduced regional differences in schooling, which nevertheless tended to persist in the relative ranking of departments.

All of these patterns should be closely tied to money. Enthusiasm for schooling beyond state requirements, national policy intended to make departments more equal in the schooling they offered, regional differences, and the systematization we have stressed should all leave their mark on educational expenditures. An analysis of those expenditures may also reveal something more about the appeal of Catholic schooling, the differential treatment of girls and boys, and the costs of expanded school programs aimed at preschoolers, adults, and those who wanted a few more years of instruction. The study of educational expenditures should, therefore, provide an opportunity both to test earlier arguments and sometimes to solidify them. In one sense, the expenditure data are the most reliable we have. There is no question about what a franc was and relatively modest variation in what it could buy.[1] For the compilers of the *Statistique*, this certainty came as a relief, enabling them to measure "with precision, the sacrifices the country had authorized."[2] Their meaning is never so unambiguous as it seems, however, and we do not have all the figures we need.

The budget figures distinguish between ordinary and extraordinary expenditures, made by commune, department, and national state primarily on the basis of the sources of revenue and the legal requirements surrounding them. By far the more important, ordinary expenses were generally those required by ordinance and used to pay rent for schoolrooms and teachers' quarters and to pay teachers' salaries as set by law (with minimums for men and women and for different classes of teachers, and diverse supplements for years of service and for pensions, etc., all of which rise with time, salaries accounted for more than nine-tenths of ordinary expenditures). These expenses were expected to be attached to regular and specified sources of income, including tuition, communal levies earmarked for education as required by the state, and continuing appropriations from higher levels of government. Extraordinary or voluntary expenses might include such optional expenditures as supplemental payments that lifted teachers' salaries above the legal minimum, improvements to a school building, additional equipment or facilities, or other supplementary needs; they might come from any surplus after ordinary expenses had been met from normal revenues, from the additional taxes that within strict limits communes and departments were permitted to assess, or from special appropriations and subsidies. Departmental expenditures supported *écoles normales* and provided both general and special subventions to needy communes and for specific projects (especially school buildings).

The legal distinctions so carefully maintained reflect the difficulties of financing a national system and fears that the cost of public schools might get out of hand and communes might not meet their obligations. Ordinary and extraordinary expenditures are categories that conflated funding and purpose; their meaning (and even the terms themselves) changed over time, and they were often interpreted differently in different departments.[3] The neatly balanced budgets and long columns that add up each centime reflect the accountant's precision, not the historian's, but one can see the increasing complexity of the system in the way these figures are recorded. Funding for the construction of school buildings became a larger but separate item, and so did the amounts (each primarily assigned to a particular level of government) spent for teachers of drawing, needlework, and applied skills; for inspectors and administrative costs; for books and printing. Nor are the budget figures complete. Until 1885, they present designated revenues but not the additional expenditures a commune might opt to make from general funds (to increase a teacher's pay, buy equipment, offer prizes, or serve some other specific purpose). When those voluntary communal expenditures were counted, the figure for national expenditure went up by about 20 percent.[4] Figures for the Seine were not included until 1863 (and were omitted twice again in that decade), and the accounts of major cities were sometimes reported separately.[5] In addition, of course, procedures were fundamentally altered as part of the Ferry Laws, and the responsibilities assigned to state, departments, and communes were redefined in 1890. These complications argue against using expenditure data in the highly elaborated ways their detail and precision make tempting. Without the risks of estimating which expenditures really went for what and adjusting for expenses not reported in the *Statistique* (although a case could be made for doing both), it remains possible to establish basic patterns.

I. Patterns and Periodization

Despite these complexities, fundamental patterns of change are clear. First, the total amount spent on public primary instruction increased impressively in the course of the century, even though revenues from specific sources often declined. The overall figures suggest a fairly complicated periodization that begins with a period of steady and significant increase prior to 1850, followed by sharper increases (and other signficant changes in funding) in the Second Empire and the early Third Republic.[6] Ordinary expenditures, officially required and reported, rose from 9,000,000 to over 12,000,000 francs from 1837 to 1850; actual costs were certainly higher, although we do not know by how much—perhaps from one-third more to twice that figure. By 1855, the first date for which reasonably good (but never entirely complete) figures are available, the total for ordinary and extraordinary expenditures surpassed 29,000,000 francs. National legislation established the framework in which this growth took place, but much of it was the collective result of thousands of local preferences and of the steadily rising norms for the amount of schooling students should receive and the qualifications teachers should have.

This pattern of steady annual rises continued after each major leap in expenditures; local commitment and systemic tendencies remained important. Although the published statistics, when they slight local and voluntary contributions, make nationally authorized expenditures seem even more overwhelmingly important than they were, there is no question that the major, sudden increases in total expenditures resulted from changes in national policy. One such dramatic increase occurred in the early 1850s, and that plus subsequent annual increases brought total expenditure to more than 40,000,000 by 1864. Another leap followed the legislation of 1867, and expenditures jumped to 57,000,000 the following year, rising above 61,000,000 by the end of the Second Empire. With the new regime, annual increases tended to be larger, but the average annual percentage of increase was lower (because the sharp rises in a single year brought by specific legislation were not so great). Total figures (still not including voluntary communal expenditures) were almost 68,000,000 by 1872.

With annual rises of nearly 5 percent, expenditures reached 78,000,000 by 1875, were more than 101,000,000 by 1878, and reached 116,000,000 by 1881. It is important to recognize the strong base thus established for the Ferry Laws as well as the extraordinary budget increase they brought: to 135,000,000 by 1883 and 142,000,000 the following year. When most (but never all) communal voluntary expenditures were added into the official figures in 1885, the total reached 171,000,000. Still, the pattern of steady increases continued, and total expenditures rose to 182,000,000 by 1891, to nearly 194,000,000 by 1894, 202,000,000 by 1896, and 214,000,000 by the end of the decade. Annual increases then tended to become larger with the turn of the century, and, pushed by the secularization measures of 1905-7, the total budget rose to more than 283,000,000 in 1907.[7] Although annual increases per capita were somewhat lower (see table Ex.1), this continuing growth in what France spent for elementary intruction remains a remarkable social and political fact: Operating budgets (which generally did not include the cost of buildings) were some twenty-five times greater in 1907 than in 1837, whereas the total budget of the French central government increased but fourfold in these seventy years.[8]

Total expenditures, then, including special appropriations, show the familiar pattern between the achievement of universal education and the system's further development and differentiation—one more piece of evidence for a periodization that sees the late 1860s and early 1870s as a period of transition between two stages. Costs per student, of course, were lower where there were more students and larger schools; reaching those not yet enrolled was relatively more expensive. Voluntary expenditures, which are a rough indicator of local enthusiasm (and wealth), like the other forms of school expenditure, all correlate with early enrollment. That is, departments that developed schooling early continued to spend more on it. Having students in school led to higher expenditures more clearly than spending money can be said to have preceded or produced higher enrollments—another side of the importance of local attitudes and practice.

The pattern of steady, almost annual, growth that was established by the time of the July Monarchy is equally important. This trend, evidence of internally generated and systemic growth, was supported by national policy. The sharpest increases (which came in the 1850s and in 1867–68, 1881–82, and 1903–5) were each the result of famous ordinances and laws. There were also important differences in regimes. Between major changes in policy, the Second Empire strove to keep annual increases quite low; in a different spirit, the Third Republic generally accepted significant yearly rises. Such increased financial commitment accompanied, and required, the greater involvement of the state.

Prior to 1850, expenditures went hand in hand with enrollment (table E.17), and the annual growth rate in enrollment (2 percent) closely paralleled that of expenditure. This relationship changed with the sharper rise in expenditures during the Second Empire, for enrollment increased by only 1 or 2 percent per year and the growth rate in the number of schools was lower still. Much of the apparent rise in expenditures during the 1850–55 period may result from better national records, but from 1855 until 1870, expenditures continued to rise (at an average annual rate of nearly 7 percent) despite frequent efforts to hold them down. Increased costs in the Second Empire reflected the establishment of a uniform salary scale at a somewhat higher level, reductions in classroom size, and the growth of *écoles maternelles*. For the system as a whole the late 1860s and early 1870s were a period of transition between two stages, one in which the achievement of universal instruction was the principle concern and one marked by the further development of the national system and by its professionalization and differentiation. The process continued in the first decade of the Third Republic at an annual rate of increase of nearly 10 percent, with salaries (now in several grades) still by far the costliest item, but with more spent on training, better facilities, administrative costs, and an array of programs, such as publications and prizes, that expressed institutional prominence and prestige. Expenditures increased more slowly following the Ferry Laws (at an annual average of 1 percent from 1882 to 1891) but increased again in the period 1891 to 1896 (at an annual rate of 8 percent).[9]

These rising expenditures on elementary education brought increased reliance on the national budget. Initially, the cost of elementary schooling had been locally borne, coming from the tuition parents paid and from local taxes, with very small amounts from higher levels of government. By 1855, communes still contributed 75 percent of the total, with the rest almost evenly divided between the national government and the departments (12 and 13 percent, respectively). Although expenditures increased in the first decade of the Second Empire, they fell still more heavily on the communes, which provided about 85 percent of the official total (and even more of actual expenditures). The national government's contribution actually fell in the 1850s, both as a proportion of the whole and in absolute amount, reaching a low of only 7 percent in 1862, when departments provided 10 percent. Only then did the state's allocation for primary schooling begin the steady rise that never ceased. In 1866, for the first time, the national government contributed more than departments, and it would do so ever after; even so, it provided only 9 percent of the total. Departmental contributions remained less important, although they also continued to rise steadily in absolute amount before leveling off in the 1880s.

Communes continued to carry the principal burden, but their share was lessening. In 1880, communes provided 53 percent of official expenditures (before most of their voluntary additional expenditures were included in these figures), the state 29 percent, departments 18 percent. Of all the changes the Ferry Laws then established, none was greater than the shift in financing. In effect taking over some of the local tax revenue and then adding to it, the state became the principal source of funds for public primary instruction. In 1882, it provided 66 percent of total expenditures, communes 20 percent, and departments 13 percent. The state's share would stay at about that level until the end of our period, increasing to 67 and then 68 percent before falling a bit toward the end of the century, while communes provided most of the rest.

A historian's preoccupation, periodization is helpful in revealing how multilayered the development of elementary schooling in nineteenth-century France really was. Fundamental though they were, expenditures give only part of the picture. They reflect local commitment, the spread of schooling, professionalization, and increased centralization—all of which contributed to the continuity of rising costs. They show the effects of national policy in the sharply increased expenditures of 1867–68, 1881–82, and 1903–5 and also in the increased proportion of the budget that came from the national ministry after 1865 and again after 1882. That is one chronology, one aspect of how universal schooling in France was shaped, but there are others.

The fundamental step, the establishment of schools, came first, and we saw three stages of development, roughly in the periods 1821–37, 1837–67, and 1876–1906, with the annual growth in the number of schools markedly slower after 1843. Two later periods of increased growth in the establishment of schools, 1850–65 (especially 1863–65) and 1876–86 (especially 1882–86), only faintly echo the far more dramatic increases in expenditures occuring at the same time,[10] and whereas the number of schools essentially ceased to grow by the 1890s, expenditures continued their steady and impressive rise.

Enrollment followed quickly upon the establishment of schools, a sign of important popular commitment to primary instruction. Analysis of enrollment also indicated three periods: 1829–50, 1863–76, and 1881–1906. With somewhat different measures, the first period could be extended, 1829–67; the second contracted, 1872–76; and the third divided into two parts, 1881–91, 1896–1906. Either way, important breaks occurred, breaks that we suggest can be understood as marking the shift to a different stage of development in the national school system, between 1850 and 1863, between 1867 and 1872, and between 1876 and 1891. By 1850 (when three-quarters of France's departments had enrollments equal to 50 percent of the school-age population and one-half the departments had enrollments equal to 60 percent of the target population), the principle of universal primary schooling had been established. By 1876, especially as a result of growth in the period after 1867 (when nearly all departments had enrollments equal to 75 percent of their school-age population and nearly two-thirds of them had enrollments equal to or even greater than their school-age population), universal primary schooling had become the national norm, with anything less viewed as deficient and laggard (table E.14). The third period, then, encompassed some growth (nine-tenths of the departments had enrollments equal to their school-age population by the 1880s), but it was characterized primarily by the increased quality and uniformity achieved through the centralized, national system of universal instruction.

This periodization provides the context within which the growth of Catholic schools and girls enrollment during the Second Empire needs to be understood. Of course, the role of clerical teachers was sharply affected by national policy, and enrollments in Catholic schools reflect it, rising sharply in the Second Empire, declining in the Third Republic, and formally eliminated in 1906. Looked at more closely, these figures also point to something else. The sharp growth in Catholic enrollment occurred from 1850 to 1863 and from 1867 to 1876 (table C.2), having continued beyond the fall of Louis Napoleon until halted with the political changes that established the Third Republic.[11] The distribution of Catholic enrollment among departments was, however, very similar in the period from 1867 to 1876 to the pattern of 1850 and after 1881; it was the extent of change and the shift of Catholic teaching from private to public schools that was exceptional (table C.4). In short, much of the dramatic change in Catholic enrollment was politically induced, but the general history of Catholic enrollment fit within the development of a national educational system. Growth came most strongly as the system itself was rapidly filling out, primarily in public schools, and as the increased enrollment of girls was the principal source of growth. Decline came after enrollment was universal and a national, public system had been established.

The great growth in girls enrollment followed the increase in the number of girls (mostly Catholic) public schools. Two-thirds of France's departments had enrollments equal to 50 percent of their school-age girls by 1850; although not yet the practice, the principle of universal instruction was only slightly less firmly established for girls than for boys. By 1867, three-quarters of the departments had enrollments equal to at least 75 percent of the number of school-age girls. Schooling was reaching most girls through the expansion of Catholic schools, which had 44 percent of girls enrollment in 1850 and 59 percent by 1876. The fight to secularize public schools could take place after the battle to establish universal schooling for girls and boys had been won (nine-tenths of the departments had girls enrollments equal to the number of school-age girls by 1881).

The experience of men and women as teachers was more different than the instruction given boys and girls, and so the data on elementary school teachers gives a somewhat different periodization. By 1837, France already had a great many men (nearly thirty thousand) whose principal occupation was teaching; their number would not quite double by 1906 (table T.1). Although the number of schools increased even less and the number of *titulaires* even less than that, everything else—enrollment, expenditures, qualifications, etc.—increased a great deal more. That is important. As early as the 1830s, *instituteurs* were fairly evenly distributed across the departments of France. Combined with the relatively limited increase in their numbers, that means that the model of the *instituteur* was well established rather early in the century. The important developments centered neither on the creation nor the expansion of that role but on the training for it, particularly in the *écoles normales*. Although departments paid most of the bill, these were in a broader sense expenses of the state,[12] and they were used to create a national cadre associated (rather like engineers) with the state. Ninety percent of the students were on scholarship. This system was expensive—the cost per student was more than the base pay of *instituteurs*—and it worked, in that an overwhelming majority of the normal school graduates then spent a lifetime in teaching.

From 1837 to 1863, the number of graduates remained steady; it then began a steady expansion that crested in 1885–87 (when the number of graduates was double what it had been in 1863) [table T.5]; in a third period, it fell from that high to remain fairly steadily at or above the level of the late 1870s. In the first period, a formal, universal standard for the preparation of male teachers was established (by 1863, one-half of France's *instituteurs* were normal school graduates). In the second period, men's normal schools expanded to meet the needs of all public boys schools, and in the third period, the production of *normaliens* was adjusted to a level that would maintain their monopoly in a mature system (table T.4). A similar pattern, with the stages coming slightly earlier, is discernable in the award of *brevets*. Prior to the 1860s, fewer were awarded than the system could use (rising in 1863 to an annual rate equal to 6 percent of the teachers); after the 1870s, more were awarded than needed (reaching a figure equal to 17 percent the number of teachers by the 1880s).[13]

Matters were quite different with regard to women teachers. The total number of women elementary school teachers in 1837 (some twenty thousand) increased to more than four times that number in 1906. Furthermore, the greatest increase came during the Second Empire, when most of the new women teachers were religious. From 1837 through 1876, in fact, a majority of the women teaching in France's public schools were in religious orders (two-thirds of them in the 1870s) [table T.1]. In contrast, independent schools, where until 1876 most female teachers were laic, did much to establish teaching as a career for women. Thus, the history of women teachers is marked by two distinct patterns. The long-term pattern from midcentury on of sharply increasing numbers breaks into two periods, one dominated by teachers in religious orders and one in which nuns were steadily replaced by lay women. In public schools, lay women outnumbered those in orders by 1882.[14] Only in 1901 did these public school *institutrices* become a majority of all women elementary teachers.

There is another trend as well: in 1837, two of every three school teachers were men; by 1863, more than half of all these elementary teachers were women.[15] Teaching in primary school was becoming a feminine occupation, but not because the government was devoted to teacher training for women. There were only ten *écoles normales* for girls by 1850, but the number then increased, especially with the Third Republic (even in the 1870s most of these normal schools were run by nuns). Girls normal schools had less favorable teacher:student ratios than those for boys, and only about 70 percent of the girls received scholarships (in contrast to 90 percent of the boys)—reduced opportunities that must have been felt locally, for communes contributed a larger proportion of the scholarships for girls in *écoles normales* than for boys. Not until 1901 did more women than men graduate from the normal schools (table T.5). The locally sponsored *cours normaux*, however, served girls primarily, and women, who as early as 1850 claimed about half the *brevets* awarded, took twice as many as men by 1873 (table T.4). In the Third Republic, women then tended to do somewhat better on these exams than men and more often to seek and win higher certification. The state had not decided that elementary teaching was a task especially suited to women, but somehow society did, through the enthusiasm of women for a career in teaching, reinforced perhaps by the fact that women were paid lower salaries and possibly by parental preference (tables T.11 and T.12).

The mature national system of universal instruction was also defined by what it was not. The steady if slow growth of *écoles maternelles* had suggested that kindergartens had social appeal; but those schools, closely associated with Catholic sisters, suffered with the policy of secularization, their enrollments declining in 1886 and 1891 and again in 1901 and 1906 (table Sys.1). Adult education, strongly favored by Duruy as a corrective to illiteracy, reached its highest enrollment in 1867. As adult literacy came to be taken for granted, adult education in the Third Republic tended to become a form of postprimary education, but that possible avenue of social mobility won very limited support. Enrollments fell. The rise in girls enrollment in secondary schools prior to 1906, several times greater than for boys, was certainly one effect of primary schooling. So were the signs of rising pressures for access to more schooling and higher certification. In France, the linkage between primary and secondary schooling was never broken, and the desire for a greater flow from one to another was bound to increase; but all the promises implicit in the growth of *cours* and *écoles primaires supérieures* before 1850 had not been fulfilled seventy years later.

II. System Building

Throughout this study, we have argued for the systemic nature of the development of elementary schooling. The term refers to three qualities, conceptually distinct, but difficult to separate: continuity, inertial energy, and increased national homogeneity. Continuity is notable in several respects. Departments that were early leaders in establishing schools tended to remain leaders one or two generations later in other measures of schooling—an effect both of self-sustaining institutionalization and also of the continuing importance of local attitudes and culture. Inertial energy describes the progressive tendency whereby the fact of having some schools leads to more, schooling for some students leads to some schooling for all, enrollment for a few years grows into enrollment for six or seven years, and the employment of trained teachers makes for higher standards of teacher preparation, and so forth. This inertial energy was sustained by a combination of factors. Not only did primary schooling come to be accepted by most parents, but the village school often became a focus of community pride. That supported a demonstration effect such that improvements in one school were likely to be adopted in others. The system itself contributed with *écoles normales* and scholarships to send promising pupils to them so that more trained teachers were available. Examiners and inspectors came to expect more of public schools, applying rising standards; they in turn pressed for and relied upon more demanding national policies. There was also pressure both within the system and from outside it to make universal instruction more similar across the nation. National policies to that end were, after all, reinforced by a strong administrative state, domestic politics, increased communication and geographic mobility, and greater economic integration.

This systemic effect, beginning with local commitment and culminating in a centralized national educational system, shows in the growth of the education budget. Despite all the variations in local circumstance and all the changes in official policies, expenditures increased from year to year, not only through steady growth in annual budgets but from more sudden increases that then proved irreversible. Bigger budgets appear, in fact, to have been more a result than a cause of increased enrollment and better schooling[16] (table E.17). Initially, enrollment tended to be higher where concentrated population made it easier to provide teachers and schools; enrollment in 1829 and for the next twenty years correlates negatively with expenditure per student. On the other hand, enrollment in 1829 correlates positively with expenditure per student in 1906; departments that were early leaders in schooling came to spend more on schools and teachers later on, well after universal enrollment had been achieved.

Systemic growth, however, brought an important change at the local level in the way schools were financed, as dependence on the fees paid by parents gave way to reliance on funds raised through taxes. Communal contributions had depended heavily on tuition payments, which accounted for considerably more than half of communal expenditures before the 1850s. From 1855 to 1870, tuition provided about half of communal ordinary expenditures on instruction, occasionally a little less and often a little more (still not counting most of the voluntary expenditures or most of the cost of buildings).[17] Total revenue from tuition reached its height in 1869, and tuition began its marked decline as a source of communal expenditure from that point on (table Ex.2), falling to 37 percent of communal ordinary expenditures by 1876 and 1877 and to only about 20 percent by 1881.[18] At the national level, revenue from tuition accounted for 30 percent of total expenditures in 1855, and that proportion rose steadily, reaching 35 percent in 1860 and 37 percent in 1863, staying at about that level through 1867. It fell to about 33 percent in the next two years, to 30 percent in 1870 and under 27 percent in 1871, declining a bit each year to 24 percent in 1873 and 21 percent in 1877.

Departments had varied in the amount of tuition charged and in their reliance upon it, receiving annually between 4 and 5.3 francs per student in 1850 (when tuition was the largest single source of local expenditure) and between 4.8 and 10.5 francs per student in 1863 (when tuition provided less than half of what communes spent). All departments exempted some parents and increasing numbers of communes exempted all from paying these fees. Socially and politically, tuition proved an inelastic source of income, and the shift away from it reflects the importance of local opinion in the development of primary schooling. Taxes also assured the predictability and institutional autonomy congenial to an established national system of public instruction. It was state policy, however, that earmarked the taxes available for education and that assured a smooth transition to them without reducing revenue. Public schooling rested on a firm tax base by the time the Ferry Laws ratified the trend and nationalized the practice.

The impact of centralization also showed in the formal distinction between ordinary and extraordinary expenditures. Ordinary expenditures came from levies (both special taxes and, more often, a percentage of regular taxes) assigned to education as required by the national government. The proportion of total expenditures classified as extraordinary can be calculated for the period from 1855 on, and they tell more about the system than about local attitudes.[19] Extraordinary expenditures represented optional additional levies assessed within the narrow limits nationally permitted. In theory they might be a useful historical indicator of added effort, maybe even of local enthusiasm, that raised money for public schooling beyond the required minimum. In 1885, ordinary expenditures accounted for over 90 percent of total expenditures in more than one-third of France's departments, over 85 percent in more than two-thirds, and over 75 percent in all but three departments. The range was not very great; meeting legal requirements was a major burden. Furthermore, those requirements tended to rise. By 1891, in only a dozen departments were ordinary expenditures less than 85 percent of the total (and in only two less than 80 percent). Heavy reliance on ordinary expenditures could indicate a strong tax base or, from the Second Empire on, a poorer department's dependence upon subsidies from Paris. Thus, extraordinary expenditures most often accounted for the highest percentage of the total budget in poor departments where total expenditures were relatively low by national standards but help from the national government was not yet substantial. That began to change by the late 1860s and disappeared with the more generous payments from the national government (counted as ordinary expenditures) in the Third Republic.[20] By then, it was largely urban departments that had the highest proportion of extraordinary expenses, but this resulted less from their higher standards than from national policy, which required the largest cities to pay most of the cost of their schools. Prosperous departments, in short, were able to meet almost all of their educational needs from the taxes assigned by the state to public schools. For poorer departments, meeting requirements was a long struggle finally relieved by the Ferry Laws and subsequent measures. For all departments, the range of optional expenditure, never large, had narrowed as educational policy in general and expenditures in particular were increasingly determined by the state.

Expenditures, then, measure the effort required more than the results produced. They correlate fairly strongly with the number of schools at midcentury but do so more and more weakly thereafter (when the number of schools changed less than other aspects of the system).[21] Similarly, for the nation as a whole, expenditures per student were generally more closely related to teachers' salaries than to enrollment (despite a high correlation in 1833) [table E.17]. From 1837 to 1850, expenditure per teacher stayed about the same, and expenditures rose, nationally, because more teachers were hired.[22] The sharpest rise in cost per teacher came between 1850 and 1863 and again between 1863 and 1868 in nearly every department, a result of a better and more universal pay scale. Thereafter, expenditure per teacher steadily increased, as salaries went up and other needs came to command more of the budget while the number of teachers stayed about the same—all matters largely decided by state policies that set salaries, determined the number of teachers needed, and authorized most other expenses.

The range among departments had never been as great on this as on many other indicators. The presence of the state was felt from the first.[23] Nor was expenditure per teacher tightly tied to quality. Salaries were higher in urban departments, which does seem to have helped them attract experienced teachers, but expenditure per teacher was also affected by years of experience, the level of certification, and the proportion of *titulaires* and *adjoints*. Thus, leaders and laggards in the other measures of schooling are mixed together at both the top and the bottom on lists of costs per teacher[24] (table Ex. 4). Higher pay acknowledged the importance of the *instituteur* and *institutrice*, and broad social engagement was involved in the remarkable growth in spending on education, an increase especially striking in the amount spent per student. During the second half of the nineteenth century, that doubled every fifteen years.[25] In a society struggling to meet the burdensome requirements for universal schooling, differences in cost per student had initially been mainly a matter of necessity, the result of higher pay in cities or scattered, small schools in the countryside.

Seen on a national scale, expanded schooling tended to be irreversible and the pressures for growth (which included local commitment and parental wishes, national requirements, and the ambitions of teachers) tended to be greater than the resistance based on custom, parental need, dislike of taxes, resentment of state instrusion, and ideological disagreement. Locally, the picture was more uneven, but it is possible to discern some common patterns. A sharp rise in a department's enrollment, for example, was often followed by a small decline before beginning again on a steady rise. The pressures that brought many new students to school brought some unwilling or unable to stay, pushed a department somewhat beyond the level local circumstances or habits could support, then established a new standard that in turn created new customs and pressures. Departments with low enrollment in the 1820s were likely to take a long time to reach full enrollment; those with high enrollment by 1832 tended to see their schools expand rapidly to a level at which enrollment equaled 110 percent or more of the school-age population. Some repeated patterns suggest the possibility of distinct stages of growth. At any time, once 70 percent of the school-age population was enrolled, full enrollment was likely to follow quickly, and the rise from 10 to 30 percent of that population enrolled also tended to be rapid. The stretch between seems often to have taken longer.

The clearest statistical evidence of resistance to pressures for more schooling is the drop in attendance during the summer months. Even that reflected personal choices as well as local attitudes. Most students went to school when they were supposed to; summer attendance was generally lower where winter attendance was very high and especially where it had only recently risen (conditions particularly common in the period from the 1840s to 1860s). A sizable minority resisted the system's more stringent demands, particularly at first, and only the more talented or privileged minority took the special examinations for the *certificat d'études*.

The growth of Catholic enrollment in the Second Empire was part of the process that built a national system. Clerical teachers taught less than one-third of France's elementary school students in 1850, when Catholic teachers had 40 percent of the enrollment in independent schools and 24 percent of the enrollment in public schools (table C.2). Then their enrollment grew much faster than that of schools with lay teachers, but it was in Catholic *public* schools that most of this growth occurred, contributing to the growth of the public system. The emphasis upon Catholic public schools in the Second Empire, which gave them an added political taint in the eyes of republicans, was also a Catholic admission that the state had a preeminent interest in schooling and that clerical teachers could not fill all the teaching posts a universal system required.

Furthermore, Catholic enrollments came primarily in regions where enrollment had been lower; clerical teachers were helping the system to spread. And Catholic schools joined in, and probably helped to accelerate, a number of trends affecting the system as a whole: the trends toward more girls schools, larger schools with assistant teachers (*adjoints*), rising attendance in the summer months, the elimination of tuition charges, and the development of *écoles maternelles*. The process of system building continued even as public schools were turned over to lay teachers in the Third Republic. That shift was widely understood as one of professionalization and the establishment of higher and more uniform standards, a continuity of development seen as natural. It was also vigorously opposed on political and religious grounds, and that spurred the establishment of many new Catholic independent schools. Resistance to laicization could also stem from a practical concern about increased cost.[26] The competition between lay public and Catholic independent schools may in turn have contributed to increased enrollments (in that sense assisting the final step in the creation of universal instruction). Private or independent schools proved politically vulnerable, however, as they became nearly synonymous with Catholic schools, bastions of a Catholic subculture in opposition to the national system of public schools.

The importance of Catholic teachers to the development of elementary schools in this period raises for historians a question much debated by contemporaries: Did Catholic schools cost less? Communes employed members of religious orders to teach in their public schools for many reasons. Four have already been discussed. Enrollment in Catholic schools, public and private, was highest in departments reputed to be very "Catholic" as indicated by measures of religious practice and clerical influence. The preference for clerical teachers was, first of all, a religious one. Second, public policy favored the use of clerical teachers in the first decade or so of the Second Empire, a policy that obviously appealed to Catholics but offered reassurance to others as well that public schools would not be nurseries of revolution; the greatest increase in the number and proportion of students sitting in front of clerical teachers occurred between 1850 and 1863. Third, girls schools were the most likely to be taught by religious, a cultural preference for having girls trained by nuns that extended beyond general attachment to the church and overlapped with a fourth reason, pragmatism. Members of religious orders were often, especially in the first two-thirds of the century, the best prepared teachers available and those most likely to divide a sizable school into several classes. A related argument for preferring that members of religious orders be hired to teach in public schools was that they cost the community less.

That claim, often asserted by those who favored Catholic schooling and denied by advocates of a secular and professional teaching corps, has similarly been disputed but not resolved by historians. It is difficult to test and not only because departmental data include both kinds of schools. The proportion of students in public schools taught by members of religious orders tended, we know, to be higher in departments that were slower to develop universal instruction and that spent less on schools. Statistically, cause and effect here are inseparable, but there are some suggestive indications. Ordinary expenditures per student tended to be lower as the proportion of public school students taught by clerical teachers increased. Such figures must be used cautiously, however, for costs per student were also likely to be lower in bigger, more urban schools of the type the congregations preferred.[27] It is useful, therefore, to try another tack. We can identify the departments with highest Catholic enrollments for a closer look. From 1850 to 1882, eleven departments were at least 1.5 times above the national mean in the proportion of their students in public schools taught by members of religious orders.[28] Four of these departments were in the bottom quartile for enrollment in 1832, five near the mean, only one a little above; we would expect them to spend less than others for schools. They did, and by a margin large enough to permit the possibility that there was some economy in using clerical teachers.[29] The indication is reinforced by comparison with the thirteen departments that remained 1.5 times below the national mean in the proportion of their public school students with clerical teachers. As a group, these departments were close to the national mean in per capita expenditures during the 1860s and a little above thereafter.[30] In 1872, the group of departments with highest Catholic public school enrollment spent 57 percent as much per capita as the group with the fewest students in Catholic public schools, and that group in 1882 spent 71 percent as much. It may well have cost communes somewhat less to employ Catholic teachers in their public schools.

For the nation as a whole, girls enrollments had never lagged far behind boys; even in 1837 the percentage of school-age girls enrolled was only about 3 percent less than the percentage of school-age boys (table E.2). Growth thereafter followed systemically, with girls enrollment a bit lower than boys (often about what boys enrollment had been ten years before) but steadily catching up, an orderly process that shows most clearly in the analysis of the octiles based on total enrollment in 1832. There was a notable absence of resistance to sending girls to school. Indeed, the pattern of expansion, with its reliance on private and Catholic schools, suggests that the desire of French parents to see their daughters in elementary school ran ahead of the facilities (schools and lay teachers) the state could provide. This can be easily overlooked, however, because girls enrollments depended heavily on mixed schools that accepted both girls and boys and on private schools, using the available resources when the state did not provide the separate, public girls schools desired in principle. But whereas there were more independent girls schools than public ones in 1863 (with about one-third the total enrollment of girls), by 1875 two-thirds of the girls schools were public ones.

Across the nation this growth of girls public schools was a growth of schools taught by nuns. Catholic girls schools were less likely to charge tuition than lay schools,[31] and the percentage of girls in them varied less department by department than did most measures of education; 44 percent of the girls in primary schools in 1850 enrolled in Catholic schools, and 59 percent did so by 1876. Then the campaign to put public schools in lay hands began, with girls enrollment already essentially universal and primarily in public schools. The relatively even distribution of Catholic girls schools also suggests that many parents felt particularly comfortable in having girls taught by nuns, and a closer analysis of the data on the rise and decline of Catholic girls schools suggested that this cultural, gender-specific preference was a principal factor in the popularity of these schools. Next in importance was local Catholic tradition, followed by national policy (favoring and then discouraging Catholic teachers in public schools), and then by institutional convenience (the fact of having a Catholic girls school at hand). As Catholic schooling retreated to independent schools, which became almost wholly Catholic and represented a conscious choice in open resistance to public policy, enrollment remained higher in private Catholic girls schools than in those for boys.

An important finding of our analysis is that in the 1860s, the national government significantly helped departments where girls enrollments increased the most to meet their rising costs. Total expenditures rose sharply during the 1860s, in the nation as a whole (at an annual rate of about 8 percent) and in those departments with the highest rise in girls enrollment, while the percentage of total expenditures paid for by communes and departments began to decline. That decline was nearly twice as great in departments where girls enrollment increased the most.[32]

The systemic development of the school system is nicely exemplified by the data on teachers. Public schools were built around *instituteurs*—male, public school teachers—understood to be professional civil servants. Thus, their additional service as communal secretary or assistant to the curé (and they often did both) would come to seem a distraction and subordination inappropriate for professionals; but in the 1830s and 1840s, those social connections undoubtedly helped to establish the *instituteur's* place in the local community. In 1837, *instituteurs* constituted half of the elementary school teachers in France (male and female, public and private), and although that proportion would decline in the second half of the century as the number of women teaching in public and independent schools increased, they remained numerous enough to define a profession.

Furthermore, they were rather well distributed across the departments of France, a familiar, national model, and they were easily subject to the rising requirements that strengthened their identity and increased their status (and accompanied a rise in salary). *Instituteurs* were more likely than other teachers to have the *brevet* and then *brevets complets*, and by 1863, half of the *instituteurs* were graduates of *écoles normales* (table T.7). Primarily the sons of artisans, peasants, and school teachers who had attended normal school on scholarship, they formed the cadre of victors in academic competition on which universal, secular schooling was built.

That required women teachers as well, however, and gender differences were striking. A majority of the women teaching in independent schools had been lay women up until 1863, but the majority of women teaching in public schools were religious from 1837 to 1882, a period in which their total number increased fivefold. The need for more women teachers had been provided rapidly and relatively inexpensively by Catholic orders. From 1876 on, however, the sisters teaching in public schools were replaced by *institutrices*, who usually had more formal training, were more eager to take examinations for *brevets*, and came to be more and more like *instituteurs* in terms of social origin, training, and certification. A majority of the elementary school teachers of France were women by 1863, but only in 1891 did women become a majority of the *titulaires*. No longer primarily *adjoints* in religious orders, they constituted half of all the public school teachers by 1906 (when they were three-quarters of all the independent school teachers); by then, the practice of women teaching in mixed classes that included boys was well established.

The fact that the great increase in women teachers came primarily from the expansion of teaching orders under the Second Empire had multiple effects. It made growth easier and faster; quite possibly, the presence of nuns also made schooling for girls more attractive, making it appear safer and more traditional than it might otherwise have seemed. The availability of women's teaching orders also allowed, and probably encouraged, the slow establishment of *écoles normales* for girls. Only ten departments had them by 1850 and only seventeen by 1875; not until the 1880s did all departments fall into line. Awareness of the religious alternative may have been a factor in the continuing tendency to encourage women less than men toward teaching as a career, to provide a smaller proportion of girls than boys with scholarships, and to pay female teachers less than their male counterparts. These practices followed from government policy (the first women inspector of schools was appointed in 1891), but social attitudes were somewhat different. The number of women seeking certification as teachers leaped ahead of male applications, and the *cours normaux* were essentially a local response (most often provided by some religious order) to the desire of girls to teach or at least become qualified to do so. Nuns may well have created a model that made teaching seem especially appropriate for women (and that tended to expect lay women teachers to display the restraint in dress and behavior of a nun). Thus, the lay, woman teacher was a recognized figure even as the Third Republic made a place for her and insisted that she be like the *instituteur* in selection and training.

This double sense of systemic growth for which we have argued throughout this book—incremental changes each building upon the last but also development driven by the system itself—is also illustrated by the changed meaning of *adjoints*. Initially, the term generally referred to less qualified assistant teachers. Hiring them was an economy attractive to departments that had lagged in providing universal schooling, and the practice was more readily adopted in departments that used a high proportion of teachers from religious orders. More flexible and less concerned with certification, religious orders also had more personnel available because they were required to live in small groups if not full-fledged communities. As the educational system was secularized, the practice of employing *adjoints* was maintained where it had been prevalent before, even as *adjoints* increasingly came to be normal school graduates in their apprenticeship years and classroom teachers in multiclass schools. The device for using less qualified teachers had been transformed into a means for raising quality by having smaller classes.

The combined factors of continuity, inertial growth, and institutionalization worked together to create a model of universal primary education, a model clear enough that we have been able to apply it statistically, retroactively using the conception of partial fulfillment of the model as a measure of a department's degree of progress along a predictable path. In analyzing the changes that took place in elementary education, it is often impossible to establish the relative importance of legislation, administrative requirements, internal tendencies shared by inspectors and *instituteurs*, and local politics and pressures. But the important point is that these diverse modes of decision making tended to work in the same direction and often with considerable local support. If professionalization felt like progress to many, so did institutionalization that brought more uniform standards, curriculum, and teachers across France. Much of French schooling had from the first been shaped by the state, by legislation requiring schools and setting revenue and pay. But centralization increased with the growing importance of *écoles normales*, examinations for *brevets*, and a corps of inspectors. So much is made of the centralized French system, however, that it is easy to forget the strong local roots the system sustained through local politics, public ceremonies, and departmental organizations even after another important local linkage through the Church was cut off.

The limitations brought by centralized institutionalization show more clearly by the end of the century as developments that might have taken place were slowed or restricted. Even then, however, parental aims and local practices resisted circumscription. As courses for adults changed in social significance from remedial offerings to something more like continuing education, the state lost interest, but enrollment in adult courses in 1876 was still higher than it had been in 1850. By 1886, although only a minority of communes offered any adult courses, three-fourths of those taking them were enrolled in *cours complémentaires* rather than elementary classes, and the number of women enrolled had risen from a tiny fraction to about one-half the number of men.[33]

Ecoles maternelles also served mixed purposes, as sources of day care, of instruction in order and cleanliness, and of preschool training. Enrollment in these schools at first correlated with early primary enrollment, but the growth stopped well short of becoming universal, and variation among departments remained high, at least in part an effect of national policy. In the 1880s, the state set higher formal standards for the qualifications required of teachers in *écoles maternelles* but lessened its financial support (in 1886), and these schools were often absorbed into elementary schools as adjunct classes. Although *écoles maternelles* were not found primarily where Catholic schooling was generally strong but in urban and industrial areas, they had developed something of their own culture, especially in the predominance of Catholic nuns, which undoubtedly made them less attractive to republican educators.

The government also tended consistently to view secondary and primary schooling as two distinct systems serving different clienteles. Departments that led in secondary schooling were not necessarily those with high elementary enrollments. Rather than assume that talented or interested elementary students would go on to secondary schools, the July Monarchy had provided for *écoles primaires supérieures*. Abandoned by the Second Empire, some of these schools continued nevertheless, presumably in response to local demand. The Third Republic established new regulations for them in the 1880s. They were to provide a two-year program and have their own faculty; in addition, a one-year higher course could be attached to elementary schools. These provisions were soon altered, expanding the e.p.s. to a three-year program and the *cours* to two years. Popular ambition for some further instruction and the social mobility it was expected to permit was manifest in the more rapid expansion of the supplementary *cours*. More than half of the students in these *cours* were girls, two-thirds of them in classes taught by religious. Only a minority of elementary students benefited from these options, but they indicate both an increasing interest and widening opportunities.[34] A small proportion of the students in e.p.s. held scholarships, but they did rather well. Of the 15 percent of the boys and 12 percent of the girls in e.p.s. who went on to other schools, some 40 percent had been on scholarships. The e.p.s. were intended, however, to provide a kind of professional training for a limited number of students aspiring to lower middle-class occupations, especially in state employment as officials and teachers; and in fact, graduates of these schools were especially likely to enter government employment on completing their studies. Nevertheless, the e.p.s., like secondary schools, had not been fostered as a natural extension of primary school. They were more likely to be found where there was higher urbanization, literacy, and wealth than in departments that had led in elementary schooling. The basis for the more integrated educational system that was created much later had already been laid, and there were signs of a popular desire for such an evolution. But that continuation of a process begun early in the century was not permitted.

III. Local and Regional Patterns

One of the aims of universal instruction was to overcome some of the local and regional differences in French society. As we have seen, however, primary schooling also incorporated many of these differences; they persisted, for example, in the number of schools a department established. These departmental differences in turn often had regional aspects (although not necessarily conforming to historic regions), as shown in our analyses of departments arranged in various geographical groupings. Differences in needs, capacity, and commitment remained, but state policy, by legislation and by equalizing expenditure, could do something to make schooling more equal across France.

Budgets thus provide a useful measure of that effort. The early differences among departments in their per capita expenditures on elementary education were greatly reduced by 1855, and the coefficient of variation among departments, 47 percent in 1837, had fallen to 31 percent by 1863. After that, however, it was reduced only slightly more, standing at 25 percent in 1886, its lowest point, and being somewhat higher from then to 1906.[35] Centralization did more to standardize instruction than it could to equalize costs. The communes and departments least able to raise the necessary funds received important subsidies, which brought their expenditures closer to the national norm, but there was a limit. The departments in which per capita expenditures were lowest at the beginning of the Third Republic had generally been in that position for a long time and would on the whole remain there, although the difference was somewhat narrowed.[36]

This reduction in difference was achieved by a significant variation among departments in the proportion of their educational expenditures that came from local (meaning primarily communal but also departmental) funds.[37] The proportion of departmental expenditures locally paid for was indeed related to its wealth as national policy intended it should be.[38] Locally financed expenditures thus correlated more strongly with per capita wealth than with the amount of schooling provided. Differences in wealth were more easily compensated for, however, than other more fundamental differences, and total departmental expenditures tended to correlate most strongly with early enrollment, literacy, and urban population than per capita wealth (table Ex.5). National policy, which lessened the gap between poorer and wealthier departments, could not eliminate other structural and cultural factors.[39]

Certainly expenditure and the tax base on which it rested mattered, and, for the nation as a whole, the departments that spent the most per capita led in enrollment and subsequently in other signs of quality. Other factors counted as much or more, however. From 1837 to 1868, the ordinary expenditures per student of the departments in the top three octiles (based on enrollment in 1832) were below the national mean.[40] Only from 1882 on did even the top two octiles begin consistently to have ordinary expenditures per student above the mean. This apparent anomaly was related to dependence on tuition as a source of income. Earlier in the century, tuition was generally an important component of the revenue that supported ordinary expenditures. The leading departments, however, which exempted more of their students from having to pay tuition and often abolished it entirely, thus often raised less money per student for ordinary expenditure (despite the fact that they raised more money per capita from tuition because more children were in school) [table Ex.2].

Culture and geography were especially important in the early history of French primary schooling. Literacy correlated more strongly with enrollment than per capita wealth or urban population; with the momentum progressives believed in, higher literacy brought larger enrollments and higher enrollments were followed by increased literacy.[41] A department's per capita wealth, although never decisive, did correlate with its enrollment, but that relationship disappeared by the Third Republic. Similarly, before 1867 but not thereafter, enrollment tended to be higher where a large part of the population was distinctly urban. In effect, some of the initial advantages of wealth and concentrated population were overcome, particularly with regard to enrollment and teachers' pay, but the picture is complex.

Because local differences remained important, patterns first visible in the 1830s remained throughout the century. If departmental rankings reveal a persistent pattern in the amounts spent on education, they can also suggest some explanations for a continuity which is all the more impressive considering the many changes during seventy years in accounting,[42] funding, services paid for, and total costs. Expenditures in 1837 might be expected to correlate with enrollment a few years earlier (because rising numbers of students required more teachers), and they did, at .88. Even by the end of the century, however, per capita expenditures still showed some correlation with enrollment in 1832 ($r = .46$); the circumstances that created an early educational lead sustained a willingness to spend more on education.[43] Although less significant than expenditure per capita, expenditures per student suggest three important elements in this pattern: the bottom third of the departments, ranked by enrollment in 1832, consistently spent less per student; expenditure per student was not a major reason for the ranking of the upper two-thirds of France's departments; and departments in the top two octiles, which had spent less per student than the national mean from 1837 to 1868, came to spend above the mean *after* 1872.[44] Pearson correlations of each department's total expenditures per capita in 1837 with expenditures at later dates reveal an impressive tenacity and point to the 1850s and the 1880s as periods of major shifts toward greater equality.[45] The octiles of departments based on their enrollment in 1832 tended to predict per capita expenditures at later dates,[46] but the statistical clusters based on a variety of indicators and described in chapter 3 clarify the picture more than the octiles (table Ex.3). The score of departments in the top two clusters remain well ahead of all the others in per capita expenditure throughout the century. The third and fourth clusters near the mean keep that position and draw closer together.[47] The remaining three clusters, containing half the departments of France, also keep their respective positions, with the four departments in the final cluster markedly behind the others.[48]

Two overlapping groups of explanations thus need to be borne in mind, one essentially structural and the other (somewhat vaguely) cultural. Expenditures were always related to the special circumstances of towns—the easier access for students and the higher pay for teachers, the more varied educational opportunities offered, the generally better level of facilities provided, and the different funding that applied to the largest cities.[49] Expenditures were considerably less closely and less consistently related, however, to a department's per capita wealth[50] (table Ex.5). From the 1860s on, a department's expenditures coming from departmental and communal funds correlated almost not at all with these other indicators,[51] an achievement of national policy.

On the other hand, even in the mature system of 1901 and 1902 voluntary expenditures reflect old commitments. A small proportion of the total budget and restricted by law, such matters were essentially a matter of communal choice (except for the largest cities, which were required to raise most of the cost of their schools). At the beginning of the new century, they still tended to be greater where summer attendance had been high in the 1830s and in departments that had been early leaders in schools and enrollment (table Ex.8). It is noteworthy, too, how many departments spent all the money the law allowed.[52]

IV. Analysis by Statistical Clusters

Historical analysis of French society has paid a great deal of attention not just to local variation but to regional differences. Although the boundaries of these regions often differ according to topic and to the scale on which analysis is conducted, French regional analysis tends powerfully to combine geographic features, a very long view of historical development, cultural characteristics including dialect and custom, and economic structure. The results, even when set forth in detailed and lengthy books, are often summarized in maps. Something similar can be done with the history of primary schooling in the nineteenth century, and many such maps have been published, none perhaps more impressive than those in the introductions to the *Statistique de l'enseignement* on which this study relies so heavily. Rather than reprint those here, despite their attractiveness and utility, we have chosen to explore the possibilities of what analysis by computer might add. There are, of course, two severe limitations. All the awkwardness of analysis in terms of departments is magnified in mapping, for even when gradations indicated on a map are so numerous as to confuse the eye, they allow much less subtlety than numbers. Furthermore, maps that combine many variables become difficult to interpret while separate maps for each variable at each data point leave continuity and change hard to visualize.

We have experimented, therefore, with maps constructed on the basis of statistical analysis in which the data are manipulated and combined statistically to produce a limited grouping of departments. The groups are statistically determined to achieve a maximum reduction of variation between departments on a single variable or multiple variables across many data points. This complicated technique, which is in effect a comparison of means within groups and over time, itself involves a good deal of statistical generalization. Its advantages are simply that these summations of differences are made numerically rather than by the eyes of draftsmen and readers and that they do not assume any configuration of departments into regions already familiar from tradition and studies of other subjects. We presented a map of this sort, combining variables to depict the geography of primary schooling's development, in figure 7 of chapter 3.

Similar techniques could be used to construct other groupings of departments for any variables, and we have considered that for six of them. The more groups, of course, the greater the reduction in variation; we have limited ourselves to seven groups. These are then constructed through an elaborate series of calculations to create seven clusters of departments that are more like each other than they are to the rest of France in their movement on that single variable across all data points assigned to it. The results are presented statistically in table Ex.7. Obviously, such statistically constructed clusters based on a single variable can reduce variance far more effectively than any grouping based on actual geography or multiple variables, but the effort is informative in other ways.

Girls enrollment, the first variable, measures girls enrollment as a percentage of the school-age population in its period of greatest change. The clusters created in effect separate out a few smaller groups of departments that changed the least and the most, familiar leaders and laggards in enrollment, from four clusters more similar in size and less extreme in the amount of change they experienced.[53] Girls enrollment here shows itself essentially a by-product of enrollment overall, and the more straightforward geographical groups of academies and the old provinces are somewhat closer to these clusters than are the clusters constructed to represent systemic development or the regional patterns of secondary schooling.

Girls enrollment as a percentage of total enrollment, however, presents a quite different picture. The issue here is gender discrimination, the difference between girls and boys enrollments whatever their level. It produces groups closer to those of the clusters of systemic development and the regions of secondary schooling than to geographically based groupings. The principal point that emerges from this analysis, however, remains the similarity in girls and boys enrollments throughout most of France. Thus, one cluster contains forty-seven departments (with a mean for girls enrollment of 45 percent in 1837 and just under 50 percent in 1876), and three clusters are composed of a single department, each of which differed notably from the nation as a whole: Corse, where girls constituted half of low enrollment in 1837 but dropped to 43 percent of total enrollment as more boys came to school; Seine, where girls constituted 38 percent of total enrollment in 1837 and 55 percent in 1876; and Haute-Loire, where girls enrollments were consistently and markedly behind those for boys, rising from 10 to 37 percent of the total.[54]

Reducing variance among departments in terms of the percentage of their enrollment in Catholic schools (during the period when those schools were most prominent) produces another set of clusters, but these, too, are closer to the clusters of systemic development and to the secondary school regions than to regional groupings—a somewhat surprising result that supports the case for the importance of Catholic schools within the larger process of expanding primary instruction. Here, too, there are some notable outliers: Loire, all by itself with the highest Catholic enrollments in France, 75 percent of total enrollment in 1850, falling to 64 percent in 1881; Corse and Haute-Vienne, a cluster of two with a sharp drop in Catholic enrollments that had never been high (falling from 35 to just over 18 percent). The other five clusters follow a similar pattern, rising sharply in the 1860s, peaking in 1876, and falling in 1881 to a level close to that of 1850; the largest of the clusters marks the national mean, one of the two next largest stays well below the mean, and two smaller clusters are above it. These clusters are not a map of Catholic conviction but of institutionalization and local choices, perhaps convenience.[55]

The use of *adjoints* in the Third Republic, also closely tied to systemic development, is another variable that produces clusters closer to groupings that measure the educational system than to those rooted in geography. Clusters did not fluctuate much on this measure;[56] institutional practices were sustained, and one would expect the Seine to use a higher percentage of *adjoints* than any other department and to stand out from all the rest. The cluster with the next highest use of *adjoints* contained departments that were urban and Catholic, and there is a cluster of departments in which the employment of *adjoints* dropped after 1872, apparently the result of rising standards for teacher qualification (some of these were poorer departments).[57] The use of *adjoints*, then, reflected demography and culture and habit but also the development of a national system with common standards.

The remaining two variables to which we applied cluster analysis proved less interesting. In the analysis of adult classes, systemic clusters and secondary school regions both significantly reduce variance, and that is suggestive; such classes tended to be offered in greater numbers where schools were well established and strong. But the enrollment in such courses throughout the nation changed very sharply (from small enrollments in 1850 and 1863 that then peaked between 1867 and 1872 before falling off in 1876), and the period was strongly affected by territorial changes. Two-thirds of the departments fall into two clusters, and the outliers reveal little.[58] For different reasons, clusters based on the ratio of students to teachers do not add much to what we already know. In a broad sense an indirect measure of quality, the ratio reached its peak in most departments in 1840 and then declined as more teachers were added. National patterns were so similar over the century, however, that even seven clusters prove less effective than usual in reducing variance, and geographical groupings are much more telling than those based on systemic development precisely because population distribution was important in determining class size.[59]

On the whole, then, the map of France (fig. 7 in chap. 3), based on clusters designed to reflect the overall development of the instructional system, holds up as the most useful picture of schooling across the entire period of this study. Based on a number of measures of (usually sequential) development, they modify familiar views. The northeast (with Savoy) does lead, but it is a smaller northeast than that more crudely described by the St. Malo–Geneva line, and its lead is not so dramatic as verbal descriptions often imply. The slightly less advanced region of the northeast is in turn immediately followed by three parallel tiers of descending levels of schooling, each close to the other. Similarly, there is a large and distinct group, which we have called the western wedge, of laggards, but it also falls into three graduated sections with the most developed close to the bottom of those middle tiers. These gradations are crucial, for they indicate an essentially national development quite early on, drawing the diverse regions of France ever closer together in terms of elementary education. These groupings also indicate the early and continuing importance of the instructional system as a counterweight to older divisions; for these statistical groups, although tending to describe regions and favoring contiguity, are not exactly contiguous nor do they recapture a great deal of the older provinces, regions as traditionally described, or academies as officially administered. The national mean was not merely statistical but had real meaning for the majority of France's departments that clustered near it. On one hand, local circumstances made a greater difference and, on the other, national trends had greater impact than emphasis on French regionalism would lead one to expect.

When the seven groups created by the cluster analysis of systemic development are analyzed separately in terms of variables other than those included in the construction of these clusters, the result tends to support the broad conclusions reached in this study. There was remarkable consistency in the relative prominence of Catholic schools among the departments of France. That consistency, however, depended on much more than religious sentiment. Catholic enrollments were highest in departments along the Rhône and in the west, but not in all of them. Their strength depended upon the early establishment of an extensive network of Catholic schools (as in the department of the Rhône) and upon a relatively large urban population, especially in smaller cities. Catholic schools prospered especially in terms of girls schooling and were therefore more prominent in departments where girls schooling grew rapidly in the 1860s (departments that had generally lagged in enrollment). The fact that Catholic enrollments were not universally high in Catholic departments and that they stood out in departments less accustomed to universal instruction may have made their subsequent secularization somewhat easier.

The largest gaps between the enrollment of boys and of girls occurred in mountainous departments with scattered populations (e.g., Hautes-Alpes), where boys enrollments were also low (Corse, Creuse, Deux-Sèvres, Haute-Loire, Pyrénées-Orientales, and also Ariège and Drôme, always below the mean in enrollment), and where boys enrollments suddenly rose and girls enrollments had not yet caught up. That differential tended to last in departments that were laggards in enrollment and had fewer Catholic schools than most (Charente, Charente-Inférieure, Corse, Pyrénées-Orientales, Deux-Sèvres, Vienne). Stronger where there were towns and commerce, girls enrollment tended to be weaker in agricultural areas.

Some departments (Hérault, Lozère, Hautes-Pyrénées, and Basses-Alpes) do seem to have sustained an earlier tradition of producing more teachers than needed locally. But the size of *écoles normales* was determined by officials who kept a close eye on local needs and not by the ambitions of primary school graduates. Of course, areas slow to develop public schools also tended to lag in establishing boys normal schools (e.g., Morbihan, Pas-de-Calais, Oise, Charente, Côtes-du-Nord, Lot, Haute-Savoie). Nevertheless, the educational system succeeded remarkably well in establishing national standards for teachers, and, because departments that led in schooling already had the teachers they needed as *écoles normales* were expanding, graduates of these schools were surprisingly evenly distributed across the nation. That process was slower and more contentious in terms of women teachers. In 1837, only two departments (Marne and Aveyron) had 85 percent of the *institutrices* they would need in 1901; by 1876, however, the number of women who sought the *brevet* correlated very strongly, department by department, with the number of men who did so—a general cultural attitude and established institutions were overcoming some traditional differences.

These different elements of the school system often reinforced each other. Among departments with large differences in girls and boys enrollment, five also stood out as laggards in the establishment of *écoles maternelles*,[60] and four of them depended almost exclusively on revenue raised for ordinary expenditures.[61] Some departments where enrollment in *écoles maternelles* was unusually low also had exceptionally low enrollments in adult classes.[62] Three departments with high Catholic enrollment also stood out for very high enrollments in their *écoles maternelles*.[63] Of those that early in the century employed nearly all the teachers they would ever need, some also stood out for large enrollments in adult courses[64] and some for high enrollments in *écoles maternelles*.[65] Such relationships were not automatic, however, and the generalizations they invite cannot be pushed very far. Local factors and momentary changes could produce great and sometimes surprising variations in the many aspects of primary schooling, while official policies pressed all toward a national norm. Analyzed in terms of national means, rank order, and variation, these complex departmental data that hide internal diversity obscure much that only local studies can reveal, even as they establish the uneven but almost inexorable movement toward a coherent national system. To emphasize the importance of sytemic development is also to underscore the importance of the fact that in each commune and department schooling had its own history.

V

The history of elementary education in the nineteenth century is related to many issues of modern social change that preoccupy social scientists, especially those having to do with the transformation of "traditional" society, gender differences, social mobility, bureaucratization, and state making. Although the quantitative analysis undertaken here speaks to these issues only indirectly, it does suggest some further questions; for once general impressions have been tested and modified and patterns of development observed in a different way, a different perspective emerges.

If schooling spread quite steadily leaving little evidence of sizable or persistant popular resistance, the pressing question becomes why attending school should have been so acceptable to so many, even to peasants and even when they had to pay for it. How did so many of the poor, often themselves illiterate, come to believe that their children would benefit from at least a few years in school? Assumptions, as natural to twentieth-century professors as they were to nineteenth-century bourgeois reformers, about the structural rigidity and intransigent attitudes of rural society may well deserve to be challenged in European history as they have been by anthropologists studying other societies. Perhaps many attitudes easily labeled bourgeois were in fact broadly shared, at least in part, by other groups in society. We need to know more about what made the same schooling seem worthwhile to people whose lives were very different.

The fact that the schooling of girls followed so closely upon boys schooling reopens questions about gender discrimination. Apparently, much of what elementary instruction was thought to accomplish was considered appropriate for girls, too. That raises another question. Peasants, it is usually assumed, sent boys to school in the hope that they would get better jobs as a result, but the spread of girls schooling occurred much more rapidly than the changes in women's employment. Perhaps the appeal of education was less narrowly or immediately practical than we have imagined. Schools were intended to maintain and even reinforce gender differences, however. Girls schools paid a lot of attention to domestic skills, which were expected to improve family life and strengthen the home but also to be a source of income in case of need. Culturally, the differences that followed from the fact that girls so often attended schools taught by nuns may have been even more important. The curriculum may well have tended to be more rudimentary than that offered boys, and these schools presumably reinforced the sense of a separate female sphere, of women as purer than men and needing special protection, destined for domesticity and motherhood. Insofar as such attitudes were already well established in society, the sisters' schools may have made protective parents more willing to send their daughters for formal instruction. Still, they sent them with relative alacrity even where the teachers were not nuns and where boys and girls shared the classroom.

In this context, it is striking how readily teaching came to be an attractive career for women. It may well have seemed a natural extension of motherhood, a kind of professionalization of skills and interests women were expected to have. Still, as a secular occupation, the possibility of teaching must have enlarged horizons for many, suggesting chances for mobility and independent respectability. The number of teenage girls who sought *brevets* rose well above any prospects for immediate employment, and the *brevet* may have seemed both a kind of insurance (in case of widowhood, ailing parents, and penury) and a certification of intellectual capacity. A girl taught by nuns in elementary schools and in teachers training courses need not feel that she was somehow breaking away from established social norms by considering such a career. We should not assume that social changes seen with hindsight to have been fundamental were necessarily experienced as a crisis.

Something similar seems to be true for the institutionalization of the school system and the professionalization of teachers. Archival evidence emphasizes the regulations through which they came about, as by fiat, and politics echoed the clashes that resulted. Yet this professionalization was more than a mere imposition, for in this as in so much else the state was an agent of greater equality of opportunity, an avenue of mobility. Teachers and communes alike had reasons to welcome certification with the assurances and prestige it brought. The state took charge of education in large part because in France, as everywhere else, only government could afford the considerable cost of universal instruction.[66] But the state that centuries earlier had grown with its capacity to provide justice as well as to tax was welcomed in elementary education for the standards and uniformity it promised as well as the money it provided.

Thus, the spread of schooling in France should not be seen simply as the imposition of an overweening state or the intrusion of middle-class goals. The history of French elementary schooling in the nineteenth century is in many respects the history of a common project in which communes and church and paying parents worked with the government and expected its participation in principle even when objecting to specific policies. The creation of a national system incorporated values very widely shared, from the patriotism schools inculcated and that was also disseminated in public ceremonies and newspapers to the bureaucratization that guaranteed that the school system would enjoy the efficiencies of the clear, hierarchical responsibility expected in the civil service and large businesses. Once established, of course, the educational system developed a life of its own, with semiautonomous goals and standards. The elites who had seen themselves as imposing standards and uniformity against the resistance of shortsighted provincials came in practice to be defining boundaries and barriers that limited how long most students could stay in school as well as how long they had to be there and that maintained the social distance between primary and secondary schools. The educational statistics strongly suggest that by the end of the century, as in the 1840s, the demand for education was greater than the supply. Universal instruction stimulated a momentum that continued to run ahead of what planners considered affordable or necessary.

The educational system has for so long been a subject of controversy in France that it is easy to overlook the shared assumptions that have given the debate its enduring vigor. Even while Catholics and anticlericals fought over who should control the system, whether clergy should teach, and whether religion should be taught, they were contributing to a national consensus about schooling. That consensus has an important place in French social and cultural history because it has proved to be so universally shared, so expandable in ambition, and so lasting. Even when disputes over education were at their bitterest, most public, and most divisive, nearly all participants assumed that elementary education should be accessible to all, that formal schools supported by taxes were the best way to ensure that French men and women could read and do sums, that everyone should be fluent in a single national tongue, that schools should in addition teach practical matters like surveying and sewing, and that instruction should instill ethical and civic values on which all ought to agree. Conservatives did not argue against universal schooling but claimed rather that the foundations for such a system had been laid in the old regime, which provided a still useful model. Catholics did not claim they could or should provide all the schools the nation needed but rather that it should accept their help in practice and their guidance in principle as the way to form character and ensure social order. Anticlericals denounced Catholic schools for slighting science and modern subjects and for propagandizing in favor of monarchy, yet the curricula in secular and religious schools were strikingly similar. Everyone meant to teach respect for parents, the value of work, the importance of honesty, and a fervent love of country, even when they differed as to the intellectual roots and ideological implications of such doctrines. That consensus, with its emphasis on the connection between personal values and citizenship and its search for *solidarité*, is important in understanding the cohesion in French society that commentators so often rediscover with surprise. The high ambitions enshrined within that consensus, refined and propagated in every debate, also implied possibilities for social mobility, civic responsibility, and shared culture that were never achieved, thus assuring that the French educational system would remain a favorite target for social critics of every type. Even in their failings, public schools had become potent symbols of the nation.

Notes

1. Prices were relatively steady in France from 1820 to 1880, when they fell sharply. This means that educational expenditures in the last twenty-five years of this study actually increased more than the raw figures indicate. Setting the price index at 100 for the years 1901–10, the index for other decades would be: 1821–30 = 136; 1831–40 = 129; 1841–50 = 122; 1851–60 = 140; 1861–70 = 136; 1871–80 = 130; 1881–90 = 102; 1891–1900 = 90. Calculated from the wholesale price indices in B. R. Mitchell, *European Historical Statistics, 1750–1970* (New York, 1975), 737–38.

2. *Statistique de l'enseignement*, II:clxxv.

3. In the Second Empire, extraordinary expenses were most often used for the maintenance of buildings, Archives Nationales, F17/10367. Later, as mentioned in the introductions to the various volumes of the *Statistique de l'enseignement*, they were more often used to support a girls school in communes of fewer than five hundred people (where separate girls schools were not required), to supplement salaries, and for increasingly varied additional needs.

4. The editors of the *Statistique* offer as a loose guess a figure of 120 million francs as the amount spent on primary education in France in 1877 (including private

schooling as well as communal extraordinary expenses), a year in which their total for communal, departmental, and state expenditures reaches 89.5 million francs, ibid., II:cxcviii.

5. The five largest cities did not receive the state subsidies that after 1882 compensated all other communes for the loss of tuition payments; these cities had to compensate instead from their own taxes but received some matching funds, and beginning in 1890, cities over 100,000 were gradually brought under the same arrangement.

6. Ordinary expenditures were slightly lower in 1840 than in 1837 and in 1837 than in 1833; they also dropped from 1870 to 1871; the most sizable decline, however, was between 1866 and 1867. In all other years reported in the *Statistique* for this period, they rose. Total expenditures rose in every year except 1867, when they were slightly below what they had been in 1866, due primarily to a fall in the return from communal taxes.

7. Where possible, these figures are taken from the more complete totals given in the introductions to the various volumes of the *Statistique de l'enseignement* rather than the printed tables, which tend to give somewhat lower figures, following formal budget categories.

8. Based on the figures in B. R. Mitchell, *European Historical Statistics, 1750–1970* (New York, 1975), 697–98.

9. These percentages are the annual growth rate in total expenditures per capita, reflecting the increased costs Frenchmen bore.

10. The rate of increase in these periods is further flattened and stretched out when the number of schools is normalized by school-age population (table S.2). Cities expenditures, on the other hand, were becoming increasingly independent of the national budget, and William B. Cohen finds the 1860s the period of greatest growth in expenditures for the cities he is currently studying.

11. Although the percentage increase in Catholic public school enrollment is almost the same for the two periods, there are some interesting differences between them. The second period, being shorter, actually saw a greater annual increase and a much greater increase in the departmental mean for Catholic public school enrollment; the spread of Catholic public schools across all departments was greater in the second period. On the other hand, in the second period, enrollment in Catholic independent schools declined in absolute terms and as a percentage of total independent school enrollment, so that the increase in Catholic enrollment in all schools was much less than it had been in the earlier period.

12. The annual expense for *écoles normales* doubled from one million to two million francs between 1837 and 1863. It was three million in 1876 and nine million in 1887, before becoming an expense of the national government in 1889.

13. The chronological grouping by number of *brevets* awarded men would be 1837–50 or 1837–63, 1863–76, and 1887–1906, with 1882 aberrant.

14. In 1891, the first woman school inspector was appointed.

15. By the turn of the century, a majority of *titulaires* were women.

16. Other measures suggest that enrollment generally preceded increased expenditure (see table S.14B); we have found none that indicates the reverse, but the nature

of the data and the distance between data points in the crucial period from 1840 to 1867 do not permit a compelling test of this proposition.

17. Tuition revenue was slightly less than that from communal taxes from 1855 through 1858, higher than income from communal taxes from 1859 through 1869 with the execption of 1865 and 1868.

18. *Statistique de l'enseignment*, vol. II, table LXXII, shows graphically how the proportions of total revenue from department, state, and commune rose sharply after 1868 while revenue from tuition remained essentially flat.

19. Aside from the insensitivity of departmental data as a measure of communal choices, extraordinary expenses were never more than supplemental.

20. In 1891, ten departments met 99 percent of their total from ordinary expenditures, with Corsica at the top of the list, followed by Creuse, Pyrénées-Orientales, Aveyron, and Charente.

21. Expenditures correlated more strongly with the number of schools than with the number of schools normalized by enrollment; schools were expensive.

22. Indeed, in one-quarter of the departments of France, expenditure per teacher apparently dropped between 1837 and 1840, and it fell in more than half of them between 1840 and 1850 (when teachers' pay depended heavily on income from tuition, it was possible for the number of teachers to increase more rapidly than total revenue or expenditure). At almost every other data point, the cost per teacher increased in each department; the system did have its internal momentum.

23. If one leaves out the Seine, however (where cost per teacher was always much higher than elsewhere in France), the variation across departments did shrink a bit across the century. Bouches-du-Rhône spent 2.8 times as much per teacher as Manche in 1840, twice as much as Hautes-Alpes in 1891.

24. An analysis by our departmental clusters based on indicators of a developed system drive the point home. Only once, in 1850, when all the clusters were close together, did the top two lead all others in expenditure per teacher (and cluster two led again in 1901); usually, the departments at or just below the mean spent more per teacher. Presumably, urban departments had the means to meet their higher costs; but demography inhibited economic efficiency for many of France's departments requiring a relatively greater effort per student but also per teacher where nearly all were *titulaires*, an effort that should not be forgotten in making departmental comparisons.

25. The national mean of ordinary expenditures per student, which did not increase from 1837 to 1850, doubled between 1850 and 1863, again between 1867 and 1882 (having increased little between 1863 and 1867), and total expenditures doubled once more between 1882 and 1896.

26. Where independent schools took a large number of students, the per pupil costs of public schools were likely to be higher. A case study, which indicates how laicization could result from stubbornness on both sides, also reveals a town council's concern about the extra expense that a laic school would entail, Richard Hemeryck, "La laicisation des écoles des frères à Lille en 1868," *95ᵉ Congrès national des sociétés savantes* (Reims, 1970), 1:867–95.

27. Note also that the published figures do not distinguish, for example, between public schools that met on church property and those in a building maintained by the

commune. Nearly all of a commune's annual expenditures in practice went for stipends to teachers. Correlations between ordinary expenses per child in public schools are always negative for 1850–96 with enrollment in Catholic schools as a percentage of all enrollment, and in Catholic public schools as a percentage of all public school enrollment. The last is most telling because it compares lay and Catholic schools of the same type: $r = .1$ for 1850; $-.34$ for 1863; $-.32$ for 1867; $-.26$ for 1876; $-.43$ for 1881; $-.42$ for 1886; $-.34$ for 1891; $-.3$ for 1896.

28. Ardèche, Bouches-du-Rhône, Côtes-du-Nord, Gard, Ille-et-Villaine, Loire, Loire-Inférieure, Mayenne, Morbihan, Rhône, and Vienne.

29. In 1863, 1868, 1872, and 1882 only one of these departments ever reached the national mean in per capita expenditures (Gard in 1882). Although some were sometimes close to the mean, many remained well below; and the mean per capita expenditure of these departments was 32 percent below the national mean in 1863, 28 percent below in 1868, 27 percent below in 1870, and 22 percent below in 1882.

30. Seven of the thirteen spent at a rate above the mean in 1863 and 1868; eight were above in 1872, nine in 1882 but even then the mean per capita expenditure for the whole group was only 9 percent above the national mean.

31. An unpublished report of 1863 declared that more than 20 percent of Catholic girls schools were free against only 10 percent of the laic girls schools, Archives Nationales, F17/9351.

32. The analysis is necessarily indirect. The first challenge was to identify those departments that experienced an extended period of rising girls enrollment. Nationally, the period of greatest growth in girls enrollment was 1863–76. We started with that. But we needed to sort out those departments in which this occurred not just in one sudden leap but in a continuing process that could be expected to show in budgets over several years. We therefore also established intervening and overlapping periods (1867–76, 1863–72, 1867–72) and constructed a list of the fifteen departments that led the nation in growth in girls enrollment in each of these four periods. Eight departments appeared in all four lists; four departments appeared at the top on three of the lists, and two appeared but twice. Having thus selected the fourteen departments (in groups of eight, four, and two) with the most consistent, continuing rise in girls enrollments, we then compared changes in them on a number of indicators with changes in the national mean, concentrating especially on changes in the crucial period from 1863 to 1868. Six of these departments had been in the upper quartile of enrollment in 1832, ten in the upper half; the change occurring in such departments would have involved getting all girls to school for the full course of study. The proportion of total expenditures paid for locally declined nationally by about 4 percent. It declined by more than that in six of the group of eight, averaging 7.4 percent in that group, 7 percent in the second group, but remaining unaffected in the third group (two departments).

33. In 1886, one commune in six offered adult courses for men, one in thirty for women. There was one woman for every twenty men enrolled in adult course in 1843, one woman for every six men in 1870, one women to two men in 1900.

34. Enrollments in the two programs rose to about one-fifteenth and then one-twelfth of elementary school enrollment; allowing for the shorter term of these courses, something between one-sixth and one-quarter of elementary school graduates

may have attended them. The combined number of students receiving the c.e.p, attending an e.p.s., or taking a *brevet* doubled between 1882 and 1906.

35. The coefficient of variation for expenditures in public schools normalized by population is as follows: 1837, 47 percent; 1840, 46; 1850, 42; 1855, 35; 1863, 31; 1868, 31; 1872, 29; 1882, 26; 1886, 25; 1891, 29; 1896, 26; 1901, 27.

36. *Statistique de l'enseignement*, II:clxxxviin, lists the ten departments whose communes in 1876 spent the least per capita on education; it is interesting to compare that with a list of departments ranked in 1886 by total expenses per capita, including departmental and national contributions in a much more centralized system: Three of those departments remain in the bottom ten, five are in the next ten (table Ex.6).

37. The coefficient of variation, 16 and 17 percent in 1863 and 1868, had increased to 64 and 59 percent in 1891 and 1896.

38. Correlations of per capita wealth with per capita expenditures from communal and departmental sources range from .41 in 1863 and .31 in 1882 up to .48 in 1872 and .57 in 1896

39. Using the octiles based on 1832 enrollment here is helpful. The octile ranks stay closer to the expected order in terms of the percentage of total expenditure paid for locally (although still with considerable fluctuation) than in terms of the actual amount of locally financed expenditures, although the octile with lowest enrollment always spends the least. The others tend to fall into two groups with a good deal of shifting in rank order. The national contribution was tied to the number of teachers and schools and the local tax base; the octiles, which predict enrollment, reflect local conditions that at some times and for some octiles did not reflect the amount of educational costs that came from local funds. Cluster analysis gives similar results.

40. The figure for each octile is, of course, an average of all the departments in that octile; as we have demonstrated, rankings in these octiles were consonant with other and later measures of elementary schooling.

41. Note the persistent correlation of a department's level of per capita expenditure on instruction with its literacy rate in 1865, which remained significant even while declining from .73 (in 1837 and .74 in 1840) to .52 at the end of the century (table Ex.5).

42. That, for example, probably explains the rise in 1886.

43. Correlations were similarly persistent between per capita expenditures and the number of schools a department had in 1821!—ranging from .85 to .35 at the end of the century.

44. Expenditure per student is a less helpful indicator than one would like because it is so sensitive to the cost of teachers, often higher in urban areas and always higher in relationship to the number of students where the population was dispersed and schools were necessarily small. The top five and the bottom three octiles are quite distinct on this measure until the 1860s; the bottom two octiles continue to be below the national mean in expenditure per student from 1868 on. The top two octiles, at or below the national mean from 1837 to 1868, rise above it after 1872. Octile number five, the most urban, tends to spend the most per student from 1868 on.

45. The Pearson correlations of total expenditures by department in 1837 with expenditures at later dates are: 1840, .98; 1850, .95; 1863, .79; 1868, .76; 1872, .72; 1882, .56; 1886, .59; 1891, .50; 1896, .51; 1901, .55.

46. Not perfectly, however. The octiles maintain the expected order for each data point from 1837 through 1868, although drawing closer together. By 1872 the most urban octile (No. 5) moves ahead one place, a position it continues to hold except in 1896 when it tops the list. Some other displacements of one position occur later. The third and fourth octiles trade places in 1882, the second and third in 1886 and 1891, the seventh and eighth in 1901.

47. In the 1860s, the fourth cluster of nineteen departments actually moved ahead of the third, containing only three deparments (Hérault, Basses-Pyrénées, and Hautes-Pyrénées) that fluctuated broadly on a number of indicators.

48. Finistère, Haute-Loire, Loire-Inférieur, and Morbihan, all with large enrollments in Catholic schools.

49. The correlation of per capita expenditure and the percentage of the population in towns of more than two thousand in 1865 ranged between .71 and .68 in 1850 and earlier, between .62 and .68 in the 1860s, and between .56 and .41 thereafter. Analysis by octile also confirms the effect of the measures taken during the Third Republic to deprive large cities of much of the national subsidy for schools. In the octile with the most urban departments, the proportion of total expenditures locally financed was higher than any other octile by the 1890s; it had contributed the smallest proportion during the Second Empire.

50. The correlation of wealth per capita in 1865 with expenditures at selected dates is: 1837, .43; 1850, .39; 1863, .22; 1868, .30; 1872, .15; 1891, .40.

51. The correlation at different dates from 1863 to 1896 with these indicators—schools in 1821, enrollment in 1832, literacy and urban population—ranges between .2 and none at all.

52. Gifts and bequests, not large enough to be significant in the overall funding of primary schooling, did tend to increase over the century, another sign of the schools' prominent place in French society. These donations tended to be highest in octile five with its concentration of urban and Catholic departments.

53. Six data points were used for this variable: 1837, 1850, 1863, 1867, 1872, and 1876. The three smallest clusters contain three, five, and eleven departments; the other groups contain fifteen, sixteen, sixteen, and twenty-four departments. The cluster of five contains departments most below the national mean: Haute-Vienne, Morbihan, Finistère, Corrèze, Moselle. The clusters of three and eleven contain departments with enrollments of girls at or above the school-age population from 1837 on: Meurthe-et-Moselle, Bas-Rhin, Moselle, Côte-d'Or, Ardennes, Jura, Doubs, Haute-Sâone, Marne, Aube, Vosges, Meurthe, Meuse, Haute-Marne.

54. The same data points were used here as for girls enrollment; the clusters contain one, one, one, nine, ten, twenty, and forty-seven departments. In the clusters of nine, ten, and twenty departments, girls accounted for a lower percentage of total enrollment than in the largest cluster, rising respectively from 22 to 45 percent, from 25 to over 48 percent, and from 35 to over 48 percent.

55. The data points used are 1850, 1863, 1867, 1876, and 1881; the clusters contain one, two, seven, eight, twenty, twenty, and thirty-one departments. The cluster of seven, always high in Catholic enrollment (varying from nearly half to almost two-thirds of total enrollment), includes Haute-Saône, Haute-Loire, Ardèche, Bouches-du-Rhône, Côtes-du-Nord, Vaucluse, and Ille-et-Vilaine. The cluster of eight, with from

39 to 57 percent of its students in Catholic schools, includes Gard, Loire-Inférieure, Maine-et-Loire, Mayenne, Aveyron, Seine-Inférieure, Morbihan, and Puy-de-Dôme. One cluster of twenty ranged from 16 to 30 percent and the other from 24 to 38 percent of its students in Catholic schools. The cluster of thirty-one had means of from 30 to 45 percent of their enrollments in Catholic schools.

56. The two that do, Côte-d'Or and Savoie, form a cluster by themselves.

57. The data points are 1872, 1876, 1882, 1886, 1891, 1896, 1901, and 1906. The clusters contain one, two, seven, nine, sixteen, twenty-two, and thirty departments. The cluster of nine was the group well above the national mean: Loire-Inférieure, Loire, Finistère, Indre, Var, Rhône, Bouches-du-Rhône, Vaucluse, and Nord. The cluster of seven, those in which the percentage of *adjoints* dropped after 1872, included Ardèche, Indre-et-Loire, Drôme, Trarn-et-Garonne, Vienne, Seine-et-Marne, and Haute-Loire.

58. The data points are 1850, 1863, 1867, 1869, 1872, and 1876; the clusters contain one, two, three, four, thirteen, thirty-one, and thirty-three departments. Haute-Savoie and Bas-Rhin statistically join Corse in the two smallest clusters. The group of three departments well above the mean include the educationally well-developed ones of Meurthe and Ardennes but more surprisingly Lozère as well. The group of four, which fluctuated more than the others, contains Côte-d'Or, Haute-Saône, Aveyron, and Vosges.

59. The data points are 1837, 1840, 1863, 1872, 1876, 1882, 1886, 1891, 1896, 1901, and 1906. The clusters group one, two, three, ten, thirteen, twenty-eight, and thirty-two departments. The Nord, with its high number of students per teachers, is the department by itself; the Vaucluse and Aube, generally with low ratios, make up the cluster of two; the cluster of three includes Bas-Rhin, Haut-Rhin, and Vosges, departments with high ratios in 1837 and 1840 when their enrollments were unusually high and in which the ratios then drop sharply. Here, too, two clusters include two-thirds of France's departments.

60. Hautes-Alpes, Corse, Creuse, Deux-Sèvres, and Pyrénées-Orientales. The departments mentioned in this paragraph are those that were among the top or bottom ten at least once on two measures.

61. As much as 99 percent of the educational budget in Corse, Creuse, Charente, and Pyrénées-Orientales came from ordinary expenditures.

62. Haute-Vienne, Cantal, Creuse.

63. Bouches-du-Rhône, Loire, and Rhône.

64. Hautes-Pyrénées and Lozère.

65. Hérault and Marne.

66. Ernest Gellner, *Nations and Nationalism* (Ithaca, 1983), 35–36.

Tables

Tables are arranged by chapter and within each chapter in the order of their relative statistical complexity, from absolute numbers and normalized data to correlations, regressions, and cluster analysis.

Chapter 2: Schools

S.1 Number of Primary Schools of All Types in France
S.2 Number of Schools Adjusted by Population
    A. Number of Schools per 1,000 Population
    B. Schools per 100 School-Age Population
S.3 Communes without Schools
S.4 Variations among Departments at Specific Times in the Size of Schools and Their Number in Relation to Population
S.5 Number of Schools per 100 School-Age Population, Above and Below the St. Malo–Geneva Line
S.6 Schools Owned by Communes and Number of Students per School, Above and Below the St. Malo–Geneva Line
S.7 The Number of Departments with Nearly All the Schools They Would Need (Fulfillment) at Specific Dates
S.8 Percentage of Schools in School Buildings Owned by Communes, Departmental Means and Ranges
S.9 Correlations: Number of Schools with Total Enrollment in Particular Years
S.10 Correlations: Number of Schools with Total Enrollment at Different Times
    A. Number of Schools with Total Enrollment Before and After
    B. Number of Schools in 1821 with Later Enrollment
    C. Number of Schools in 1906 with the Number of Schools at Earlier Dates
S.11 Correlations: Number of Students per School with the Number of Schools and with Total Enrollment
S.12 Correlations: Ordinary Expenditures with the Absolute Number of Schools and with Total Enrollment

S.13 Correlations: Ordinary Expenditures with the Number of Schools, Normalized by School-Age Population
S.14 Correlations: Schools in 1821
   A. Schools in 1821 with Indicators of School Quality in the Third Republic
   B. Schools per School-Age Population in 1821 with Ordinary Expenditure per Student at Later Dates
S.15 Proportion of Variation in the Availability of Schools Removed by Grouping Departments at Selected Dates
S.16 Regression Analysis: Total Enrollment per Population at Specific Dates on the Number of Schools per Population for All Available Data Points

Chapter 3: Enrollment

E.1 Number of Students Enrolled in Primary Schools
E.2 Number of Boys and Girls Enrolled in Primary Schools
E.3 Number of Boys and Girls Enrolled in Public and Private Primary Schools
E.4 Number of Students with Scholarships (*boursiers*)
E.5 Number of Candidates for *Certificats d'études primaires* and Number of *Certificats* Awarded, by Gender
E.6 Total Enrollment in Primary Schools per 100 Children Six to Thirteen Years Old, Departmental Means and Ranges
E.7 Enrollment per 100 Children Six to Thirteen Years Old, Above and Below the St. Malo–Geneva Line
E.8 Percentage of Children Six to Thirteen Years Old Enrolled in Primary Schools
E.9 Number of Departments Enrolling 50, 60, 70, and 80 Percent of Children Five to Fifteen Years Old
E.10 Summer Attendance as a Percentage of Winter Enrollment
E.11 Summer Attendance per 100 Children Six to Thirteen Years Old, Departmental Means and Ranges
E.12 Enrollment in *Ecoles Maternelles* per 100 Children Five and Six Years Old, Departmental Means and Ranges, Octiles
E.13 Percentage of Thirteen-Year-Olds Seeking and Receiving *Certificats*, Departmental Means and Ranges
E.14 Dates at Which Departments Reached Enrollments Equal to 50, 75, and 100 Percent of the Number of Children Six to Thirteen Years Old
E.15 Date at Which Summer Attendance in Departments Reached a Number Equal to Various Percentages of the Population Six to Thirteen Years Old

E.16 Enrollment per 100 Children Six to Thirteen Years Old in Five Groups of Departments Arranged by Their Degree of Urbanization in 1876
E.17 Correlations: Expenditures with Enrollment
    A. Gross Expenditures with Enrollment per School-Age Population
    B. Ordinary Expenses per Student with Enrollment per School-Age Population
    C. Voluntary Expenses in 1901 and 1906 with Earlier Enrollment per School-Age Population
E.18 Correlations: Enrollment in *Ecoles Maternelles* per Population and *Certificats d'études primaires* per Thirteen Year Olds with Primary School Enrollment and with Attendance
E.19 Correlations: *Certificats d'études primaires* per Thirteen Year Olds with Socioeconomic Factors
E.20 Correlations: Enrollment per School-Age Population with Urbanization, Wealth, and Literacy
E.21 Regression Analysis: Variance in Enrollment Accounted for by Grouping Departments

Chapter 4: Catholic Schools

C.1 Number of Students in Catholic and Lay Primary Schools
C.2 Number of Students in Public and Independent Schools
C.3 Enrollment Growth in All Schools and in Catholic Schools, 1850–76
C.4 Changes in Enrollment in Various Types of Schools, 1866–76
C.5 Percentage of Boys and Girls Enrolled in Catholic Schools
C.6 Number of Boys in Catholic Schools, 1876–1901
C.7 Number of Students with Scholarships (*boursiers*) in Various Types of Schools
C.8 Catholic Enrollment as a Percentage of Total Enrollment, Arranged by 1832 Octiles
C.9 Departments with More than Half of Their Enrollment in Catholic Schools in 1850
C.10 Correlations: Departmental Population in Communes of Various Sizes with Membership in Teaching Religious Orders, 1861, and with Percentage of Enrollment in Catholic Schools

Chapter Five: Girls

G.1 Number of Girls Schools, Public and Independent
G.2 Boys and Girls Enrollment per Population Six to Thirteen Years Old

      A. Assuming Boys and Girls Are Each 50 Percent of School-Age Cohort
      B. Using Census Figures by Department for Percentage of Boys and Girls in School-Age Cohort
      C. Coefficient of Variation
G.3 Enrollment of Boys and Girls Per Population Six to Thirteen Years Old, Above and Below the St. Malo–Geneva Line
G.4 Percentage of Communes without Any Girls School, by Department
G.5 Dates by Which Departments Reached Enrollment Equal to 50, 75, and 100 Percent of the Girls Six to Thirteen Years Old
G.6 Girls Enrollment per Number of Girls Six to Thirteen Years Old, by Octiles (based on total enrollment in 1832)
G.7 Female and Male Literacy in 1872
      A. Departmental Ranges
      B. Correlations: Female Literacy in 1872 with Girls Enrollment at Other Dates
G.8 Correlations: Girls and Boys Enrollment per Population Six to Thirteen Years Old with Social Factors
G.9 Correlations: Boys Enrollment with Girls Enrollment at Various Dates
G.10 Regression Analysis: Girls Enrollment with Socioeconomic Factors
      A. Girls Enrollment in 1837
      B. Girls Enrollment in 1876

Chapter 6: Teachers

T.1 The Number of Teachers
      A. *Titulaires* in Public Schools, Male Lay and Religious, Female Lay and Religious
      B. All Teachers in Public Schools, Male Lay and Religious, Female Lay and Religious
      C. *Titulaires* in Independent Schools, Male Lay and Religious, Female Lay and Religious
      D. All Teachers in Independent Schools, Male Lay and Religious, Female Lay and Religious
      E. *Titulaires* in Public Schools, Male, Female, Lay, and Religious
      F. All Teachers in Public Schools, Male, Female, Lay, and Religious
      G. *Titulaires* in Independent Schools, Male, Female, Lay, and Religious
      H. All Teachers in Independent Schools, Male, Female, Lay, and Religious

　　　　I. *Titulaires*, All Schools, Male, Female, Lay, and Religious
　　　　J. All Teachers, All Schools, Male, Female, Lay, and Religious
T.2　Percentage of Teachers Who Were Female and Percentage of Teachers Who Were Lay
T.3　Teachers in All Categories as a Percentage of Total Teaching Personnel
　　　　A. In Public Schools
　　　　B. In Independent Schools
T.4　Number of *Brevets élémentaires* (or *simples*) Awarded, by Year
T.5　Number of Graduates of *Ecoles Normales*, National Totals, Departmental Means and Ranges
　　　　A. Male, Annual
　　　　B. Male, Cumulative Five-Year Totals
　　　　C. Female, Annual
　　　　D. Female, Cumulative Five-Year Totals
T.6　Number of Advanced *Brevets* Awarded, Absolute Numbers and Ratio of Higher *Brevets* to Elementary *Brevets*
T.7　Number of Teachers with and without *Brevets*, 1876–77
　　　　A. Public Schools
　　　　B. Independent Schools
T.8　Student:Teacher Ratio, Departmental Means and Ranges
T.9　Student:*Adjoint* Ratio, Departmental Means and Ranges
T.10　Teaching Personnel, Departmental Means and Ranges
　　　　A. Absolute Numbers
　　　　B. Normalized by Number of Schools
　　　　C. Normalized by Enrollment per 1,000 Students
T.11　Number of *Brevets élémentaires* Awarded to Females, Departmental Means and Ranges
　　　　A. Normalized by 100 Female, Lay Teachers
　　　　B. Normalized by 7,000 Female Students
T.12　Number of *Brevets* Awarded to Males
　　　　A. Normalized by 100 Male, Lay Teachers
　　　　B. Normalized by 7,000 Male Students
T.13　*Adjoints* as Percentage of All Teachers, by Octiles
T.14　Student:Teacher Ratio, by Octiles
T.15　Student:*Adjoint* Ratio, by Octiles
T.16　Dates at Which Departments Had 85 Percent of the Teachers They Would Have in 1901
　　　　A. All Teachers
　　　　B. Male, Lay Public School Teachers
T.17　Percentage of Candidates Who Passed the *Brevet* Examination, Departmental Means and Ranges, 1882–1906

    A. Elementary *Brevets*
    B. Advanced *Brevets*
    C. Advanced *Brevets* as Percentage of All *Brevets* Granted, 1837–1906

Chapter 7: The System Circumscribed

Sys.1 Number of Students in *Ecoles Maternelles*
    A. By Gender
    B. By Type of School
Sys.2 The Percentage of Students Enrolled in *Ecoles Maternelles* Who Enrolled in Catholic Schools
Sys.3 Correlations: Enrollment in Primary Schools with Enrollment in *Ecoles Maternelles*
Sys.4 Correlations: Certification of Primary School Graduates with the Early Establishment of Schooling and with Socioeconomic Factors
Sys.5 Correlations: Number of Books in *Bibliothèques scolaires* in Public Schools (normalized by enrollment) with Socioeconomic Factors and the Early Establishment of Schooling

Chapter 8: Expenditures

Ex.1 Annual Percentage Growth in Total Expenditures and Total Enrollment, Normalized by Population
Ex.2 Tuition in Public Schools, Means, Octiles, Maximums, and Minimums
    A. Per Student
    B. Per Capita
Ex.3 Total Expenditures for Public Schools (normalized by population), Arranged by Clusters
Ex.4 Total Expenditures per Teacher, Arranged by Clusters
Ex.5 Correlations: Total Expenditures Normalized by Population with Socioeconomic Factors
Ex.6 Correlations: Expenditures at Different Dates, Normalized by Population
Ex.7 Reduction in Variance by Cannonical Discriminant Analysis (same results by K-means) for Various Clusters or Groups of Departments
Ex.8 Voluntary (Facultative) Expenses in 1901 and 1906
    A. Correlations
    B. By Octiles

Table S.1. Number of Primary Schools of All Types in France (to nearest hundred)

Date		Annual Compound Growth Rate (in percentage)	Girls Schools	Boys Schools	Mixed Schools	Boys and Mixed Schools
1813	23,300+ (est.)	—				19,600
1821	33,500+ (est.)	4.6				28,200
1829	36,200+ (est.)	1.0				30,500
1832	42,100	5.2				31,400
1833	45,000 (est.)	6.9				33,800
1837	52,800	4.1	14,100	17,900	20,900	38,700
1840	55,300	1.6				39,500
1843	59,800	2.6				42,600
1850	60,600	0.2				
1863	68,800	1.0	27,300	23,700	17,800	
1865	69,700	0.7				
1867	69,100	−0.4				
1872	70,200	0.3	28,500	24,500	17,200	
1876	71,500	0.5	29,100	25,400	17,000	
1882	75,600	0.9	31,300	26,600	17,700	
1886	79,900	1.4				
1891	81,200	0.3	34,400	27,900	19,100	
1896	82,300	0.3				
1901	83,700	0.3				
1906	79,900	−0.9				

Note: Figures for the Restoration period are problematic. There was a general underreporting, especially of schools in isolated areas (see *Statistique de l'enseignement,* II: xix–xx, lii–lvii) and for girls schools (see Jean Perrel, "Les écoles de filles dans la France d'Ancien Régime," and Gerard Cholvy, "Une école des pauvres au début du 19e siècle: 'pieuse filles,' béates ou soeurs des campagnes," in *The Making of Frenchmen: Current Directions in the History of Education in France, 1679–1979,* ed. Donald N. Baker and Patrick J. Harrigan [Waterloo, Ont., 1980], 75–84, 135–44). For some dates, girls schools were not reported, only the boys in mixed schools were counted, etc. We created estimates of the number of girls schools for 1833 (by linear adjustment from the data for 1832 and 1837), for 1829 (by comparing enrollment data for girls in 1829 and 1832 and assuming the enrollment:school ratios did not change between the two dates), for 1821 (by assuming that the ratio of girls schools to other schools was the same as in 1832), and for 1813 (by assuming that the 40 percent of the department that did not report in 1813 had the same proportion of the nation's school as they had in 1821). We regard the totals prior to 1837 as minimums, but the schools not reported were probably the poorest and least stable and often privately run. The apparent growth between 1829 and 1832 is undoubtedly exaggerated (as the earnest compilers of the *Statistique de l'enseignement,* II:liii, remind us). Our adjustments are not entirely satisfactory, but they at least avoid the inconsistencies and misleading comparisons of totals for one type of school with those for another that creep in even to the summary table of the *Statistique* (II:liv) and have undoubtedly ever since affected the historiography that hails the impressive growth following the Guizot Law. The statistical evidence of slower growth in the last years of the Restoration fits with Maurice Gontard's picture of an educational reversal under the government of the Ultras, *L'enseignement primaire en France de la Révolution à la loi Guizot, 1789–1933* (Paris, 1959), 360–95.

Table S.2. Number of Schools Adjusted by Population

A. Number of Schools per 1,000 Population

Date	Mean		Coefficient of Variation	Compound Growth Rate by Population
1813	[0.82]	0.69	71%	—
1821	[1.12]	0.94	59%	(4.0%) 3.9%
1829	[1.13]	0.95	56%	(0.1%) 0.1%
1833	[1.47]	1.10	49%	(6.8%) 3.7%
1837		1.60	40%	(2.1%) 9.8%[a]
1850		1.80	39%	0.9%
1863		2.00	39%	0.8%
1867		2.10	38%	1.2%
1876		2.20	36%	0.5%
1882		2.30	36%	0.7%
1886		2.40	35%	1.1%
1891		2.50	35%	0.8%
1896		2.50	36%	0.0%
1901		2.60	37%	0.8%
1906		2.50	37%	−0.8%

B. Schools per 100 School-Age Population

Date	Mean		Maximum	Minimum	Coefficient of Variation	Compound Growth Rate by School-Age Population
1813	[.39]	0.33	1.02	.06	73%	— —
1821	[.53]	0.45	1.14	.07	61%	(3.9%) 4.0%
1829	[.58]	0.49	1.16	.07	59%	(1.1%) 1.1%
1833	[.74]	0.55	1.38	.10	51%	(6.3%) 2.9%
1837		0.86	1.80	.24	41%	(3.8%) 11.8%[a]
1850		1.01	2.54	.35	39%	1.2%
1863		1.15	3.15	.44	38%	1.0%
1867		1.19	3.33	.41	37%	0.9%
1876		1.26	2.69	.42	36%	0.6%
1882[b]		1.34	2.87	.44	37%	1.0%
1886		1.37	3.04	.47	35%	0.7%
1891		1.42	2.79	.43	34%	0.7%
1896		1.48	2.87	.38	35%	0.8%
1901		1.51	3.03	.38	34%	0.4%
1906		1.51	3.11	.37	36%	0.0%

Note: The coefficient of variation is the result of the division of the standard deviation by mean (for all departments). A high coefficient indicates great diversity among departments; a low one indicates homogeneity.

[a] Exaggerated by first inclusion of girls schools. Figures prior to 1837 are for boys and mixed schools only. Brackets indicate mean of estimated total of all schools. Parentheses indicate growth rate based on estimated total of all schools.
[b] Growth in this year is slightly exaggerated by the redefinition of school-age.

Table S.3. Communes without Schools

Date	Total Communes	Communes without Schools	Percentage of Communes without Schools	Departments at the 25th Percentile	Departments at the 75th Percentile
1837	37,234	5,667	15.0	4.9%	31.3%
1850	36,786	2,690	7.0	1.6%	12.1%
1863	37,510	818	2.0	0.0%	3.3%
1876	37,056	312	0.8	0.0%	1.3%

Note: When two neighboring communes combined to support a single school, both were counted as having a school. A comparison of departments at the 25th percentile (one quarter of all departments had a lower percentage of communes without schools) and at the 75th percentile (one quarter of all departments had a higher percentage of communes without schools) demonstrates the rapid closing of a spread that initially was very great.

Table S.4. Variations among Departments at Specific Times in the Size of Schools and Their Number in Relation to Population

	Coefficients of Variation			Ratio of Highest to Lowest Department in Number of Schools per School-Age Population
Date	Schools per School-Age Population	Schools per Population	Number of Students per School	
1813	73%	71%	—	17.0
1821	61%	59%	—	16.0
1829	59%	56%	37%	17.0
1833	51%	49%	34%	14.0
1837	41%	40%	29%	8.0
1850	39%	39%	25%	7.0
1863	38%	39%	25%	7.0
1867	37%	38%	24%	8.0
1876	36%	36%	28%	6.0
1881	37%	36%	38%	6.5
1886	35%	35%	34%	7.0
1891	34%	35%	36%	6.5
1896	35%	36%	47%	7.5
1901	34%	37%	42%	8.0
1906	36%	37%	42%	8.5

Table S.5. Number of Schools per 100 School-Age Population, Above and Below the St. Malo–Geneva Line

Date		Mean	Coefficient of Variation	Growth Rates between Data Points	Ratio: Above to Below
1813	Above	0.60	48%	—	2.5
	Below	0.24	63%	—	
1812	Above	0.72	32%	20%	2.3
	Below	0.31	58%	30%	
1829	Above	0.75	28%	3%	2.1
	Below	0.36	60%	14%	
1834	Above	0.76	23%	2%	1.7
	Below	0.45	57%	21%	
1837	Above	1.07	24%	40%	1.4
	Below	0.75	47%	69%	
1850	Above	1.17	25%	8%	1.3
	Below	0.93	46%	23%	
1863	Above	1.32	25%	13%	1.2
	Below	1.07	43%	15%	
1867	Above	1.34	25%	1%	1.2
	Below	1.12	42%	5%	
1876	Above	1.44	28%	7%	1.2
	Below	1.19	39%	6%	
1882	Above	1.49	33%	3%	1.2
	Below	1.26	38%	6%	
1886	Above	1.47	28%	−2%	1.1
	Below	1.34	38%	6%	
1891	Above	1.50	29%	2%	1.1
	Below	1.39	37%	5%	
1896	Above	1.53	31%	2%	1.0
	Below	1.46	37%	5%	
1901	Above	1.54	30%	0%	1.0
	Below	1.49	36%	2%	
1906	Above	1.50	31%	−3%	1.0
	Below	1.52	38%	2%	

Table S.6. Schools Owned by Communes and Number of Students per School, Above and Below the St. Malo–Geneva Line

Date		Percentage of Schools in School Buildings Owned by the Commune		Students per School	
		Mean	Coefficient of Variation	Mean	Coefficient of Variation
1834	Above	45	53	53.18	20%
	Below	16	58	33.54	38%
1863	Above	75	25	67.17	24%
	Below	39	37	59.34	24%
1876	Above	76	20	63.31	36%
	Below	47	33	65.59	25%
1906	Above	83	11	68.32	54%
	Below	63	18	63.38	33%

Table S.7. **The Number of Departments with Nearly All the Schools They Would Need (Fulfillment) at Specific Dates**

	By School-Age Population		By Total Population	
Date	First Achieving Fulfillment	Total Having Achieved Fulfillment	First Achieving Fulfillment	Total Having Achieved Fulfillment
1821	3	3	3	3
1829	1	4	2	5
1834	—	—	—	5
1837	8	12	10	15
1850	5	17	8	23
1863	12	29	14	37
1867	3	32	1	38
1876	11	43	14	52
1882	18	61	15	67
1886	14	75	11	78
1891	8	83	6	84
1901	4	87	3	87

Note: A department is said to have achieved fulfillment when its ratio of schools to school-age cohort or to total population is 85 percent of that ratio in 1906. Nationally, the ratio by school-age population was achieved in 1876; by total population it was achieved in 1867.

Department Names, by Date of Achieved Fulfillment (by school-age cohort)

1813 [Moselle, Bas-Rhin, Meurthe, lost in 1870]
1821 Nord, Pas-de-Calais, Seine
1829 Seine-Inférieure
1834 (none)
1837 Bouches-du-Rhoâne, Doubs, Gironde, Hérault, Marne, Rhoâne, Seine-et-Oise, Var
1850 Loire, Loire-Inférieure, Pyrénées-Orientales, Haut-Rhin, Vosges
1863 Aisne, Alpes-Maritimes, Ardennes, Aube, Calvados, Ille-et-Vilaine, Lozère, Manche, Meuse, Oise, Savoie, Somme
1867 Gard, Haute-Marne, Seine-et-Marne
1876 Ain, Hautes-Alpes, Aude, Charente, Charente-Inférieure, Corse, Côte-d'Or, Eure, Loiret, Haute-Saone, Meurthe-et-Moselle
1882 Basses-Alpes, Corrèze, Creuse, Drome, Eure-et-Loir, Haute-Garonne, Indre, Indre-et-Loire, Isère, Jura, Landes, Basses-Pyrénées, Hautes-Pyrénées, Saône-et-Loire, Sarthe, Vaucluse, Haute-Vienne, Yonne
1886 Allier, Ariège, Cantal, Finistère, Loire-et-Cher, Haute-Loire, Lot-et-Garonne, Nièvre, Orne, Puy-de-Dome, Haute-Savoie, Deux-Sèvres, Vendée, Vienne
1891 Ardèche, Cher, Côtes-du-Nord, Dordogne, Gers, Morbihan, Tarn, Tarn-et-Garonne
1901 Aveyron, Lot, Maine-et-Loire, Mayenne

Table S.8. Percentage of Schools in School Buildings Owned by Communes, Departmental Means and Ranges

Date	Mean	Minimum	Maximum	Coefficient of Variation	Compound Annual Growth Rate
1834	26%	2%	86%	83%	−2.6%
1840	29%	3.5%	82%	70%	6.5%
1850	43%	4%	100%	59%	4.0%
1863	51%	6%	100%	42%	1.3%
1872	55%	6%	93%	37%	0.8%
1876	56%	5%	94%	37%	0.5%
1886	59%	5%	88%	28%	0.9%
1891	63%	12%	90%	26%	1.3%
1896	63%	11%	90%	24%	0.0%
1901	63%	13%	89%	23%	0.0%
1906	69%	16%	92%	21%	1.8%

Note: The correlations of percentage of schools in school buildings owned by communes with the number of schools per population are as follows:

1834	1837	1850	1863	1867/1872	1876	1886	1891	1896	1901	1906
.45	.38	.25	.19	.18	.22	.08	.09	.14	.15	.14

Table S.9. Correlations: Number of Schools with Total Enrollment in Particular Years

	Per Population		Per School-Age Population	
Date	Spearman (rank order)	Pearson (weighted)	Spearman	Pearson
1829	.90	.87	.90	.88
1832	.75	.78	.80	.77
1833	.88	.82	.88	.84
1837	.83	.73	.83	.76
1850	.79	.76	.80	.76
1863	.71	.68	.75	.70
1867	.69	.72	.77	.71
1876	.66	.75	.83	.80
1882	.49	.66	.75	.78
1886	.42	.60	.76	.75
1891	.38	.62	.75	.73
1896	.32	.57	.72	.71
1901	.34	.60	.49	.51
1906	.21	.44	.62	.62

Note: Throughout these tables, departments are the units for correlational analysis. Those few departments not part of France for all data points are excluded. Unless otherwise noted, correlations are Pearson Correlations.

Table S.10 Correlations: Number of Schools with Total Enrollment at Different Times

A. Number of Schools with Total Enrollment Before and After

Date	Schools with Enrollment Thirty Years Later	Enrollment with Schools Thirty Years Later	Enrollment with Enrollment Thirty Years Later
1821:1850	.68	—[a]	—[a]
1829:1867	.68	.39	.73
1837:1876	.68	.53	.60
1850:1882	.62	.63	.47
1863:1891	.60	.55	.50
1876:1906	.46	.45	.72

B. Number of Schools in 1821 with Later Enrollment (both normalized by population)

1829	.88	1872	.51
1832	.86	1876	.60
1834	.89	1882	.30
1837	.84	1886	.24
1840	.77	1891	.27
1850	.73	1896	.33
1863	.74	1901	.38
1867	.72	1906	.28

C. Number of Schools in 1906 with the Number of Schools at Earlier Dates (normalized by school-age population)

1813	.08	1867	.84
1821	.23	1876	.89
1829	.31	1882	.89
1834	.47	1886	.94
1837	.55	1891	.97
1850	.67	1896	.94
1863	.80	1901	.99

[a] Enrollment data are not available before 1829.

Table S.11. Correlations: Number of Students per School with the Number of Schools and with Total Enrollment

Date	Number of Schools by School-Age Population	Enrollment by Population
1829	.26	.67
1833	.12	.64
1837	−.01	.63
1850	−.26	.42
1863	−.63	.04
1867	−.68	.00
1876	−.84	−.32
1886	−.84	−.17
1891	−.83	−.14
1901	−.80	−.21
1906	−.81	−.05

Table S.12. Correlations: Ordinary Expenditures with the Absolute Number of Schools and with Total Enrollment

Date	Schools at Same Date	Schools in 1821	Date of Highest Correlation Earlier	Date of Highest Correlation Later
1833	.86	.86	.87 (1829)	.82 (1863)
1837	.78	.92	.93 (1829)	.80 (1850)
1840	—	.88	.90 (1829)	.82 (1863)
1850	.83	.81	.81 (1829)	.83 (1863)
1855	—	.86	.88 (1833)	.86 (1863)
1863	.83	.82	.82 (1821)	.81 (1867)
1867	.80	.80	.84 (1863), .81 (1833)	.76 (1876)
1868	—	.55	.79 (1863)	.78 (1876)
1872	—	.54	.84 (1867)	.86 (1876)
1876	.77	.40	.76 (1867)	.75 (1882)
1882	.74	.38	.75 (1876)	.74 (1886)
1886	.67	.27	.65 (1882)	.65 (1891)
1891	.58	.22	.59 (1886)	—

Note: Data for expenditures are available for somewhat different years than the data for other variables.

Table S.13. Correlations: Ordinary Expenditures with the Number of Schools, Normalized by School-Age Population

Date	Schools at Same Date	Schools in 1821	Date of Highest Correlation	
			Earlier	Later
1833	.41	.60	.60 (1821)	.29 (1837)
1837	.45	.74	.58 (1833)	.29 (1850)
1840	—	.68	—	—
1850	.18	.61	.36 (1837)	.15 (1863)
1855	—	.62	—	—
1863	.09	.56	.13 (1850)	.06 (1867)
1867	.07	.55	.10 (1863)	.06 (1876)
1868	—	.30	−.04 (1863)	−.14 (1876)
1872	—	.24	−.09 (1867)	−.16 (1876)
1876	−.23	.13	−.16 (1867)	—
1882	−.23	.12	−.14 (1867)	−.30 (1891)
1886	−.29	.05	−.25 (1876)	−.26 (1891)
1891	−.30	.02	−.26 (1882)	−.32 (1901)

Table S.14. Correlations: Schools in 1821

A. Schools in 1821 with Indicators of School Quality in the Third Republic

Date	Schools per Population with Enrollment (per population) in Ecoles Maternelles	School per School-Age Population with Certificates des Etudes Primaires (per estimated number of 13 year olds)	Number of Books in School Libraries
1876	—	.48	
1881	.41	.50	.70
1886	.42	.28	.53
1891	.31	.28	.58
1896	—	.28	.51
1901	.24	.27	.49
1906	.29	.27	.45

B. Schools per School-Age Population in 1821 with Ordinary Expenditure per Student at Later Dates
Date

1850	.17
1863	.17
1867	.20
1868	.26
1872	.38
1883	.61

Table S.15. Proportion of Variation in the Availabilty of Schools Removed by Grouping Departments at Selected Dates

Date	Ancien Régime Provinces Approximated (15)	Geographical Academies (17)	Regions (10)	k-Means Clusters (15)
1821	.60	.56	.52	—
1829	.58	.50	.53	.97
1850	.39	.48	.34	—
1863	.41	.47	.31	.97
1906	.43	.50	.30	.90

Note: The ten geographical groups are those used in Patrick Harrigan with Victor Neglia, *Lycéens et Collégians sous le Second Empire: étude et statistique sur les fonctions sociales de l'enseignement secondaire d'après l'enquête de Victor Duruy (1864–1865)* (Paris, 1979). Mathematically, one expects that the more groupings, the higher the R^2.

Table S.16. Regression Analysis: Total Enrollment per Population at Specific Dates on the Number of Schools per Population for All Available Data Points

Date	Two Years with Best Fit	Three Years with Best Fit
1906	1863, 1867	1829, 1863, 1867
1901	1829, 1863	1829, 1863, 1867
1896	1863, 1896	1863, 1876, 1896
1891	1829, 1863	1829, 1863, 1867
1886	1829, 1863	1829, 1834, 1863
1881	1829, 1876	1829, 1837, 1876
1876	1837, 1876	1829, 1837, 1876
1867	1829, 1850	1829, 1834, 1850
1863	1829, 1850	1829, 1837, 1850
1850	1821, 1850	1821, 1850, 1901

Table E.1. Number of Students Enrolled in Primary Schools

Date	Students	Annual Compound Growth Rate	Students per 10,000 Population
1829	1,357,934	—	417
1829[a]	1,556,340	—	478
1832	1,937,582	8.0%	596
1833	1,654,328	—	508
1833[a]	1,987,101	3.0%	610
1837	2,690,035	8.0%	752
1840	2,896,934	2.5%	864
1843	3,164,297	3.0%	924
1847	3,530,135	3.0%	997
1850	3,321,423	−2.0%	967
1861	4,286,641	2.0%	1,147
1863	4,336,368	1.0%	1,160
1865	4,436,470	1.0%	1,165
1866	4,515,967	2.0%	1,186
1872	4,722,754	1.0%	1,303
1875	4,809,728	1.0%	1,303
1876–77[b]	4,716,935	−2.0%	1,303
	4,918,890	1.0%	1,281
1881–82	5,341,211	2.0%	1,418
1883–84	5,468,681	1.0%	1,430
1886–87	5,526,365	1.0%	1,446
1891	5,471,402	0.0%	1,427
1896	5,427,211	0.0%	1,388
1901	5,433,302	0.0%	1,395
1906	5,451,094	0.0%	1,389

[a]These figures are adjusted to compensate for the absence of girls schools in the censuses of 1829 and 1833. Annual compound growth rates are based on the adjusted figures. The inquiries of 1832 and 1837 included girls schools as well as boys, as do all subsequent ones. The 1829 and 1833 inquiries, however, included only schools taught by *instituteurs,* thus excluding schools taught by women, which were nearly always schools for girls. We have thus made two simple adjustments. The 1829 figures do note the number of girls taught by *instituteurs,* and to complete the total we assumed that the proportion of girls enrolled in mixed and girls schools at that date was the same as in 1837, the first date for which a complete breakdown is given. The estimate of girls in girls schools was then added to the figures for 1829.

The census for the year 1833 made no differentiation between boys and girls (in 1829 at least the number of girls in schools taught by an *instituteur* was noted). As a result we have made a simple linear adjustment—subtracting the 402,636 girls found to be in mixed schools during the 1837 census from the boys total in 1833 and adding to that the girls enrollment for 1832. The resulting figure (1,987,101) enlarges the total in the *Statistique* by 20 percent. A more sophisticated adjustment, taking into account the annual increase in enrollments during those years, would have enlarged the figure still more, by about 25 percent; but we have used the figure less supportive of our argument.

[b]The first figure for 1876–77 is from the *Statistique* of 1876–77 and is used in computing the 1876–82 growth rate. The second figure comes from the reports of the rectors of academies in 1876–77.

Table E.2. Number of Boys and Girls Enrolled in Primary Schools

Date	Boys	Annual Compound Growth Rate	Girls	Annual Compound Growth Rate	Difference
1837	1,579,888	—	1,119,147	—	460,741
1850	1,793,657	1.0%	1,528,756	2.4%	264,901
1863	2,265,738	2.0%	2,070,612	2.4%	196,126
1867	2,343,781	1.0%	2,172,186	1.0%	171,595
1872	2,445,207	1.0%	2,277,538	1.0%	167,669
1876	2,401,165	−0.5%	2,315,753	4.0%	85,412
1881	2,708,510	2.4%	2,632,701	2.6%	75,809
1886	2,789,685	1.0%	2,736,680	1.0%	53,005
1891	2,757,566	0.0%	2,713,836	0.0%	43,730
1896	2,719,674	0.0%	2,707,532	0.0%	12,142
1901	2,705,616	0.0%	2,727,686	0.0%	(22,070)
1906	2,726,895	0.0%	2,724,199	0.0%	2,696

Note: Parentheses indicate more girls than boys. Decimals are used only if between .39 and .61.

Table E.3. Number of Boys and Girls Enrolled in Public and Private Primary Schools

	Boys		Girls	
Date	Public	Private	Public	Private
1833[a]	1,289,230	365,598	—	—
1837	1,292,558	287,330	753,897	365,250
1840	—	—	—	—
1850	1,564,821	228,836	1,036,788	491,968
1863	2,053,665	212,073	1,360,156	710,456
1867	2,114,988	228,793	1,422,721	749,465
1872	2,245,801	199,406	1,590,181	687,357
1876	2,197,935	203,230	1,625,696	690,357
1881–82	2,442,581	265,929	1,916,675	716,026
1886	2,462,422	327,263	1,982,146	754,534
1891	2,310,662	446,904	1,896,766	817,070
1896	2,260,096	459,578	1,838,743	868,789
1901	2,264,533	441,083	1,808,571	919,115
1906	2,393,617	333,278	2,068,724	655,475

[a]See note to table E.1; approximately 290,479 girls in mixed schools are included in the 1833 figures for boys.

Table E.4. Number of Students with Scholarships *(boursiers)*

All	Date	Total	Variation among Department	Compound Annual Growth Rate
	1833	377,164[a]	92%	—
	1850	1,197,212	69%	7%
	1863	1,532,590	80%	2%
	1867	1,710,710	75%	3%
	1872	2,324,437	67%	6%
	1876[b]	2,193,047	—	–1%
Boys				
	1833	377,164	92%	—
	1850	739,388	66%	4%
	1863	821,467	74%	1%
	1867	931,979	69%	3%
	1872	1,277,741	63%	7%
Girls				
	1850	457,824	78%	—
	1863	711,123	87%	3%
	1867	778,731	85%	2%
	1872	1,046,696	73%	6%

[a] Includes only students in a school taught by an *instituteur*.
[b] Figures for 1876 include only *boursiers* in public schools. Those were 89 percent of all *boursiers* in 1872. Scholarships in public schools increased by 6 percent between 1872 and 1876.

Table E.5. Number of Candidates for *Certificats d'études primaires* and Number of *Certificats* Awarded, by Gender

Candidates Date	Boys	Girls	Percentage of Girls	Total	Growth Rate
1872	5,146	2,447	32	7,593	—
1873	12,861	5,221	29	18,082	138%
1874	16,849	6,289	27	23,169	28%
1875	23,169	8,571	25	31,740	37%
1876	29,315	9,813	25	39,128	23%
1877	40,467	15,099	27	55,546	42%
1878	43,148	18,735	30	61,883	11%
1882	80,301	54,138	40	134,439	21%
1886	114,418	88,863	44	203,281	11%
1892	124,716	101,613	43	226,329	2%
1897	127,463	105,915	45	233,378	1%
1902	136,289	112,930	45	249,219	1%
1907	142,521	117,422	45	259,943	1%

Awarded Date	Boys	Girls	Total	Growth Rate	Percentage of Success, All	Percentage of Success, Girls
1872	3,572	1,586	5,158	—	68	65
1873	7,254	2,617	9,871	91%	55	50
1874	11,380	4,190	15,570	58%	67	67
1875	15,457	6,293	21,750	40%	69	73
1876	19,271	6,884	26,155	20%	67	70
1877	26,057	10,784	38,841	49%	70	71
1878	27,948	12,589	40,537	4%	66	67
1882	53,156	37,997	91,153	23%	68	70
1886	80,372	63,674	144,046	12%	71	72
1892	95,776	78,741	174,517	3%	77	82
1897	99,939	83,648	183,587	1%	79	79
1902	110,394	94,021	204,415	2%	82	83
1907	117,713	100,307	218,020	1%	84	85

Table E.6. Total Enrollment in Primary Schools per 100 Children Six to Thirteen Years Old, Departmental Means and Ranges

Date	Mean	Median	Maximum	Minimum	Annual Compound Growth Rate	Coefficient of Variation
1829	30	19	97	4	—	80%
1829[a]	35	22	111	5	—	80%
1832	43	32	121	6	8%	70%
1833	38	27	101	7	—	66%
1833[a]	45	37	138	10	4%	66%
1837	61	52	137	17	8%	51%
1840	66	62	144	21	3%	48%
1850	75	71	139	28	1%	39%
1863	96	95	150	48	2%	26%
1867	101	101	151	49	1%	24%
1872	109	108	159	58	2%	20%
1876	108	106	150	62	0%	15%
1881	120	120	166	76	2%	13%
1886	120	119	163	79	0%	11%
1891	120	120	155	77	0%	10%
1896	120	119	151	94	0%	9%
1901	119	118	140	96	0%	8%
1906	124	124	150	99	1%	8%

[a] See note to table E.1.

Table E.7. Enrollment per 100 Children Six to Thirteen Years Old, Above and Below the St. Malo–Geneva Line

Date		Mean	Variance	Growth Rate
1829[a]	Above	66	36%	—
	Below	18	53%	—
1832	Above	78	29%	26%
	Below	25	45%	60%
1833[a]	Above	94	30%	−17%
	Below	43	48%	−9%
1837	Above	98	25%	45%
	Below	49	36%	87%
1840	Above	102	24%	4%
	Below	60	42%	14%
1850	Above	121	19%	4%
	Below	84	35%	23%
1863	Above	122	13%	18%
	Below	90	22%	40%
1867	Above	124	13%	1%
	Below	103	21%	7%
1872	Above	120	21%	1%
	Below	102	18%	15%
1876	Above	124	10%	−3%
	Below	119	15%	0%
1881	Above	123	11%	8%
	Below	119	14%	18%
1886	Above	124	7%	0%
	Below	118	13%	0%
1891	Above	124	6%	1%
	Below	118	12%	−1%
1896	Above	124	7%	0%
	Below	118	10%	0%
1901	Above	124	5%	0%
	Below	116	9%	−1%
1906	Above	126	7%	2%
	Below	123	9%	5%

[a]Girls in girls schools are not reported.

Table E.8. Percentage of Children Six to Thirteen Years Old Enrolled in Primary Schools

Date	Mean	Departmental Minimum	Coefficient of Variance
1863[a]	77.0	—	—
1881	97.8	64.4	10%
1886	101.0	70.8	8%
1891	98.3	67.9	7%
1896	96.4	65.6	7%
1901	95.3	66.4	10%
1906	99.9	84.2	5%

[a] An archival document (F17*/5160) for 1863 listed the school-age population (six to thirteen year olds) as 4,018,449; the enrollment of that age group as 3,093,652; the number of students who were older than thirteen as 519,092; the number of students who were younger than six as 741,160. Total enrollment as given in this source is .4% higher than that in table E.1, based on the published *Statistiques*.

Table E.9. Number of Departments Enrolling 50, 60, 70, and 80 Percent of Children Five to Fifteen Years Old

Date	Depts.	50 Percent Enrolled Five Years of Schooling		Depts.	60 Percent Enrolled Six Years of Schooling	
		Relative Percentage	Cumulative Percentage		Relative Percentage	Cumulative Percentage
1829	1 (10)	1 (11)	11	0 (6)	0 (7)	7
1832	16 (7)	18 (8)	19	12 (6)	13	13
1837	10	11	30	8	9	22
1840	7	8	38	4	4	27
1850	11	12	50	4	4	31
1863	30	33	83	27	30	61
1867	1	1	84	10	11	72
1872	11	12	97	16	18	90
1876	1	1	98	3	3	93
1881	2	2	100	4	4	98
1886	—	—	—	2	2	100

Date	Depts.	70 Percent Enrolled Seven Years of Schooling		Depts.	80 Percent Enrolled Eight Years of Schooling	
		Relative Percentage	Cumulative Percentage		Relative Percentage	Cumulative Percentage
1829	0 (1)	0 (1)	0 (1)	0	0	0
1832	4 (3)	4 (3)	4	2	2	2
1837	8	9	13	5	6	8
1840	2	2	15	2	2	10
1850	6	7	22	6	7	17
1863	21	23	46	7	8	25
1867	6	7	52	5	6	30
1872	19	21	73	9	10	40
1876	5	6	79	2	2	42
1881	13	14	93	21	23	66
1886	3	3	97	6	7	72
1891	1	1	98	7	8	80
1896	—	—	—	1	1	81
1901	1	1	99	—	—	—
1906	—	—	—	4	4	86
Never	1	1	—	13	14	—

Note: Parentheses indicate adjusted data; see note to table E.1.

Table E.10. Summer Attendance as a Percentage of Winter Enrollment

Date	Percentage
1829	60
1832	64
1833	54
1837	61
1840	62
1850	66
1876	79
1882	81
1886	71 (86)
1891	71 (86)
1896	72 (84)
1901	74
1906	74 (84)

Note: Figures in parentheses represent attendance in independent schools. Before 1886, the single figure is for students in both public and independent schools.

Table E.11. Summer Attendance per 100 Children Six to Thirteen Years Old, Departmental Means and Ranges

Date	Mean	Median	Maximum	Minimum	Ratio Max. to Minimum	Coefficient of Variation	Annual Compound Growth Rate
1829	15	11	63	2	31:1	76%	—
1829[a]	17	13	72	2	36:1	76%	—
1832	25	21	74	4	19:1	62%	14%
1833	17	15	43	5	9:1	56%	—
1833[a]	21	18	51	6	9:1	56%	−16%
1837	34	31	69	13	5:1	42%	13%
1840	37	33	77	15	5:1	42%	3%
1850	47	45	106	20	5:1	38%	2%
1863[b]	68	67	105	36	3:1	23%	3%
1876	85	86	109	44	2.5:1	14%	2%
1881	96	97	123	53	2.3:1	13%	3%
1886	85	85	104	54	1.9:1	12%	2%
1891	85	85	102	52	1.7:1	11%	0%
1896	86	86	103	59	1.7:1	10%	0%
1901	87	86	130	59	2.2:1	11%	0%
1906	92	92	105	70	1.5:1	8%	1%

[a] See note to table E.1.
[b] Figures for summer attendance in 1863 are extrapolated (assuming attendance then was the mean of attendance in 1850 and 1876 and dividing by the school-age population in 1863).

Table E.12. Enrollment in *Écoles Maternelles* per 100 Children Five and Six Years Old, Departmental Means and Ranges, Octiles

Date	Mean	Maximum	Minimum	Variation
1837	4	26	0	127%
1850	22	78	0	74%
1863	54	178	8	66%
1867	60	208	9	67%
1876	77	281	23	66%
1881	90	253	21	58%
1886	98	248	21	54%
1891	88	238	21	52%
1896	90	241	21	50%
1901	92	256	21	53%
1906	80	204	21	55%

	By Octiles								By St. Malo–Geneva Line	
Date	1	2	3	4	5	6	7	8	Below	Above
1837	3	3	4	3	8	4	6	6	3	5
1850	13	17	22	18	26	28	23	31	18	30
1863	27	34	40	46	60	74	64	90	41	79
1867	31	36	47	50	65	81	71	103	45	89
1876	34	60	66	65	86	101	83	123	63	104
1881	42	61	74	82	108	109	103	141	72	127
1886	49	68	82	92	122	118	111	149	80	134
1891	47	66	73	83	122	105	94	116	77	112
1896	49	71	78	85	124	107	94	116	79	112
1901	51	73	77	88	133	110	95	112	82	113
1906	48	61	64	78	116	94	75	103	70	98

Note: Number of five and six year olds is estimated as one-seventh of six to thirteen age cohort or one-tenth of five to fifteen age cohort.

Table E.13. Percentage of Thirteen Year Olds Seeking and Receiving *Certificats*, Departmental Means and Ranges

Date	Mean	Maximum	Minimum	Coefficient of Variation
1876 applied for	8.6	39.4	0.0	86%
awarded	5.8	31.9	0.0	104%
1881 applied for	20.5	54.0	9.3	42%
awarded	14.3	43.9	5.3	51%
1886 applied for	29.3	54.0	10.2	34%
awarded	20.8	45.9	7.7	39%
1891 applied for	32.3	66.8	12.4	27%
awarded	25.0	51.6	8.6	29%
1896 applied for	34.0	59.8	17.0	25%
awarded	27.0	46.2	12.4	23%
1901 applied for	35.3	69.6	17.3	24%
awarded	31.1	60.0	14.9	27%
1906 applied for	38.6	67.8	22.1	21%
awarded	30.5	54.4	16.6	25%

Note: Number of thirteen year olds is calculated as one-seventh of six to thirteen age cohort.

Table E.14. Dates at Which Departments Reached Enrollments Equal to 50, 75, and 100 Percent of the Number of Children Six to Thirteen Years Old

	Date	Number of Departments	Relative Percentage	Cumulative Percentage
50%				
	1829	2 (25)	2 (28)	2 (28)
	1832	28 (5)	31 (6)	33
	1837	17	19	52
	1840	5	6	58
	1850	16	18	76
	1863	20	22	98
	1867	1	1	99
	1876	1	1	100
75%				
	1829	0 (9)	0 (10)	0 (10)
	1832	16 (7)	18 (8)	18
	1837	9	10	28
	1840	5	4	32
	1850	7	8	40
	1863	36	40	80
	1867	3	3	83
	1872	10	11	94
	1876	3	3	98
	1881	2	2	100
100%				
	1829	0 (1)	0 (1)	0 (1)
	1832	4 (3)	4 (3)	6
	1837	8	9	13
	1840	2	2	16
	1850	6	7	22
	1863	21	23	46
	1867	6	7	52
	1872	19	21	73
	1876	5	6	79
	1881	13	14	93
	1886	3	3	97
	1891	1	1	98
	1901	1	1	99
	Never	1	1	—

Note: Parentheses indicate adjusted data; see note to table E.1.

Table E.15. Date at Which Summer Attendance in Departments Reached a Number Equal to Various Percentages of the Population Six to Thirteen Years Old

Date	50%			71.4% (equal to attendance of entire cohort for five years)		
	Number of Departments	Relative Percent	Cumulative Percent	Number of Departments	Relative Percent	Cumulative Percent
1829	2	2	2	1	1	1
1832	5	6	8	—	—	—
1837	8	9	17	—	—	—
1840	12	13	30	2	3	—
1850	12	13	43	6	7	10
1863[a]	35	39	82	42	47	57
1876	17	19	99	28	31	88
1881	—	—	—	7	8	96
1886	—	—	—	—	—	—
1891	—	—	—	—	—	—
1896	—	—	—	1	1	97
Never	—	—	—	3	3	—

Date	85.7% (equal to attendance of entire cohort for six years)			100%		
	Number of Departments	Relative Percent	Cumulative Percent	Number of Departments	Relative Percent	Cumulative Percent
1850	4	4	4	2	3	3
1863[a]	7	8	12	1	1	4
1876	35	39	51	3	3	8
1881	30	33	84	32	36	42
1886	1	1	85	1	1	43
1891	2	2	88	—	—	—
1896	1	1	89	—	—	—
1901	—	—	—	2	2	45
1906	3	3	92	1	1	47
Never	7	8	—	48	53	—

[a] For extrapolation of data for 1863, see note to table E.11.

Table E.16. Enrollment per 100 Children Six to Thirteen Years Old in Five Groups of Departments Arranged by Their Degree of Urbanization in 1876

Date	Group 1	2	3	4	5
1829	42	27	39	30	26
1832	60	40	53	41	40
1833	47	30	46	37	34
1837	77	57	70	57	59
1840	82	66	72	61	66
1850	90	73	80	70	74
1863	102	94	99	94	96
1867	104	100	102	99	102
1872	93[a]	109	113	109	114
1876	106	104	112	106	112
1881	117	116	123	123	130
1886	117	116	126	124	129
1891	119	119	124	123	129
1901	124	126	126	132	124
1906	124	129	133	127	132

Note: Groups are defined as follows:
1: The eleven departments with more than 50 percent of their population in communes of more than 2,000 people in 1876.
2: The five departments with 40 to 50 percent of their population in communes of more than 2,000 people in 1876.
3: The six departments with 30 to 40 percent of their population in communes of more than 2,000 people in 1876.
4: The thirty-three departments with 20 to 30 percent of their population in communes of more than 2,000 people in 1876.
5: The thirty-four departments with less than 20 percent of their population in communes of more than 2,000 people in 1876.
[a] Departments of Alsace-Lorraine (early leaders) disappear.

Table E.17. Correlations: Expenditures with Enrollment

A. Gross Expenditures with Enrollment per School-Age Population

Date	1906 Expenditures with Enrollment at Earlier Dates	Expenditures and Enrollment at Same Date
1829	.57	—
1832	.56	—
1833	.55	.63
1837	.59	.78
1840	.50	.65
1850	.46	.57
1863	.49	.50
1867	.47	.47
1872	.36	.12
1876	.34	.07
1881	.09	−.05
1886	.05	−.05
1891	.13	−.03
1896	.14	—
1901	.23	—
1906	.06	.06

B. Ordinary Expenses per Student with Enrollment per School-Age Population

Date	Enrollment in 1829 with Later Expenses per Student	Enrollment and Expenses per Student at Same Date
1833	−.68	−.78
1837	−.12	−.33
1840	−.03	−.33
1850	−.07	−.21
1863	−.10	−.11
1867	.18	.01
1868	.16	—
1872	.27	.27
1876	.35	.36
1882	.59	.39
1886	.45	.41
1891	.40	.33
1906	.46	.48

C. Voluntary Expenses in 1901 and 1906 with Earlier Enrollment per School-Age Population

Expenditure in	Schools 1821	Enrollment 1832	Present in Summer 1832	Enrollment 1837	Present in Summer 1837
1901 per student	.29	.33	.43	.35	.48
1901 per capita	.34	.39	.49	.40	.50
1906 per student	.27	.28	.43	.30	.46
1906 per capita	.31	.33	.48	.34	.48

Note: 97 percent of all voluntary (facultative) expenses were paid by town councils in 1906.

Table E.18. Correlations: Enrollment in *Écoles Maternelles* per Population and *Certificats d'études primaires* per Thirteen Year Olds with Primary School Enrollment and with Attendance (per school-age population)

Écoles Maternelles	Primary School Enrollment			Primary School Attendance		
	Same Date	1829	1832	Same Date	1829	1832
1867	.41	.54	.53	—	.28	.36
1876	.21	.38	.37	.30	.26	.20
1881	−.06	.44	.45	.00	.14	.21
1886	−.08	.44	.46	.03	.14	.18
1891	−.01	.26	.27	.12	.09	.15
1901	−.04	.14	.13	.04	.10	.10
Certificats d'études primaires						
1876 applied for	.47	.61	.60	.45	.40	.39
awarded	.45	.61	.61	.46	.40	.42
1881 applied for	.43	.63	.65	.42	.35	.42
awarded	.40	.63	.65	.42	.32	.40
1886 applied for	.35	.59	.60	.53	.38	.41
awarded	.33	.64	.64	.54	.36	.38
1891 applied for	.37	.47	.51	.55	.31	.35
awarded	.39	.49	.52	.60	.27	.31
1896 applied for	.13	.49	.51	.50	.32	.34
awarded	.08	.49	.51	.54	.32	.33
1901 applied for	.24	.31	.30	.51	.30	.32
awarded	.33	.33	.35	.47	.26	.35
1906 applied for	.25	.23	.25	.48	.18	.23
awarded	.16	.27	.26	.50	.23	.28

Table E.19. Correlations: *Certificats d'études primaires* per Thirteen Year Olds with Socioeconomic Factors

Certificats	Agricultural Population (1861)	Urban Population 1865	Literacy 1865	Literacy 1851	Population Growth 1841–66
1886	−.43	.01	.40	.47	.04
1891	−.46	.11	.46	.49	.20
1896	−.40	.13	.43	.46	.20
1901	−.51	.32	.33	.34	.43
1906	.34	.29	.30	.30	.33

Note: The correlations with certificates applied for and certificates awarded are approximately the same.

Table E.20. Correlations: Enrollment per School-Age Population with Urbanization, Wealth, and Literacy

Enrollment in	Density of Pop. 1865	Percent Urban 1865	Population in Small Cities[a] 1865	Wealth	Literacy 1865
1829 (adj.)	−.05	.03	.50	.53	.72
1832	−.02	.06	.52	.49	.80
1833	−.05	.00	.56	.52	.78
1837	−.01	.05	.53	.50	.85
1840	−.01	.03	.52	.44	.86
1850	−.05	.04	.48	.43	.86
1863	−.02	−.01	.54	.47	.88
1867	−.07	−.06	.55	.44	.86
1872	−.10	−.18	.53	.30	.67
1876	−.02	−.10	.66	.28	.79
1881	−.11	−.23	.54	.06	.52
1886	−.06	−.22	.51	.07	.46
1891	−.06	−.20	.47	.16	.56
1896	−.13	−.27	.50	.06	.56
1901	−.05	−.01	.41	.13	.60
1906	−.13	−.19	.36	.01	.48

[a]Percentage of total population residing in towns of 2,000 to 10,000 inhabitants.

Table E. 21. Regression Analysis: Variance in Enrollment Accounted for by Grouping Departments

Date	k-Means Clusters	Provinces	Academy	Regions[a]
1829	.98	.75	.66	.76
1863	.91	.69	.65	.53
1872	.90	.42	.66	.31
1881	—	.47	.55	.31
1901	.86[a]	.59	.58	.47

[a]See note to table S.15.

Table C.1. Number of Students in Catholic and Lay Primary Schools

Date	Enrollment (public and independent) in Catholic Schools	Annual Compound Growth Rate (in percentage)	Annual Enrollment in All Lay Schools	Compound Growth Rate (in percentage)
1850	953,793	—	2,367,630	—
1863	1,610,674	4	2,725,694	1
1865	—	—	—	—
1867	1,695,297	1	2,820,670	1
1872	—	—	—	—
1876	2,068,373	2	2,648,562	−1
1881	1,773,350	−3	3,567,861	6
1886	1,707,256	−1	3,819,109	1
1891	1,640,373	−1	3,831,029	0
1896	1,553,451	−1	3,873,760	0
1901	1,488,055	−1	3,945,247	0
1906	216,686[a]	−32	5,234,408	6

[a] 216,765 if public and private totals are summed. Minor discrepancies sometimes exist for different combinations of subtotals. Totals for lay schools are obtained by subtraction of figures for Catholic schools from the national total. For total enrollment figures, see table E.1.

Table C.2. Number of Students in Public and Independent Schools

Date	Public Schools		Mean Percent Catholic Enrollment By Department	Independent Schools		Mean Percent Catholic Enrollment By Department
	Total	Catholic		Total	Catholic	
1833	1,289,230	—	—	365,598	—	—
1837	2,046,455	—	—	643,580	—	—
1850	2,601,619	676,769	26	720,804	277,024	39
1863	3,413,830	1,110,047	31	922,538	500,627	55
1867	3,537,709	1,150,998	32	978,258	544,299	59
1872	3,835,991	—	—	886,763	—	—
1876	3,823,348	1,628,289	44	893,587	440,084	49
1881	4,359,256	1,009,483	22	981,955	763,867	82
1886	4,444,568	800,009	17	1,081,797	907,246	87
1891	4,207,428	523,340	12	1,263,974	1,117,033	91
1896	4,098,839	405,825	11	1,328,367	1,197,626	92
1901	4,073,104	251,423	6	1,360,198	1,235,105	93
1906	4,462,341	40,529	1	988,023	176,236	3

Note: In 1876 a category of *écoles tenant lieu des écoles publiques* was introduced. These were generally Catholic schools—a result of the law of August 10, 1867, encouraging communes to convert independent schools into public ones. See different totals in *Statistique comparée,* 1876 (Paris, 1880), introduction, 135–37. See also chap. 4, n.12; 142,134 students would have been counted as in Catholic independent schools by the criteria of other censuses. Minor discrepancies exist in some subtables and between our computer addition and that in the *Statistiques.* The mean percentage given is the mean among departments. The national mean, which never differs from the former by more than 1 percent, can be calculated by dividing the first column into the second.

Table C.3. Enrollment Growth in All Schools and in Catholic Schools, 1850–76

Date	All Schools	Catholic Schools	Catholic Percent of Total Growth
1850–63	1,014,945	656,881	65
1863–67	179,599	84,623	47
1867–76	200,968	373,076	186
1876–81	624,276	−295,023	—
1881–86	185,154	−66,094	—
1850–76	1,395,512	1,114,580	80

Table C.4. Changes in Enrollment in Various Types of Schools, 1866–76

	Boys	Girls	Total
Independent Schools			
Laic	−41,230	−81,360	−122,590
Catholic	365	−104,580	−104,215
Total	−40,865	−185,940	−226,805
Public Schools			
Laic	−91,803	42,285	−49,518
Catholic	189,769	287,522	477,291
Total	97,966	329,807	427,773
Laic Schools			
Independent	−41,230	−81,360	—
Public	−91,803	42,285	—
Total	−133,033	−39,075	−172,108
Catholic Schools			
Independent	365	−104,580	
Public	189,769	287,522	
Total	190,134	182,942	373,076

Note: Total enrollment in 1866 was 4,515,967; in 1876, 4,716,935: the number gained was 200,968.

Table C.5. Percentage of Boys and Girls Enrolled in Catholic Schools

Date	Nationally		Departments with High Catholic Enrollment		Departments with High Early Enrollment	
	Girls	Boys	Girls	Boys	Girls	Boys
1850	44	16	64	33	38	7
1863	53	22	71	45	49	11
1867	55	21	76	42	50	11
1876	59	27	80	45	54	19
1881	49	16	72	33	42	9
1886	45	14	68	30	38	9
1891	43	14	66	28	36	11
1896	42	15	65	29	33	10
1901	38	14	60	28	28	9
1906	5	1	12	3	2	1

Table C.6. Number of Boys in Catholic Schools, 1876–1901

Date	Public	Private	Total
1876	587,351	94,263	681,614
1881	254,094	199,932	454,026
1886	169,360	267,023	436,383
1891	36,290	393,330	429,620
1896	25,187	411,539	436,726
1901	15,880	395,526	411,406

Table C.7. Number of Students with Scholarships *(boursiers)* in Various Types of Schools

Date	All Schools	Public Schools	Catholic Schools	Lay Schools	Boys	Girls
1833	24	—	—	—	—	—
1837	—	37	—	—	—	—
1850	36	41	67	32	41	30
1863	33	37	57	27	36	34
1867	36	40	59	32	40	36
1872	48	53	—	—	52	46
1876	—	56	66	52	—	—

Note: See also table E.4.

Table C.8. Catholic Enrollment as a Percentage of Total Enrollment, Arranged by 1832 Octiles (= based on total enrollment per school-age cohort)

Date	Octiles							
	1	2	3	4	5	6	7	8
1850	.31	.32	.30	.25	.38	.28	.21	.21
1863	.40	.39	.40	.33	.46	.38	.26	.27
1867	.41	.40	.41	.33	.45	.39	.27	.28
1876	.46	.44	.46	.39	.49	.44	.33	.37
1881	.35	.35	.37	.28	.36	.32	.23	.25
1886	.31	.33	.34	.26	.34	.30	.21	.23
1891	.29	.32	.33	.26	.33	.28	.21	.23
1896	.30	.32	.34	.26	.32	.27	.20	.21
1901	.28	.29	.32	.24	.29	.25	.17	.18
1906	.05	.04	.02	.01	.03	.03	.01	.01

Table C.9. Departments with More than Half of Their Enrollment in Catholic Schools in 1850

	Percentage in Catholic Schools	Percentage in Independent Schools		Percentage of School-Age Population in School
	1850	1850	1876	1850
Loire	75	17	17	72
Vaucluse	60	35	15	65
Haute-Loire	59	44	36	50
Rhône	58	35	27	80
Côtes-du-Nord	55	29	16	42

Table C.10. Correlations: Departmental Population in Communes of Various Sizes with Membership in Teaching Religious Orders, 1861, and with Percentage of Enrollment in Catholic Schools

1862 Commune Size	Population (in thousands)	Enrollment in Catholic Schools, 1850	Number in Female Teaching Orders	Number in Male Teaching Orders
More than 80,000	3,159	.24	.55	.81
10,001–15,000	749	.20	.46	.48
5,001–10,000	1,981	.32	.43	.39
1,001–5,000	15,236	.41	.43	.23
20,001–30,000	602	–.03	.25	.21
30,001–40,000	445	.08	.17	.12
15,001–20,000	548	.09	.16	.15
40,000–50,000	455	–.02	.16	–.05
501–1,000	8,281	–.51	.09	–.22
Less than 500	5,458	–.52	–.09	–.27
50,001–60,000	434	.02	.04	–.02
60,001–80,000	142	.08	.02	–.01

Table G.1. Number of Girls Schools, Public and Independent

	Public Schools			Independent Schools			
Date	Total	Lay	Catholic	Total	Lay	Catholic	Total
1837	4,343	—	—	8,606	—	—	14,059
1840	6,000	4,032	3,798	9,882	6,759	2,698	15,882
1843	7,830	—	—	9,457	—	—	17,287
1847	7,926	—	—	11,488	—	—	19,414
1850	9,415	4,178	5,237	11,774	8,325	3,449	21,189
1863	14,059	5,998	8,061	13,208	7,637	5,571	27,267
1865	14,721	6,339	8,322	12,839	6,983	5,856	27,560
1866	14,099	5,569	8,530	13,115	7,079	6,036	28,214
1872	17,461	8,479	8,982	10,998	5,292	5,706	28,459
1875	20,360	9,229	11,131	8,719	4,236	4,476	29,072
1876	19,257	9,417	9,840	9,869	4,091	5,778	29,126

Table G.2. Boys and Girls Enrollment per Population Six to Thirteen Years Old

A. Assuming Boys and Girls Are Each 50 Percent of School-Age Cohort

Date	Mean Boys	Mean Girls	Minimum Boys	Minimum Girls	Maximum Boys	Maximum Girls
1833	—	—	—	—	—	—
1837	72	49	22	7	145	131
1850	81	68	31	14	141	136
1863	102	90	55	29	160	143
1867	106	95	54	32	163	146
1872	114	104	65	25	170	148
1876	111	105	67	57	157	142
1881	123	118	78	73	172	160
1886	122	118	83	75	168	158
1891	121	118	81	74	162	149
1896	121	119	99	90	165	148
1901	118	119	97	94	144	140
1906	124	123	103	95	154	156

B. Using Census Figures by Department for Percentage of Boys and Girls in School-Age Cohort

Date	Mean Boys	Mean Girls	Minimum Boys	Minimum Girls	Maximum Boys	Maximum Girls
1833	—	—	—	—	—	—
1837	69	48	22	7	144	131
1850	79	68	31	14	140	138
1863	100	91	54	30	160	147
1867	104	96	53	33	160	147
1872	114	106	63	53	165	153
1876	110	106	66	57	154	145
1881	121	119	76	75	168	164
1886	120	120	82	76	164	161
1891	120	120	80	75	158	152
1896	119	121	97	92	152	151
1901	117	120	98	94	140	144
1906	123	124	101	97	150	152

C. Coefficient of Variation

Date	Boys	Girls
1833	—	—
1837	43%	65%
1850	36%	44%
1863	25%	30%
1867	22%	27%
1872	20%	21%
1876	15%	17%
1881	14%	14%
1886	12%	12%
1891	10%	11%
1896	10%	11%
1901	9%	9%
1906	9%	9%

Table G.3. Enrollment of Boys and Girls per Population Six to Thirteen Years Old, Above and Below the St. Malo–Geneva Line

	Above Line		Below Line	
Date	Boys	Girls	Boys	Girls
1837	103	85	55	30
1850	108	97	67	53
1863	124	118	91	76
1867	125	120	97	83
1872	125	122	109	96
1876	120	119	107	98
1881	124	124	122	115
1886	123	123	121	116
1891	123	125	120	115
1896	123	125	119	116
1901	122	125	117	116
1906	125	127	124	122

Table G.4. Percentage of Communes without Any Girls School, by Department

Date	Mean	Minimum	Maximum
1863	45	1	78
1876	41	0	89
1882	34	0	67
1886	32	0	70
1891	35	0	74
1896	36	0	75
1901	2	0	23
1906	1	0	9

Note: For all schools, see table S.3.

Table G.5. Dates by Which Departments Reached Enrollment Equal to 50, 75, and 100 Percent of the Girls Six to Thirteen Years Old

A. (50 percent)	Number of Departments	Percentage	Cumulative Percentage
1850	25 (25)	28	66
1863	23 (23)	26	91
1867	4 (4)	4	96
1872	3 (3)	3	99
1876	1 (1)	1	100

B. (75 percent)	Number of Departments	Percentage	Cumulative Percentage
1837	20 (19)	22	22
1850	13 (14)	14	37
1863	32 (32)	36	72
1867	3 (4)	3	76
1872	13 (13)	14	90
1876	3 (3)	3	93
1881	4 (3)	4	98
1886	2 (2)	2	100

C. (100 percent)	Number of Departments	Percentage	Cumulative Percentage
1837	9 (9)	10	10
1850	10 (11)	11	21
1863	15 (16)	17	38
1867	6 (4)	7	45
1872	12 (11)	13	58
1876	4 (8)	4	62
1881	23 (23)	26	88
1886	5 (4)	6	93
1891	1 (1)	1	95
1896	2 (1)	2	97
1906	2 (1)	2	99
Never	1 (2)	1	100

Note: Numbers in parentheses indicate the figure if the school-age cohort is set according to the percent of boys in the six to thirteen school-age cohort in 1872 in each department (50.6 percent nationally with a range of 48.5 to 52.9) rather than at 50 percent for each department.

Table G.6. Girls Enrollment per Number of Girls Six to Thirteen Years Old, by Octiles (based on total enrollment in 1832)

Date	Octile							
	1	2	3	4	5	6	7	8
1837	0.25	0.24	0.24	0.30	0.45	0.55	0.79	1.06
1850	0.36	0.43	0.51	0.49	0.73	0.80	0.98	1.10
1863	0.57	0.69	0.75	0.77	0.95	1.07	1.14	1.26
1867	0.63	0.74	0.86	0.82	0.98	1.10	1.17	1.28
1872	0.76	0.90	0.95	0.96	1.08	1.15	1.27	1.24
1876	0.82	0.93	1.00	0.98	1.09	1.08	1.20	1.24
1881	1.00	1.14	1.14	1.16	1.19	1.20	1.28	1.29
1886	1.04	1.16	1.12	1.18	1.20	1.20	1.24	1.27
1891	1.07	1.16	1.10	1.13	1.22	1.20	1.28	1.26
1896	1.08	1.16	1.13	1.17	1.20	1.21	1.28	1.27
1901	1.09	1.13	1.11	1.17	1.22	1.20	1.28	1.26
1906	1.15	1.20	1.18	1.20	1.25	1.23	1.30	1.29

Table G.7. Female and Male Literacy in 1872

A. Departmental Ranges

	Minimum	25 Percent	Median	Mean	75 Percent	Maximum
Read only	2 (2)	7 (4)	11 (7)	13 (8)	18 (10)	39 (29)
Age: 6-20	20 (34)	49 (57)	59 (65)	59 (66)	70 (74)	90 (91)
Age: over 20	18 (32)	32 (49)	45 (60)	47 (61)	62 (73)	83 (90)

Note: Figures for males are in parentheses.

B. Correlations: Female Literacy in 1872 with Girls Enrollment per School-Age Population at Other Dates

1832	.82	1872	.76
1837	.83	1876	.74
1840	.83	1881	.45
1850	.79	1886	.41
1863	.83	1891	.50
1867	.81	1896	.51

Table G.8. Correlations: Girls and Boys Enrollment per Population Six to Thirteen Years Old With Social Factors

Date	Percentage of Literacy 1861–65	Per Capita Wealth in 1866	Percentage of 1866 Population	
			Agriculture	Industry
1837	.80 (.85)	.50 (.45)	−.44 (−.37)	−.45 (.34)
1850	.85 (.84)	.48 (.37)	−.38 (−.26)	.40 (.26)
1863	.87 (.85)	.55 (.38)	−.40 (−.16)	.40 (.17)
1867	.84 (.83)	.51 (.33)	−.32 (−.11)	.33 (.11)
1872	.71 (.59)	.40 (.19)	−.13 (.08)	.11 (−.10)
1876	.82 (.70)	.40 (.15)	−.19 (.07)	.15 (−.10)
1881	.61 (.40)	.19 (−.07)	.04 (.27)	−.06 (−.28)
1886	.55 (.33)	.20 (−.06)	.06 (.30)	−.01 (−.32)
1891	.66 (.44)	.30 (.02)	−.03 (.22)	.04 (−.20)
1896	.69 (.40)	.22 (−.08)	−.01 (.24)	.00 (−.25)
1901	.68 (.45)	.23 (−.01)	−.22 (.04)	.15 (−.10)
1906	.59 (.36)	.13 (−.10)	.13 (.30)	−.06 (−.27)

Date	Percentage of 1866 Population			Communes of 2,000–10,000
	Commerce	Professions	Urban	
1837	.25 (.24)	.29 (.37)	.03 (.02)	−.47 (−.56)
1850	.23 (.14)	.21 (.21)	.09 (.00)	−.44 (−.50)
1863	.28 (.06)	.22 (.19)	.09 (−.12)	−.48 (−.58)
1867	.21 (.003)	.17 (.18)	.03 (−.15)	−.49 (−.58)
1872	.07 (−.15)	.14 (.12)	−.01 (−.24)	−.52 (−.51)
1876	.15 (−.11)	.15 (.11)	.01 (−.20)	−.63 (−.64)
1881	.00 (−.24)	.06 (.0003)	−.12 (−.33)	−.57 (−.48)
1886	.01 (−.24)	.07 (.0079)	−.11 (−.32)	−.53 (−.45)
1891	.01 (−.26)	−.01 (−.07)	−.05 (−.28)	−.48 (−.41)
1896	−.03 (−.29)	.09 (.03)	−.14 (−.34)	−.54 (−.41)
1901	.17 (−.10)	.23 (.18)	.13 (−.11)	−.44 (−.34)
1906	−.07 (−.30)	−.04 (−.11)	−.08 (−.27)	−.39 (−.31)

Note: Correlations for boys are in parentheses.

Table G.9. Correlations: Boys Enrollment with Girls Enrollment at Various Dates

Date	Boys Enrollment in 1837 with Boys Enrollment at Other Dates[a]	Boys Enrollment with Girls Enrollment at Same Date	Girls Enrollment in 1837 with Boys Enrollment at Other Date
1850	.88	.89	.91
1863	.86	.94	.88
1867	.86	.88	.85
1872	.62	.88	.66
1876	.72	.90	.72
1881	.43	.84	.45
1886	.36	.87	.42
1891	.42	.86	.54
1896	.44	.82	.57
1901	.51	.82	.60
1906	.42	.87	.46

[a] All figures are adjusted by school-age population.

Table G.10. Regression Analysis: Girls Enrollment with Socioeconomic Factors

A. Girls Enrollment in 1837 (as percentage of total enrollment)

(1) Agricultural population (as percentage of population)	–.40
(2) Urban population (1865)	.47
(3) Wealth (1865)	.49
(4) Percent population in commerce	.51
(5) Enrollment in Catholic secondary schools as percentage of all enrollment	.52
(6) Percent population in industry	.53
(7) Schools per school-age population in 1821	.53

B. Girls Enrollment in 1876 (as percentage of total enrollment)

	Simple R	Cumulative (multiple) R
Percent population in agriculture (1865)	–.53	.53
Wealth	.47	.55
Percent population in industry	.43	.57
Enrollment in Catholic secondary schools	.11	.60
Percent urban population (1876)	.00	.60
Percent commercial population	.50	.60

Table T.1. The Number of Teachers

A. *Titulaires* in Public Schools, Male Lay and Religious, Female Lay and Religious

Date	Male, Lay	Male, Rel.	Female, Lay	Female, Rel.	Total
1850	32,168	1,007	4,195	5,240	42,610
1863	33,767	1,996	7,579	9,133	52,445
1872	33,438	2,020	10,786	10,149	56,393
1876	32,585	2,188	11,128	10,895	56,796
1882	35,631	1,454	16,101	9,811	69,088
1886	37,250	926	20,326	8,171	62,297
1891	37,810	NA	21,827	6,597	66,307
1896	37,342	NA	23,777	5,338	66,457
1901	36,809	0	26,737	3,528	66,610
1906	36,165	0	30,636	449	67,250

B. All Teachers in Public Schools, Male Lay and Religious, Female Lay and Religious

Date	Male, Lay	Male, Rel.	Female, Lay	Female, Rel.	Total
1837	29,333	1,404	2,835	4,842	38,975 (38,414)
1840	31,147	1,590	2,649	5,446	40,843
1863	36,457	6,319	8,388	19,099	70,441
1872	37,928	6,416	12,217	18,386	75,053
1876	39,533	6,867	13,707	19,956	80,063
1882	46,591	4,117	21,326	16,186	88,220
1886	52,280	2,542	29,304	13,165	97,291
1891	54,442	NA	34,437	11,233	100,790 (100,052)
1896	54,920	NA	38,800	8,915	102,786 (102,635)
1901	55,160	0	44,461	5,643	106,338 (105,264)
1906	56,151	0	54,961	626	112,281 (111,738)

C. *Titulaires* in Independent Schools, Male Lay and Religious, Female Lay and Religious

Date	Male, Lay	Male, Rel.	Female, Lay	Female, Rel.	Total
1850	4,059	347	7,294	3,252	14,961
1863	2,572	536	7,637	5,571	16,326
1872	1,841	673	5,424	5,282	13,710
1876	1,493	627	4,236	5,932	12,299
1882	1,047	1,202	3,431	6,958	12,638
1886	949	1,568	2,987	7,997	13,501
1891	737	2,473	2,681	9,254	15,145
1896	585	2,707	2,246	10,404	15,942
1901	551	2,840	1,991	11,836	17,218
1906	2,550	201	9,004	1,197	12,952

Note: There are very minor discrepancies (always less than .01, usually in the order of .001) among subcategories. These exist in the original data and the figures in parentheses give the totals that result from adding the subcategories. The editors of the *Statistique* warn that there is less precision in the counting and categorization of teachers than for other educational data. One obvious source of divergency concerns *personnel supplémentaire*, a category added in 1891 and found mainly among female religious.

D. All Teachers in Independent Schools, Male Lay and Religious, Female Lay and Religious

Date	Male, Lay	Male, Rel.	Female, Lay	Female, Rel.	Total
1837	8,038	527	8,560	4,245	21,270
1840	7,221	548	9,804	5,015	22,566
1863	4,360	2,447	12,544	18,979	38,358
1872	3,165	2,925	9,723	19,353	35,176
1876	2,716	2,601	8,069	17,270	30,646
1882	2,143	5,286	7,682	21,634	36,745
1886	1,826	6,504	6,897	24,297	39,524
1891	1,407	9,159	6,158	27,071	43,795
1896	1,273	9,559	5,711	19,756	46,059
1901	1,220	10,021	5,134	33,535	49,910
1906	7,091	1,068	23,240	4,515	35,914

E. *Titulaires* in Public Schools, Male, Female, Lay, and Religious

Date	Male	Female	Lay	Religious	Total
1850	33,175	9,455	36,363	6,247	42,610
1863	35,733	1,672	41,346	11,099	52,445
1872	35,458	20,935	44,224	12,169	56,393
1876	34,773	22,023	43,713	13,083	56,796
1882	37,085	25,912	51,732	11,265	63,717
1886	38,176	28,497	57,576	9,097	66,673
1891	37,810	28,424	59,637	6,797	66,234
1896	37,342	29,115	61,119	5,338	66,457
1901	36,809	29,801	63,082	3,528	66,610
1906	36,165	31,805	66,082	449	67,250

F. All Teachers in Public Schools, Male, Female, Lay, and Religious

Date	Male	Female	Lay	Religious	Total
1837	30,737	7,727	32,618	6,807	38,975
1840	32,737	8,095	33,796	7,047	40,843
1863	42,776	27,487	44,845	25,596	70,441
1872	44,344	30,603	50,145	24,908	75,043
1876	46,400	33,663	53,240	26,823	80,063
1882	50,708	37,512	67,917	20,303	88,220
1886	54,822	42,469	81,584	15,707	97,291
1891	54,442	45,670	88,879	11,911	100,790
1896	54,920	47,710	93,720	9,066	102,786
1901	55,160	50,104	99,621	5,643	105,264
1906	56,151	55,587	111,112	1,169	112,281

G. *Titulaires* in Independent Schools, Male, Female, Lay, and Religious

Date	Male	Female	Lay	Religious	Total
1850	4,415	10,546	7,311	7,650	14,961
1863	3,118	13,208	10,209	6,117	16,323
1872	3,004	10,706	7,265	6,445	13,710
1876	2,111	10,188	5,749	6,550	12,299
1882	4,478	10,389	4,478	10,389	14,867
1886	3,936	10,904	3,936	10,904	14,840
1891	3,418	11,935	3,418	11,935	15,353
1896	2,831	12,650	2,831	12,650	15,481
1901	2,542	13,827	2,542	13,845	16,369
1906	2,751	10,201	11,554	1,398	12,952

H. All Teachers in Independent Schools, Male, Female, Lay, and Religious

Date	Male	Female	Lay	Religious	Total
1837	9,015	12,705	16,498	47,472	21,270
1840	7,667	14,899	17,105	5,461	22,566
1863	6,835	31,523	16,904	21,454	38,358
1872	6,100	29,076	12,888	22,288	35,176
1876	5,307	25,339	10,785	19,861	30,646
1882	7,429	29,316	9,825	26,920	36,745
1886	8,330	31,194	8,723	30,801	39,524
1891	10,566	33,229	7,568	36,227	43,795
1896	10,832	35,227	6,744	39,315	46,059
1901	11,241	38,669	6,354	43,556	49,910
1906	8,159	27,755	30,331	5,583	35,914

I. *Titulaires,* All Schools, Male, Female, Lay, and Religious

Date	Male	Female	Lay	Religious	Total	
1850	37,590	19,981	43,674	13,897	57,571	
1863	30,851	29,920	51,555	17,216	68,771	
1872	38,532	31,641	51,489	18,614	70,103	
1876	36,884	32,211	49,462	19,633	69,095	
1882	38,132	36,301	56,210	18,223	74,433	
1886	42,309	39,401	61,512	20,198	81,710	
1891	41,020	40,359	63,055	18,354	81,379	
1896	35,234	41,765	63,950	18,449	82,399	(80,094)
1901	40,200	43,628	65,624	18,204	83,828	
1906	38,196	42,006	78,355	1,847	80,202	

J. All Teachers, All Schools, Male, Female, Lay, and Religious

Date	Male	Female	Lay	Religious	Total
1837	39,815	20,432	48,666	11,579	60,245
1840	40,415	22,994	50,901	12,508	63,409
1863	49,739	59,010	61,749	47,050	108,799
1872	50,550	59,679	63,033	47,196	110,229
1876	51,707	59,002	64,025	46,684	110,709
1882	58,135	66,828	77,742	47,221	124,963
1886	63,152	73,663	90,307	46,508	136,815
1891	65,686	78,899	96,447	48,138	144,585
1896	65,903	82,942	100,464	48,381	148,845
1901	67,475	88,773	105,975	50,273	156,248
1906	65,595	83,342	141,443	7,494	148,937

Table T.2. Percentage of Teachers Who Were Female and Percentage of Teachers Who Were Lay

	Teachers All Schools		*Titulaires* All Schools		*Titulaires* Public Schools		Teachers Public Schools		*Titulaires* Independent Schools		Teachers Independent Schools	
Date	F	L	F	L	F	L	F	L	F	L	F	L
1837	34	81	—	—	—	—	20	83	—	—	60	78
1840	36	80	—	—	—	—	20	83	—	—	66	76
1850	—	—	35	76	22	85	—	—	70	49	—	—
1863	54	57	44	75	32	79	39	64	81	63	82	44
1872	54	57	45	73	37	78	41	67	78	53	83	37
1876	53	58	47	72	39	77	42	66	83	47	83	35
1882	53	62	49	76	43	82	43	77	70	30	80	32
1886	54	66	48	75	43	86	44	84	73	27	79	24
1891	55	67	51	78	43	90	45	88	78	22	76	19
1896	56	67	51	78	44	92	46	91	82	18	76	15
1901	57	68	52	78	45	95	48	95	84	15	77	13
1906	56	95	52	98	47	99	50	99	79	89	77	84

Table T.3. Teachers in All Categories as a Percentage of Total Teaching Personnel

A. In Public Schools

Date	Male, Lay	Male, Rel.	Female, Lay	Female, Rel.	Total
1840	49	3	4	9	64
1863	34	6	8	18	65
1872	34	6	11	17	68
1876	36	6	12	18	72
1882	37	3	17	13	71
1886	38	2	21	10	71
1891	38	0[a]	24	8	70
1896	36	0	26	6	69
1901	35	0	28	4	68
1906	38	0	37	0	76

B. In Independent Schools

Date	Male, Lay	Male, Rel.	Female, Lay	Female, Rel.	Total
1840	11	1	16	8	36
1863	4	2	12	17	35
1872	3	3	9	18	32
1876	2	2	7	16	28
1882	2	4	6	17	29
1886	1	5	5	18	28
1891	1	6	4	19	30
1896	1	6	9	20	31
1901	1	6	3	21	32
1906	5	1	16	3	24

[a]Zero means less than .5 percent.

Table T.4. Number of *Brevets élémentaires* (or *simples*) Awarded, by Year

Date	Male	Female
1833	947	0
1837	1,422	398
1840	1,243	535
1845	1,502	782
1850	2,044	1,305
1855	1,747	1,637
1860	2,067	1,991
1865	2,177	2,258
1867	2,012	2,667
1870	2,264	3,357
1876[a]	2,740	5,769
1882	7,997	18,194
1887	3,636	8,963
1891	3,706	10,524
1897	4,327	11,601
1901	5,563	13,685
1906	6,136	15,000
1876–80[a]	15,874	34,468
1881–85	41,042	87,528
1886–90	16,863	48,088

[a] Because the examination was given at a number of times during the year during the Third Republic, summary totals can differ depending upon whether one uses the calendar year or the school year.

Table T.5. Number of Graduates of *Écoles Normales*, National Totals, Departmental Means and Ranges

A. Male, Annual

Year	National Total	Dept. Mean	Maximum	Minimum	Coefficient of Variation
1837	860	9.7	27	0	76%
1863	875	10.2	27	0	58%
1877	1,101	12.8	26	0	46%
1882	1,303	15.2	41	0	49%
1886–87	1,665	19.4	57	0	41%
1891–92	1,284	15.1	40	5	46%
1896–97	1,265	14.7	47	0	52%
1901–2	1,214	14.1	48	3	58%
1906–7	1,583	18.2	57	3	49%

B. Male, Cumulative Five-Year Totals

Year	National Total	Dept. Mean	Maximum	Minimum	Coefficient of Variation
1882	5,800	67.4	149	0	46%
1886	7,555	87.9	264	0	42%
1891	7,423	87.3	246	40	39%
1896	6,050	70.3	232	0	51%
1901	5,887	68.5	224	18	50%
1906	6,574	75.6	262	18	48%

C. Female, Annual

Year	National Total	Dept. Mean	Maximum	Minimum	Coefficient of Variation
1863	122	1.4	29	0	334%
1877	216	2.5	39	0	263%
1882	363	4.2	30	0	159%
1886	963	11.2	40	0	78%
1891	1,214	14.1	51	0	45%
1896	1,248	14.5	46	0	47%
1901	1,319	15.3	71	4	58%
1906	1,647	18.9	48	5	38%

D. Female, Cumulative Five-Year Totals

Year	National Total	Dept. Mean	Maximum	Minimum	Coefficient of Variation
1882	1,038	12.2	118	0	225%
1886	3,518	40.9	144	0	86%
1891	5,547	64.5	246	40	39%
1896	6,034	70.2	219	0	44%
1901	6,225	72.4	230	24	43%
1906	7,649	87.9	237	28	38%

Table T.6. Number of Advanced *Brevets* Awarded, Absolute Numbers and Ratio of Higher *Brevets* to Elementary *Brevets*

	Men			Women		
Date	Advanced	Elementary	Ratio of Elementary to Higher	Advanced	Elementary	Ratio of Elementary to Higher
1837	194	1,422	7.3	55	398	7.2
1840	131	1,243	9.5	51	535	10.5
1850	104	2,044	19.7	170	1,305	7.7
1863	221	2,196	9.9	168	2,082	12.4
1867	169	2,012	11.9	249	2,667	10.7
1872	339	2,614	7.7	619	4,364	7.1
1876	429	2,740	6.4	838	5,769	6.9
1882	1,680	7,997	4.8	1,658	18,194	10.8
1887	1,676	3,636	2.2	2,680	8,963	3.3
1892	1,165	3,706	3.2	2,160	10,524	4.9
1897	1,178	4,327	3.7	2,453	11,601	4.7
1901	1,291	5,563	4.3	5,532	13,685	2.5
1907	3,013	6,136	2.0	5,510	15,000	2.7

Table T.7. Number of Teachers with and without *Brevets*, 1876–77

A. Public Schools

		Brevets	*Non-Brevets*	Totals		
Men						
Titulaires	Lay	32,585	—	32,585	34,773	
	Cong.	2,188	—	2,188		45408
Adjoints	Lay	5,580	1,368	6,948	11,635	
	Cong.	548	4,139	4,687		
Women						
Titulaires	Lay	10,822	306	11,128	22,023	
	Cong.	2,434	8,461	10,895		33,663
Adjoints	Lay	2,032	547	2,579	11,640	
	Cong.	695	8,366	9,061		

B. Independent Schools

		Brevets	*Non-Brevets*	Totals		
Men						
Titulaires	Lay	1,493	—	1,493	2,126	
	Cong.	633	—	633		5,309
Adjoints	Lay	513	710	1,223	3,183	
	Cong.	399	1,561	1,960		
Women						
Titulaires	Lay	4,108	139	4,247	10,173	
	Cong.	1,187	4,739	5,926		25,329
Adjoints	Lay	2,363	1,459	3,822	15,156	
	Cong.	1,417	9,917	11,334		
						—
						110,709

Source: F17/10897

Table T.8. Student:Teacher Ratio, Departmental Means and Ranges

Date	Mean	Maximum	Minimum	Coefficient of Variation
1837	43	80	21	28%
1840	45	82	23	28%
1863	40	62	23	19%
1872	43	60	28	17%
1876	42	56	29	17%
1882	43	60	31	16%
1886	40	59	27	16%
1891	37	55	25	16%
1896	36	54	23	17%
1901	34	53	22	17%
1906	36	51	24	16%

Table T.9. Student:*Adjoint* Ratio, Departmental Means and Ranges

Date	Mean	Maximum	Minimum	Coefficient of Variation
1863	127	435	50	43%
1872	142	315	54	39%
1876	130	235	68	29%
1882	128	269	50	33%
1886	114	209	52	27%
1891	98	158	50	23%
1896	92	142	48	21%
1901	84	125	43	19%
1906	91	142	45	22%

Table T.10. Teaching Personnel, Departmental Mean and Ranges

A. Absolute Numbers

Date	Mean	Maximum	Minimum
1837	701	1,668	222
1840	737	1,907	187
1863	1,222	4,903	515
1872	1,267	5,367	189
1876	1,272	5,340	246
1882	1,436	7,173	282
1886	1,572	7,972	331
1891	1,662	8,449	354
1896	1,711	9,101	376
1901	1,796	10,498	391
1906	1,710	10,340	363

B. Normalized by Number of Schools

Date	Mean	Maximum	Minimum	Coefficient of Variation
1837	1.15	2.07	0.80	17%
1840	1.23	2.71	0.85	23%
1863	1.57	2.85	1.14	18%
1872	1.59	2.99	1.17	19%
1876	1.53	3.05	1.10	21%
1882	1.63	3.94	0.99	29%
1886	1.68	4.20	1.19	27%
1891	1.73	4.65	1.26	28%
1896	1.79	5.02	1.31	28%
1901	1.81	5.90	1.31	34%
1906	1.80	5.86	1.25	35%

C. Normalized by Enrollment per 1,000 Students

1837	25	47	13	28%
1840	24	44	12	29%
1863	26	44	16	19%
1872	24	36	17	11%
1876	24	35	18	17%
1882	24	32	17	17%

Table T.11. Number of *Brevets Elémentaires* Awarded to Females, Departmental Means and Ranges

A. Normalized by 100 Female, Lay Teachers

Date	Mean	Median	Coefficient of Variation	Maximum	Minimum	Number of Depts. Awarding *Brevets* That Year
1837	9.2	0.0	94%	45.9	28.0	
1840	8.2	3.2	75%	38.0	1.6	51
1850	16.2	9.0	61%	68.0	4.7	57
1863	11.1	9.7	50%	32.0	2.6	84
1872	21.2	18.2	57%	88.0	5.0	85
1876	29.6	23.1	80%	210.0	6.9	85
1882	81.4	48.5	153%	1,097.0	16.5	All
1886	25.6	20.8	99%	207.0	5.1	All
1891	25.4	20.7	77%	129.0	7.7	All
1896	24.7	21.2	80%	152.0	7.3	All
1901	24.1	19.5	69%	94.0	6.7	All
1906	16.4	13.7	54%	60.0	3.0	All
1886–1906 (average)	23.3	18.6	70%	125.0	8.0	All

B. Normalized by 7,000[a] Female Students

Date	Mean	Median	Coefficient of Variation	Maximum	Minimum
1837	16.5	0.0	92%	63	2.7
1840	5.6	2.1	77%	25	0.5
1850	9.3	4.8	60%	27	1.1
1863	8.1	6.7	60%	25	2.7
1867	9.7	7.6	58%	27	2.4
1872	12.9	10.5	48%	30	4.5
1876	16.7	14.7	43%	45	6.7
1882	52.5	36.8	129%	642	11.0
1886	21.8	17.0	80%	149	6.4
1891	25.5	20.1	70%	133	6.6
1896	27.6	23.1	71%	167	6.9
1901	30.8	24.7	59%	118	7.3
1906	34.3	30.5	53%	119	8.4
1886–1906 (average)	28.0	24.3	58%	128	8.2

[a] Assuming full enrollment, one-seventh of students would graduate each year.

Table T.12. Number of *Brevets* Awarded to Males

A. Normalized by 100 Male, Lay Teachers

Year	Mean	Median	Maximum	Minimum	Coefficient of Variation	Number of Depts. Awarding *Brevets* That Year
1837	5.7	4.8	24	0.6	59%	65
1840	4.9	3.8	27	0.9	69%	70
1850	6.1	4.9	25	1.4	58%	70
1863	6.0	5.3	15	2.6	40%	85
1872	5.9	5.1	16	1.4	41%	85
1876	6.5	6.1	14	1.9	32%	86
1882	17.1	14.8	58	5.8	51%	All
1886	6.6	5.9	16	1.7	46%	All
1891	6.4	5.5	22	1.6	67%	All
1896	7.4	6.1	37	2.4	67%	All
1901	8.9	7.4	37	3.0	67%	All
1906	8.8	8.5	23	1.9	45%	All

B. Normalized by 7,000 Male Students[a]

Year	Mean	Median	Maximum	Minimum	Coefficient of Variation
1837	9.0	7.1	22	0.9	47%
1840	9.0	6.7	24	1.3	53%
1850	9.5	8.0	23	2.5	45%
1863	7.4	6.8	20	1.9	40%
1867	7.2	6.7	19	1.4	41%
1872	6.8	6.1	14	2.0	38%
1876	8.0	7.7	14	3.1	32%
1882	21.6	18.4	89	7.6	53%
1886	9.1	8.1	23	2.3	42%
1891	9.1	8.2	34	2.8	54%
1896	10.9	10.0	57	4.1	60%
1901	13.3	11.3	55	4.8	57%
1906	15.0	13.8	40	3.7	43%

[a] See note to table T.11, section B.

Table T.13. *Adjoints* as Percentage of All Teachers, by Octiles (based on enrollment in 1832)

	Octile							
Date	1	2	3	4	5	6	7	8
1863	37	38	38	36	41	35	28	27
1872	59	35	38	34	39	33	27	26
1876	37	37	34	34	45	34	30	26
1882	42	39	36	37	44	37	28	28
1886	43	40	36	39	45	39	28	29
1891	45	42	38	41	47	40	32	32
1896	45	42	39	42	48	41	33	34
1901	47	43	39	43	49	43	35	35
1906	46	42	37	42	48	42	34	34

Table T.14. Student: Teacher Ratio, by Octiles (based on enrollment in 1832)

	Octile							
Date	1	2	3	4	5	6	7	8
1837	33	35	36	41	38	48	55	55
1840	36	38	38	42	39	51	54	57
1863	38	39	34	38	35	43	42	45
1872	44	45	35	44	39	44	44	44
1876	48	46	38	43	38	41	42	41
1882	50	48	41	45	38	42	40	38
1886	47	44	38	41	35	39	38	38
1891	44	40	35	38	32	37	36	36
1896	42	38	32	36	31	36	35	35
1901	39	35	30	35	30	34	34	34
1906	40	36	31	36	32	36	36	36

Table T.15. Student: Adjoint Ratio, by Octiles (based on enrollment in 1832)

	Octile							
Date	1	2	3	4	5	6	7	8
1863	110	107	93	115	103	135	160	184
1872	124	139	98	135	125	146	177	183
1876	136	132	121	138	90	132	143	160
1882	125	130	118	131	112	122	153	138
1886	111	118	107	108	93	110	134	133
1891	99	100	92	95	78	97	117	111
1896	94	92	84	90	74	90	110	104
1901	84	84	79	82	68	83	100	98
1906	91	88	85	90	76	90	109	106

Table T.16. Dates at Which Departments Had 85 Percent of the Teachers They Would Have in 1901

A. All Teachers

Date	Number of Departments	Percentage of Departments	Cumulative Percentage
1837	5	6	6
1840	0	0	6
1850[a]	0	0	6
1863	8	9	14
1872	10	11	26
1876	1	1	27
1881	10	11	38
1886	40	44	82
1891	11	12	94
1896	5	6	100

B. Male, Lay, Public School Teachers

Date	Number of Departments	Percentage of Departments	Cumulative Percentage
1837	12	13	13
1840	2	2	16
1850[a]	8	9	25
1863	3	3	28
1872	3	3	31
1876	3	3	34
1881	24	27	84
1886	26	29	90
1891	7	8	98
1896	1	1	99
Never	1	1	100

[a] A department is said to have achieved fulfillment when the ratio of teachers at one date is 85 percent of the total teachers (in the two categories) that it had in 1901.

Table T.17. Percentage of Candidates Who Passed the *Brevet* Examinations, Departmental Means and Ranges, 1882–1906

A. Elementary *Brevets*

Date	Mean			Minimum			Maximum			Coefficient of Variation		
	Female	Male	Total	Female	Male	Total	Female	Male	Total	Female	Male	Total
1882	52	39	47	31	16	23	82	73	74	18	29	20
1886	44	42	43	17	12	20	65	71	62	25	29	22
1891	59	51	56	27	24	31	97	88	89	23	23	17
1896	63	66	64	20	26	30	94	100	86	25	29	26
1901	54	52	54	25	31	26	80	82	78	18	23	16
1906	48	48	48	19	28	23	66	76	68	21	22	19

B. Advanced *Brevets*

Date	Mean			Minimum			Maximum			Coefficient of Variation		
	Female	Male	Total	Female	Male	Total	Female	Male	Total	Female	Male	Total
1882	39	38	38	8	13	12	67	61	65	20	41	29
1886	43	45	43	13	14	18	78	82	70	33	33	27
1891	63	66	63	34	0	42	100	86	82	23	29	20
1896	63	66	64	20	26	30	100	100	94	25	29	21
1901	62	75	65	31	40	39	78	90	100	21	23	18
1906	61	70	64	27	25	28	95	100	96	25	22	21

C. Advanced *Brevets* as Percentage of All *Brevets* Granted, 1937–1906

1837	14%	1886	32%
1840	9%	1891	27%
1850	4%	1896	24%
1863	9%	1901	22%
1876	12%	1906	37%
1882	18%		

Table Sys.1. Number of Students in *Écoles Maternelles*

A. By Gender

Date	Boys	Girls	Total	Annual Growth Rate
1837	—	—	29,514	—
1850	—	—	160,244	34%
1863	—	—	383,856	11%
1867	—	—	432,141	3%
1876	—	—	531,077	3%
1881	327,318	317,066	644,384	4%
1886	368,670	372,554	741,224	3%
1891	341,084	340,664	681,748	−1%
1896	346,200	348,700	703,644	1%
1901	364,789	363,780	728,569	0%
1906	316,150	310,155	626,305	−3%

B. By Type of School

	Public		Independent	
Date	Lay	Religious	Lay	Religious
1881	189,091	291,521	15,326	148,456
1886	293,163	225,661	12,492	306,852
1891	311,847	125,364	12,210	232,327
1896	342,150	89,830	9,466	261,918
1901	393,058	52,416	7,630	275,465
1906	501,747	4,101	80,437	40,020

Table Sys.2. Percentage of Students Enrolled in *Écoles Maternelles* Who Enrolled in Catholic Schools

Date	Mean	Maximum	Minimum	Coefficient of Variation
1863	85	100	38	16%
1867	86	100	42	15%
1876	87	100	39	15%
1881	78	100	14	22%
1886	67	100	14	26%
1891	61	109	16	31%
1896	58	98	7	32%
1901	52	86	12	32%
1906	7	42	0	129%

Table Sys.3. Correlations: Enrollment in Primary Schools with Enrollment in *Écoles Maternelles*

Enrollment in Écoles Maternelles	Primary School Enrollment	
	in 1832	at Same Date
1837	.10	—
1850	.29	—
1863	.53	.44
1867	.54	.43
1876	.43	.25
1881	.54	.02
1886	.51	−.02
1891	.40	.04
1896	.36	−.02
1901	.31	.22
1906	.33	.04

Table Sys.4. Correlations: Certification of Primary School Graduates with the Early Establishment of Schooling and with Socioeconomic Factors

	Enrollment	Number of Schools	Percentage in Catholic Schools	Literacy	Percentage of Population in Urban Areas	Wealth
Date	1832	1821	1850	1865	1866	1865
1882	.60	.45	−.20	.45	.07	.27
1886	.65	.54	−.30	.36	.06	.31
1891	.48	.30	−.15	.42	.25	.38
1896	.44	.31	−.23	.45	.30	.37
1901	.26	.29	−.29	.42	.19	.40
1906	.27	.20	−.14	.35	.44	.32

Note: Certification figures include number of *certificats d'études*, plus *brevets*, plus one-half of enrollment in *écoles primaires supérieures*, all normalized by school-age population.

Table Sys.5. Correlations: Numbers of Books in *Bibliothèques Scolaires* in Public Schools (normalized by enrollment) with Socioeconomic Factors and the Early Establishment of Schooling

Date	Percentage of Population in Urban Areas	Enrollment 1832	Schools 1821	Wealth 1865	Literacy 1865
1882	−.20	.83	.75	.35	.51
1886	−.14	.85	.78	.41	.56
1891	−.17	.86	.77	.38	.56
1896	−.18	.84	.77	.38	.57
1901	−.21	.76	.70	.35	.53
1906	−.19	.84	.77	.40	.56

Table Ex.1. Annual Percentage Growth in Total Expenditures and Total Enrollment, Normalized by Population

Date	Expenditures	Enrollment
1837–40	2	2.5
1840–50	2	1.0
1850–63	16	2.0
1863–68	8	1.0
1868–72	7	2.0
1872–82	50	1.0
1882–91	1	0.0
1891–96	8	0.0
1896–1901	0	0.0

Table Ex.2. Tuition in Public Schools, Means, Octiles, Maximums, and Minimums (based on enrollment in 1832)

A. Per Student

Date	National Mean	Octiles								Maximum Dept. Mean	Minimum Dept. Mean
		1	2	3	4	5	6	7	8		
1850	4.0	4.6	4.5	5.4	4.9	3.3	3.4	3.7	2.3	9.3	1.30
1863	4.8	5.9	5.2	6.9	5.9	4.0	3.9	4.3	3.2	10.0	0.90
1867	4.7	5.5	4.9	6.9	5.9	4.2	3.8	4.3	3.2	9.5	0.96
1868	5.6	5.6	5.5	8.0	7.1	4.9	4.9	5.3	3.9	11.6	1.30
1872	4.8	4.5	4.7	6.9	6.0	4.0	4.7	4.7	3.7	10.5	0.30
1876	5.3	5.0	5.4	7.4	6.9	4.6	4.9	5.2	3.7	10.8	1.00

B. Per Capita

Date	National Mean	Octiles								Maximum Dept. Mean	Minimum Dept. Mean
		1	2	3	4	5	6	7	8		
1850	.26	.16	.21	.25	.27	.20	.28	.37	.31	0.68	.05
1863	.41	.34	.37	.45	.47	.34	.42	.51	.45	1.10	.04
1867	.43	.34	.38	.47	.50	.38	.43	.52	.47	1.14	.14
1868	.52	.37	.46	.58	.63	.45	.52	.64	.56	1.09	.06
1872	.50	.38	.47	.58	.62	.41	.50	.61	.52	1.02	.02
1876	.55	.47	.55	.65	.70	.48	.53	.63	.47	0.98	.11

Table Ex.3. Total Expenditures for Public Schools (normalized by population), Arranged by Clusters

Dates	1	2	3	4	5	6	7
1837	55	46	35	28	23	19	10
1840	56	46	37	30	24	20	12
1850	67	53	40	36	29	26	18
1855	135	116	110	86	79	77	42
1863	170	140	120	110	100	99	59
1868	233	201	148	166	143	139	70
1872	247	235	207	193	189	178	88
1882	345	333	295	295	288	269	147
1886	752	749	611	644	582	553	352
1891	467	474	421	428	367	340	219
1896	550	548	469	502	452	410	281
1901	523	524	469	444	443	14	386

Note: Clusters are defined in chapter 3.

Table Ex.4. Total Expenditures per Teacher, Arranged by Clusters

Date	1	2	3	4	5	6	7
1837	204	220	264	245	253	271	321
1840	198	237	263	259	260	262	285
1850	258	257	238	240	210	199	227
1863	514	547	561	598	589	605	614
1868	703	797	643	910	750	754	706
1872	736	868	856	1,016	907	880	812
1882	1,034	1,126	1,102	1,298	1,157	1,110	985
1886	1,297	1,449	1,203	1,634	1,231	1,150	1,117
1891	1,352	1,456	1,440	1,691	1,293	1,205	1,138
1896	1,552	1,659	1,554	1,922	1,558	1,404	1,396
1901	1,424	1,556	1,486	1,547	1,425	1,366	1,292

Note: Clusters are defined in chapter 2.

Table Ex.5. Correlations: Total Expenditures Normalized by Population with Socioeconomic Factors

Date	1821 Schools	1832 Enrollment	1865 Literacy	1865 Urbanization	1865 Wealth
1837	.85	.88	.73	.69	.43
1840	.83	.87	.74	.68	.44
1850	.78	.83	.71	.71	.39
1863	.63	.65	.61	.62	.22
1868	.58	.67	.67	.67	.30
1872	.46	.53	.50	.61	.15
1886	.45	.55	.53	.53	.23
1891	.39	.48	.53	.41	.40
1896	.35	.46	.52	.45	.33

Table Ex.6. Correlations: Expenditures at Different Dates, Normalized by Population

1837 With	
1840	.98
1850	.95
1863	.79
1868	.76
1872	.72
1882	.56
1886	.64
1891	.50
1896	.51
1901	.55

Table Ex.7. Reduction in Variance by Canonical Discriminant Analysis (same results by *k*-Means) for Various Clusters or Groups of Departments

	Seven Clusters Based on Best Possible Statistical Fit for Each Variable[a]	Original Enrollment Cluster in Chap. 3	By Academy	Ten Regions[b]	Ancien Régime Provinces Approximated	St. Malo–Geneva Line
1837–76 girls enrollment as percentage of school-age population	.90	.17	.31	.13	.24	.03
1837–76 percentage of enrollment that was female	.85	.53	.23	.48	.20	.07
1850–81 percentage of enrollment in Catholic schools	.90	.54	.23	.50	.22	.08
1872–1906 percentage of teachers who were *adjoints*	.89	.53	.24	.50	.22	.08
1850–96 adult enrollment as percentage of population	.80	.25	.46	.23	.37	.08
1837—1906 student:teacher ratio	.70	.17	.48	.38	.41	.13

[a]The clusters distinguish the mean for each department over the years represented and compare it to the mean for all the departments for the same period. They also compare the variation in each year for each department from the national mean.
[b]See note to table S.15.

Table Ex.8. Voluntary *(Facultative)* Expenses in 1901 and 1906 per Student

A. Correlations	Schools in 1821	Enrollment 1832	Present in Summer 1832	Enrollment 1837	Present in Summer 1837
1901 *facultative* per student	.29	.33	.43	.35	.48
1901 *facultative* per Capita	.34	.39	.49	.40	.50
1906 *facultative* per student	.27	.28	.43	.30	.46
1906 *facultative* per capita	.31	.33	.48	.34	.48

B. By Octiles (based on enrollment in 1832)	1	2	3	4	5	6	7	8
1901 *faculative* per student	1.10	1.60	2.20	2.50	7.00	3.80	6.80	4.90
1901 *faculative* per capita	0.15	0.20	0.24	0.31	0.69	0.47	0.79	0.56
1906 *facultative* per student	0.20	0.28	0.27	0.39	0.85	0.50	0.86	0.58
1906 *facultative* per capita	1.60	2.40	2.60	3.50	8.50	4.30	7.50	5.20

Note: 97 percent of expenses come from communes.

Index

Academic year, 66–67
Academies as administrative units, 37, 73, 95
Adult education, 185–86, 208, 216; and Catholic enrollment, 186; courses for, 59, 184, 225, 232; enrollment, 83n.27, 185; growth of, 181, 182–83; women's enrollment, 185
Ain, 15, 52n.21; and normal school graduates, 178n.65; women teachers in, 143n.42
Aisne, 52n.21; adult education in, 200n.8; availability of schools in, 39; Catholic schools in, 94; mixed schools in, 142n.35
Allier, 52n.21; availability of schools in, 49n.12; *écoles maternelles* in, 202n.31; girls schools in, 144n.52; and normal school graduates, 179n.69, 179n.70
Alpes-Maritimes: *brevets* for women, 174n.37; mixed schools in, 142n.35
Anticlericalism, 32, 91, 102, 105, 107, 237
Ardèche, 50n.13, 52n.21; adult education in, 199n.5; availability of schools in, 39; *brevets* for women, 174n.37; Catholic enrollment, 105, 106, 114n.23, 118n.47, 118n.49, 119n.50, 119n.52, 242n.55; employment of *adjoints*, 243n.57; employment of *titulaires*, 175n.50; expenditures, 240n.28
Ardennes, 50n.13, 52n.21, 53n.23, 170n.6; adult enrollment, 243n.58; Catholic enrollment, 112n.9; girls enrollment, 140n.19, 242n.53; mixed schools in, 142n.35
Ariège, 52n.21, 80n.3; adult education in, 199n.5, 200n.8; availability of schools in, 49n.12; Catholic enrollment, 105; *écoles maternelles* in, 202n.31; girls enrollment, 144n.48, 233; mixed schools in, 142n.34
Attendance, 27n.26, 27n.28, 65–68, 83n.24, 114n.27; and age, 80n.9; boys, 66; and enrollment, 56; measurement of, 84n.28; summer, 67, 68, 78, 86n.33, 86n.34, 89n.50, 114n.27, 220, 229
Aube, 52n.21, 53n.23, 80n.3; adult education in, 200n.8; availability of schools in, 49n.12; Catholic schools in, 94; girls enrollment, 140n.19, 242n.53; mixed schools in, 142n.34, 142n.35; student-teacher ratios in, 243n.59
Aude, 52n.21, 80n.3; availability of schools in, 49n.12; Catholic enrollment, 119n.52; mixed schools in, 142n.34
Aveyron, 52n.21, 80n.3, 152; adult enrollment, 243n.58; availability of schools in, 49n.12; Catholic enrollment, 105, 118n.45, 118n.47, 118n.49, 119n.50, 119n.52, 242n.55; employment of *titulaires*, 175n.50; expenditures, 239n.20; girls enrollment, 140n.17; mixed schools in, 142n.35; women teachers in, 233

315

Bas-Rhin, 42, 168, 169, 170n.6; adult enrollment, 243n.58; availability of schools in, 49n.12; *écoles maternelles* in, 202n.30; girls enrollment, 242n.53; mixed schools in, 142n.35; student-teacher ratios in, 243n.59

Basses-Alpes, 42, 50n.13, 52n.21, 170n.6, 173n.35; adult education in, 199n.5; *brevets* for women, 174n.37; Catholic enrollment, 105; teachers in, 158, 233; training of teachers, 158; women teachers, 143n.42

Basses-Pyrénées, 52n.21, 80n.3, 118n.49; and *certificats d'études primaires*, 75; expenditures, 242n.47; mixed schools in, 142n.34; and normal school graduates, 178n.65

Bouches-du-Rhône, 42, 44, 52n.21, 112n.7, 160, 176n.58; adult education in, 200n.8; Catholic enrollment, 106, 114n.23, 118n.47, 118n.49, 120n.56, 242n.55; *écoles maternelles* in, 202n.30, 243n.63; employment of *adjoints*, 243n.57; expenditures, 239n.23, 240n.28; girls enrollment, 140n.17; mixed schools in, 142n.34, 142n.35; and normal school graduates, 179n.69; secondary school enrollment, 203n.40

Brevet complet, 167, 223

Brevet élémentaire, 157, 161

Brevets, 9, 13, 152, 198; in *écoles maternelles*, 190; importance of, 225; number awarded, 156; standards for, 155–56, 160–61, 162; and teaching, 158; and women, 174n.39, 235

Brevet simple, 167

Brevet supérieur, 152, 162, 175n.43, 175n.47; test for, 161; women graduates with, 153, 161

Budget. *See* Expenditures

Calvados, 52n.21; availability of schools in, 49n.12; girls enrollment, 140n.20; mixed schools in, 142n.36

Cantal, 52n.21, 80n.3; adult education in, 200n.8; availability of schools in, 49n.12; Catholic enrollment, 118n.47, 118n.49, 119n.52; *écoles maternelles* in, 202n.31, 243n.62; girls enrollment, 140n.14; girls schools in, 144n.52; mixed schools in, 142n.35

Catholic schools, 100, 136, 207, 220, 225, 233; and *cours complémentaires*, 196; enrollment, 56, 92–94, 96, 99, 101–4, 105, 107, 109, 110, 112n.12, 119n.53, 213, 238n.11; expenditures, 69, 208, 221; and girls, 99, 106, 130–32, 135, 160, 222, 233; and laicization of public schools, 101–2, 108–9; and population, 94; private, and public schools, 91–92; and Second Empire, 213; and summer attendance, 67; and Third Republic, 213; tuition at, 99–100, 119n.53

Certificat de l'aptitude, 190

Certificat d'études primaires, 28n.32, 46, 69–71, 102, 110, 196–97, 198; and the *école normale*, 127; for girls, 126–27; as measure of quality, 166; number of, 75

Charente, 52n.21, 80n.3, 171n.14; anticlericalism in, 94, 105, 119n.52; Catholic enrollment, 119n.52; *écoles maternelles* in, 243n.61; employment of *titulaires*, 175n.50; expenditures, 239n.20; girls enrollment, 140n.16, 233; mixed schools in, 142n.36; normal schools in, 233

Charente-Inférieure, 52n.21; *brevets* for women, 174n.37; Catholic enrollment, 112n.9, 119n.52; girls enrollment, 140n.16, 233; mixed schools in, 142n.34

Cher, 15, 52n.21; availability of schools in, 49n.12; girls enrollment, 140n.18; and normal school graduates, 179n.69

Collège communale, 194

Collèges. *See* Secondary schools

Communes: and adult education, 183; and clerical teachers, 221; and *écoles maternelles*, 190; and *écoles primaires supérieures*, 194; expenditures by, 208, 210, 211, 212, 217; and girls instruction, 122–23, 128, 129, 141; girls scholarships, 153, 215; initiative of, 45–46; rural, 167; and schools, 31, 34–35, 39, 46; and subsidies, 227; and teachers' pay, 150

Corrèze, 52n.21, 80n.3, 173n.35; adult education in, 200n.8; *écoles maternelles* in, 202n.31; girls enrollment, 242n.53; and normal school graduates, 179n.69

Corse, 80n.3, 87n.39, 173n.35; adult enrollment, 243n.58; Catholic enrollment, 105, 231; *écoles maternelles* in, 202n.31, 243n.60, 243n.61; expenditures, 239n.20; girls enrollment, 123, 140n.16, 144n.48, 231, 233; girls schools in, 144n.52; mixed schools in, 142n.34, 142n.36; women teachers in, 143n.42

Costs of schooling. *See* Expenditures

Côte-d'Or, 52n.21; adult education in, 199n.5; adult enrollment, 243n.58; Catholic enrollment, 112n.9; employment of *adjoints*, 243n.56; girls enrollment, 242n.53; mixed schools in, 142n.35

Côtes-du-Nord, 52n.21, 112n.7, 171n.14; availability of schools in, 49n.12; Catholic enrollment, 105, 113n.18, 114n.23, 117n.43, 118n.48, 118n.49, 242n.55; and *certificats d'études primaires*, 75; employment of *titulaires*, 175n.50; expenditures, 240n.28; girls enrollment, 140n.20; mixed schools in, 142n.33, 142n.35; and normal school graduates, 178n.67, 179n.70; normal schools in, 233; teachers in, 175n.44

Cours complémentaires, 184, 194, 196, 198, 225; graduates of, 198

Cours normaux, 154–55, 215, 224

Cousin, Victor, 3, 128

Creuse, 52n.21; adult education in, 199n.5, 200n.8; anticlericalism in, 94, 105, 119n.52; Catholic enrollment, 105, 112n.8, 117n.42, 119n.52; *écoles maternelles* in, 202n.31, 243n.60, 243n.61, 243n.62; expenditures, 239n.20; girls enrollment, 144n.48, 233; girls schools in, 144n.52; and normal school graduates, 179n.69

D'Angeville, Adolphe, 38

Departments, 21; as academy, 95; agricultural, 71; anticlerical, 105; *brevets* awarded, 156–58; Catholic enrollment, 98–99, 105, 222; and Catholic schools, 94, 96–97; differences among, 45–46, 55–57; and *écoles maternelles*, 234; enrollment, 56, 58–59; expenditures by, 208, 212, 227–29; and girls enrollment, 223; grouping of, 230; and number of schools, 35; patterns of growth, 77–79; ranking of, 36–37; rural, 88n.44; and school-age population, 80n.5; and secondary education, 193, 226; urban, 239n.24; wealth of, 87n.42, 227, 228

Deries, M. L., 15

Deux-Sèvres, 52n.21, 53n.23; *brevets* for women, 174n.37; Catholic enrollment, 112n.9, 119n.52; *écoles maternelles* in, 202n.31, 243n.60; girls enrollment, 140n.16, 144n.48, 233; mixed schools in, 142n.34

Dordogne, 52n.21; Catholic enrollment, 112n.9; *écoles maternelles* in, 202n.31

Doubs, 15, 27n.28, 42, 52n.21; adult education in, 199n.5; availability of schools in, 49n.12; *brevets* for women, 174n.37; Catholic enrollment, 112n.9, 118n.49; girls enrollment, 242n.53; mixed schools in, 142n.36

Drôme, 52n.21, 80n.3; employment of *adjoints*, 243n.57; girls enrollment, 144n.48, 233
Dupin, Charles, 38
Duruy, Victor, 4, 15, 16, 17, 86n.35, 115n.30, 130, 183, 194, 216; and adult education, 185; and professionalization of teaching, 147

Ecoles maternelles, 7, 13, 61, 70, 186, 188, 201n.24, 201n.26, 208, 234; and the *brevet*, 190; Catholic role in, 103, 188; and Catholic schools, 100, 220; enrollment in, 117n.38, 120n.59, 187–89, 202n.30, 202n.31, 234; financial support, 226; growth of, 79, 100, 181, 191, 216, 220; legislation for, 117n.38; purpose of, 225–26; teachers in, 130, 190, 226; and urban needs, 189
Ecoles normales, 216, 223, 225; access to, 154; and the *brevet*, 96, 152; and the *certificat d'études primaires*, 127; and *collège*, 154; cost per student, 152; curriculum of, 150–51; for girls, 149, 153, 215, 224; graduates of, 168–69, 172n.23; and *lycée*, 154; scholarships in, 151; size of, 233; students in, 151, 154; teachers in, 132, 150, 151
Ecoles normales supérieures, 154
Ecoles primaires secondaires: enrollment in, 83n.27
Ecoles primaires supérieures, 152, 182, 195–96, 216, 226; enrollment in, 83n.27; entrance into, 163; and government employment, 226; graduates of, 197–98; growth of, 194; scholarships for, 198, 226; and urbanization, 226
Enrollment, 7–8, 55–61, 82n.15, 89n.49, 93–93, 125, 126, 213, 222; and age, 66; and availability of schools, 45; of boys, 83n.27, 88n.45; data for, 60–61, 62, 63–64; of girls, 56, 63, 88n.45; growth of, 62–63, 77–79, 82n.17; and literacy, 228; and school-age population, 20, 66, 79n.2, 80n.10; social factors of, 71–72; and tuition fees, 69, 87n.38; and urban population, 228; and wealth, 27n.29, 72, 87n.42
Eure, 52n.21; *écoles maternelles* in, 202n.31; girls schools in, 144n.52; mixed schools in, 142n.36; and normal school graduates, 179n.70; women teachers in, 143n.42
Eure-et-Loir, 15, 27n.28, 52n.21, 53n.23, 169; adult education in, 200n.8; Catholic enrollment, 112n.9; mixed schools in, 142n.34, 142n.35; and normal school graduates, 179n.70; teachers in, 175n.44
Expenditures, 45, 47, 69, 210–12, 217–19, 229; by communes, 208; data for, 209; by departments, 208; and enrollment, 211, 227, 228; extraordinary, 209, 218; increases in, 63, 81n.14, 211–12; and literacy, 227; ordinary, 209, 218; patterns of change, 209–12; per student, 88n.45, 211, 219, 241n.44; per teacher, 239n.22; and salary scale, 211, 219; and tuition, 217–18, 228; and urban population, 227; and wealth, 227, 229

Falloux Law, 4, 91, 95, 102, 130, 156, 194, 207; and the *brevet*, 149; and Catholic teaching, 96; and the church, 95–96, 98, 108; and girls schools, 122, 124; and religious orders, 92
Ferry, Jules, 4, 15, 16, 99, 194
Ferry Laws, 59–60, 69, 72, 91, 109–10, 123, 157, 181; bias of, 32; and *certificats d'études primaires*, 70; and enrollment, 28n.32, 56, 62; and expenditures, 209, 210, 211, 212; and growth rates, 31–32; and summer attendance, 67, 68; and taxes, 218
Finistère, 44, 52n.21, 73, 176n.58;

adult education in, 200n.8; availability of schools in, 49n.12; Catholic enrollment, 118n.48, 118n.49, 120n.56; employment of *adjoints*, 243n.57; employment of *titulaires*, 175n.50; expenditures, 242n.48; girls enrollment, 140n.20, 242n.53; mixed schools in, 142n.33, 142n.35; and normal school graduates, 179n.69
Fortoul, Hyppolyte, 143n.43
French Revolution, 38, 121; goals of, 5
Frontiers, changes in, 19, 64
Fulfillment, concept of, and number of schools, 40, 42, 43, 52n.20; number of teachers, 164

Gambetta, Léon, 4
Gard, 52n.21; adult education in, 199n.4, 200n.8; Catholic enrollment, 105, 114n.23, 118n.47, 118n.49, 119n.51, 242n.55; *écoles maternelles* in, 202n.30, 202n.31; employment of *titulaires*, 175n.50; expenditures, 240n.28
Gers, 44, 52n.21, 80n.3; adult education in, 199n.5; *brevets* for women, 174n.37
Girls: attendance of, 85n.32; enrollment of, 56, 63, 87n.38, 123, 124, 133, 134, 135, 213, 214, 222, 230, 233, 240n.32; scholarships for, 87n.38, 123, 139n.7, 153, 215; separate schooling for, 127–28; summer attendance of, 67
Girls schooling, 207, 235; in agricultural areas, 133, 233; in Catholic schools, 122; and the church, 130–31; and job opportunities, 134; and literacy, 133; resistance to, 138; weaknesses of, 124; and wealth, 133
Girls schools, 47n.2, 48n.3, 95, 96, 99, 235; Catholic, 222; curriculum in, 121; independent, 222; and literacy, 136; and nuns as teachers, 221; public, 130, 222

Gironde, 42, 52n.21, 80n.3; adult education in, 199n.4, 199n.5; *brevets* for women, 174n.37; girls enrollment, 140n.17; mixed schools in, 142n.35; and normal school graduates, 178n.65
Guérry, André Michel, 38
Guizot, François, 11, 16
Guizot Law, 7, 33, 34, 46, 47n.2, 91, 151, 182, 192, 207; and availability of schools, 45; and enrollment, 56; and funding of schools, 113n.21; and girls schools, 122; and growth rates, 31–32; and religion, 92

Haute-Garonne, 49n.12, 52n.21; Catholic enrollment, 119n.52; mixed schools in, 142n.34
Haute-Loire, 17, 52n.21; adult education in, 200n.10; availability of schools in, 49n.12; Catholic enrollment, 105, 106, 113n.18, 117n.43, 118n.47, 118n.49, 119n.50, 242n.55; Catholic schools in, 94; employment of *adjoints*, 243n.57; expenditures, 242n.48; girls enrollment, 144n.48, 231, 233; mixed schools in, 142n.35; and normal school graduates, 179n.69
Haute-Marne, 52n.21, 53n.23, 80n.3, 170n.6; availability of schools in, 49n.12; girls enrollment, 242n.53; and normal school graduates, 179n.70
Hautes-Alpes, 14, 41, 50n.13, 52n.21, 80n.3; adult education in, 199n.5, 200n.8; availability of schools in, 39, 49n.12; Catholic enrollment, 105, 112n.9; *écoles maternelles* in, 202n.31, 243n.60; employment of *titulaires*, 175n.50; expenditures, 239n.23; girls enrollment, 140n.16, 233; mixed schools in, 142n.33, 142n.35
Haute-Saône, 44, 52n.21; adult education in, 200n.8; adult enrollment,

Haute-Saône (*continued*)
243n.58; Catholic enrollment, 105, 242n.55; Catholic schools in, 94; girls enrollment, 242n.53
Haute-Savoie, 87n.39, 171n.14; adult enrollment, 243n.58; *brevets* for women, 174n.37; Catholic enrollment, 118n.49; *écoles maternelles* in, 202n.31; normal schools in, 233
Hautes-Pyrénées, 52n.21, 173n.35; adult education in, 199n.5, 200n.8; availability of schools in, 49n.12; Catholic enrollment, 105, 112n.9, 118n.49; *écoles maternelles* in, 243n.64; expenditures, 242n.47; mixed schools in, 142n.34; and normal school graduates, 178n.65; teachers in, 233; teaching, 158
Haute-Vienne, 52n.21; adult education in, 200n.8; availability of schools in, 49n.12; Catholic enrollment, 119n.52, 231; *écoles maternelles* in, 202n.31, 243n.62; girls enrollment, 242n.53; mixed schools in, 142n.34; and normal school graduates, 178n.66
Haut-Rhin: adult education in, 200n.10; Catholic enrollment, 118n.49; *écoles maternelles* in, 202n.30; employment of *titulaires*, 175n.50; student teacher ratios in, 243n.59
Hérault, 42, 44, 50n.13, 52n.21, 80n.3, 112n.7, 148, 173n.35; availability of schools in, 49n.12; *écoles maternelles* in, 202n.30, 202n.31, 243n.65; employment of *titulaires*, 175n.50; expenditures, 242n.47; girls enrollment, 140n.17; teachers in, 233; and teaching, 158

Ille-et-Vilaine, 52n.21, 173n.34, 173n.35, 176n.58; availability of schools in, 49n.12; Catholic enrollment, 105, 106, 114n.23, 118n.48, 118n.49, 119n.51, 242n.55; expenditures, 240n.28; girls enrollment, 140n.20; and normal school graduates, 179n.69, 179n.70; and training of teachers, 158; women teachers in, 143n.42
Independent schools, 13, 92, 112n.15, 132; Catholic, 102–3, 116n.37, 221–22; Catholic teachers in, 94–95, 97, 103; enrollment, 56, 94, 104, 116n.37; women teachers in, 215
Indre, 52n.21, 173n.35; adult education in, 200n.10; availability of schools in, 49n.12; and *certificats d'études primaires*, 119n.53; employment of *adjoints*, 243n.57; and normal school graduates, 179n.69
Indre-et-Loire, 52n.21; adult education in, 199n.4; employment of *adjoints*, 243n.57; and normal school graduates, 178n.66, 179n.70
Inspectors, 66, 86, 111n.2, 162, 183; frustrations of, 71; on girls schools, 99, 136; on private instruction, 130; and secular schools, 100; women, 224
Instituteurs. *See* Teachers
Institutionalization, 225, 235–36
Institutrices. *See* Teachers
Isère, 52n.21, 80n.3; availability of schools in, 49n.12; and normal school graduates, 178n.65

July Monarchy, 4, 10, 33, 121, 155, 181; adult education during, 182; and attendance, 33; and *écoles primaires supérieures*, 226; and elementary schools, 47; and girls schooling, 122; and primary education, 35; and schools, 31
Jura, 52n.21; Catholic enrollment, 105, 112n.9; girls enrollment, 242n.53

Kindergartens. *See Ecoles maternelles*

Landes, 52n.21, 80n.3; availability of schools in, 49n.12; *écoles maternelles* in, 202n.31; girls schools in, 144n.52
Libraries, 166

Literacy, 2, 21, 72; of adults, 216; and age distribution, 137; and enrollment, 228; and girls schooling, 133; and independent schools, 117n.40; of women, 121–22, 136

Loire, 52n.21, 112n.7, 176n.58; Catholic enrollment, 105, 106, 113n.18, 114n.23, 115n.29, 117n.43, 118n.47, 118n.49, 231; Catholic schools in, 94; *écoles maternelles* in, 202n.30, 243n.63; employment of *adjoints*, 243n.57; expenditures, 240n.28; girls enrollment, 140n.18; and normal school graduates, 179n.69

Loire-Inférieure, 52n.21, 73, 112n.7; Catholic enrollment, 105, 114n.23, 118n.49, 119n.52, 120n.56; employment of *adjoints*, 243n.57; expenditures in, 240n.28, 242n.48; mixed schools in, 142n.35

Loiret, 52n.21; adult education in, 199n.4, 199n.5; Catholic enrollment, 118n.45; mixed schools in, 142n.34; and normal school graduates, 179n.69, 179n.70

Loir-et-Cher, 52n.21; adult education in, 199n.4, 200n.8

Lorain, Paul, 14, 15, 16, 66

Lot, 44, 52n.21, 80n.3, 171n.14; adult education in, 199n.5; Catholic enrollment, 118n.47, 118n.49; *écoles maternelles* in, 202n.31; employment of *titulaires*, 175n.50; mixed schools in, 142n.35; normal schools in, 233

Lot-et-Garonne, 52n.21

Lozère, 12, 44, 52n.21, 80n.3, 173n.35; adult education in, 200n.8, 200n.10; adult enrollment, 243n.58; availability of schools in, 39, 49n.12; Catholic enrollment, 118n.49, 119n.52; *écoles maternelles* in, 202n.31, 243n.64; employment of *titulaires*, 175n.50; mixed schools in, 142n.34; teachers in, 233; teaching in, 158; women teachers in, 143n.42

Lycées. See Secondary schools

Maggiolo, Louis, 38, 136, 137

Maine-et-Loire, 52n.21; adult education in, 199n.5, 200n.8; Catholic enrollment, 105, 118n.45, 118n.48, 118n.49, 242n.55; *écoles maternelles* in, 202n.30, 202n.31; girls enrollment, 140n.14, 140n.20; and normal school graduates, 179n.70

Malte-Brun, Conrad, 38

Manche, 15, 27n.28, 52n.21, 80n.3, 169; Catholic enrollment, 112n.9, 118n.48, 118n.49; expenditures, 239n.23; girls enrollment, 140n.20; girls schools in, 144n.52; mixed schools in, 142n.33, 142n.35

Marne, 52n.21, 53n.23, 80n.3, 80n.9, 152, 170n.6; Catholic enrollment, 112n.9; *écoles maternelles* in, 202n.30, 243n.65; girls enrollment, 242n.53; mixed schools in, 142n.34, 142n.35, 142n.36; women teachers in, 233

Mayenne, 52n.21, 87n.39; availability of schools in, 49n.12; Catholic enrollment, 105, 114n.23, 118n.45, 118n.48, 118n.49, 242n.55; expenditures, 240n.28; girls enrollment, 140n.20; mixed schools in, 142n.34, 142n.35; and normal school graduates, 179n.69, 179n.70

Meurthe, 42, 142n.34, 168, 170n.6; adult enrollment, 243n.58; availability of schools in, 49n.12; *écoles maternelles* in, 202n.30; girls enrollment, 242n.53

Meurthe-et-Moselle, 53n.23; *écoles maternelles* in, 202n.30

Meuse, 15, 27n.28, 44, 52n.21, 80n.3, 170n.6; adult education in, 199n.5; availability of schools in, 49n.12; *brevets* for women, 174n.37; *écoles maternelles* in, 202n.30, 202n.31; girls enrollment, 140n.19, 242n.53; mixed schools in, 142n.34, 142n.36

Mixed schools, 47n.2, 127, 128, 129; enrollment of girls in, 128–29

Montalivet, Camille, 14

Morbihan, 52n.21, 67, 73, 171n.14; availability of schools in, 49n.12; Catholic enrollment, 106, 114n.23, 115n.29, 118n.48, 118n.49, 242n.55; expenditures, 240n.28, 242n.48; girls enrollment, 140n.20, 242n.53; mixed schools in, 142n.33, 142n.35; normal schools in, 233

Moselle, 15, 27n.28, 42; adult education in, 199n.4; availability of schools in, 49n.12; *écoles maternelles* in, 202n.30; girls enrollment, 242n.53; mixed schools in, 142n.35

Nièvre, 52n.21; availability of schools in, 49n.12

Nord, 42, 44, 52n.21, 176n.58; adult education in, 199n.4; availability of schools in, 49n.12; Catholic enrollment, 118n.49, 120n.56; and *certificats d'études primaires*, 75; *écoles maternelles* in, 202n.30; employment of *adjoints*, 243n.57; mixed schools in, 142n.35; student-teacher ratios in, 243n.59

Normal schools. See *Ecoles normales*

Oise, 52n.21, 80n.3, 171n.14; Catholic enrollment, 112n.9; mixed schools in, 142n.35, 142n.36; and normal school graduates, 178n.67; normal schools in, 233

Ordinances of 1828, 98

Orne, 52n.21, 169; adult education in, 199n.4; mixed schools in, 142n.36

Parents: aims of, 28n.31, 216, 225; and girls schooling, 138, 222

Pas-de-Calais, 42, 52n.21, 171n.14; adult education in, 199n.4; availability of schools in, 49n.12; mixed schools in, 142n.35; and normal school graduates, 178n.67; normal schools in, 233

Pestalozzi, J. H., 186

Population, school-age, 20, 66, 79n.2, 80n.10, 119n.53

Privat, H., 38

Private schools. See Independent schools

Provinces, reconstituted, 37, 76

Public schools, 91–92, 133; attendance, 68; Catholic, 214, 220, 222, 238n.11; clerical teachers in, 116n.35; cost of, 209; enrollment, 116n.36; funds for, 13; growth of, 214; image of, 108; secularization of, 100–107, 214; teachers in, 223

Puy-de-Dôme, 17, 52n.21, 80n.3; Catholic enrollment, 118n.47, 118n.49, 242n.55

Pyrénées-Orientales, 52n.21, 94; *brevets* for women, 174n.37; Catholic enrollment, 105; *écoles maternelles* in, 202n.31, 243n.60, 243n.61; expenditures, 239n.20; girls enrollment, 140n.16, 144n.48, 233; mixed schools in, 142n.34, 142n.35; and normal school graduates, 178n.66, 179n.69

Restoration government, 19, 31; and adult education, 182; and the Church, 4; and elementary schools, 47

Rhône, 52n.21, 80n.3, 112n.7; adult education in, 199n.4, 199n.5, 200n.8; Catholic enrollment, 105, 106, 107, 113n.18, 114n.23, 115n.29, 117n.43, 118n.47, 118n.49; Catholic schools in, 94; *écoles maternelles* in, 202n.30, 202n.31, 243n.63; employment of *adjoints*, 243n.57; expenditures, 240n.28; girls enrollment, 140n.18; mixed schools in, 142n.35; and normal school graduates, 179n.69

Ribot Commission, 193–94

Rouland, Gustave, 115n.30

Rousseau, Jean-Jacques, 186

St. Malo–Geneva line, 38–39, 40, 42, 51n.17, 72, 112n.15, 123, 158, 168, 178n.65, 232

Salles d'asiles, 186, 188. See also *Ecoles maternelles*
Salvandy, Narcise, 182
Saône-et-Loire, 52n.21; adult education in, 200n.8; availability of schools in, 49n.12; and normal school graduates, 178n.65
Sarthe, 52n.21; adult education in, 199n.4; *écoles maternelles* in, 202n.31; girls enrollment, 140n.20
Savoie: availability of schools in, 49n.12; *brevets* for women, 174n.37; employment of *adjoints*, 243n.56
Scholarships, 151, 198, 215–16, 224, 226; from communes, 153, 215; for girls, 87n.38, 139n.7, 153, 215
Schooling, 5–6, 9, 212, 216–17; availability of, 39–40; demand for, 16, 45–46; development of, 65–66, 77, 101, 121, 213, 227; government role in, 107–8; historiography of French, 1–6, 16, 72; institutionalization of, 16, 64–65, 108, 110; quality of, 47; roots of, 17; universal, 40, 42. See also Catholic schools; Enrollment; Expenditures; Girls schooling
Schools: for apprentices, 61; availability of, 33–36, 38; class size in, 46; creation of, 31; data on, 91; establishment of, 212–13; number of, 31–32, 35; physical facilities for, 114n.24; and population, 32, 49n.10; size of, 114n.26. See also *types of schools*
Secondary schools, 191–93, 196–98, 208; girls enrollment, 216
Second Empire, 4, 13, 32, 59, 95, 97, 156, 181; and the academic year, 67; and Catholic schools, 105, 207, 213, 220; and *certificats d'études primaires*, 70; and clerical teachers, 100, 221; and *écoles maternelles*, 188, 191; and *écoles primaires supérieures*, 226; expenditures, 209, 210, 211, 212, 218, 237n.3; and girls schools, 122; and growth rates, 31; policy of, 108; and tuition, 115n.30; and women teachers, 153, 224

Second Republic: and *écoles maternelles*, 187
Seine, 42, 44, 52n.21, 53n.23, 160, 173n.35, 176n.58; adult education in, 199n.4; availability of schools in, 39; and *certificats d'études primaires*, 75; *écoles maternelles* in, 202n.30, 202n.31; expenditures, 239n.23; girls enrollment, 140n.14, 231; mixed schools in, 142n.35; and normal school graduates, 178n.66; secondary school enrollment, 203n.40
Seine-et-Marne, 52n.21, 53n.23; anti-clericalism in, 105; Catholic enrollment, 105; Catholic schools in, 94; *écoles maternelles* in, 202n.30; employment of *adjoints*, 243n.57; mixed schools in, 142n.34, 142n.35
Seine-et-Oise, 52n.21, 80n.3; adult education in, 199n.4, 199n.5, 200n.8; and *certificats d'études primaires*, 75; *écoles maternelles* in, 202n.30, 202n.31; girls enrollment, 140n.19; mixed schools in, 142n.35; secondary school enrollment, 203n.40
Seine-Inférieure, 52n.21; Catholic enrollment, 118n.49, 242n.55; girls schools in, 144n.52; mixed schools in, 142n.35
Siegfried, André, 38, 103
Simon, Jules, 4, 123, 128
Somme, 52n.21, 170n.6; girls enrollment, 140n.19; mixed schools in, 142n.35
Statistics, 10; cluster analyses, 22–23, 29n.42, 34, 40, 44, 49n.9, 78; correlations, 21–22; k-means clusters, 39–40, 51n.19; octiles, 22; regression analysis, 45; standard deviation, 22
Statistique de l'enseignement, 12–13; analysis of, 18–22, 62, 229
Statistique générale de la France, 18, 38
Student-teacher ratio, 166–67, 176n.55, 176n.58

Tableau de l'instruction primaire (Lorain), 14
Tarn, 52n.21, 87n.39; Catholic enrollment, 118n.49; and normal school graduates, 179n.69
Tarn-et-Garonne, 17, 52n.21; availability of schools in, 49n.12; Catholic enrollment, 119n.52; *écoles maternelles* in, 202n.31; employment of *adjoints*, 243n.57; and normal school graduates, 179n.69
Teachers, 8–9, 81n.14, 95, 224; *adjoints*, 151, 162, 165–66, 167, 172n.23, 175n.45, 176n.54, 176n.58, 224, 225; clerical, 100, 101, 107, 112n.10, 114n.22, 116n.35, 147, 149, 162, 163, 225; and *écoles normales*, 214–15; jobs for, 148–49, 165; lay, 101, 132, 133, 162; policy toward, 147; professional status of, 162, 163, 168; in public schools, 223; qualifications of, 9, 96, 116n.34, 155–56, 164, 233; salaries of, 95, 150, 167; *titulaires*, 148, 151, 157, 162, 163, 164, 165, 166, 172n.23, 175n.45, 176n.57, 214, 224; training of, 207, 214; women, 130, 149, 163, 215, 223–24, 235. See also *Brevets*
Territory of Belfort, 160, 173n.34, 174n.37
Third Republic: and the academic year, 67; adult education in, 182; and attendance, 33; and the *brevet supérieur*, 161; and Catholic schools, 3, 91, 97; *certificats d'études primaires*, 126; and *écoles maternelles*, 190; *écoles normales* in, 152, 155, 169; and *écoles primaires supérieures*, 226; and enrollment, 59, 62, 63; expenditures, 69, 209, 211, 218; and girls normal schools, 215; and lay teachers, 220; policies of, 4–6, 46, 100, 181; use of *adjoints*, 231; and women teachers, 149, 224

Tuition, 69, 87n.38, 99–100, 217–18, 228

Unions pédagogiques, 168

Var, 42, 52n.21, 176n.58; *brevets* for women, 174n.37; and *certificats d'études primaires*, 75; *écoles maternelles* in, 202n.30, 202n.31; employment of *adjoints*, 243n.57; mixed schools in, 142n.35
Vaucluse, 52n.21, 176n.58; adult education in, 199n.4; Catholic enrollment, 106, 113n.18, 114n.23, 117n.43, 118n.47, 118n.49, 242n.55; *écoles maternelles* in, 202n.30, 202n.31; employment of *adjoints*, 243n.57; mixed schools in, 142n.35; student-teacher ratios in, 243n.59
Vendée, 52n.21, 176n.58; availability of schools in, 49n.12; Catholic enrollment, 119n.52
Veuillot, Louis, 108
Vienne, 52n.21; adult education in, 199n.5; employment of *adjoints*, 243n.57; expenditures, 240n.28; girls enrollment, 140n.16, 233
Vosges, 52n.21; adult enrollment, 243n.58; *écoles maternelles* in, 202n.30; employment of *titulaires*, 175n.50; girls enrollment, 242n.53; mixed schools in, 142n.34, 142n.35; student-teacher ratios in, 243n.59

Waldeck-Rousseau, René, 4
Women teachers, 215, 223–24, 233; and the *brevet*, 149, 215, 234; and religious orders, 99; as *titulaires*, 149. See also Girls; Teachers

Yonne, 52n.21, 53n.23; adult education in, 199n.4, 199n.5; anticlericalism in, 105; availability of schools in, 49n.12; Catholic enrollment, 105, 112n.9; mixed schools in, 142n.35